ISBN 978-1-396-01107-8
PIBN 11190458

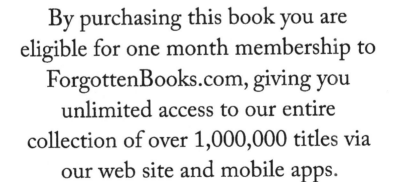

English
Français
Deutsche
Italiano
Español
Português

www.forgottenbooks.com

Mythology Photography **Fiction**
Fishing Christianity **Art** Cooking
Essays Buddhism Freemasonry
Medicine **Biology** Music **Ancient
Egypt** Evolution Carpentry Physics
Dance Geology **Mathematics** Fitness
Shakespeare **Folklore** Yoga Marketing
Confidence Immortality Biographies
Poetry **Psychology** Witchcraft
Electronics Chemistry History **Law**
Accounting **Philosophy** Anthropology
Alchemy Drama Quantum Mechanics
Atheism Sexual Health **Ancient History**
Entrepreneurship Languages Sport
Paleontology Needlework Islam
Metaphysics Investment Archaeology
Parenting Statistics Criminology
Motivational

Oxford English Classics.

DR. JOHNSON'S WORKS.

THE

ADVENTURER AND IDLER.

THE

WORKS

OF

SAMUEL JOHNSON, LL.D.

IN NINE VOLUMES.

4

VOLUME THE FOURTH.

OXFORD.

PUBLISHED BY TALBOYS AND WHEELER;

AND W. PICKERING, LONDON.

MDCCCXXV.

TALBOYS AND WHEELER, PRINTERS, OXFORD.

PREFATORY NOTICE

TO

THE ADVENTURER.

THE Adventurer was projected in the year 1752, by Dr. John Hawkesworth. He was partly induced to undertake the work by his admiration of the Rambler, which had now ceased to appear, the style and sentiments of which evidently, from his commencement, he made the models of his imitation.

The first number was published on the seventh of November, 1752. The quantity and price were the same as the Rambler, and also the days of its appearance. He was joined in his labours by Dr. Johnson in 1753, whose first paper is dated March 3, of that year; and after its publication Johnson applied to his friend, Dr. Joseph Warton, for his assistance, which was afforded: and the writers then were, besides the projector Dr. Hawkesworth, Dr. Johnson, Dr. Joseph Warton, Dr. Bathurst, Colman, Mrs. Chapone and the Hon. Hamilton Boyle, the accomplished son of Lord Orrery[a].

· Our business, however, in the present pages, does not lie with the Adventurer in general, but only with Dr. Johnson's contributions; which amount to the number of twenty-nine, beginning with N°. 34, and ending with N°. 138.

---

[a] For the general history of the Adventurer, the reader may be referred to Chalmers' British Essayists, xxiii, Dr. Drake's Essays on Rambler, Adventurer, &c. ii, and Boswell's Journal, 3rd edit. p. 240.

Much criticism has been employed in appropriating some of them, and the carelessness of editors has overlooked several that have been satisfactorily proved to be Johnson's own[b].

Mr. Boswell relies on internal evidence, which is unnecessary, since in Dr. Warton's copy (and his authority on the subject will scarcely be disputed) the following remark was found at the end : " The papers marked T were written by Mr. S. Johnson." Mrs. Anna Williams asserted that he dictated most of these to Dr. Bathurst, to whom he presented the profits. The anecdote may well be believed from the usual benevolence of Johnson and his well-known attachment to that amiable physician, whose professional knowledge might undoubtedly have enabled him to offer hints to Johnson in the progress of composition. Thus we may account for the references to recondite medical writers in Nº. 39, which so staggered Boswell and Malone in pronouncing on the genuineness of this paper. Those who are familiar with Johnson's writings can have little hesitation, we conceive, in recognising his style, and manner, and sentiments in those papers which are now published under his name. They may be considered as a continuation of the Rambler. The same subjects are discussed; the interests of literature and of literary men, the emptiness of praise and the vanity of human wishes. The same intimate knowledge of the town and its manners is displayed[c]; and occasionally we are amused with humorous delineation of adventure and of character[d].

From the greater variety of its subjects, aided, perhaps, by a growing taste for periodical literature, the sale of the Adventurer was greater than that of the Rambler on its first appearance. But still there were those, who " talked of it as a catch-penny

---

[b] Five of these, Nᵒˢ. 39, 67, 74, 81, and 128, which Sir John Hawkins omitted to arrange among the writings of Johnson, are given in this edition.

[c] See particularly the Letters of Misargyrus.

[d] The description in Nº. 84, of the incidents of a stage-coach journey, so often imitated by succeeding writers, but, perhaps, never surpassed, will exemplify the above remark.

performance, carried on by a set of needy and obscure scribblers[e]."
So slowly is a national taste for letters diffused, and so hardly do
works of sterling merit, which deal not in party-politics, nor
exemplify their ethical discussions by holding out living characters to censure or contempt, win the applause of those, whose
passions leave them no leisure for abstracted truth, and whom
virtue itself cannot please by its naked dignity. But, by such,
Johnson professed, that he had little expectation of his writings
being perused. Keeping then our main object more immediately in view, the elucidation of Johnson's real character and
motives, we cannot but admire the prompt benevolence, with
which he joined Hawkesworth in his task, and the ready zeal, with
which he embraced any opportunity of promoting the interests of
morality and virtue. "To a benevolent disposition every state
of life will afford some opportunities of contributing to the welfare
of mankind," is the characteristic opening of his first Adventurer.
And when we have admired the real excellence of his heart, we
must wonder at the vigour of a mind, which could so abstract
itself from its own sorrows and misfortunes, which too often
deaden our feelings of pity, as to sympathise with others in affliction, and even to promote innocent cheerfulness. Bowed down
by the loss of a wife[f], on whom he had called from amidst the
horrors of a hopeless melancholy, to "hide him from the ills of
life," and depressed by poverty, "that numbs the soul with icy
hand," his genius sank not beneath a load, which might have
crushed the loftiest; but the "incumbrances of his fortune were
shaken from his mind, ' as dew-drops from a lion's mane[g].'"

The same pure and exalted morality, which stamps their chief
value on the pages of the Rambler, instructs us in the lessons of
the Adventurer. Here is no cold doctrine of expediency or

---

[e] See Lounger, No. 30.

[f] "I have heard, he means to occasionally throw some papers into the Daily
Advertiser; but he has not begun yet, as he is in great affliction, I fear, poor
man, for the loss of his wife."—Letter from Miss Talbot to Mrs. Carter. Mrs.
Johnson died March 17, 1752.

[g] See the Preface to Shakespeare.

dangerous speculations on moral approbation, no easy virtue which can be practised without a struggle, and which interdicts the gratification of no passion but malice : here is no compromise of personal sensuality, for an endurance of others' frailties, amounting to an indifference of moral distinctions altogether. Johnson boldly and, at once, propounds the real motives to Christian conduct ; and does not, with some ethical writers, in a slavish dread of interfering with the more immediate office of the divine, hold out slender inducements to virtuous action, which can never give us strength to stem the torrent of passion ; but holding with the acute Owen Feltham [h], " that, as true religion cannot be without morality, no more can morality, that is right, be without religion," Johnson ever directs our attention, not to the world's smile or frown, but to the discharge of the duty which Providence assigns us, by the consideration of the awful approach of that night when no man can work. To conclude with the appropriate words of an eloquent writer, " in his sublime discussions of the most sacred truths, as no style can be too lofty nor conceptions too grand for such a subject, so has the great master never exerted the powers of his great genius with more signal success. Impiety shrinks beneath his rebuke ; the atheist trembles and repents ; the dying sinner catches a gleam of revealed hope ; and all acknowledge the just dispensations of eternal Wisdom [i]."

[h] Owen Feltham's Resolves.
[i] Indian Observer, N°. 1, 1793. See likewise Adventurers, N°ˢ. 120, 126, 128.

PREFATORY NOTICE

TO

THE IDLER.

THE Idler may be ranked among the best attempts which have been made to render our common newspapers the medium of rational amusement; and it maintained its ground in this character longer than any of the papers which have been brought forward by Colman and others on the same plan [a]. Dr. Johnson first inserted this production in the Universal Chronicle, or Weekly Gazette, April 15, 1758, four years after he had desisted from his labours as an essayist. It would seem probable, that Newbery, the publisher of the Chronicle, projected it as a vehicle for Johnson's essays, since it ceased to appear when its pages were no longer enlivened by the humour of the Idler.

It is well known, that Johnson was not "built of the press and pen [b]" when he composed the Rambler; but his sphere of observation had been much enlarged since its publication, and his more ample means no longer suffered his genius to be " limited by the narrow conversation, to which men in want are inevitably condemned [c]." " The sublime philosophy of the Rambler cannot properly be said to have portrayed the manners of the times; it has seldom touched on subjects so transient and fugitive, but has displayed the more fixed and invariable operations of the human

---

[a] The Genius was published by Colman in the St. James's Chronicle, 1761, 1762. The Gentleman, by the same author, came out in the London-Packet, 1775. The Grumbler was the production of the Antiquary Grose, and appeared in the English Chronicle, 1791.

[b] Owen Feltham.   [c] Preface to Shakespeare.

heart [d]." But the Idler breathes more of a worldly spirit, and savours less of the closet than Johnson's earlier essays; and, accordingly, we find delineated in its diversified pages the manners and characters of the day in amusing variety and contrast.

Written professedly for a paper of miscellaneous intelligence, the Idler dwells on the passing incidents of the day, whether serious or light [e], and abounds with party and political allusion. Johnson ever surveyed mankind with the eye of a philosopher; but his own easier circumstances would now present the world's aspect to him in brighter, fairer colours. Besides, he could, with more propriety and less risk of misapprehension, venture to trifle now, than when first he addressed the public.

The World [f] had diffused its precepts, and corrected the fluctuating manners of fashion, in the tone of fashionable raillery; and the Connoisseur [g], by its gay and sparkling effusions, had forwarded the advance of the public mind to that last stage of intellectual refinement, in which alone a relish exists for delicate and half latent irony. The plain and literal citizens of an earlier period, who conned over what was " so nominated in the bond," would have misapprehended that graceful playfulness of satire, elegant and fanciful as ever charmed the leisure of the literary loungers of Athens. For, in the writings of Bonnel Thornton and Colman, the philosophy of Aristippus may indeed be said to be revived [h]. We would not, however, be supposed, by these allusions, to imply that all the papers of the Idler are light and sportive; or that Johnson for a moment lost sight of a grand moral end in all his discussions. His mind only accommodated itself to the circumstances in which it was placed, and diligently sought to avail itself of each varying opportunity to admonish and to benefit, whether from the chair of philosophic reproof or in the cheerful, social circle. Whatever faults have been charged upon the Idler may be traced, we conceive, to this source. Nobody at times,

[d] Country Spectator, No. 1.   [e] Idler, No. 6.
[f] The World was published in 1753.   [g] The Connoisseur appeared in 1754.
[h] See Dr. Drake's Essays, II.

said Johnson, talks more laxly than I do[i]. And this acknowledged propensity may well be presumed to have affected the humorous and almost conversational tone of the work before us. In
the conscious pride of mental might and in the easier moments of
conversations, that illuminated the minds of Reynolds[k] and of
Burke, Johnson delighted to indulge in a lively sophistry which
might sometimes deceive himself, when at first he merely wished
to sport in elegant raillery or ludicrous paradox. When these
sallies were recorded and brought to bear against him on future
occasions, irritated at their misconstruction and conscious to himself of an upright intention, or at most of only a wish to promote
innocent cheerfulness, he was too stubborn in retracting what. he
had thus advanced. Hence, when menaced with a prosecution
for his definition of Excise in his Dictionary, so far from offering
apology or promising alteration, he called, in his Idler, a Commissioner of Excise the lowest of human beings, and classes him
with the scribbler for a party[l]. So strange a definition and still
less pardonable adherence to it can only be justified on the
ground of Johnson's warm feelings for the comfort of the middle
class of society. He knew that the execution of the excise laws
involved an intrusion into the privacies of domestic life, and often
violated the fireside of the unoffending and quiet tradesman. He,
therefore, disliked those laws altogether, and his warm-hearted
disposition would not allow him to calculate on their abstract advantages with modern political economists, who, in their generaliz-
ing doctrines, too frequently overlook individual comfort and interests. His remarks, in the same paper, on the edition of the
Pleas of the Crown cannot be thus vindicated, and we must here
lament an error in an otherwise honest and well-intentioned
mind[m]. Every impartial reader of his works may thus easily
trace to their origin Johnson's chief political errors, and his re-

---

[i] Journal of a Tour to the Hebrides.
[k] See life of Sir Joshua Reynolds, prefixed to his Works by Malone, i. 28, &c.
[l] See Idler, No. 65 and Mr. Chalmers' Preface to vol. 33 of the British
Essayists.
[m] See Gentleman's Magazine 1706. p. 272.

search must terminate in admiration of a writer, who never pro-
stituted his pen to fear or favour ; and who, though erroneous
often in his estimate of men and measures, still, in his support of
a party, firmly believed himself to be the advocate of morality and
right.   His tenderness of spirit, his firm principles and his deep
sense of the emptiness of human pursuits are visible amidst the
lighter papers of the Idler, and his serious reflections are, perhaps, more strikingly affecting as contrasted with mirthfulness
and pleasantry.

His concluding paper and the one[n] on the death of his
mother have, perhaps, never been surpassed.   Here is no affectation of sentimentality, no morbid and puling complaints, but the
dignified and chastened expression of sorrow, which a mind, con-
stituted as Johnson's, must have experienced on the departure
of a mother.   A heart, tender and susceptible of pathetic
emotion, as his was, must have deeply felt, how dreary it is to
walk downward to the grave unregarded by her "who has looked
on our childhood."   Occasions for more violent and perturbed
grief may occur to us in our passage through life, but the gentle,
quiet death of a mother speaks to us with "still small voice" of
our wasting years, and breaks completely and, at once, our earliest
and most cherished associations.   This tenderness of spirit seems
ever to have actuated Johnson, and he is surely greatest when he
breathes it forth over the sorrows and miseries of man.   Even in
his humorous papers, he never wounds feeling for the sake of
raising a laugh, nor sports with folly, but in the hope of reclaim-
ing the vicious and with the design of warning the young of the
delusion and danger of an example, which can only be imitated
by the forfeiture of virtue and the practice of vice.   "In whatever he undertook, it was his determined purpose to rectify the
heart, to purify the passions, to give ardour to virtue and confidence to truth[o]."

a Idler, N°. 41.
• See Pursuits of Literature, Dialogue I. note.

CONTENTS OF THE FOURTH VOLUME.

THE ADVENTURER.

THE IDLER.

ADVENTURER.

———

Nº. 34. SATURDAY, MARCH 3, 1753.

———

Has toties optata exegit gloria pœnas.   Juv. Sat. x. 187.
Such fate pursues the votaries of praise.

TO THE ADVENTURER.

SIR,   Fleet Prison, Feb. 24.

To a benevolent disposition, every state of life will afford some opportunities of contributing to the welfare of mankind. Opulence and splendour are enabled to dispel the cloud of adversity, to dry up the tears of the widow and the orphan, and to increase the felicity of all around them: their example will animate virtue, and retard the progress of vice. And even indigence and obscurity, though without power to confer happiness, may at least prevent misery, and apprize those who are blinded by their passions, that they are on the brink of irremediable calamity.

Pleased, therefore, with the thought of recovering others from that folly which has embittered my own days, I have presumed to address the ADVENTURER from the dreary mansions of wretchedness and despair, of which the gates are so wonderfully constructed, as to fly open for the re-

ception of strangers, though they are impervious as a rock
of adamant to such as are within them :

> —— *Facilis descensus Averni:*
> *Noctes atque dies patet atri janua Ditis :*
> *Sed revocare gradum, superasque evadere ad auras,*
> *Hoc opus, hic labor est,——————*   VIRG. Æn. vi. 126.

> The gates of hell are open night and day ;
> Smooth the descent, and easy is the way :
> But to return and view the cheerful skies ;
> In this the task and mighty labour lies.   DRYDEN.

Suffer me to acquaint you, Sir, that I have glittered at
the ball, and sparkled in the circle ; that I have had the
happiness to be the unknown favourite of au unknown
lady at the masquerade, have been the delight of tables of
the first fashion, and envy of my brother beaux ; and to
descend a little lower, it is, I believe, still remembered,
that Messrs. Velours and d'Espagne stand indebted for a
great part of their present influence at Guildhall, to the
elegance of my shape, and the graceful freedom of my
carriage.

> —— *Sed quæ præclara et prospera tanti,*
> *Ut rebus lætis par sit mensura malorum?*   JUV. Sat. x. 97.

> See the wild purchase of the bold and vain,
> Where every bliss is bought with equal pain !

As I entered into the world very young, with an elegant
person and a large estate, it was not long before I disentangled myself from the shackles of religion ; for I was
determined to the pursuit of pleasure, which according to
my notions consisted in the unrestrained and unlimited
gratifications of every passion and every appetite ; and as
this could not be obtained under the frowns of a perpetual
dictator, I considered religion as my enemy ; and proceed-
ing to treat her with contempt and derision, was not a
little delighted, that the unfashionableness of her appearance, and the unanimated uniformity of her motions, afforded frequent opportunities for the sallies of my imagination.

Conceiving now that I was sufficiently qualified to laugh

away scruples, I imparted my remarks to those among my
female favourites, whose virtue I intended to attack; for
I was well assured, that pride would be able to make but
a weak defence, when religion was subverted; nor was
my success below my expectation: the love of pleasure is
too strongly implanted in the female breast, to suffer them
scrupulously to examine the validity of arguments designed
to weaken restraint; all are easily led to believe, that
whatever thwarts their inclination must be wrong: little
more, therefore, was required, than by the addition of
some circumstances, and the exaggeration of others, to
make merriment supply the place of demonstration; nor
was I so senseless as to offer arguments to such as could
not attend to them, and with whom a repartee or catch
would more effectually answer the same purpose. This
being effected, there remained only " the dread of the
world:" but Roxana soared too high, to think the opinion
of others worthy her notice; Lætitia seemed to think
of it only to declare, that " if all her hairs were worlds,"
she should reckon them "well lost for love;" and Pas-
torella fondly conceived, that she could dwell for ever by
the side of a bubbling fountain, content with her swain and
fleecy care; without considering that stillness and solitude
can afford satisfaction only to innocence.

It is not the desire of new acquisitions, but the glory of
conquests, that fires the soldier's breast; as indeed the
town is seldom worth much, when it has suffered the de-
vastations of a siege; so that though I did not openly
declare the effects of my own prowess, which is forbidden
by the laws of honour, it cannot be supposed that I was
very solicitous to bury my reputation, or to hinder accidental discoveries. To have gained one victory, is an in-
ducement to hazard a second engagement: and though the
success of the general should be a reason for increasing
the strength of the fortification, it becomes, with many, a
pretence for an immediate surrender, under the notion
that no power is able to withstand so formidable an adversary; while others brave the danger, and think it mean

to surrender, and dastardly to fly. Melissa, indeed, knew better; and though she could not boast the apathy, steadiness, and inflexibility of a Cato, wanted not the more prudent virtue of Scipio, and gained the victory by declining the contest.

You must not, however, imagine, that I was, during this state of abandoned libertinism, so fully convinced of the fitness of my own conduct, as to be free from uneasiness. I knew very well, that I might justly be deemed the pest of society, and that such proceedings must terminate in the destruction of my health and fortune; but to admit thoughts of this kind was to live upon the rack: I fled, therefore, to the regions of mirth and jollity, as they are called, and endeavoured with Burgundy, and a continual rotation of company, to free myself from the pangs of reflection. From these orgies we frequently sallied forth in quest of adventures, to the no small terrour and consternation of all the sober stragglers that came in our way: and though we never injured, like our illustrious progenitors, the Mohocks, either life or limbs; yet we have in the midst of Covent Garden buried a tailor, who had been troublesome to some of our fine gentlemen, beneath a heap of cabbage-leaves and stalks, with this conceit,

Satia te caule quem semper cupisti.

Glut yourself with cabbage, of which you have always been greedy.

There can be no reason for mentioning the common exploits of breaking windows and bruising the watch; unless it be to tell you of the device of producing before the justice broken lanterns, which have been paid for an hundred times; or their appearances with patches on their heads, under pretence of being cut by the sword that was never drawn: nor need I say any thing of the more formidable attack of sturdy chairmen, armed with poles; by a slight stroke of which, the pride of Ned Revel's face was at once laid flat, and that effected in an instant, which its most mortal foe had for years assayed in vain. I shall pass over the accidents that attended attempts to scale windows, and endeavours to dislodge signs from their hooks: there are many "hair-breadth 'scapes," besides those in the "imminent deadly breach;" but the rake's life, though it be equally hazardous with that of the soldier, is neither accompanied with present honour nor with pleasing retrospect; such is, and such ought to be, the difference between the enemy and the preserver of his country.

Amidst such giddy and thoughtless extravagance, it will not seem strange, that I was often the dupe of coarse flattery. When Mons. L'Allonge assured me, that I thrust quart over arm better than any man in England, what could I less than present him with a sword that cost me thirty pieces? I was bound for a hundred pounds for Tom Trippet, because he had declared that he would dance a minuet with any man in the three kingdoms except myself. But I often parted with money against my inclination, either because I wanted the resolution to refuse, or dreaded the appellation of a niggardly fellow; and I may be truly said to have squandered my estate, without honour, without friends, and without pleasure. The last may, perhaps, appear strange to men unacquainted with the masquerade of life: I deceived others, and I endeavoured to deceive myself; and have worn the face of pleasantry and gaiety, while my heart suffered the most exquisite torture.

By the instigation and encouragement of my friends, I became at length ambitious of a seat in parliament; and accordingly set out for the town of Wallop in the west, where my arrival was welcomed by a thousand throats, and I was in three days sure of a majority: but after drinking out one hundred and fifty hogsheads of wine, and bribing two-thirds of the corporation twice over, I had the mortification to find that the borough had been before sold to Mr. Courtly.

In a life of this kind, my fortune, though considerable, was presently dissipated; and as the attraction grows more strong the nearer any body approaches the earth, when once a man begins to sink into poverty, he falls with velocity always increasing; every supply is purchased at a higher and higher price, and every office of kindness obtained with greater and greater difficulty. Having now acquainted you with my state of elevation, I shall, if you encourage the continuance of my correspondence, shew you by what steps I descended from a first floor in Pall-Mall to my present habitation [a].

I am, Sir,

Your humble servant,

MISARGYRUS.

N°. 39.   TUESDAY, MARCH 20, 1753.

—'Οδυσεὺς φύλλοισι καλύψατο· τῷ δ' ἄρ' 'Αθήνη
"Υπνον ἐπ' ὄμμασι χεῦ', ἵνα μιν παύσειε τάχιστα
Δυσπονέος καμάτοιο.——————   Hom. E'. 491.

—Pallas pour'd sweet slumbers on his soul ;
And balmy dreams, the gift of soft repose,
Calm'd all his pains, and banish'd all his woes.   POPE.

IF every day did not produce fresh instances of the ingratitude of mankind, we might, perhaps, be at a loss, why so liberal and impartial a benefactor as sleep, should meet with so few historians or panegyrists. Writers are so totally absorbed by the business of the day, as never to turn their attention to that power, whose officious hand so seasonably suspends the burthen of life ; and without whose interposition man would not be able to endure the fatigue of labour, however rewarded, or the struggle with opposition, however successful.

Night, though she divides to many the longest part of life, and to almost all the most innocent and happy, is yet unthankfully neglected, except by those who pervert her gifts.

The astronomers, indeed, expect her with impatience, and felicitate themselves upon her arrival: Fontenelle has

---

[a] For an account of the disputes raised on this paper, and on the other letters of Misargyrus, see Preface.

not failed to celebrate her praises; and to chide the sun for hiding from his view the worlds, which he imagines to appear in every constellation. Nor have the poets been always deficient in her praises: Milton has observed of the night, that it is " the pleasant time, the cool, the silent."

These men may, indeed, well be expected to pay particular homage to night; since they are indebted to her, not only for cessation of pain, but increase of pleasure; not only for slumber, but for knowledge. But the greater part of her avowed votaries are the sons of luxury; who appropriate to festivity the hours designed for rest; who consider the reign of pleasure as commencing when day begins to withdraw her busy multitudes, and ceases to dissipate attention by intrusive and unwelcome variety; who begin to awake to joy when the rest of the world sinks into insensibility; and revel in the soft affluence of flattering and artificial lights, which " more shadowy set off the face of things."

Without touching upon the fatal consequences of a custom, which, as Ramazzini observes, will be for ever condemned, and for ever retained; it may be observed, that however sleep may be put off from time to time, yet the demand is of so importunate a nature, as not to remain long unsatisfied: and if, as some have done, we consider it as the tax of life, we cannot but observe it as a tax that must be paid, unless we could cease to be men; for Alexander declared, that nothing convinced him that he was not a divinity, but his not being able to live without sleep.

To live without sleep in our present fluctuating state, however desirable it might seem to the lady in Clelia, can surely be the wish only of the young or the ignorant; to every one else, a perpetual vigil will appear to be a state of wretchedness, second only to that of the miserable beings, whom Swift has in his travels so elegantly described, as " supremely cursed with immortality."

Sleep is necessary to the happy to prevent satiety, and

to endear life by a short absence; and to the miserable, to relieve them by intervals of quiet. Life is to most, such as could not be endured without frequent intermission of existence: Homer, therefore, has thought it an office worthy of the goddess of wisdom, to lay Ulysses asleep when landed on Phæacia.

It is related of Barretier, whose early advances in literature scarce any human mind has equalled, that he spent twelve hours of the four-and-twenty in sleep: yet this appears from the bad state of his health, and the shortness of his life, to have been too small a respite for a mind so vigorously and intensely employed: it is to be regretted, therefore, that he did not exercise his mind less, and his body more: since by this means, it is highly probable, that though he would not then have astonished with the blaze of a comet, he would yet have shone with the permanent radiance of a fixed star.

Nor should it be objected, that there have been many men who daily spend fifteen or sixteen hours in study: for by some of whom this is reported it has never been done; others have done it for a short time only; and of the rest it appears, that they employed their minds in such operations as required neither celerity nor strength, in the low drudgery of collating copies, comparing authorities, digesting dictionaries, or accumulating compilations.

Men of study and imagination are frequently upbraided by the industrious and plodding sons of care, with passing too great a part of their life in a state of inaction. But these defiers of sleep seem not to remember that though it must be granted them that they are crawling about before the break of day, it can seldom be said that they are perfectly awake; they exhaust no spirits, and require no repairs; but lie torpid as a toad in marble, or at least are known to live only by an inert and sluggish loco-motive faculty, and may be said, like a wounded snake, to " drag their slow length along."

Man has been long known among philosophers by the appellation of the microcosm, or epitome of the world:

the resemblance between the great and little world might, by a rational observer, be detailed to many particulars; and to many more by a fanciful speculatist. I know not in which of these two classes I shall be ranged for observing, that as the total quantity of light and darkness allotted in the course of the year to every region of the earth is the same, though distributed at various times and in different portions; so, perhaps, to each individual of the human species, nature has ordained the same quantity of wakefulness and sleep; though divided by some into a total quiescence and vigorous exertion of their faculties, and, blended by others in a kind of twilight of existence, in a state between dreaming and reasoning, in which they either think without action, or act without thought.

The poets are generally well affected to sleep: as men who think with vigour, they require respite from thought; and gladly resign themselves to that gentle power, who not only bestows rest, but frequently leads them to happier regions, where patrons are always kind, and audiences are always candid; where they are feasted in the bowers of imagination, and crowned with flowers divested of their prickles, and laurels of unfading verdure.

The more refined and penetrating part of mankind, who take wide surveys of the wilds of life, who see the innumerable terrours and distresses that are perpetually preying on the heart of man, and discern with unhappy perspicuity, calamities yet latent in their causes, are glad to close their eyes upon the gloomy prospect, and lose in a short insensibility the remembrance of others' miseries and their own. The hero has no higher hope, than that, after having routed legions after legions, and added kingdom to kingdom, he shall retire to milder happiness, and close his days in social festivity. The wit or the sage can expect no greater happiness, than that, after having harassed his reason in deep researches, and fatigued his fancy in boundless excursions, he shall sink at night in the tranquillity of sleep.

The poets, among all those that enjoy the blessings of

sleep, have been least ashamed to acknowledge their benefactor.   How much Statius considered the evils of life as
assuaged and softened by the balm of slumber, we may.
discover by that pathetick invocation, which he poured out`
in his waking nights: and that Cowley, among the other
felicities of his darling solitude, did not forget to number
the privilege of sleeping without disturbance, we may
learn from the rank that he assigns among the gifts of nature to the poppy, " which is scattered," says he, " over
the fields of corn, that all the needs of man may be easily
satisfied, and that bread and sleep may be found together."

Si quis invisum Cereri benignæ
Me putat germen, vehementer errat ;
Illa me in partem recipit libenter
                          Fertilis agri.

Meque frumentumque simul per omnes
Consulens mundo Dea spargit oras;
Crescite, O! dixit, duo magna susten-
                          tacula vitæ.

Carpe, mortalis, mea dona lætus,
Carpe, nec plantas alias require,
Sed satur panis, satur et soporis,
                          Cætera sperne.

He wildly errs who thinks I yield
Precedence in the well-cloth'd field,
   Tho' mix'd with wheat I grow :
Indulgent Ceres knew my worth,
And to adorn the teeming earth,
   She bade the Poppy blow.

Nor vainly gay the sight to please,
But blest with pow'r mankind to ease,
   The goddess saw me rise :
" Thrive with the life-supporting grain,"
She cried, " the solace of the swain,
   The cordial of his eyes.

Seize, happy mortal, seize the good ;
My hand supplies thy sleep and food,
   And makes thee truly blest :
With plenteous meals enjoy the day,
 In slumbers pass the night away,
   And leave to fate the rest."   C. B.

Sleep, therefore, as the chief of all earthly blessings,
is justly appropriated to industry and temperance ; the re-

freshing rest, and the peaceful night, are the portion only
of him who lies down weary with honest labour, and free
from the fumes of indigested luxury; it is the just doom
of laziness and gluttony, to be inactive without ease, and
drowsy without tranquillity.

Sleep has been often mentioned as the image of death[b];
" so like it," says Sir Thomas Brown, " that I dare not
trust it without my prayers :" their resemblance is, indeed,
apparent and striking; they both, when they seize the
body, leave the soul at liberty : and wise is he that remembers of both, that they can be safe and happy only
by virtue.

<hr>

N°. 41.   TUESDAY, MARCH 27, 1753.

————*Si mutabile pectus*
Est tibi, consiliis, non curribus, utere nostris ;
Dum potes, et solidis etiamnum sedibus adstas,
Dumque male optatos nondum premis inscius axes. Ovid. Met. ii. 143.

———— Th' attempt forsake,
And not my chariot but my counsel take ;
While yet securely on the earth you stand ;
Nor touch the horses with too rash a hand.   Addison.

TO THE ADVENTURER.

SIR,   Fleet, March 24.

I NOW send you the sequel of my story, which
had not been so long delayed, if I could have brought
myself to imagine, that any real impatience was felt for
the fate of Misargyrus; who has travelled no unbeaten
track to misery, and consequently can present the reader
only with such incidents as occur in daily life.

You have seen me, Sir, in the zenith of my glory, not
dispensing the kindly warmth of an all-cheering sun: but,

---

[b] Lovely sleep! thou beautiful image of terrible death,
Be thou my pillow-companion, my angel of rest!
Come, O sleep! for thine are the joys of living and dying:
Life without sorrow, and death with no anguish, no pain.
From the German of Schmidt.

like another Phaëton, scorching and blasting every thing round me. I shall proceed, therefore, to finish my career, and pass as rapidly as possible through the remaining vicissitudes of my life.

When I first began to be in want of money, I made no doubt of an immediate supply. The newspapers were perpetually offering directions to men, who seemed to have no other business than to gather heaps of gold for those who place their supreme felicity in scattering it. I posted away, therefore, to one of these advertisers, who by his proposals seemed· to deal in thousands; and was not a little chagrined to find, that this general benefactor would have nothing to do with any larger sum than thirty pounds, nor would venture that without a joint note from myself and a reputable housekeeper, or for a longer time than three months.

It was not yet so bad with me, as that I needed to solicit surety for thirty pounds: yet partly from the greediness that extravagance always produces, and partly from a desire of seeing the humour of a petty usurer, a character of which I had hitherto lived in ignorance, I condescended to listen to his terms. He proceeded to inform me of my great felicity in not falling into the hands of an extortioner; and assured me, that I should find him extremely moderate in his demands: he was not, indeed, certain that he could furnish me with the whole sum, for people were at this particular time extremely pressing and importunate for money: yet, as I had the appearance of a gentleman, he would try what he could do, and give me his answer in three days.

At the expiration of the time, I called upon him again; and was again informed of the great demand for money, and that, "money was money now:" he then advised me to be punctual in my payment, as that might induce him to befriend me hereafter; and delivered me the money, deducting at the rate of five and thirty *per cent.* with another panegyrick upon his own moderation.

I will not tire you with the various practices of usurious

oppression; but cannot omit my transaction with Squeeze on Tower-hill, who, finding me a young man of considerable expectations, employed an agent to persuade me to borrow five hundred pounds, to be refunded by an annual payment of twenty *per cent.* during the joint lives of his daughter Nancy Squeeze and myself. The negociator came prepared to enforce his proposal with all his art; but, finding that I caught his offer with the eagerness of necessity, he grew cold and languid; " he had mentioned it out of kindness; he would try to serve me: Mr. Squeeze was an honest man, but extremely cautious." In three days he came to tell me, that his endeavours had been ineffectual, Mr. Squeeze having no good opinion of my life; but that there was one expedient remaining: Mrs. Squeeze could influence her husband, and her good will might be gained by a compliment. I waited that afternoon on Mrs. Squeeze, and poured out before her the flatteries which usually gain access to rank and beauty: I did not then know, that there are places in which the only compliment is a bribe. Having yet credit with a jeweller, I afterwards procured a ring of thirty guineas, which I humbly presented, and was soon admitted to a treaty with Mr. Squeeze. He appeared peevish and backward, and my old friend whispered me, that he would never make a dry bargain: I therefore invited him to a tavern. Nine times we met on the affair; nine times I paid four pounds for the supper and claret; and nine guineas I gave the agent for good offices. I then obtained the money, paying ten *per cent.* advance ; and at the tenth meeting gave another supper, and disbursed fifteen pounds for the writings.

Others who styled themselves brokers, would only trust their money upon goods: that I might, therefore, try every art of expensive folly, I took a house and furnished it. I amused myself with despoiling my moveables of their glossy appearance, for fear of alarming the lender with suspicions: and in this I succeeded so well, that he favoured me with one hundred and sixty pounds upon that which was rated at seven hundred. I then found that I was to maintain a guardian about me to prevent the goods from being broken or removed. This was, indeed, an unexpected tax; but it was too late to recede: and I comforted myself, that I might prevent a creditor, of whom I had some apprehensions, from seizing, by having a prior execution always in the house.

By such means I had so embarrassed myself, that my whole attention was engaged in contriving excuses, and raising small sums to quiet such as words would no longer mollify. It cost me eighty pounds in presents to Mr. Leech the attorney, for his forbearance of one hundred, which he solicited me to take when I had no need. I was perpetually harassed with importunate demands, and insulted by wretches, who a few months before would not have dared to raise their eyes from the dust before me. I lived in continual terrour, frighted by every noise at the door, and terrified at the approach of every step quicker than common. I never retired to rest without feeling the justness of the Spanish proverb, " Let him who sleeps too much, borrow the pillow of a debtor:" my solicitude and vexation kept me long waking; and when I had closed my eyes, I was pursued or insulted by visionary bailiffs.

When I reflected upon the meanness of the shifts I had reduced myself to, I could not but curse the folly and extravagance that had overwhelmed me in a sea of troubles, from which it was highly improbable that I should ever emerge. I had some time lived in hopes of an estate, at the death of my uncle; but he disappointed me by marrying his housekeeper; and, catching an opportunity soon after of quarrelling with me, for settling twenty pounds a year upon a girl whom I had seduced, told me that he would take care to prevent his fortune from being squandered upon prostitutes.

Nothing now remained, but the chance of extricating myself by marriage; a scheme which, I flattered myself, nothing but my present distress would have made me think on with patience. I determined, therefore, to look out for a tender novice, with a large fortune, at her own

· disposal; and accordingly fixed my eyes upon Miss Biddy Simper. I had now paid her six or seven visits; and so fully convinced her of my being a gentleman and a rake, that I made no doubt that both her person and fortune would be soon mine.

At this critical time, Miss Gripe called upon me, in a chariot bought with my money, and loaded with trinkets that I had, in my days of affluence, lavished on her. Those days were now over; and there was little hope that they would ever return. She was not able to withstand the temptation of ten pounds that Talon the bailiff offered her, but brought him into my apartment disguised in a livery; and taking my sword to the window, under pretence of admiring the workmanship, beckoned him to seize me.

Delay would have been expensive without use, as the debt was too considerable for payment or bail: I, therefore, suffered myself to be immediately conducted to goal.

> *Vestibulum ante ipsum, primisque in faucibus Orci,*
> *Luctus et ultrices posuere cubilia curæ :*
> *Pallentesque habitant morbi, tristisque senectus,*
> *Et metus, et malesuada fames, et turpis egestas.*   Virg. Æn. vi. 273.

> Just in the gate and in the jaws of hell,
> Revengeful cares and sullen sorrows dwell;
> And pale diseases, and repining age;
> Want, fear, and famine's unresisted rage.   Dryden.

Confinement of any kind is dreadful; a prison is sometimes able to shock those, who endure it in a good cause: let your imagination, therefore, acquaint you with what I have not words to express, and conceive, if possible, the horrours of imprisonment attended with reproach and ignominy, of involuntary association with the refuse of mankind, with wretches who were before too abandoned for society, but, being now freed from shame or fear, are hourly improving their vices by consorting with each other.

There are, however, a few, whom, like myself, imprisonment has rather mortified than hardened: with these only I converse; and of these you may, perhaps, hereafter receive some account from

Your humble servant,   MISARGYRUS.

N°. 45. TUESDAY, APRIL 10, 1753

Nulla fides regni sociis, omnisque potestas
Impatiens consortis erit.————   Lucan. Lib. i. 92.

No faith of partnership dominion owns :
Still discord hovers o'er divided thrones.

IT is well known, that many things appear plausible in speculation, which can never be reduced to practice ; and that of the numberless projects that have flattered mankind with theoretical speciousness, few have served any other purpose than to show the ingenuity of their contrivers. A voyage to the moon, however romantick and absurd the scheme may now appear, since the properties of air have been better understood, seemed highly probable to many of the aspiring wits in the last century, who began to dote upon their glossy plumes, and fluttered with impatience for the hour of their departure :

————————————*Pereunt vestigia mille*
Ante fugam, absentemque ferit gravis ungula campum.

Hills, vales and floods appear already crost ;
And, ere he starts, a thousand steps are lost.   POPE.

Among the fallacies which only experience can detect, there are some, of which scarcely experience itself can destroy the influence ; some which, by a captivating show of indubitable certainty, are perpetually gaining upon the human mind ; and which, though every trial ends in disappointment, obtain new credit as the sense of miscarriage wears gradually away, persuade us to try again what we have tried already, and expose us by the same failure to double vexation.

Of this tempting, this delusive kind, is the expectation of great performances by confederated strength. The speculatist, when he has carefully observed how much may be performed by a single hand, calculates by a very easy operation the force of thousands, and goes on accumulating power till resistance vanishes before it ; then rejoices in the success of his new scheme, and wonders at the folly or idleness of former ages, who have lived in want of what might so readily be procured, and suffered themselves to be debarred from happiness by obstacles which one united effort would have so easily surmounted.

But this gigantick phantom of collective power vanishes at once into air and emptiness, at the first attempt to put it into action. The different apprehensions, the discordant passions, the jarring interests of men, will scarcely permit that many should unite in one undertaking.

Of a great and complicated design, some will never be brought to discern the end; and of the several means by which it may be accomplished, the choice will be a perpetual subject of debate, as every man is swayed in his determination by his own knowledge or convenience. In a long series of action some will languish with fatigue, and some be drawn off by present gratifications; some will loiter because others labour, and some will cease to labour because others loiter: and if once they come within prospect of success and profit, some will be greedy and others envious; some will undertake more than they can perform, to enlarge their claims of advantage; some will perform less than they undertake, lest their labours should chiefly turn to the benefit of others.

The history of mankind informs us that a single power is very seldom broken by a confederacy. States of different interests, and aspects malevolent to each other, may be united for a time by common distress; and in the ardour of self-preservation fall unanimously upon an enemy, by whom they are all equally endangered. But if their first attack can be withstood, time will never fail to dissolve their union: success and miscarriage will be equally destructive: after the conquest of a province, they will quarrel in the division; after the loss of a battle, all will be endeavouring to secure themselves by abandoning the rest.

From the impossibility of confining numbers to the constant and uniform prosecution of a common interest, arises the difficulty of securing subjects against the encroachment of governours. Power is always gradually stealing away from the many to the few, because the few are more vigilant and consistent; it still contracts to a smaller number, till in time it centres in a single person.

Thus all the forms of governments instituted among mankind, perpetually tend towards monarchy; and power, however diffused through the whole community, is, by negligence or corruption, commotion or distress, reposed at last in the chief magistrate.

" There never appear," says Swift, " more than five or six men of genius in an age; but if they were united, the world could not stand before them." It is happy, therefore, for mankind, that of this union there is· no probability. As men take in a wider compass of intellectual survey, they are more likely to choose different objects of pursuit; as they see more ways to the same end, they will be less easily persuaded to travel together; as each is better qualified to form an independent scheme of private greatness, he will reject with greater obstinacy the project of another; as each is more able to distinguish himself as the head of a party, he will less readily be made a follower or an associate.

The reigning philosophy informs us, that the vast bodies which constitute the universe, are regulated in their progress through the ethereal spaces by the perpetual agency of contrary forces; by one of which they are restrained from deserting their orbits, and losing themselves in the immensity of heaven; and held off by the other from rushing together, and clustering round their centre with everlasting cohesion.

The same contrariety of impulse may be perhaps discovered in the motions of men: we are formed for society, not for combination; we are equally unqualified to live in a close connexion with our fellow-beings, and in total separation from them; we are attracted towards each other by general sympathy, but kept back from contact by private interests.

Some philosophers have been foolish enough to imagine, that improvements might be made in the system of the universe, by a different arrangement of the orbs of heaven; and politicians, equally ignorant and equally presumptuous, may easily be led to suppose, that the happiness of our world would be promoted by a different tendency of the human mind. It appears, indeed, to a slight and superficial observer, that many things impracticable in our present state, might be easily effected, if mankind were better disposed to union and co-operation: but a little reflection will discover, that if confederacies were easily formed, they would lose their efficacy, since numbers would be opposed to numbers, and unanimity to unanimity; and instead of the present petty competitions of individuals or single families, multitudes would be supplanting multitudes, and thousands plotting against thousands.

There is no class of the human species, of which the union seems to have been more expected, than of the learned: the rest of the world have almost always agreed to shut scholars up together in colleges and cloisters; surely not without hope, that they would look for that happiness in concord, which they were debarred from finding in variety; and that such conjunctions of intellect would recompense the munificence of founders and patrons, by performances above the reach of any single mind.

But discord, who found means to roll her apple into the banqueting chamber of the goddesses, has had the address to scatter her laurels in the seminaries of learning. The friendship of students and of beauties is for the most part equally sincere, and equally durable: as both depend for happiness on the regard of others, on that of which the value arises merely from comparison, they are both exposed to perpetual jealousies, and both incessantly employed in schemes to intercept the praises of each other.

I am, however, far from intending to inculcate that this confinement of the studious to studious companions, has been wholly without advantage to the publick: neighbourhood, where it does not conciliate friendship, incites competition; and he that would contentedly rest in a lower degree of excellence, where he had no rival to dread, will be urged by his impatience of inferiority to incessant endeavours after great attainments.

These stimulations of honest rivalry are, perhaps, the chief effects of academies and societies; for whatever be the bulk of their joint labours, every single piece is always the production of an individual, that owes nothing to his colleagues but the contagion of diligence, a resolution to write, because the rest are writing, and the scorn of obscurity while the rest are illustrious[c].

[c] It may not be uninteresting to place in immediate comparison with this finished paper its first rough draught as given in Boswell, vol. i.

'Confederacies difficult; why.

"Seldom in war a match for single persons—nor in peace; therefore kings make themselves absolute. Confederacies in learning—every great work the work of one. *Bruy.* Scholars friendship like ladies. Scribebamus, &c. Mart. The apple of discord—the laurel of discord—the poverty of criticism. Swift's opinion of the power of six geniuses united. That union scarce possible. His remarks just;—man a social, not steady nature. Drawn to man by words, repelled by passions. Orb drawn by attraction, rep. [*repelled*] by centrifugal.

"Common danger unites by crushing other passions—but they return. Equality hinders compliance. Superiority produces insolence and envy. Too much regard in each to private interest;—too little.

"The mischiefs of private and exclusive societies.—The fitness of social attraction diffused through the whole. The mischiefs of too partial love of our country. Contraction of moral duties. Οἱ φίλοι, οὖ φίλος.

"Every man moves upon his own centre, and therefore repels others from too near a contact, though he may comply with some general laws. Of confederacy with superiors every one knows the inconvenience. With equals no authority;—every man his own opinion—his own interest.

"Man and wife hardly united;—scarce ever without children. Computation, if two to one against two, how many against five? If confederacies were easy—useless;—many oppresses many.—If possible only to some, dangerous. *Principum amicitias.*"

N°. 50. SATURDAY, APRIL 28, 1753.

Quicunque turpi fraude semel innotuit,
Etiamsi verum dicit, amittit fidem.   PHÆD. Lib. i. Fab. x. 1.

The wretch that often has deceiv'd,
Though truth he speaks, is ne'er believ'd.

WHEN Aristotle was once asked, what a man could gain by uttering falsehoods? he replied, " Not to be credited when he shall tell the truth."

The character of a liar is at once so hateful and contemptible, that even of those who have lost their virtue it might be expected that from the violation of truth they should be restrained by their pride. Almost every other vice that disgraces human nature, may be kept in countenance by applause and association: the corrupter of virgin innocence sees himself envied by the men, and at least not detested by the women; the drunkard may easily unite with beings, devoted like himself to noisy merriments or silent insensibility, who will celebrate his victories over the novices of intemperance, boast themselves the companions of his prowess, and tell with rapture of the multitudes whom unsuccessful emulation has hurried to the grave; even the robber and the cut-throat have their followers, who admire their address and intrepidity, their stratagems of rapine, and their fidelity to the gang.

The liar, and only the liar, is invariably and universally despised, abandoned, and disowned: he has no domestick consolations, which he can oppose to the censure of mankind; he can retire to no fraternity, where his crimes may stand in the place of virtues; but is given up to the hisses of the multitude, without friend and without apologist. It is the peculiar condition of falsehood, to be equally detested by the good and bad: " The devils," says Sir Thomas Brown, " do not tell lies to one another; for truth is necessary to all societies: nor can the society of hell subsist without it."

It is natural to expect, that a crime thus generally detested should be generally avoided; at least, that none should expose himself to unabated and unpitied infamy, without an adequate temptation; and that to guilt so easily detected, and so severely punished, an adequate temptation would not readily be found.

Yet so it is, that in defiance of censure and contempt, truth is frequently violated; and scarcely the most vigilant and unremitted circumspection will secure him that mixes with mankind, from being hourly deceived by men of whom it can scarcely be imagined, that they mean any injury to him or profit to themselves: even where the subject of conversation could not have been expected to put the passions in motion, or to have excited either hope or fear, or zeal or malignity, sufficient to induce any man to put his reputation in hazard, however little he might value it, or to overpower the love of truth, however weak might be its influence.

The casuists have very diligently distinguished lies into their several classes, according to their various degrees of malignity: but they have, I think, generally omitted that which is most common, and perhaps, not least mischievous; which, since the moralists have not given it a name, I shall distinguish as (the *lie of vanity.*)

To vanity may justly be imputed most of the falsehoods which every man perceives hourly playing upon his ear, and, perhaps, most of those that are propagated with success. To the lie of commerce, and the lie of malice, the motive is so apparent, that they are seldom negligently or implicitly received; suspicion is always watchful over the practices of interest; and whatever the hope of gain, or desire of mischief, can prompt one man to assert, another is by reasons equally cogent incited to refute. But vanity pleases herself with such slight gratifications, and looks forward to pleasure so remotely consequential, that her practices raise no alarm, and her stratagems are not easily discovered.

Vanity is, indeed, often suffered to pass unpursued by

suspicion, because he that would watch her motions, can never be at rest: fraud and malice are bounded in their influence; some opportunity of time and place is necessary to their agency; but scarce any man is abstracted one moment from his vanity; and he, to whom truth affords no gratifications, is generally inclined to seek them in false-hoods.

It is remarked by Sir Kenelm Digby, " that every man has a desire to appear superior to others, though it were only in having seen what they have not seen." Such an accidental advantage, since it neither implies merit, nor confers dignity, one would think should not be desired so much as to be counterfeited: yet even this vanity, trifling as it is, produces innumerable narratives, all equally false; but more or less credible in proportion to the skill or confidence of the relater. How many may a man of diffusive conversation count among his acquaintances, whose lives have been signalized by numberless· escapes; who never cross the river but in a storm, or take a journey into the country without more adventures than befel the knights-errant of ancient times in pathless forests or enchanted castles! How many must he know, to whom portents and prodigies are of daily·occurrence; and for whom nature is hourly working wonders invisible to every other eye, only to supply them with subjects of conversation.

Others there are that amuse themselves with the dis-semination of falsehood, at greater hazard of detection and disgrace; men marked out by some lucky planet for uni-versal confidence and friendship, who have been consulted in every difficulty, intrusted with every secret, and sum-moned to every transaction: it is the supreme felicity of these men, to stun all companies with noisy information; to still doubt, and overbear opposition, with certain know-ledge or authentick intelligence. A liar of this kind, with a strong memory or brisk imagination, is often the oracle of an obscure club, and, till time discovers his impostures, dictates to his hearers with uncontrouled authority; for if a publick question be started, he was present at the debate;

if a new fashion be mentioned, he was at court the first
day of its appearance; if a new performance of literature
draws the attention of the publick, he has patronized the
author, and seen his work in manuscript; if a criminal of
eminence be condemned to die, he often predicted his
fate, and endeavoured his reformation: and who that lives
at a distance from the scene of action, will dare to contradict a man, who reports from his own eyes and ears, and
to whom all persons and affairs are thus intimately known?

This kind of falsehood is generally successful for a time,
because it is practised at first with timidity and caution:
but the prosperity of the liar is of short duration; the reception of one story is always an incitement to the forgery
of another less probable; and he goes on to triumph over
tacit credulity, till pride or reason rises up against him,
and his companions will no longer endure to see him wiser
than themselves.

It is apparent, that the inventors of all these fictions intend some exaltation of themselves, and are led off by the
pursuit of honour from their attendance upon truth: their
narratives always imply some consequence in favour of
their courage, their sagacity, or their activity, their familiarity with the learned, or their reception among the great;
they are always bribed by the present pleasure of seeing
themselves superior to those that surround them, and receiving the homage of silent attention and envious admiration.

But vanity is sometimes excited to fiction by less visible
gratifications: the present age abounds with a race of liars
who are content with the consciousness of falsehood, and
whose pride is to deceive others without any gain or glory
to themselves. Of this tribe it is the supreme pleasure
to remark a lady in the playhouse or the park, and to publish, under the character of a man suddenly enamoured,
an advertisement in the news of the next day, containing
a minute description of her person and her dress. From
this artifice, however, no other effect can be expected,
than perturbations which the writer can never see, and

conjectures of which he never can be informed; some mischief, however, he hopes he has done; and to have done mischief, is of some importance.　He sets his invention to work again, and produces a narrative of a robbery or a murder, with all the circumstances of time and place accurately adjusted.　This is a jest of greater effect and longer ＼ duration: if he fixes his scene at a proper distance, he may for several days keep a wife in terrour for her husband, or a mother for her son; and please himself with reflecting, that by his abilities and address some addition is made to the miseries of life.

There is, I think, an ancient law of Scotland, by which *leasing-making* was capitally punished.　I am, indeed, far from desiring to increase in this kingdom the number of executions; yet I cannot but think, that they who destroy the confidence of society, weaken the credit of intelligence, and interrupt the security of life; harass the delicate with shame, and perplex the timorous with alarms; might very properly be awakened to a sense of their crimes, by denunciations of a whipping-post or pillory: since many are so insensible of right and wrong, that they have no standard of action but the law; nor feel guilt, but as they dread punishment.

Nᵒ. 53.　TUESDAY, MAY 8, 1753.

Quisque suos patimur manes.　　　　VIRG. Æn. Lib. vi. 743.

Each has his lot, and bears the fate he drew.

SIR,　　　　　　　　　　　　　　　Fleet, May 6.

IN consequence of my engagements, I address you once more from the habitations of misery.　In this place, from which business and pleasure are equally excluded, and in which our only employment and diversion is to hear the narratives of each other, I might much sooner have gathered materials for a letter, had I not hoped to have been reminded of my promise; but since I find myself

placed in the regions of oblivion, where I am no less neglected by you than by the rest of mankind, I resolved no
longer to wait for solicitation, but stole early this evening
from between gloomy sullenness and riotous merriment, to
give you an account of part of my companions.

One of the most eminent members of our club is Mr.
Edward Scamper, a man of whose name the Olympick
heroes would not have been ashamed. Ned was born to a
small estate, which he determined to improve; and therefore, as soon as he became of age, mortgaged part of his
land to buy a mare and stallion, and bred horses for the
course. He was at first very successful, and gained several
of the king's plates, as he is now every day boasting, at
the expense of very little more than ten times their value.
At last, however, he discovered, that victory brought him
more honour than profit: resolving, therefore, to be rich as
well as illustrious, he replenished his pockets by another
mortgage, became on a sudden a daring bettor, and resolving not to trust a jockey with his fortune, rode his
horse himself, distanced two of his competitors the first
heat, and at last won the race by forcing his horse on a
descent to full speed at the hazard of his neck. His estate
was thus repaired, and some friends that had no souls
advised him to give over; but Ned now knew the way to
riches, and therefore without caution increased his expenses. From this hour he talked and dreamed of nothing
but a horse-race; and rising soon to the summit of equestrian reputation, he was constantly expected on every
course, divided all his time between lords and jockeys,
and, as the unexperienced regulated their bets by his example, gained a great deal of money by laying openly on
one horse and secretly on the other. Ned was now so sure
of growing rich, that he involved his estate in a third
mortgage, borrowed money of all his friends, and risked
his whole fortune upon Bay Lincoln. He mounted with
beating heart, started fair, and won the first heat; but in
the second, as he was pushing against the foremost of his
rivals, his girth broke, his shoulder was dislocated, and

before he was dismissed by the surgeon, two bailiffs fastened upon him, and he saw Newmarket no more. His daily amusement for four years has been to blow the signal for starting, to make imaginary matches, to repeat the pedigree of Bay Lincoln, and to form resolutions against trusting another groom with the choice of his girth.

The next in seniority is Mr. Timothy Snug, a man of deep contrivance and impenetrable secrecy. His father died with the reputation of more wealth than he possessed : Tim, therefore, entered the world with a reputed fortune of ten thousand pounds. Of this he very well knew that eight thousand was imaginary : but being a man of refined policy, and knowing how much honour is annexed to riches, he resolved never to detect his own poverty ; but furnished his house with elegance, scattered his money with profusion, encouraged every scheme of costly pleasure, spoke of petty losses with negligence, and on the day before an execution entered his doors, had proclaimed at a public table his resolution to be jolted no longer in a hackney coach.

Another of my companions is the magnanimous Jack Scatter, the son of a country gentleman, who, having no other care than to leave him rich, considered that literature could not be had without expense ; masters would not teach for nothing ; and when a book was bought and read, it would sell for little. Jack was, therefore, taught to read and write by the butler ; and when this acquisition was made, was left to pass his days in the kitchen and the stable, where he heard no crime censured but covetousness and distrust of poor honest servants, and where all the praise was bestowed on good housekeeping, and a free heart. At the death of his father, Jack set himself to retrieve the honour of his family : he abandoned his cellar to the butler, ordered his groom to provide hay and corn at discretion, took his housekeeper's word for the expenses of the kitchen, allowed all his servants to do their work by deputies, permitted his domesticks to keep his house open to their relations and acquaintance, and in ten years was conveyed hither, without having purchased by the loss of his patrimony either honour or pleasure, or obtained any other gratification than that of having corrupted the neighbouring villagers by luxury and idleness.

Dick Serge was a draper in Cornhill, and passed eight years in prosperous diligence, without any care but to keep his books, or any ambition but to be in time an alderman: but then, by some unaccountable revolution in his understanding, he became enamoured of wit and humour, despised the conversation of pedlars and stock-jobbers, and rambled every night to the regions of gaiety, in quest of company suited to his taste. The wits at first flocked about him for sport, and afterwards for interest; some found their way into his books, and some into his pockets; the man of adventure was equipped from his shop for the pursuit of a fortune; and he had sometimes the honour to have his security accepted when his friends were in distress. Elated with these associations, he soon learned to neglect his shop; and having drawn his money out of the funds, to avoid the necessity of teasing men of honour for trifling debts, he has been forced at last to retire hither, till his friends can procure him a post at court.

Another that joins in the same mess is Bob Cornice, whose life has been spent in fitting up a house. About ten years ago Bob purchased the country habitation of a bankrupt: the mere shell of a building Bob holds no great matter; the inside is the test of elegance. Of this house he was no sooner master than he summoned twenty workmen to his assistance, tore up the floors and laid them anew, stripped off the wainscot, drew the windows from their frames, altered the disposition of doors and fire-places, and cast the whole fabrick into a new form: his next care was to have his ceilings painted, his pannels gilt, and his chimney-pieces carved: every thing was executed by the ablest hands: Bob's business was to follow the workmen with a microscope, and call upon them to retouch their performances, and heighten excellence to perfection. The reputation of his house now brings round him a daily confluence of visitants, and every one tells him of some elegance which he has hitherto overlooked, some convenience not yet procured, or some new mode in ornament or furniture. Bob, who had no wish but to be admired, nor any guide but the fashion, thought every thing beautiful in proportion as it was new, and considered his work as unfinished, while any observer could suggest an addition; some alteration was therefore every day made, without any other motive than the charms of novelty. A traveller at last suggested to him the convenience of a grotto: Bob immediately ordered the mount of his garden to be excavated: and having laid out a large sum in shells and minerals, was busy in regulating the disposition of the colours and lustres, when two gentlemen, who had asked permission to see his gardens, presented him a writ, and led him off to less elegant apartments.

I know not, Sir, whether among this fraternity of sorrow you will think any much to be pitied; nor indeed do many of them appear to solicit compassion, for they generally applaud their own conduct, and despise those whom want of taste or spirit suffers to grow rich. It were happy if the prisons of the kingdom were filled only with characters like these, men whom prosperity could not make useful, and whom ruin cannot make wise: but there are among us many who raise different sensations, many that owe their present misery to the seductions of treachery, the strokes of casualty, or the tenderness of pity; many whose sufferings disgrace society, and whose virtues would adorn it: of these, when familiarity shall have enabled me to recount their stories without horrour, you may expect another narrative from

Sir,

Your most humble servant,

MISARGYRUS.

N°. 58. SATURDAY, MAY 25, 1753.

Damnant quod non intelligunt.   Cic.

They condemn what they do not understand.

EURIPIDES, having presented Socrates with the writings
of Heraclitus[d], a philosopher famed for involution and
obscurity, inquired afterwards his opinion of their merit.
" What I understand," said Socrates, " I find to be excellent; and, therefore, believe that to be of equal value
which I cannot understand."

The reflection of every man who reads this passage will
suggest to him the difference between the practice of Socrates, and that of modern criticks: Socrates, who had, by
long observation upon himself and others, discovered the
weakness of the strongest, and the dimness of the most
enlightened intellect, was afraid to decide hastily in his
own favour, or to conclude that an author had written
without meaning, because he could not immediately catch
his ideas; he knew that the faults of books are often more
justly imputable to the reader, who sometimes wants attention, and sometimes penetration; whose understanding
is often obstructed by prejudice, and often dissipated by
remissness; who comes sometimes to a new study, unfur-
nished with knowledge previously necessary; and finds
difficulties insuperable, for want of ardour sufficient to encounter them.

Obscurity and clearness are relative terms: to some
readers scarce any book is easy, to others not many are
difficult: and surely they, whom neither any exuberant

---

[d] The obscurity of this philosopher's style is complained of by Aristotle in his
treatise on Rhetoric, iii. 5. We make the reference with the view of recommending to attention the whole of that book, which is interspersed with the
most acute remarks, and with rules of criticism founded deeply on the
workings of the human mind. It is undervalued only by those who have not
scholarship to read it, and surely merits this slight tribute of admiration from
an Editor of Johnson's works, with whom a Translation of the Rhetoric was
long a favourite project.

praise bestowed by others, nor any eminent conquests over stubborn problems, have entitled to exalt themselves above the common orders of mankind, might condescend to imitate the candour of Socrates ; and where they find incontestable proofs of superior genius, be content to think that there is justness in the connexion which they cannot trace, and cogency in the reasoning which they cannot comprehend.

This diffidence is never more reasonable than in the perusal of the authors of antiquity ; of those whose works have been the delight of ages, and transmitted as the great inheritance of mankind from one generation to another : surely, no man can, without the utmost arrogance, imagine that he brings any superiority of understanding to the perusal of these books which have been preserved in the devastation of cities, and snatched up from the wreck of nations ; which those who fled before barbarians have been careful to carry off in the hurry of migration, and of which barbarians have repented the destruction. If in books thus made venerable by the uniform attestation of successive ages, any passages shall appear unworthy of that praise which they have formerly received, let us not immediately determine, that they owed their reputation to dulness or bigotry ; but suspect at least that our ancestors had some reasons for their opinions, and that our ignorance of those reasons makes us differ from them.

It often happens that an author's reputation is endangered in succeeding times, by that which raised the loudest applause among his contemporaries : nothing is read with greater pleasure than allusions to recent facts, reigning opinions, or present controversies ; but when facts are forgotten, and controversies extinguished, these favourite touches lose all their graces ; and the author in his descent to posterity must be left to the mercy of chance, without any power of ascertaining the memory of those things, to which he owed his luckiest thoughts and his kindest reception.

On such occasions, every reader should remember the

diffidence of Socrates, and repair by his candour the injuries of time: he should impute the seeming defects of his
author to some chasm of intelligence, and suppose that the
sense which is now weak was once forcible, and the expression which is now dubious formerly determinate.

How much the mutilation of ancient history has taken
away from the beauty of poetical performances, may be
conjectured from the light which a lucky commentator
sometimes effuses, by the recovery of an incident that had
been long forgotten: thus, in the third book of Horace,
Juno's denunciations against those that should presume to
raise again the walls of Troy, could for many ages please
only by splendid images and swelling language, of which
no man discovered the use or propriety, till Le Fevre, by
showing on what occasion the Ode was written, changed
wonder to rational delight.   Many passages yet undoubtedly remain in the same author, which an exacter knowledge of the incidents of his time would clear from objections.   Among these I have always numbered the following lines:

> *Aurum per medios ire satellites,*
> *Et perrumpere amat saxa, potentius*
>   *Ictu fulmineo.   Concidit auguris*
>   *Argivi domus ob lucrum*
> *Demersa exitio   Diffidit urbium*
> *Portas vir Macedo, et subruit æmulos*
>   *Regis muneribus:* Munera navium
>   Sævos illaqueant duces.   Hor. Lib. iii. Ode xvi. 9.

> Stronger than thunder's winged force,
> All-powerful gold can spread its course,
> 'Thro' watchful guards its passage make,
> And loves thro' solid walls to break:
> From gold the overwhelming woes
> That crush'd the Grecian augur rose:
> Philip with gold thro' cities broke,
> And rival monarchs felt his yoke;
> *Captains of ships to gold are slaves,*
> *Tho' fierce as their own winds and waves.*   FRANCIS.

The close of this passage, by which every reader is now
disappointed and offended, was probably the delight of the

Roman Court: it cannot be imagined, that Horace, after having given to gold the force of thunder, and told of its power to storm cities and to conquer kings, would have concluded his account of its efficacy with its influence over naval commanders, had he not alluded to some fact then current in the mouths of men, and therefore more interesting for a time than the conquests of Philip. Of the like kind may be reckoned another stanza in the same book:

—*Jussa coram non sine conscio*
Surgit marito, seu vocat institor,
  Seu navis Hispanæ magister,
    Dedecorum pretiosus emptor.   Hor. Lib. iii. Ode. vi. 29.

The conscious husband bids her rise,
When some rich factor courts her charms,
Who calls the wanton to his arms,
And, prodigal of wealth and fame,
Profusely buys the costly shame.   Francis.

He has little knowledge of Horace who imagines that the *factor*, or the *Spanish merchant*, are mentioned by chance: there was undoubtedly some popular story of an intrigue, which those names recalled to the memory of his reader.

The flame of his genius in other parts, though somewhat dimmed by time, is not totally eclipsed; his address and judgment yet appear, though much of the spirit and vigour of his sentiment is lost: this has happened in the twentieth Ode of the first book:

Vile potabis modicis Sabinum
Cantharis, Græcâ quod ego ipse testâ
Conditum levi, datus in theatro
    Cum tibi plausus,
Care Mæcenas eques: ut paterni
Fluminis ripæ, simul et jocosa
Redderet laudes tibi Vaticani
    Montis imago.

A poet's beverage humbly cheap,
  (Should great Mæcenas be my guest,)
The vintage of the Sabine grape,
  But yet in sober cups shall crown the feast:

> 'Twas rack'd into a Grecian cask,
>   Its rougher juice to melt away ;
> I seal'd it too—a pleasing task !
>   With annual joy to maik the glorious day,
> When in applausive shouts thy name
>   Spread from the theatre around,
> Floating on thy own Tiber's stream,
>   And Echo, playful nymph, return'd the sound.   FRANCIS.

We here easily remark the intertexture of a happy compliment with an humble invitation ; but certainly are less
delighted than those, to whom the mention of the applause
bestowed upon Mæcenas, gave occasion to recount the actions or words that produced it.

Two lines which have exercised the ingenuity of modern
criticks, may, I think, be reconciled to the judgment, by
an easy supposition : Horace thus addresses Agrippa :

> Scriberis Vario fortis, et hostium
> Victor, Mæonii carminis alite.   HOR. Lib. i. Ode vi. 1.
>
> Varius, a swan of Homer's wing,
> Shall brave Agrippa's conquests sing.

That Varius should be called " A bird of Homeric song,"
appears so harsh to modern ears, that an emendation of
the text has been proposed : but surely the learning of the
ancients had been long ago obliterated, had every man
thought himself at liberty to corrupt the lines which he
did not understand.   If we imagine that Varius had been
by any of his contemporaries celebrated under the appellation of *Musarum ales*, " the swan of the Muses," the language of Horace becomes graceful and familiar ; and that
such a compliment was at least possible, we know from the
transformation feigned by Horace of himself.

The most elegant compliment that was paid to Addison,
is of this obscure and perishable kind ;

> When panting Virtue her last efforts made,
> You brought your Clio to the virgin's aid.

These lines must please as long as they are understood ;
but can be understood only by those that have observed
Addison's signatures in the Spectator,

The nicety of these minute allusions I shall exemplify by another instance, which I take this occasion to mention, because, as I am told, the commentators have omitted it. Tibullus addressed Cynthia in this manner:

Te spectem, suprema mihi cum venerit hora,
  Te teneam moriens deficiente manu.   Lib. i. El. i. 73.
Before my closing eyes dear Cynthia stand,
Held weakly by my fainting trembling hand.

To these lines Ovid thus refers in his Elegy on the death of Tibullus:

Cynthia discedens, Felicius, inquit, amata
  Sum tibi ; vixisti dum tuus ignis eram.
Cui Nemesis, quid, ait, tibi sint mea damna dolori ?
  Me tenuit moriens deficiente manu.   Am. Lib. iii. El. ix. 56.

Blest was my reign, retiring Cynthia cry'd ;
Not till he left my breast, Tibullus dy'd.
Forbear, said Nemesis, my loss to moan,
The *fainting trembling hand* was mine alone.

The beauty of this passage, which consists in the appropriation made by Nemesis of the line originally directed to Cynthia, had been wholly imperceptible to succeeding ages, had chance, which has destroyed so many greater volumes, deprived us likewise of the poems of Tibullus.

N°. 62.   SATURDAY, JUNE 9, 1753.

O fortuna viris, invida fortibus
Quam non æqua bonis præmia dividis.   SENECA.

Capricious Fortune ever joys,
With partial hand to deal the prize,
To crush the brave and cheat the wise.

TO THE ADVENTURER.

SIR,   Fleet, June 6.
    To the account of such of my companions as are imprisoned without being miserable, or are miserable without any claim to compassion, I promised to add the

histories of those, whose virtue has made them unhappy or whose misfortunes are at least without a crime. That this catalogue should be very numerous, neither you nor your readers ought to expect: *rari quippe boni;* " the good are few." Virtue is uncommon in all the classes of humanity; and I suppose it will scarcely be imagined more frequent in a prison than in other places.

Yet in these gloomy regions is to be found the tenderness, the generosity, the philanthropy of Serenus, who might have lived in competence and ease, if he could have looked without emotion on the miseries of another. Serenus was one of those exalted minds, whom knowledge and sagacity could not make suspicious; who poured out his soul in boundless intimacy, and thought community of possessions the law of friendship. The friend of Serenus was arrested for debt, and after many endeavours to soften his creditor, sent his wife to solicit that assistance which never was refused. The tears and importunity of female distress were more than was necessary to move the heart of Serenus; he hasted immediately away, and conferring a long time with his friend, found him confident that if the present pressure was taken off, he should soon be able to re-establish his affairs. Serenus, accustomed to believe, and afraid to aggravate distress, did not attempt to detect the fallacies of hope, nor reflect that every man overwhelmed with calamity believes, that if that was removed he shall immediately be happy: he, therefore, with little hesitation offered himself as surety.

In the first raptures of escape all was joy, gratitude, and confidence: the friend of Serenus displayed his prospects, and counted over the sums of which he should infallibly be master before the day of payment. Serenus in a short time began to find his danger, but could not prevail with himself to repent of beneficence; and therefore suffered himself still to be amused with projects which he durst not consider, for fear of finding them impracticable. The debtor, after he had tried every method of raising money which art or indigence could prompt, wanted either fidelity or resolution to surrender himself to prison, and left Serenus to take his place.

Serenus has often proposed to the creditor, to pay him whatever he shall appear to have lost by the flight of his friend: but however reasonable this proposal may be thought, avarice and brutality have been hitherto inexorable, and Serenus still continues to languish in prison.

In this place, however, where want makes almost every man selfish, or desperation gloomy, it is the good fortune of Serenus not to live without a friend: he passes most of his hours in the conversation of Candidus, a man whom the same virtuous ductility has, with some difference of circumstances, made equally unhappy. Candidus, when he was young, helpless, and ignorant, found a patron that educated, protected, and supported him; his patron being more vigilant for others than himself, left at his death an only son, destitute and friendless. Candidus was eager to repay the benefits he had received; and having maintained the youth for a few years at his own house, afterwards placed him with a merchant of eminence, and gave bonds to a great value as a security for his conduct.

The young man, removed too early from the only eye of which he dreaded the observation, and deprived of the only instruction which he heard with reverence, soon learned to consider virtue as restraint, and restraint as oppression: and to look with a longing eye at every expense to which he could not reach, and every pleasure which he could not partake: by degrees he deviated from his first regularity, and unhappily mingling among young men busy in dissipating the gains of their fathers' industry, he forgot the precepts of Candidus, spent the evening in parties of pleasure, and the morning in expedients to support his riots. He was, however, dexterous and active in business: and his master, being secured against any consequences of dishonesty, was very little solicitous to inspect his manners, or to inquire how he passed those hours, which were not immediately devoted to the business of his profession: when he was informed of the young man's ex-

travagance or debauchery, " let his bondsman look to
that," said he, " I have taken care of myself."

Thus the unhappy spendthrift proceeded from folly to
folly, and from vice to vice, with the connivance, if not the
encouragement, of his master; till in the heat of a nocturnal revel he committed such violences in the street as
drew upon him a criminal prosecution. Guilty and unexperienced, he knew not what course to take; to confess
his crime to Candidus, and solicit his interposition, was
little less dreadful than to stand before the frown of a
court of justice. Having, therefore, passed the day with
anguish in his heart and distraction in his looks, he seized
at night a very large sum of money in the compting-house,
and setting out he knew not whither, was heard of no
more.

The consequence of his flight was the ruin of Candidus;
ruin surely undeserved and irreproachable, and such as
the laws of a just government ought either to prevent or
repair: nothing is more inequitable than that one man
should suffer for the crimes of another, for crimes which
he neither prompted nor permitted, which he could neither
foresee nor prevent. When we consider the weakness of
human resolutions and the inconsistency of human conduct, it must appear absurd that one man shall engage for
another, that he will not change his opinions or alter his
conduct.

It is, I think, worthy of consideration, whether, since
no wager is binding without a possibility of loss on each
side, it is not equally reasonable, that no contract should
be valid without reciprocal stipulations; but in this case,
and others of the same kind, what is stipulated on his side
to whom the bond is given? he takes advantage of the
security, neglects his affairs, omits his duty, suffers timorous wickedness to grow daring by degrees, permits appetite to call for new gratifications, and, perhaps, secretly
longs for the time in which he shall have power to seize
the forfeiture; and if virtue or gratitude should prove too
strong for temptation, and a young man persist in honesty,

however instigated by his passions, what can secure him at last against a false accusation? I for my part always shall suspect, that he who can by such methods secure his property, will go one step further to increase it; nor can I think that man safely trusted with the means of mischief, who, by his desire to have them in his hands, gives an evident proof how much less he values his neighbour's happiness than his own.

Another of our companions is Lentulus, a man whose dignity of birth was very ill supported by his fortune. As some of the first offices in the kingdom were filled by his relations, he was early invited to court, and encouraged by caresses and promises to attendance and solicitation; a constant appearance in splendid company necessarily required magnificence of dress; and a frequent participation of fashionable amusements forced him into expense: but these measures were requisite to his success; since every body knows, that to be lost to sight is to be lost to remembrance, and that he who desires to fill a vacancy, must be always at hand, lest some man of greater vigilance should step in before him.

By this course of life his little fortune was every day made less: but he received so many distinctions in publick, and was known to resort so familiarly to the houses of the great, that every man looked on his preferment as certain, and believed that its value would compensate for its slowness: he, therefore, found no difficulty in obtaining credit for all that his rank or his vanity made necessary: and, as ready payment was not expected, the bills were proportionably enlarged, and the value of the hazard or delay was adjusted solely by the equity of the creditor. At length death deprived Lentulus of one of his patrons, and a revolution in the ministry of another; so that all his prospects vanished at once, and those that had before encouraged his expenses, began to perceive that their money was in danger; there was now no other contention but who should first seize upon his person, and, by forcing immediate payment, deliver him up naked to the vengeance of the rest.

In pursuance of this scheme, one of them invited him to a tavern, and procured him to be arrested at the door; but Lentulus, instead of endeavouring secretly to pacify him by payment, gave notice to the rest, and offered to divide amongst them the remnant of his fortune: they feasted six hours at his expense, to deliberate on his proposal; and at last determined, that as he could not offer more than five shillings in the pound, it would be more prudent to keep him in prison, till he could procure from his relations.the payment of his debts.

Lentulus is not the only man confined within these walls, on the same account: the like procedure, upon the like motives, is common among men whom yet the law allows to partake the use of fire and water with the compassionate and the just; who frequent the assemblies of commerce in open day, and talk with detestation and contempt of highwaymen or housebreakers: but, surely, that man must be confessedly robbed, who is compelled, by whatever means, to pay the debts which he does not owe: nor can I look with equal hatred upon him, who, at the hazard of his life, holds out his pistol and demands my purse, as on him who plunders under shelter of the law, and by detaining my son or my friend in prison, extorts from me the price of their liberty. No man can be more an enemy to society than he, by whose machinations our virtues are turned to our disadvantage; he is less destructive to mankind that plunders cowardice, than he that preys upon compassion.

I believe, Mr. Adventurer, you will readily confess, that though not one of these, if tried before a commercial judicature, can be wholly acquitted from imprudence or temerity; yet that, in the eye of all who can consider virtue as distinct from wealth, the fault of two of them, at least, is outweighed by the merit; and that of the third is so much extenuated by the circumstances of his life, as not to deserve a perpetual prison: yet must these, with multitudes equally blameless, languish in confinement, till malevolence shall relent, or the law be changed.

I am, Sir,

Your humble servant, MISARGYRUS.

N°. 67. TUESDAY, JUNE 26, 1753.

Inventas——vitam excoluere per artes.　　VIRG. Æn. vi. 663.
They polish life by useful arts.

THAT familiarity produces neglect, has been long observed. The effect of all external objects, however great or splendid, ceases with their novelty ; the courtier stands without emotion in the royal presence ; the rustick tramples under his foot the beauties of the spring with little attention to their colours or their fragrance ; and the inhabitant of the coast darts his eye upon the immense diffusion of waters, without awe, wonder, or terrour.

Those who have past much of their lives in this great city, look upon its opulence and its multitudes, its extent and variety, with cold indifference ; but an inhabitant of the remoter parts of the kingdom is immediately distinguished by a kind of dissipated curiosity, a busy endeavour to divide his attention amongst a thousand objects, and a wild confusion of astonishment and alarm.

The attention of a new comer is generally first struck by the multiplicity of cries that stun him in the streets, and the variety of merchandize and manufactures which the shopkeepers expose on every hand ; and he is apt, by unwary bursts of admiration, to excite the merriment and contempt of those who mistake the use of their eyes for effects of their understanding, and confound accidental knowledge with just reasoning.

But, surely, these are subjects on which any man may without reproach employ his meditations : the innumerable occupations, among which the thousands that swarm in the streets of London, are distributed, may furnish employment to minds of every cast, and capacities of every degree. He that contemplates the extent of this wonderful city, finds it difficult to conceive, by what method plenty is maintained in our markets, and how the inhabitants are regularly supplied with the necessaries of life ; but when he examines the shops and warehouses, sees the immense stores of every kind of merchandize piled up for sale, and runs over all the manufactures of art and products of nature, which are every where attracting his eye and soliciting his purse, he will be inclined to conclude, that such quantities cannot easily be exhausted, and that part of mankind must soon stand still for want of employment, till the wares already provided shall be worn out and destroyed.

As Socrates was passing through the fair at Athens, and casting his eyes over the shops and customers, "how many things are here," says he, " that I do not want!" The same sentiment is every moment rising in the mind of him that walks the streets of London, however inferior in philosophy to Socrates: he beholds a thousand shops crowded with goods, of which he can scarcely tell the use, and which, therefore, he is apt to consider as of no value: and indeed, many of the arts by which families are supported, and wealth is heaped together, are of that minute and superfluous kind, which nothing but experience could evince possible to be prosecuted with advantage, and which, as the world might easily want, it could scarcely be expected to encourage.

But so it is, that custom, curiosity, or wantonness, supplies every art with patrons, and finds purchasers for every manufacture; the world is so adjusted, that not only bread, but riches may be obtained without great abilities or arduous performances: the most unskilful hand and unenlightened mind have sufficient incitements to industry; for he that is resolutely busy, can scarcely be in want. There is, indeed, no employment, however despicable, from which a man may not promise himself more than competence, when he sees thousands and myriads raised to dignity, by no other merit than that of contributing to supply their neighbours with the means of sucking smoke through a tube of clay; and others raising contributions upon those, whose elegance disdains the grossness of smoky luxury, by grinding the same materials into a powder that may at once gratify and impair the smell.

Not only by these popular and modish trifles, but by a thousand unheeded and evanescent kinds of business, are the multitudes of this city preserved from idleness, and consequently from want. In the endless variety of tastes and circumstances that diversify mankind, nothing is so superfluous, but that some one desires it: or so common, but that some one is compelled to buy it. As nothing is useless but because it is in improper hands, what is thrown away by one is gathered up by another; and the refuse of part of mankind furnishes a subordinate class with the materials necessary to their support.

When I look round upon those who are thus variously exerting their qualifications, I cannot but admire the secret concatenation of society that links together the great and the mean, the illustrious and the obscure; and consider with benevolent satisfaction, that no man, unless his body or mind be totally disabled, has need to suffer the mortification of seeing himself useless or burthensome to the community: he that will diligently labour, in whatever occupation, will deserve the sustenance which he obtains, and the protection which he enjoys; and may lie down every night with the pleasing consciousness of having contributed something to the happiness of life.

Contempt and admiration are equally incident to narrow minds: he whose comprehension can take in the whole subordination of mankind, and whose perspicacity can pierce to the real state of things through the thin veils of fortune or of fashion, will discover meanness in the highest stations, and dignity in the meanest; and find that no man can become venerable but by virtue, or contemptible but by wickedness.

In the midst of this universal hurry, no man ought to be so little influenced by example, or so void of honest emulation, as to stand a lazy spectator of incessant labour; or please himself with the mean happiness of a drone, while the active swarms are buzzin'[7] about him: no man is without some quality, by the due application of which he might deserve well of the world; and whoever he be that has but little in his power, should be in haste to do that little, lest he be confounded with him that can do nothing.

By this general concurrence of endeavours, arts of every kind have been so long cultivated, that all the wants of man may be immediately supplied; idleness can scarcely form a wish which she may not gratify by the toil of others, or curiosity dream of a toy, which the shops are not ready to afford her.

Happiness is enjoyed only in proportion as it is known; and such is the state or folly of man, that it is known only by experience of its contrary: we who have long lived amidst the conveniencies of a town immensely populous, have scarce an idea of a place where desire cannot be gratified by money. In order to have a just sense of this artificial plenty, it is necessary to have passed some time in a distant colony, or those parts of our island which are thinly inhabited: he that has once known how many trades every man in such situations is compelled to exercise, with how much labour the products of nature must be accommodated to human use, how long the loss or defect of any common utensil must be endured, or by what awkward expedients it must be supplied, how far men may wander with money in their hands before any can sell them what they wish to buy, will know how to rate at its proper value the plenty and ease of a great city.

But that the happiness of man may still remain imperfect, as wants in this place are easily supplied, new wants likewise are easily created; every man, in surveying the shops of London, sees numberless instruments and conveniencies, of which, while he did not know them, he never felt the need; and yet, when use has made them familiar, wonders how life could be supported without them. Thus it comes to pass, that our desires always increase with our possessions; the knowledge that something remains yet unenjoyed, impairs our enjoyment of the good before us.

They who have been accustomed to the refinements of science, and multiplications of contrivance, soon lose their confidence in the unassisted powers of nature, forget the paucity of our real necessities, and overlook the easy methods by which they may be supplied. It were a speculation worthy of a philosophical mind, to examine how much is taken away from our native abilities, as well as added to them, by artificial expedients. We are so accustomed to give and receive assistance, that each of us singly can do little for himself; and there is scarce any one among us, however contracted may be his form of life, who does not enjoy the labour of a thousand artists.

But a survey of the various nations that inhabit the earth will inform us, that life may be supported with less assistance; and that the dexterity, which practice enforced by necessity produces, is able to effect much by very scanty means. The nations of Mexico and Peru erected cities and temples without the use of iron; and at this day the rude Indian supplies himself with all the necessaries of life: sent like the rest of mankind naked into the world, as soon as his parents have nursed him up to strength, he is to provide by his own labour for his own support. His first care is to find a sharp flint among the rocks; with this he undertakes to fell the trees of the forest; he shapes his bow, heads his arrows, builds his cottage, and hollows his canoe, and from that time lives in a state of plenty and prosperity; he is sheltered from the storms, he is fortified against beasts of prey, he is enabled to pursue the fish of the sea, and the deer of the mountains; and as he does not know, does not envy the happiness of polished nations, where gold can supply the want of fortitude and skill, and he whose laborious ancestors have made him rich, may lie stretched upon a couch, and see all the treasures of all the elements poured down before him.

This picture of a savage life if it shows how much individuals may perform, shows likewise how much society is to be desired. Though the perseverance and address of the Indian excite our admiration, they nevertheless cannot procure him the conveniencies which are enjoyed by the vagrant beggar of a civilized country: he hunts like a wild beast to satisfy his hunger; and when he lies down to rest after a successful chase, cannot pronounce himself secure against the danger of perishing in a few days: he is, perhaps, content with his condition, because he knows not that a better is attainable by man; as he that is born blind does not long for the perception of light, because he cannot conceive the advantages which light would afford him; but hunger, wounds, and weariness, are real evils, though he believes them equally incident to all his fellow-creatures; and when a tempest compels him to lie starving in his hut, he cannot justly be concluded equally happy with those whom art has exempted from the power of chance, and who make the foregoing year provide for the following.

To receive and to communicate assistance, constitutes the happiness of human life: man may, indeed, preserve his existence in solitude, but can enjoy it only in society; the greatest understanding of an individual, doomed to procure food and clothing for himself, will barely supply him with expedients to keep off death from day to day; but as one of a large community performing only his share of the common business, he gains leisure for intellectual pleasures, and enjoys the happiness of reason and reflection.

N°. 69. TUESDAY, JULY 3, 1753.

Ferè libenter homines id quod volunt credunt.   CÆSAR.

Men willingly believe what they wish to be true.

TULLY has long ago observed, that no man, however weakened by long life, is so conscious of his own decrepitude, as not to imagine that he may yet hold his station in the world for another year.

Of the truth of this remark every day furnishes new confirmation: there is no time of life, in which men for the most part seem less to expect the stroke of death, than when every other eye sees it impending; or are more busy in providing for another year, than when it is plain to all but themselves, that at another year they cannot arrive. Though every funeral that passes before their eyes evinces the deceitfulness of such expectations, since every man who is born to the grave thought himself equally certain of living at least to the next year; the survivor still continues to flatter himself, and is never at a loss for some reason why his life should be protracted, and the voracity of death continue to be pacified with some other prey.

But this is only one of the innumerable artifices practised in the universal conspiracy of mankind against themselves: every age and every condition indulges some darling fallacy; every man amuses himself with projects which he knows to be improbable, and which, therefore, he resolves to pursue without daring to examine them. Whatever any man ardently desires, he very readily believes that he shall some time attain: he whose intemperance has overwhelmed him with diseases, while he languishes in the spring, expects vigour and recovery from the summer sun; and while he melts away in the summer, transfers his hopes to the frosts of winter: he that gazes upon elegance or pleasure, which want of money hinders him from imitating or partaking, comforts himself that the time of distress will soon be at an end, and that every day brings him nearer to a state of happiness; though he knows it has passed not only without acquisition of advantage, but perhaps without endeavours after it, in the formation of schemes that cannot be executed, and in the contemplation of prospects which cannot be approached.

Such is the general dream in which we all slumber out our time: every man thinks the day coming, in which he shall be gratified with all his wishes, in which he shall leave all those competitors behind, who are now rejoicing like himself in the expectation of victory; the day is always coming to the servile in which they shall be powerful, to the obscure in which they shall be eminent, and to the deformed in which they shall be beautiful.

If any of my readers has looked with so little attention

on the world about him, as to imagine this representation exaggerated beyond probability, let him reflect a little upon his own life; let him consider what were his hopes and prospects ten years ago, and what additions he then expected to be made by ten years to his happiness; those years are now elapsed; have they made good the promise that was extorted from them? have they advanced his fortune, enlarged his knowledge, or reformed his conduct, to the degree that was once expected? I am afraid, every man that recollects his hopes must confess his disappointment; and own that day has glided unprofitably after day, and that he is still at the same distance from the point of happiness.

With what consolations can those, who have thus miscarried in their chief design, elude the memory of their ill success?. with what amusements can they pacify their discontent, after the loss of so large a portion of life? they can give themselves up again to the same delusions, they can form new schemes of airy gratifications, and fix another period of felicity; they can again resolve to trust the promise which they know will be broken, they can walk in a circle with their eyes shut, and persuade themselves to think that they go forward.

Of every great and complicated event, part depends upon causes out of our power, and part must be effected by vigour and perseverance. With regard to that which is styled in common language the work of chance, men will always find reasons for confidence or distrust, according to their different tempers or inclinations; and he that has been long accustomed to please himself with possibilities of fortuitous happiness, will not easily or willingly be reclaimed from his mistake. But the effects of human industry and skill are more easily subjected to calculation: whatever can be completed in a year, is divisible into parts, of which each may be performed in the compass of a day; he, therefore, that has passed the day without attention to the task assigned him, may be certain, that the lapse of life has brought him no nearer to his object; for whatever idleness may expect from time, its produce will be only in proportion to the diligence with which it has been used. He that floats lazily down the stream, in pursuit of something borne along by the same current, will find himself indeed move forward; but unless he lays his hand to the oar, and increases his speed by his own labour, must be always at the same distance from that which he is following.

There have happened in every age some contingencies of unexpected and undeserved success, by which those who are determined to believe whatever favours their inclinations, have been encouraged to delight themselves with future advantages; they support confidence by considerations, of which the only proper use is to chase away despair: it is equally absurd to sit down in idleness because some have been enriched without labour, as to leap a precipice because some have fallen and escaped with life, or to put to sea in a storm because some have been driven from a wreck upon the coast to which they are bound.

We are all ready to confess, that belief ought to be proportioned to evidence or probability: let any man, therefore, compare the number of those who have been thus favoured by fortune, and of those who have failed of their expectations, and he will easily determine, with what justness he has registered himself in the lucky catalogue.

But there is no need on these occasions for deep inquiries or laborious calculations; there is a far easier method of distinguishing the hopes of folly from those of reason, of finding the difference between prospects that exist before the eyes, and those that are only painted on a (fond imagination.) Tom Drowsy had accustomed himself to compute the profit of a darling project till he had no longer any doubt of its success; it was at last matured by close consideration, all the measures were accurately adjusted, and he wanted only five hundred pounds to become master of a fortune that might be envied by a director of a trading company. Tom was generous and

grateful, and was resolved to recompense this small assistance with an ample fortune; he, therefore, deliberated
for a time, to whom amongst his friends he should declare
his necessities; not that he suspected a refusal, but because he could not suddenly determine which of them
would make the best use of riches, and was, therefore,
most worthy of his favour. At last his choice was settled; and knowing that in order to borrow he must shew
the probability of repayment, he prepared for a minute
and copious explanation of his project. But here the
golden dream was at an end: he soon discovered the impossibility of imposing upon others the notions by which
he had so long imposed upon himself; which way soever
he turned his thoughts, impossibility and absurdity arose
in opposition on every side; even credulity and prejudice
were at last forced to give way, and he grew ashamed of
crediting himself what shame would not suffer him to communicate to another.

To this test let every man bring his imaginations, before they have been too long predominant in his mind.
Whatever is true will bear to be related, whatever is rational will endure to be explained; but when we delight
to brood in secret over future happiness, and silently to
employ our meditations upon schemes of which we are
conscious that the bare mention would expose us to derision and contempt; we should then remember, that we
are cheating ourselves by voluntary delusions; and giving
up to the unreal mockeries of fancy, those hours in which
solid advantages might be attained by sober thought and
rational assiduity.

There is, indeed, so little certainty in human affairs,
that the most cautious and severe examiner may be allowed to indulge some hopes which he cannot prove to be
much favoured by probability; since, after his utmost endeavours to ascertain events, he must often leave the issue
in the hands of chance. And so scanty is our present
allowance of happiness, that in many situations life could
scarcely be supported, if hope were not allowed to relieve

the present hour by pleasures borrowed from futurity;
and reanimate the languor of dejection to new efforts, by
pointing to distant regions of felicity, which yet no resolution or perseverance shall ever reach.

But these, like all other cordials, though they may invi-
gorate in a small quantity, intoxicate in a greater; these
pleasures, like the rest, are lawful only in certain circumstances, and to certain degrees; they may be useful in a
due subserviency to nobler purposes, but become dangerous and destructive when once they gain the ascendant in
the heart: to soothe the mind to tranquillity by hope, even
when that hope is likely to deceive us, may be sometimes
useful; but to lull our faculties in a lethargy is poor and
despicable.

Vices and errours are differently modified, according to
the state of the minds to which they are incident; to indulge hope beyond the warrant of reason, is the failure
alike of mean and elevated understandings; but its foundation and its effects are totally different: the man of
high courage and great abilities is apt to place too much
confidence in himself, and to expect, from a vigorous exertion of his powers, more than spirit or diligence can attain: between him and his wish he sees obstacles indeed,
but he expects to overleap or break them; his mistaken
ardour hurries him forward; and though, perhaps, he
misses his end, he nevertheless obtains some collateral
good, and performs something useful to mankind, and
honourable to himself.

The drone of timidity presumes likewise to hope, but
without ground and without consequence; the bliss with
which he solaces his hours he always expects from others,
though very often he knows not from whom: he folds his
arms about him, and sits in expectation of some revolution in the state that shall raise him to greatness, or some
golden shower that shall load him with wealth; he dozes
away the day in musing upon the morrow; and at the end
of life is roused from his dream only to discover that the

time of action is past, and that he can now shew his wisdom only by repentance.

~~~~~~~~~~~~~~~~~~~~~~~~

N°. 74. SATURDAY, JULY 21, 1753.

Insanientis dum sapientiæ
Consultus erro.——   Hor. Lib. i. Od. xxxiv. 2.

I miss'd my end, and lost my way,
By crack-brain'd wisdom led astray.

TO THE ADVENTURER.

SIR,

IT has long been charged by one part of mankind upon the other, that they will not take advice; that counsel and instruction are generally thrown away; and that, in defiance both of admonition and example, all claim the right to choose their own measures, and to regulate their own lives.

That there is something in advice very useful and salutary, seems to be equally confessed on all hands: since even those that reject it, allow for the most part that rejection to be wrong, but charge the fault upon the unskilful manner in which it is given: they admit the efficacy of the medicine, but abhor the nauseousness of the vehicle.

Thus mankind have gone on from century to century: some have been advising others how to act, and some have been teaching the advisers how to advise; yet very little alteration has been made in the world. As we must all by the law of nature enter life in ignorance, we must all make our way through it by the light of our own experience; and for any security that advice has been yet able to afford, must endeavour after success at the hazard of miscarriage, and learn to do right by venturing to do wrong.

By advice I would not be understood to mean, the everlasting and invariable principles of moral and religious truth, from which no change of external circumstances can justify any deviation; but such directions as respect merely the prudential part of conduct, and which may be followed or neglected without any violation of essential duties.

It is, indeed, not so frequently to make us good as to make us wise, that our friends employ the officiousness of counsel; and among the rejectors of advice, who are mentioned by the grave and sententious with so much acrimony, you will not so often find the vicious and abandoned, as the pert and the petulant, the vivacious and the giddy.

As the great end of female education is to get a husband, this likewise is the general subject of female advice: and the dreadful denunciation against those volatile girls, who will not listen patiently to the lectures of wrinkled wisdom, is, that they will die unmarried,- or throw themselves away upon some worthless fellow, who will never be able to keep them a coach.

I being naturally of a ductile and easy temper, without strong desires or quick resentments, was always a favourite amongst the elderly ladies, because I never rebelled against seniority, nor could be charged with thinking myself wise before my time; but heard every opinion with submissive silence, professed myself ready to learn from all who seemed inclined to teach me, paid the same grateful acknowledgments for precepts contradictory to each other, and if any controversy arose, was careful to side with her who presided in the company.

Of this compliance I very early found the advantage; for my aunt Matilda left me a very large addition to my fortune, for this reason chiefly, as she herself declared, because I was not above hearing good counsel, but would sit from morning till night to be instructed, while my sister Sukey, who was a year younger than myself, and was, therefore, in greater want of information, was so much conceited of her own knowledge, that whenever the good lady in the ardour of benevolence reproved or instructed her, she would pout or titter, interrupt her with questions, or embarrass her with objections.

I had no design to supplant my sister by this complaisant attention; nor, when the consequence of my obsequiousness came to be known, did Sukey so much envy as despise me: I was, however, very well pleased with my success; and having received, from the concurrent opinion of all mankind, a notion that to be rich was to be great and happy, I thought I had obtained my advantages at an easy rate, and resolved to continue the same passive attention, since I found myself so powerfully recommended by it to kindness and esteem.

The desire of advising has a very extensive prevalence; and since advice cannot be given but to those that will hear it, a patient listener is necessary to the accommodation of all those who desire to be confirmed in the opinion of their own wisdom: a patient listener, however, is not always to be had; the present age, whatever age is present, is so vitiated and disordered that young people are readier to talk than to attend, and good counsel is only thrown away upon those who are full of their own perfections.

I was, therefore, in this scarcity of good sense, a general favourite; and seldom saw a day in which some sober matron did not invite me to her house, or take me out in her chariot, for the sake of instructing me how to keep my character in this censorious age, how to conduct myself in the time of courtship, how to stipulate for a settlement, how to manage a husband of every character, regulate my family, and educate my children.

We are all naturally credulous in our own favour. Having been so often caressed and applauded for docility, I was willing to believe myself really enlightened by instruction, and completely qualified for the task of life. I did not doubt but I was entering the world with a mind furnished against all exigencies, with expedients to extricate myself from every difficulty, and sagacity to provide against every danger; I was, therefore, in haste to give some specimen of my prudence, and to show that this liberality of instruction had not been idly lavished upon a mind incapable of improvement.

My purpose, for why should I deny it? was like that of other women, to obtain a husband of rank and fortune superior to my own; and in this I had the concurrence of all those that had assumed the province of directing me. That the woman was undone who married below herself, was universally agreed: and though some ventured to assert, that the richer man ought invariably to be preferred, and that money was a sufficient compensation for a defective ancestry; yet the majority declared warmly for a gentleman, and were of opinion that upstarts should not be encouraged.

With regard to other qualifications I had (an irreconcilable variety) of instructions. I was sometimes told that deformity was no defect in a man; and that he who was not encouraged to intrigue by an opinion of his person, was more likely to value the tenderness of his wife: but a grave widow directed me to choose a man who might imagine himself agreeable to me, for that the deformed were always insupportably vigilant, and apt to sink into sullenness, or burst into rage, if they found their wife's eye wandering for a moment to a good face or a handsome shape.

They were, however, all unanimous in warning me, with repeated cautions, against all thoughts of union with a wit, as a being with whom no happiness could possibly be enjoyed: men of every other kind I was taught to govern, but a wit was an animal for whom no arts of taming had been yet discovered: the woman whom he could once get within his power, was considered as lost to all hope of dominion or of quiet: for he would detect artifice and defeat allurement; and if once he discovered any failure of conduct, would believe his own eyes, in defiance of tears, caresses, and protestations.

In pursuance of these sage principles, I proceeded to

form my schemes; and while I was yet in the first bloom of youth, was taken out at an assembly by Mr. Frisk.   I am afraid my cheeks glowed, and my eyes sparkled; for I observed the looks of all my superintendants fixed anxiously upon me; and I was next day cautioned against him from all hands, as a man of the most dangerous and formidable kind, who had writ verses to one lady, and then forsaken her only because she could not read them, and had lampooned another for no other fault than defaming his sister.

Having been hitherto accustomed to obey, I ventured to dismiss Mr. Frisk, who happily did not think me worth the labour of a lampoon.   I was then addressed by Mr. Sturdy, and congratulated by all my friends on the manors of which I was shortly to be lady: but Sturdy's conversation was so gross, that after the third visit I could endure him no longer; and incurred, by dismissing him, the censure of all my friends, who declared that my nicety was greater than my prudence, and that they feared it would be my fate at last to be wretched with a wit.

By a wit, however, I was never afterwards attacked, but lovers of every other class, or pretended lovers, I have often had; and, notwithstanding the advice constantly given me, to have no regard in my choice to my own inclinations, I could not forbear to discard some for vice, and some for rudeness.   I was once loudly censured for refusing an old gentleman who offered an enormous jointure, and died of the phthisic a year after; and was so baited with incessant importunities, that I should have given my hand to Drone the stock-jobber, had not the reduction of interest made him afraid of the expenses of matrimony.

Some, indeed, I was permitted to encourage; but miscarried of the main end, by treating them according to the rules of art which had been prescribed me.   Altilis, an old maid, infused into me so much haughtiness and reserve, that some of my lovers withdrew themselves from my frown, and returned no more; others were driven away, by the demands of settlement which the widow Trapland directed me to make; and I have learned, by many experiments, that to ask advice is to lose opportunity.

I am, Sir,

Your humble servant,

PERDITA.

~~~~~~~~~~~~~~~~~~~~~~~~

<div style="text-align:center">

N°. 81.   TUESDAY, AUGUST 14, 1753.

———

</div>

Nil desperandum.   HOR. Lib. i. Od. vii. 27.
Avaunt despair!

I HAVE sometimes heard it disputed· in conversation, whether it be more laudable or desirable, that a man should think too highly or too meanly of himself: it is on all hands agreed to be best, that he should think rightly; but since a fallible being will always make some deviations from exact rectitude, it is not wholly useless to inquire towards which side it is safer to decline.

The prejudices of mankind seem to favour him who errs by under-rating his own powers: he is considered as a modest and harmless member of society, not likely to break the peace by competition, to endeavour after such splendour of reputation as may dim the lustre of others, or to interrupt any in the enjoyment of themselves; he is no man's rival, and, therefore, may be every man's friend.

The opinion which a man entertains of himself ought to be distinguished, in order to an accurate discussion of this question, as it relates to persons or to things. To think highly of ourselves in comparison with others, to assume by our own authority that precedence which none is willing to grant, must be always invidious and offensive; but to rate our powers high in proportion to things, and imagine ourselves equal to great undertakings, while we leave others in possession of the same abilities, cannot with equal justice provoke censure.

It must be confessed, that self-love may dispose us to decide too hastily in our own favour: but who is hurt by the mistake? If we are incited by this vain opinion to attempt more than we can perform, ours is the labour, and ours is the disgrace.

But he that dares to think well of himself, will not always prove to be mistaken; and the good effects of his confidence will then appear in great attempts and great performances: if he should not fully complete his design, he will at least advance it so far as to leave an easier task for him that succeeds him; and even though he should wholly fail, he will fail with honour.

But from the opposite errour, from torpid despondency, can come no advantage; it is the frost of the soul, which binds up all its powers, and congeals life in perpetual sterility. He that has no hopes of success, will make no attempts; and where nothing is attempted, nothing can be done.

Every man should, therefore, endeavour to maintain in himself a favourable opinion of the powers of the human mind; which are, perhaps, in every man, greater than they appear, and might, by diligent cultivation, be exalted to a degree beyond what their possessor presumes to believe. There is scarce any man but has found himself able, at the instigation of necessity, to do what in a state of leisure and deliberation he would have concluded impossible; and some of our species have signalized themselves by such achievements, as prove that there are few things above human hope.

It has been the policy of all nations to preserve, by some public monuments, the memory of those who have served their country by great exploits: there is the same reason for continuing or reviving the names of those, whose extensive abilities have dignified humanity. An honest emulation may be alike excited; and the philosopher's curiosity may be inflamed by a catalogue of the works of Boyle or Bacon, as Themistocles was kept awake by the trophies of Miltiades.

Among the favourites of nature that have from time to time appeared in the world, enriched with various endow-

ments and contrarieties of excellence, none seems to have
been exalted above the common rate of humanity, than the
man known about two centuries ago by the appellation of
the Admirable Crichton ; of whose history, whatever we
may suppress as surpassing credibility, yet we shall, upon
incontestable authority, relate enough to rank him among
prodigies.

" Virtue," says Virgil, " is better accepted when it
comes in a pleasing form :" the person of Crichton was
eminently beautiful ; but his beauty was consistent with
such activity and strength, that in fencing he would spring
at one bound the length of twenty feet upon his antagonist ;
and he used the sword in either hand with such force and
dexterity, that scarce any one had courage to engage him.

Having studied at St. Andrew's in Scotland, he went to
Paris in his twenty-first year, and affixed on the gate of
the college of Navarre a kind of challenge to the learned
of that university to dispute with him on a certain day :
offering to his opponents, whoever they should be, the
choice of ten languages, and of all faculties and sciences.
On the day appointed three thousand auditors assembled,
when four doctors of the church and fifty masters appeared
against him ; and one of his antagonists confesses, that the
doctors were defeated ; that he gave proofs of knowledge
above the reach of man ; and that a hundred years passed
without food or sleep, would not be sufficient for the attainment of his learning. After a disputation of nine hours,
he was presented by the president and professors with a
diamond and a purse of gold, and dismissed with repeated
acclamations.

From Paris he went away to Rome, where he made the
same challenge, and had in the presence of the pope and
cardinals the same success. Afterwards he contracted at
Venice an acquaintance with Aldus Manutius, by whom
he was introduced to the learned of that city : then visited
Padua, where he engaged in another publick disputation,
beginning his performance with an extemporal poem in
praise of the city and the assembly then present, and con-

cluding with an oration equally unpremeditated in commendation of ignorance.

He afterwards published another challenge, in which he declared himself ready to detect the errours of Aristotle and all his commentators, either in the common forms of logick, or in any which his antagonists should propose of a hundred different kinds of verse.

These acquisitions of learning, however stupendous, were not gained at the expense of any pleasure which youth generally indulges, or by the omission of any accomplishment in which it becomes a gentleman to excel : he practised in great perfection the arts of drawing and painting, he was an eminent performer in both vocal and instrumental musick, he danced with uncommon gracefulness, and, on the day after his disputation at Paris, exhibited his skill in horsemanship before the court of France, where at a publick match of tilting, he bore away the ring upon his lance fifteen times together.

He excelled likewise in domestic games of less dignity and reputation : and in the interval between his challenge and disputation at Paris, he spent so much of his time at cards, dice, and tennis, that a lampoon was fixed upon the gate of the Sorbonne, directing those that would see this monster of erudition, to look for him at the tavern.

So extensive was his acquaintance with life and manners, that in an Italian comedy composed by himself, and exhibited before the court of Mantua, he is said to have personated fifteen different characters ; in all which he might succeed without great difficulty, since he had such power of retention, that once hearing an oration of an hour, he would repeat it exactly, and in the recital follow the speaker through all his variety of tone and gesticulation.

Nor was his skill in arms less than in learning, or his courage inferior to his skill : there was a prize-fighter at Mantua, who travelling about the world, according to the barbarous custom of that age, as a general challenger, had defeated the most celebrated masters in many parts of Europe ; and in Mantua, where he then resided, had killed three that appeared against him. The duke repented that he had granted him his protection; when Crichton, looking on his sanguinary success with indignation, offered to stake fifteen hundred pistoles, and mount the stage against him. The duke with some reluctance consented, and on the day fixed the combatants appeared: their weapon seems to have been single rapier, which was then newly introduced in Italy. The prize-fighter advanced with great violence and fierceness, and Crichton contented himself calmly to ward his passes, and suffered him to exhaust his vigour by his own fury. Crichton then became the assailant; and pressed upon him with such force and agility, that he thrust him thrice through the body, and saw him expire: he then divided the prize he had won among the widows whose husbands had been killed.

The death of this wonderful man I should be willing to conceal, did I not know that every reader will inquire curiously after that fatal hour, which is common to all human beings, however distinguished from each other by nature or by fortune.

The duke of Mantua, having received so many proofs of his various merit, made him tutor to his son Vicentio di Gonzaga, a prince of loose manners and turbulent disposition. On this occasion it was, that he composed the comedy in which he exhibited so many different characters with exact propriety. But his honour was of short continuance; for as he was one night in the time of Carnival rambling about the streets, with his guitar in his hand, he was attacked by six men masked. Neither his courage nor skill in his exigence deserted him: he opposed them with such activity and spirit, that he soon dispersed them, and disarmed their leader, who throwing off his mask, discovered himself to be the prince his pupil. Crichton, falling on his knees, took his own sword by the point, and presented it to the prince; who immediately seized it, and instigated, as some say, by jealousy, according to others, only by drunken fury and brutal resentment, thrust him through the heart.

Thus was the Admirable Crichton brought into that state, in which he could excel the meanest of mankind only by a few empty honours paid to his memory: the court of Mantua testified their esteem by a publick mourning, the contemporary wits were profuse of their encomiums, and the palaces of Italy were adorned with pictures, representing him on horseback with a lance in one hand and a book in the other[e].

* * *

N°. 84. SATURDAY, AUGUST 25, 1753.

——————————— *Tolle periclum,*
Jam vaga prosiliet frenis natura remotis.   HOR. Lib. ii. Sat. vii. 73.

But take the danger and the shame away,
And vagrant nature bounds upon her prey.   FRANCIS.

TO THE ADVENTURER.

SIR,

IT has been observed, I think, by Sir William Temple, and after him by almost every other writer, that England affords a greater variety of characters than the rest of the world. This is ascribed to the liberty prevailing amongst us, which gives every man the privilege of being wise or foolish his own way, and preserves him from the necessity of hypocrisy or the servility of imitation.

That the position itself is true, I am not completely satisfied. To be nearly acquainted with the people of different countries can happen to very few; and in life, as in every thing else beheld at a distance, there appears an even uniformity: the petty discriminations which diversify the natural character, are not discoverable but by a close inspection; we, therefore, find them most at home,

---

[e] This paper is enumerated by Chalmers among those which Johnson dictated, not to Bathurst, but to Hawkesworth. It is an elegant summary of Crichton's life which is in Mackenzie's Writers of the Scotch Nation. See a fuller account by the Earl of Buchan and Dr. Kippis in the Biog. Brit. and the recently published one by Mr. Frazer Tytler.

because there we have most opportunities of remarking them. Much less am I convinced, that this peculiar diversification, if it be real, is the consequence of peculiar liberty; for where is the government to be found that superintends individuals with so much vigilance, as not to leave their private conduct without restraint? Can it enter into a reasonable mind to imagine, that men of every other nation are not equally masters of their own time or houses with ourselves, and equally at liberty to be parsimonious or profuse, frolick or sullen, abstinent or luxurious? Liberty is certainly necessary to the full play of predominant humours; but such liberty is to be found alike under the government of the many or the few, in monarchies or commonwealths.

How readily the predominant passion snatches an interval of liberty, and how fast it expands itself when the weight of restraint is taken away, I had lately an opportunity to discover, as I took a journey into the country in a stage-coach; which, as every journey is a kind of adventure, may be very properly related to you, though I can display no such extraordinary assembly as Cervantes has collected at Don Quixote's inn[f].

In a stage coach, the passengers are for the most part wholly unknown to one another, and without expectation of ever meeting again when their journey is at an end; one should therefore imagine, that it was of little importance to any of them, what conjectures the rest should form concerning him. Yet so it is, that as all think them-

[f] Johnson has made impressive allusion to the immortal work of Cervantes in his second Rambler. Every reflecting man must arise from its perusal with feelings of the deepest melancholy, with the most tender commiseration for the weakness and lot of humanity. To such a man its moral must ever be "profoundly sad." Vulgar minds cannot know it. Hence it has ever been the favorite with the intellectual class, while Gil Blas has more generally won the applause of men of the world. An amusing anecdote of the almost universal admiration for the *chef d'œuvre* of Le Sage may be found in Butler's Reminiscences. That bigotted, yet extraordinary man, Alva, predicted, with prophetic precision, the effects which the satire on Chivalry would produce in Spain. See *Broad Stone of Honour; or Rules for the Gentlemen of England.*

selves secure from detection, all assume that character of which they are most desirous, and on no occasion is the general ambition of superiority more apparently indulged.

On the day of our departure, in the twilight of the morning, I ascended the vehicle with three men and two women, my fellow travellers. It was easy to observe the affected elevation of mien with which every one entered, and the supercilious servility with which they paid their compliments to each other. When the first ceremony was despatched, we sat silent for a long time, all employed in collecting importance into our faces, and endeavouring to strike reverence and submission into our companions.

It is always observable that silence propagates itself, and that the longer talk has been suspended, the more difficult it is to find any thing to say. We began now to wish for conversation; but no one seemed inclined to descend from his dignity, or first propose a topick of discourse. At last a corpulent gentleman, who had equipped himself for this expedition with a scarlet surtout and a large hat with a broad lace, drew out his watch, looked on it in silence, and then held it dangling at his finger. This was, I suppose, understood by all the company as an invitation to ask the time of the day, but nobody appeared to heed his overture; and his desire to be talking so far overcame his resentment, that he let us know of his own accord it was past five, and that in two hours we should be at breakfast.

His condescension was thrown away: we continued all obdurate; the ladies held up their heads; I amused myself with watching their behaviour; and of the other two, one seemed to employ himself in counting the trees as we drove by them, the other drew his hat over his eyes, and counterfeited a slumber. The man of benevolence, to shew that he was not depressed by our neglect, hummed a tune, and beat time upon his snuff-box.

Thus universally displeased with one another, and not much delighted with ourselves, we came at last to the little inn appointed for our repast; and all began at once to recompense themselves for the constraint of silence, by innumerable questions and orders to the people that attended us. At last, what every one had called for was got, or declared impossible to be got at that time, and we were persuaded to sit round the same table; when the gentleman in the red surtout looked again upon his watch, told us that we had half an hour to spare, but he was sorry to see so little merriment among us; that all fellow travellers were for the time upon the level, and that it was always his way to make himself one of the company. " I remember," says he, " it was on just such a morning as this, that I and my Lord Mumble and the Duke of Tenterden were out upon a ramble: we called at a little house as it might be this; and my landlady, I warrant you, not suspecting to whom she was talking, was so jocular and facetious, and made so many merry answers to our questions, that we were all ready to burst with laughter. At last the good woman happening to overhear me whisper the duke and call him by his title, was so surprised and confounded, that we could scarcely get a word from her; and the duke never met me from that day to this, but he talks of the little house, and quarrels with me for terrifying the landlady."

He had scarcely time to congratulate himself on the veneration which this narrative must have procured for him from the company, when one of the ladies having reached out for a plate on a distant part of the table, began to remark, " the inconveniencies of travelling, and the difficulty which they who never sat at home without a great number of attendants, found in performing for themselves such offices as the road required; but that people of quality often travelled in disguise, and might be generally known from the vulgar by their condescension to poor inn-keepers, and the allowance which they made for any defect in their entertainment; that for her part, while people were civil and meant well, it was never her custom to find fault, for one was not to expect upon a journey all that one enjoyed at one's own house."

A general emulation seemed now to be excited. One of the men who had hitherto said nothing, called for the last newspaper; and having perused it a while with deep pensiveness, " It is impossible," says he, " for any man to guess how to act with regard to the stocks; last week it was the general opinion that they would fall; and I sold out twenty thousand pounds in order to a purchase: they have now risen unexpectedly; and I make no doubt but at my return to London I shall risk thirty thousand pounds among them again."

A young man, who had hitherto distinguished himself only by the vivacity of his looks, and a frequent diversion of his eyes from one object to another, upon this closed his snuff-box, and told us that " he had a hundred times talked with the chancellor and the judges on the subject of the stocks; that for his part he did not pretend to be well acquainted with the principles on which they were established, but had always heard them reckoned pernicious to trade, uncertain in their produce, and unsolid in their foundation; and that he had been advised by three judges, his most intimate friends, never to venture his money in the funds, but to put it out upon land security, till he could light upon an estate in his own country."

It might be expected, that upon these glimpses of latent dignity, we should all have begun to look round us with veneration; and have behaved like the princes of romance, when the enchantment that disguises them is dissolved, and they discover the dignity of each other; yet it happened, that none of these hints made much impression on the company; every one was apparently suspected of endeavouring to impose false appearances upon the rest; all continued their haughtiness in hopes to enforce their claims; and all grew every hour more sullen, because they found their representations of themselves without effect.

Thus we travelled on four days with malevolence perpetually increasing, and without any endeavour but to outvie each other in superciliousness and neglect; and when any two of us could separate ourselves for a moment we vented our indignation at the sauciness of the rest.

At length the journey was at an end; and time and chance, that strip off all disguises, have discovered that the intimate of lords and dukes is a nobleman's butler, who has furnished a shop with the money he has saved; the man who deals so largely in the funds, is the clerk of a broker in Change-alley; the lady who so carefully concealed her quality, keeps a cook-shop behind the Exchange; and the young man who is so happy in the friendship of the judges, engrosses and transcribes for bread in a garret of the Temple. Of one of the women only I could make no disadvantageous detection, because she had assumed no character, but accommodated herself to the scene before her, without any struggle for distinction or superiority.

I could not forbear to reflect on the folly of practising a fraud, which, as the event showed, had been already practised too often to succeed, and by the success of which no advantage could have been obtained; of assuming a character, which was to end with the day; and of claiming upon false pretences honours which must perish with the breath that paid them.

But, Mr. Adventurer, let not those who laugh at me and my companions, think this folly confined to a stage-coach. Every man in the journey of life takes the same advantage of the ignorance of his fellow travellers, disguises himself in counterfeited merit, and hears those praises with complacency which his conscience reproaches him for accepting. Every man deceives himself while he thinks he is deceiving others; and forgets that the time is at hand when every illusion shall cease, when fictitious excellence shall be torn away, and *all* must be shown to *all* in their realestate.

I am, Sir, your humble servant,
VIATOR.

N°. 85 TUESDAY, AUGUST 28, 1753.

Qui studet optatam cursu contingere metam,
Multa tulit fecitque puer.   Hor. De Ar. Poet. 412.

The youth, who hopes th' Olympic prize to gain,
All arts must try, and every toil sustain.   Francis.

It is observed by Bacon, that " reading makes a full man, conversation a ready man, and writing an exact man."

As Bacon attained to degrees of knowledge scarcely ever reached by any other man, the directions which he gives for study have certainly a just claim to our regard; for who can teach an art with so great authority, as he that has practised it with undisputed success?

Under the protection of so great a name, I shall, therefore, venture to inculcate to my ingenious contemporaries, the necessity of reading, the fitness of consulting other understandings than their own, and of considering the sentiments and opinions of those who, however neglected in the present age, had in their own times, and many of them a long time afterwards, such reputation for knowledge and acuteness as will scarcely ever be attained by those that despise them.

An opinion has of late been, I know not how, propagated among us, that libraries are filled only with useless lumber; that men of parts stand in need of no assistance; and that to spend life in poring upon books, is only to imbibe prejudices, to obstruct and embarrass the powers of nature, to cultivate memory at the expense of judgment, and to bury reason under a chaos of indigested learning.

Such is the talk of many who think themselves wise, and of some who are thought wise by others; of whom part probably believe their own tenets, and part may be justly suspected of endeavouring to shelter their ignorance in multitudes, and of wishing to destroy that reputation which they have no hopes to share. It will, I believe, be found invariably true, that learning was never decried by any learned man; and what credit can be given to those who venture to condemn that which they do not know?

If reason has the power ascribed to it by its advocates, if so much is to be discovered by attention and meditation, it is hard to believe, that so many millions, equally participating of the bounties of nature with ourselves, have been for ages upon ages meditating in vain: if the wits of the present time expect the regard of posterity, which will then inherit the reason which is now thought superior to instruction, surely they may allow themselves to be instructed by the reason of former generations. When, therefore, an author declares, that he has been able to learn nothing from the writings of his predecessors, and such a declaration has been lately made, nothing but a degree of arrogance unpardonable in the greatest human understanding, can hinder him from perceiving that he is raising prejudices against his own performance; for with what hopes of success can he attempt that in which greater abilities have hitherto miscarried? or with what peculiar force does he suppose himself invigorated, that difficulties hitherto invincible should give way before him?

Of those whom Providence has qualified to make any additions to human knowledge, the number is extremely small; and what can be added by each single mind, even of this superior class, is very little: the greatest part of mankind must owe all their knowledge, and all must owe far the larger part of it, to the information of others. To understand the works of celebrated authors, to comprehend their systems, and retain their reasonings, is a task more than equal to common intellects; and he is by no means to be accounted useless or idle, who has stored his mind with acquired knowledge, and can detail it occasionally to others who have less leisure or weaker abilities.

Persius has justly observed, that knowledge is nothing to him who is not known by others to possess it[g]: to the scholar himself it is nothing with respect either to honour or advantage, for the world cannot reward those qualities which

[g] Scire tuum nihil est, nisi te scire hoc sciat alter.   Sat. i. 27.

are concealed from it; with respect to others it is nothing, because it affords no help to ignorance or errour.

It is with justice, therefore, that in an accomplished
character, Horace unites just sentiments with the power of
expressing them; and he that has once accumulated learning, is next to consider, how he shall most widely diffuse
and most agreeably impart it.

A ready man is made by conversation. He that buries
himself among his manuscripts, " besprent," as Pope expresses it, " with learned dust," and wears out his days
and nights in perpetual research and solitary meditation,
is too apt to lose in his elocution what he adds to his wisdom ; and when he comes into the world, to appear over-
loaded with his own notions, like a man armed with weapons which he cannot wield. He has no facility of incul-
cating his speculations, of adapting himself to the various
degrees of. intellect which the accidents of conversation
will present; but will talk to most unintelligibly, and to all
unpleasantly.

I was once present at the lectures of a profound philosopher, a man really skilled in the science which he professed, who having occasion to explain the terms *opacum*
and *pellucidum*, told us, after some hesitation, that *opacum*
was, as one might say, *opake*, and that *pellucidum* signified
pellucid. Such was the dexterity with which this learned
reader facilitated to his auditors the intricacies of science;
and so true is it, that a man may know what he cannot
teach.

Boerhaave complains, that the writers who have treated
of chymistry before him, are useless to the greater part of
students, because they presuppose their readers to have
such degrees of skill as are not often to be found. Into
the same errour are all men apt to fall, who have familiarized any subject to themselves in solitude : they discourse,
as if they thought every other man had been employed in
the same inquiries; and expect that short hints and obscure allusions will produce in others the same train of
ideas which they excite in themselves.

Nor is this the only inconvenience which the man of study·suffers from a recluse life. When he meets with an opinion that pleases him, he catches it up with eagerness; looks only after such arguments as tend to his confirmation; or spares himself the trouble of discussion, and adopts it with very little proof; indulges it long without suspicion, and in time unites it to the general body of his knowledge, and treasures it up among incontestable truths: but when he comes into the world among men who, arguing upon dissimilar principles, have been led to different conclusions, and being placed in various situations, view the same object on many sides; he finds his darling position attacked, and himself in no condition to defend it: having thought always in one train, he is in the state of a man who having fenced always with the same master, is perplexed and amazed by a new posture of his antagonist; he is entangled in unexpected difficulties, he is harassed by sudden objections, he is unprovided with solutions or replies; his surprise impedes his natural powers of reasoning, his thoughts are scattered and confounded, and he gratifies the pride of airy petulance with an easy victory.

It is difficult to imagine, with what obstinacy truths which one mind perceives almost by intuition, will be rejected by another; and how many artifices must be practised, to procure admission for the most evident propositions into understandings frighted by their novelty, or hardened against them by accidental prejudice; it can scarcely be conceived, how frequently, in these extemporaneous controversies, the dull will be subtle, and the acute absurd; how often stupidity will elude the force of argument, by involving itself in its own gloom; and mistaken ingenuity will weave artful fallacies, which reason can scarcely find means to disentangle.

In these encounters the learning of the recluse usually fails him: nothing but long habit and frequent experiments can confer the power of changing a position into various forms, presenting it in different points of view, connecting it with known and granted truths, fortifying it with intelligible arguments, and illustrating it by apt similitudes; and he, therefore, that has collected his knowledge in solitude, must learn its application by mixing with mankind.

But while the various opportunities of conversation invite us to try every mode of argument, and every art of recommending our sentiments, we are frequently betrayed to the use of such as are not in themselves strictly defensible: a man heated in talk, and eager of victory, takes advantage of the mistakes or ignorance of his adversary, lays hold of concessions to which he knows he has no right, and urges proofs likely to prevail on his opponent, though he knows himself that they have no force: thus the severity of reason is relaxed, many topicks are accumulated, but without just arrangement or distinction; we learn to satisfy ourselves with such ratiocination as silences others; and seldom recall to a close examination, that discourse which has gratified our vanity with victory and applause.

Some caution, therefore, must be used lest copiousness and facility be made less valuable by inaccuracy and confusion. To fix the thoughts by writing, and subject them to frequent examinations and reviews, is the best method of enabling the mind to detect its own sophisms, and keep it on guard against the fallacies which it practises on others: in conversation we naturally diffuse our thoughts, and in writing we contract them; method is the excellence of writing, and unconstraint the grace of conversation.

To read, write, and converse in due proportions, is, therefore, the business of a man of letters. For all these there is not often equal opportunity; excellence, therefore, is not often attainable; and most men fail in one or other of the ends proposed, and are full without readiness, or without exactness. Some deficiency must be forgiven all, because all are men; and more must be allowed to pass uncensured in the greater part of the world, because none can confer upon himself abilities, and few have the choice of situations proper for the improvement of those which nature has bestowed: it is, however, reasonable to have *perfection* in our eye; that we may always advance towards it, though we know it never can be reached.

~~~~~~~~~~~~~~~~~~~~~~

Nᵒ. 92. SATURDAY, SEPTEMBER 22, 1753.

Cum tabulis animum censoris sumet honesti.   Hor. Lib. ii. Ep. ii. 110.

Bold be the critick, zealous to his trust,
Like the firm judge inexorably just.

TO THE ADVENTURER.

SIR,

In the papers of criticism which you have given to the publick, I have remarked a spirit of candour and love of truth equally remote from bigotry and captiousness; a just distribution of praise amongst the ancients and the moderns: a sober deference to reputation long established, without a blind adoration of antiquity; and a willingness to favour later performances, without a light or puerile fondness for novelty.

I shall, therefore, venture to lay before you, such observations as have risen to my mind in the consideration of Virgil's pastorals, without any inquiry how far my sentiments deviate from established rules or common opinions.

If we survey the ten pastorals in a general view, it will be found that Virgil can derive from them very little claim to the praise of an inventor. To search into the antiquity of this kind of poetry is not my present purpose; that it has long subsisted in the east, the *Sacred Writings* sufficiently inform us; and we may conjecture, with great probability, that it was sometimes the devotion, and sometimes the entertainment of the first generations of mankind. Theocritus united elegance with simplicity; and taught his shepherds to sing with so much ease and harmony, that his countrymen, despairing to excel, forbore to imitate him; and the Greeks, however vain or ambitious, left him in quiet possession of the garlands which the wood-nymphs had bestowed upon him.

Virgil, however, taking advantage of another language, ventured to copy or _to rival the _Sicilian bard:_ he has written with greater splendour of diction, and elevation of sentiment: but as the magnificence of his performances was more, the simplicity was less; and, perhaps, where he excels Theocritus, he sometimes obtains his superiority by deviating from the pastoral character, and performing what Theocritus never attempted.

Yet, though I would willingly pay to Theocritus the honour which is always due to an original author, I am far from intending to depreciate Virgil: of whom Horace justly declares, that the rural muses have appropriated to him their elegance and sweetness, and who, as he copied Theocritus in his design, has resembled him likewise in his success; for, if we except Calphurnius, an obscure author of the lower ages, I know not that a single pastoral was written after him by any poet, till the revival of literature.

But though his general merit has been universally acknowledged, I am far from thinking all the productions of his rural Thalia equally excellent; there is, indeed, in all his pastorals a strain of versification which it is vain to seek in any other poet; but if we except the first and the tenth, they seem liable either wholly or in part to considerable objections.

The second, though we should forget the great charge against it, which I am afraid can never be refuted, might, I think, have perished, without any diminution of the praise of its author; for I know not that it contains one affecting sentiment or pleasing description, or one passage that strikes the imagination or awakens the passions.

The third contains a contest between two shepherds, begun with a quarrel of which some particulars might well be spared, carried on with sprightliness and elegance, and terminated at last in a reconciliation: but, surely, whether the invectives with which they attack each other be true or false, they are too much degraded from the dignity of pastoral innocence; and instead of rejoicing that they are both victorious, I should not have grieved could they have been both defeated.

The poem to Pollio is, indeed, of another kind: it is filled with images at once splendid and pleasing, and is elevated with grandeur of language worthy of the first of Roman poets; but I am not able to reconcile myself to the disproportion between the performance and the occasion that produced it: that the golden age should return because Pollio had a son, appears so wild a fiction, that I am ready to suspect the poet of having written, for some other purpose, what he took this opportunity of producing to the publick.

The fifth contains a celebration of Daphnis, which has stood to all succeeding ages as the model of pastoral elegies. To deny praise to a performance which so many thousands have laboured to imitate, would be to judge with too little deference for the opinion of mankind: yet whoever shall read it with impartiality, will find that most of the images are of the mythological kind, and therefore easily invented; and that there are few sentiments of rational praise or natural lamentation.

In the Silenus he again rises to the dignity of philosophick sentiments, and heroick poetry. The address to Varus is eminently beautiful: but since the compliment paid to Gallus fixes the transaction to his own time, the fiction of Silenus seems injudicious: nor has any sufficient reason yet been found, to justify his choice of those fables that make the subject of the song.

The seventh exhibits another contest of the tuneful shepherds: and, surely, it is not without some reproach to his inventive power, that of ten pastorals Virgil has written two upon the same plan. One of the shepherds now gains an acknowledged victory, but without any apparent superiority, and the reader, when he sees the prize adjudged, is not able to discover how it was deserved.

Of the eighth pastoral, so little is properly the work of Virgil, that he has no claim to other praise or blame than that of a translator. -

Of the ninth, it is scarce possible to discover the design or tendency; it is said, I know not upon what authority, to have been composed from fragments of other poems; and except a few lines in which the author touches upon his own misfortunes, there is nothing that seems appropriated to any time or place, or of which any other use can be discovered than to fill up the poem.

The first and the tenth pastorals, whatever be determined of the rest, are sufficient to place their author above the reach of rivalry. The complaint of Gallus disappointed in his love, is full of such sentiments as disappointed love naturally produces; his wishes are wild, his resentment is tender, and his purposes are inconstant. In the genuine language of despair, he soothes himself awhile with the pity that shall be paid him after his death.

> ————Tamen cantabitis, Arcades, inquit,
> Montibus hæc vestris : soli cantare periti
> Arcades. O mihi tum quam molliter ossa quiescant,
> Vestra meos olim si fistula dicat amores! Virg. Ec. x. 31.

> ————Yet, O Arcadian swains,
> Ye best artificers of soothing strains !
> Tune your soft reeds, and teach your rocks my woes,
> So shall my shade in sweeter rest repose.
> O that your birth and business had been mine;
> To feed the flock, and prune the spreading vine ! WARTON.

Discontented with his present condition, and desirous to be any thing but what he is, he wishes himself one of the shepherds. He then catches the idea of rural tranquillity; but soon discovers how much happier he should be in these happy regions, with Lycoris at his side:

> Hic gelidi fontes, hic mollia prata, Lycori :
> Hic nemus, hic ipso tecum consumerer ævo.
> Nunc insanus amor duri me Martis in armis
> Tela inter media atque adversos detinet hostes.
> Tu procul a patria (nec sit mihi credere) tantum
> Alpinas, ah dura, nives, et frigora Rheni
> Me sine sola vides. Ah te ne frigora lædant !
> Ah tibi ne teneras glacies secet aspera plantas! Ec. x. 42.

> Here cooling fountains roll through flow'ry meads,
> Here woods, Lycoris, lift their verdant heads;

Here could I wear my careless life away,
And in thy arms insensibly decay.
Instead of that, me frantick love detains,
'Mid foes, and dreadful darts, and bloody plains :
While you—and can my soul the tale believe,
Far from your country, lonely wand'ring leave
Me, me your lover, barbarous fugitive!
Seek the rough Alps where snows eternal shine,
And joyless borders of the frozen Rhine.
Ah! may no cold e'er blast my dearest maid,
Nor pointed ice thy tender feet invade.   WARTON.

He then turns his thoughts on every side, in quest of something that may solace or amuse him: he proposes happiness to himself, first in one scene and then in another: and at last finds that nothing will satisfy:

Jam neque Hamadryades rursum, nec carmina nobis
Ipsa placent: ipsæ rursum concedite sylvæ.
Non illum nostri possunt mutare labores ;
Nec si frigoribus mediis Hebrumque bibamus,
Sithoniasque nives hyemis subeamus aquosæ:
Nec si, cum moriens alta liber aret in ulmo
Æthiopum versemus oves sub sidere Cancri.
Omnia vincit amor ; et nos cedamus amori.   Ec. x. 62.

But now again no more the woodland maids,
Nor pastoral songs delight—Farewell, ye shades—
No toils of ours the cruel god can change,
Tho' lost in frozen deserts we should range ;
Tho' we should drink where chilling Hebrus flows,
Endure bleak winter blasts, and Thracian snows :
Or on hot India's plains our flocks should feed,
Where the parch'd elm declines his sickening head,
Beneath fierce-glowing Cancer's fiery beams,
Far from cool breezes and refreshing streams.
Love over all maintains resistless sway,
And let us love's all-conquering power obey.   WARTON.

But notwithstanding the excellence of the tenth pastoral, I cannot forbear to give the preference to the first, which is equally natural and more diversified. The complaint of the shepherd, who saw his old companion at ease in the shade, while himself was driving his little flock he knew not whither, is such as, with variation of circumstances, misery always utters at the sight of prosperity:

Nos patriæ fines, et dulcia linquimus arva ;
Nos patriam fugimus: Tu, Tityre, lentus in umbra
Formosam resonare doces Amaryllida sylvas.   Ec. i. 3.

We leave our country's bounds, our much-lov'd plains ;
We from our country fly, unhappy swains!
You, Tit'rus, in the groves at leisure laid,
Teach Amaryllis' name to every shade.   WARTON.

His account of the difficulties of his journey, gives a
very tender image of pastoral distress :.

————————*En ipse capellas*
Protenus æger ago : hanc etiam vix, Tityre, duco:
Hic inter densas corylos modo namque gemellos,
Spem gregis, ah! silice in nuda connixa reliquit.   Ec. i. 12.

And lo! sad partner of the general care,
Weary and faint I drive my goats afar!
While scarcely this my leading hand sustains,
Tired with the way, and recent from her pains ;
For 'mid yon tangled hazels as we past.
On the bare flints her hapless twin she cast,
The hopes and promise of my ruin'd fold!   WARTON.

The description of Virgil's happiness in his little farm,
combines almost all the images of rural pleasure ; and he,
therefore, that can read it with indifference, has no sense
of pastoral poetry :

Fortunate senex ! ergo tua rura manebunt,
Et tibi magna satis ; quamvis lapis omnia nudus,
Limosoque palus obducat pascua junco :
Non insueta graves tentabunt pabula fœtas,
Nec mala vicini pecoris contagia lædent.
Fortunate senex! hic inter flumina nota,
Et fontes sacros, frigus captabis opacum.
Hinc tibi, quæ semper vicino ab limite sepes,
Hyblæis apibus florem depasta salicti,
Sæpe levi somnum suadebit inire susurro.
Hinc alta sub rupe canet frondator ad auras.
Nec tamen interea raucæ, tua cura, palumbes,
Nec gemere aëria cessabit turtur ab ulmo.   Ec. i. 47.

Happy old man! then still thy farms restored,
Enough for thee, shall bless thy frugal board.
What tho' rough stones the naked soil o'erspread,
Or marshy bulrush rear its wat'ry head,
No foreign food thy teeming ewes shall fear,
No touch contagious spread its influence here.

Happy old man ! here 'mid th' accustom'd streams
And sacred springs, you'll shun the scorching beams;
While from yon willow-fence, thy picture's bound,
The bees that suck their flow'ry stores around,
Shall sweetly mingle with the whispering boughs
Their lulling murmurs, and invite repose :
While from steep rocks the pruner's song is heard ;
Nor the soft-cooing dove, thy fav'rite bird,
Meanwhile shall cease to breathe her melting strain,
Nor turtles from th' aërial elm to 'plain.   WARTON.

It may be observed, that these two poems were produced by events that really happened; and may, therefore, be of use to prove, that we can always feel more
than we can imagine, and that the most artful fiction must
give way to truth.

I am, Sir,
Your humble servant,
DUBIUS.

<hr>

Nᵒ. 95.   TUESDAY, OCTOBER 2, 1753.

——*Dulcique animos novitate tenebo.*   OVID. Met. iv. 284.

And with sweet novelty your soul detain.

IT is often charged upon writers, that with all their pretensions to genius and discoveries, they do little more than
copy one another; and that compositions obtruded upon
the world with the pomp of novelty, contain only tedious
repetitions of common sentiments, or at best exhibit a
transposition of known images, and give a new appearance
to truth only by some slight difference of dress and decoration.

The allegation of resemblance between authors is in-
disputably true; but the charge of plagiarism; which is
raised upon it, is not to be allowed with equal readiness.
A coincidence of sentiment may easily happen without any
communication, since there are many occasions in which all
reasonable men will nearly think alike. Writers of all
ages have had the same sentiments, because they have in

all ages had the same objects of speculation; the interests and passions, the virtues and vices of mankind, have been diversified iu different times, only by unessential and casual varieties: and we must, therefore, expect in the works of all those who attempt to describe them, such a likeness as we find in the pictures of the same person drawn in different periods of his life.

It is necessary, therefore, that before an author be charged with plagiarism, one of the most reproachful, though, perhaps, not the most atrocious of literary crimes, the subject on which he treats should be carefully considered. We do not wonder, that historians, relating the same facts, agree in their narration; or that authors, delivering the elements of science, advance the same theorems, and lay down the same definitions: yet it is not wholly without use to mankind, that books are multiplied, and that different authors lay out their labours on the same subject; for there will always be some reason why one should on particular occasions, or to particular persons, be preferable to another; some will be clear where others are obscure, some will please by their style and others by their method, some by their embellishments and others by their simplicity, some by closeness and others by diffusion.

The same indulgence is to be shown to the writers of morality: right and wrong are immutable; and those, therefore, who teach us to distinguish them, if they all teach us right, must agree with one another. The relations of social life, and the duties resulting from them, must be the same at all times and in all nations: some petty differences may be, indeed, produced, by forms of government or arbitrary customs; but the general doctrine can receive no alteration.

Yet it is not to be desired, that morality should be considered as interdicted to all future writers: men will always be tempted to deviate from their duty, and will, therefore, always want a monitor to recall them; and a new book often seizes the attention of the publick, without any other claim than that it is new. There is likewise in composition, as in other things, a perpetual vicissitude of fashion ; and truth is recommended at one time to regard, by appearances which at another would expose it to neglect; the author, therefore, who has judgment to discern the taste of his contemporaries, and skill to gratify it, will have always an opportunity to deserve well of mankind, by conveying instruction to them in a grateful vehicle.

There are likewise many modes of composition, by which a moralist may deserve the name of an original writer : he may familiarize his system by dialogues after the manner of the ancients, or subtilize it into a series of syllogistick arguments : he may enforce his doctrine by seriousness and solemnity, or enliven it by sprightliness and gaiety : he may deliver his sentiments in naked precepts, or illustrate them by historical examples : he may detain the studious by the artful concatenation of a continued discourse, or relieve the busy by short strictures, and unconnected essays.

To excel in any of these forms of writing will require a particular cultivation of the genius : whoever can attain to excellence, will be certain to engage a set of readers, whom no other method would have equally allured ; and he that communicates truth with success, must be numbered among the first benefactors to mankind.

The same observation may be extended likewise to the passions : their influence is uniform, and their effects nearly the same in every human breast : a man loves and hates, desires and avoids, exactly like his neighbour ; resentment and ambition, avarice and indolence, discover themselves by the same symptoms in minds distant a thousand years from one another.

Nothing, therefore, can be more unjust, than to charge an author with plagiarism, merely because he assigns to every cause its natural effect ; and makes his personages act, as others in like circumstances have always done. There are conceptions in which all men will agree, though each derives them from his own observation : whoever has been in love, will represent a lover impatient of every idea that inter-

rupts his meditations on his mistress, retiring to shades
and solitude, that he may muse without disturbance on his
approaching happiness, or associating himself with some
friend that flatters his passion, and talking away the hours
of absence upon his darling subject.   Whoever has been
so unhappy as to have felt the miseries of long-continued
hatred, will, without any assistance from ancient volumes,
be able to relate how the passions are kept in perpetual
agitation, by the recollection of injury and meditations of
revenge; how the blood boils at the name of the enemy,
and life is worn away in contrivances of mischief.

Every other passion is alike simple and limited, if it be
considered only with regard to the breast which it inhabits;
the anatomy of the mind, as that of the body, must perpetually exhibit the same appearances; and though by the
continued industry of successive inquirers, new movements
will be from time to time discovered, they can affect only
the minuter parts, and are commonly of more curiosity
than importance.

It will now be natural to inquire, by what arts are the
writers of the present and future ages to attract the notice
and favour of mankind.   They are to observe the alterations which time is always making in the modes of life,
that they may gratify every generation with a picture of
themselves.   Thus love is uniform, but courtship is perpetually varying: the different arts of gallantry, which
beauty has inspired, would of themselves be sufficient to
fill a volume; sometimes balls and serenades, sometimes
tournaments and adventures, have been employed to melt
the hearts of ladies, who in another century have been
sensible of scarce any other merit than that of riches, and
listened only to jointures and pin-money.   Thus the ambitious man has at all times been eager of wealth and
power; but these hopes have been gratified in some countries by supplicating the people, and in others by flattering
the prince: honour in some states has been only the reward of military achievements, in others it has been gained
by noisy turbulence and popular clamours. (Avarice has

worn a different form, as she actuated the usurer of Rome, and the stock-jobber of England; and idleness itself, how little soever inclined to the trouble of invention, has been forced from time to time to change its amusements, and contrive different methods of wearing out the day.

Here then is the fund, from which those who study mankind may fill their compositions with an inexhaustible variety of images and allusions: and he must be confessed to look with little attention upon scenes thus perpetually changing, who cannot catch some of the figures before they are made vulgar by reiterated descriptions.

It has been discovered by Sir Isaac Newton, that the distinct and primogenial colours are only seven; but every eye can witness, that from various mixtures, in various proportions, infinite diversifications of tints may be produced. In like manner, the passions of the mind, which put the world in motion, and produce all the bustle and eagerness of the busy crowds that swarm upon the earth; the passions, from whence arise all the pleasures and pains that we see and hear of, if we analyze the mind of man, are very few; but those few agitated and combined, as external causes shall happen to operate, and modified by prevailing opinions and accidental caprices, make such frequent alterations on the surface of life, that the show, while we are busied in delineating it, vanishes from the view, and a new set of objects succeed, doomed to the same shortness of duration with the former: thus curiosity may always find employment, and the busy part of mankind will furnish the contemplative with the materials of speculation to the end of time.

The complaint, therefore, that all topicks are preoccupied, is nothing more than the murmur of ignorance or idleness, by which some discourage others, and some themselves; the mutability of mankind will always furnish writers with new images, and the luxuriance of fancy may always embellish them with new decorations.

N°. 99.   TUESDAY, OCTOBER 16, 1753.

——*Magnis tamen excidit ausis.*   Ovid. Met. Lib. ii. 328.

But in the glorious enterprise he died.   Addison.

It has always been the practice of mankind, to judge of actions by the event. The same attempts, conducted in the same manner, but terminated by different success, produce different judgments: they who attain their wishes, never want celebrators of their wisdom and their virtue; and they that miscarry, are quickly discovered to have been defective not only in mental but in moral qualities. The world will never be long without some good reason to hate the unhappy; their real faults are immediately detected; and if those are not sufficient to sink them into infamy, an additional weight of calumny will be superadded: he that fails in his endeavours after wealth or power, will not long retain either honesty or courage.

This species of injustice has so long prevailed in universal practice, that it seems likewise to have infected speculation: so few minds are able to separate the ideas of greatness and prosperity, that even Sir William Temple has determined, " that he who can deserve the name of a hero, must not only be virtuous but fortunate."

By this unreasonable distribution of praise and blame, none have suffered oftener than projectors, whose rapidity of imagination and vastness of design raise such envy in their fellow mortals, that every eye watches for their fall, and every heart exults at their distresses: yet even a projector may gain favour by success; and the tongue that was prepared to hiss, then endeavours to excel others in loudness of applause.

When Coriolanus, in Shakespeare, deserted to Aufidius, the Volscian servants at first insulted him, even while he stood under the protection of the household gods: but when they saw that the project took effect, and the stranger was seated at the head of the table, one of them very judiciously observes, "that he always thought there was' more in him than he could think."

· Machiavel has justly animadverted on the different notice taken by all succeeding times, of the two great projectors, Cataline and Cæsar. Both formed the same project, and intended to raise themselves to power, by subverting the commonwealth: they pursued their design, perhaps, with equal abilities, and with equal virtue; but Cataline perished in the field, and Cæsar returned from Pharsalia with unlimited authority: and from that time, every monarch of the earth has thought himself honoured by a comparison with Cæsar; and Cataline has been never mentioned, but that his name might be applied to traitors and incendiaries.

In an age more remote, Xerxes projected the conquest of Greece, and brought down the power of Asia against it: but after the world had been filled with expectation and terrour, his army was beaten, his fleet was destroyed, and Xerxes has been never mentioned without contempt.

A few years afterwards, Greece likewise had her turn of giving birth to a projector; who invading Asia with a small army, went forward in search of adventures, and by his escape from one danger, gained only more rashness to rush into another: he stormed city after city, over-ran kingdom after kingdom, fought battles only for barren victory, and invaded nations only that he might make his way through them to new invasions: but having been fortunate in the execution of his projects, he died with the name of Alexander the Great.

These are, indeed, events of ancient times; but human nature is always the same, and every age will afford us instances of publick censures influenced by events. The great business of the middle centuries, was the holy war; which undoubtedly was a noble project, and was for a long time prosecuted with a spirit equal to that with which it had been contrived; but the ardour of the European heroes only hurried them to destruction; for a long time they could not gain the territories for which they fought, and, when at last gained, they could not keep them : their expeditions, therefore, have been the scoff of idleness and ignorance, their understanding and their virtue have been equally vilified, their conduct has been ridiculed, and their cause has been defamed.

When Columbus had engaged king Ferdinand in the discovery of the other hemisphere, the sailors, with whom he embarked in the expedition, had so little confidence in their commander, that after having been long at sea looking for coasts which they expected never to find, they raised a general mutiny, and demanded to return. He found means to sooth them into a permission to continue the same course three days longer, and on the evening of the third day descried land. Had the impatience of his crew denied him a few hours of the time requested, what had been his fate but to have come back with the infamy of a vain projector, who had betrayed the king's credulity to useless expenses, and risked his life in seeking countries that had no existence ? how would those that had rejected his proposals have triumphed in their acuteness ! and when would his name have been mentioned, but with the makers of potable gold and malleable glass ?

The last royal projectors with whom the world has been troubled, were Charles of Sweden and the Czar of Muscovy. Charles, if any judgment may be formed of his designs by his measures and his inquiries, had purposed first to dethrone the Czar, then to lead his army through pathless deserts into China, thence to make his way by the sword through the whole circuit of Asia, and by the conquest of Turkey to unite Sweden with his new dominions : but this mighty project was crushed at Pultowa; and Charles has since been considered as a madman by those powers, who sent their ambassadors to solicit his friendship, and their generals " to learn under him the art of war."

The Czar found employment sufficient in his own dominions, and amused himself in digging canals, and building cities: murdering his subjects with insufferable fatigues, and transplanting nations from one corner of his dominions to another, without regretting the thousands that perished on the way: but he attained his end, he made his people formidable, and is numbered by fame among the demigods.

I am far from intending to vindicate the sanguinary projects of heroes and conquerors, and would wish rather to diminish the reputation of their success, than the infamy of their miscarriages: for I cannot conceive, why he that has burned cities, wasted nations, and filled the world with horrour and desolation, should be more kindly regarded by mankind, than he that died in the rudiments of wickedness; why he that accomplished mischief should be glorious, and he that only endeavoured it should be criminal. I would wish Cæsar and Catiline, Xerxes and Alexander, Charles and Peter, huddled together in obscurity or detestation.

But there is another species of projectors, to whom I would willingly conciliate mankind; whose ends are generally laudable, and whose labours are innocent; who are searching out new powers of nature, or contriving new works of art; but who are yet persecuted with incessant obloquy, and whom the universal contempt with which they are treated, often debars from that success which their industry would obtain, if it were permitted to act without opposition.

They who find themselves inclined to censure new undertakings, only because they are new, should consider, that the folly of projection is very seldom the folly of a fool; it is commonly the ebullition of a capacious mind, crowded with variety of knowledge, and heated with intenseness of thought; it proceeds often from the consciousness of uncommon powers, from the confidence of those, who having already done much, are easily persuaded that they can do more. When Rowley had completed the orrery, he attempted the perpetual motion; when Boyle had exhausted the secrets of vulgar chymistry, he turned his thoughts to the work of transmutation [b].

A projector generally unites those qualities which have the fairest claim to veneration, extent of knowledge and greatness of design; it was said of Catiline, "*immoderata, incredibilia, nimis alta semper cupiebat.*" Projectors of all kinds agree in their intellects, though they differ in their morals; they all fail by attempting things beyond their power, by despising vulgar attainments, and aspiring to performances to which, perhaps, nature has not proportioned the force of man: when they fail, therefore, they fail not by idleness or timidity, but by rash adventure and fruitless diligence.

That the attempts of such men will often miscarry, we may reasonably expect; yet from such men, and such only, are we to hope for the cultivation of those parts of nature which lie yet waste, and the invention of those arts which are yet wanting to the felicity of life. If they are, therefore, universally discouraged, art and discovery can make no advances. Whatever is attempted without previous certainty of success, may be considered as a project, and amongst narrow minds may, therefore, expose its author to censure and contempt; and if the liberty of laughing be once indulged, every man will laugh at what he does not understand, every project will be considered as madness, and every great or new design will be censured as a project. Men unaccustomed to reason and researches, think every enterprise impracticable, which is extended beyond common effects, or comprises many intermediate operations. Many that presume to laugh at projectors, would consider a flight through the air in a winged chariot, and the movement of a mighty engine by the steam of

[b] Sir Richard Steele was infatuated with notions of Alchemy, and wasted money in its visionary projects. He had a laboratory at Poplar. Addisoniana, vol i. p. 10.

The readers of Washington Irving's Brace-Bridge Hall will recollect a pleasing and popular exposition of the alternately splendid and benevolent, and always passionate reveries of the Alchemist, in the affecting story of the Student of Salamanca.

water as equally the dreams of mechanick lunacy; and would hear, with equal negligence, of the union of the Thames and Severn by a canal, and the scheme of Albuquerque, the viceroy of the Indies, who in the rage of hostility had contrived to make Egypt a barren desert, by turning the Nile into the Red Sea.

Those who have attempted much, have seldom failed to perform more than those who never deviate from the common roads of action : many valuable preparations of chymistry are supposed to have risen from unsuccessful inquiries after the grand elixir: it is, therefore, just to encourage those who endeavour to enlarge the power of art, since they often succeed beyond expectation; and when they fail, may sometimes benefit the world even by their miscarriages.

N°. 102. SATURDAY, OCTOBER 27, 1753.

———: Quid tam dextro pede concipis, ut te
Conatus non pæniteat votique peracti ?　　　Juv. Sat. x. 5.

What in the conduct of our life appears
So well design'd, so luckily begun,
But when we have our wish, we wish undone.　　Dryden.

TO THE ADVENTURER.

SIR,

I HAVE been for many years a trader in London. My beginning was narrow, and my stock small; I was, therefore, a long time brow-beaten and despised by those, who, having more money, thought they had more merit than myself. I did not, however, suffer my resentment to instigate me to any mean arts of supplantation, nor my eagerness of riches to betray me to any indireot methods of gain; I pursued my business with incessant assiduity, supported by the hope of being one day richer than those who contemned me; and had, upon every annual review of my books, the satisfaction of finding my fortune increased beyond my expectation.

In a few years my industry and probity were fully re-compensed, my wealth was really great, and my reputation for wealth still greater. I had large warehouses crowded with goods, and considerable sums in the publick funds; I was caressed upon the Exchange by the most eminent merchants; became the oracle of the common council; was solicited to engage in all commercial undertakings; was flattered with the hopes of becoming in a short time one of the directors of a wealthy company, and, to complete my mercantile honours, enjoyed the expensive happiness of fining for sheriff.

Riches, you know, easily produce riches; when I had arrived to this degree of wealth, I had no longer any obstruction or opposition to fear; new acquisitions were hourly brought within my reach, and I continued for some years longer to heap thousands upon thousands.

At last I resolved to complete the circle of a citizen's prosperity by the purchase of an estate in the country, and to close my life in retirement. From the hour that this design entered my imagination, I found the fatigues of my employment every day more oppressive, and per-suaded myself that I was no longer equal to perpetual at-tention, and that my health would soon be destroyed by the torment and distraction of extensive business. I could image to myself no happiness, but in vacant jollity, and uninterrupted leisure: nor entertain my friends with any other topick than the vexation and uncertainty of trade, and the happiness of rural privacy.

But, notwithstanding these declarations, I could not at once reconcile myself to the thoughts of ceasing to get money; and though I was every day inquiring for a pur-chase, I found some reason for rejecting all that were offered me; and, indeed, had accumulated so many beau-ties and conveniencies in my idea of the spot where I was finally to be happy, that, perhaps, the world might have been travelled over without discovery of a place which would not have been defective in some particular.

Thus I went on, still talking of retirement, and still refusing to retire; my friends began to laugh at my delays, and I grew ashamed to trifle longer with my own inclinations; an estate was at length purchased, I transferred my stock to a prudent young man who had married my daughter, went down into the country, and commenced lord of a spacious manor.

Here for some time I found happiness equal to my expectation. I reformed the old house according to the advice of the best architects, I threw down the walls of the garden, and enclosed it with palisades, planted long avenues of trees, filled a green-house with exotick plants, dug a new canal, and threw the earth into the old moat.

The fame of these expensive improvements brought in all the country to see the show. I entertained my visitors with great liberality, led them round my gardens, showed them my apartments, laid before them plans for new decorations, and was gratified by the wonder of some and the envy of others.

I was envied: but how little can one man judge of the condition of another! The time was now coming, in which affluence and splendour could no longer make me pleased with myself. I had built till the imagination of the architect was exhausted; I had added one convenience to another, till I knew not what more to wish or to design; I had laid out my gardens, planted my park, and completed my water-works; and what now remained to be done? what, but to look up to turrets, of which when they were once raised I had no further use, to range over apartments where time was tarnishing the furniture, to stand by the cascade of which I scarcely now perceived the sound, and to watch the growth of woods that must give their shade to a distant generation.

In this gloomy inactivity, is every day begun and ended: the happiness that I have been so long procuring is now at an end, because it has been procured; I wander from room to room, till I am weary of myself; I ride out to a neighbouring hill in the centre of my estate, from whence all my lands lie in prospect round me; I see nothing that

I have not seen before, and return home disappointed, though I knew that I had nothing to expect.

In my happy days of business I had been accustomed to rise early in the morning; and remember the time when I grieved that the night came so soon upon me, and obliged me for a few hours to shut out affluence and prosperity. I now seldom see the rising sun, but to " tell him," with the fallen angel, " how I hate his beams[i]." I awake from sleep as to languor or imprisonment, and have no employment for the first hour but to consider by what art I shall rid myself of the second. I protract the breakfast as long as I can, because when it is ended I have no call for my attention, till I can with some degree of decency grow impatient for my dinner. If I could dine all my life, I should be happy; I eat not because I am hungry, but because I am idle: but, alas! the time quickly comes when I can eat no longer; and so ill does my constitution second my inclination, that I cannot bear strong liquors: seven hours must then be endured before I shall sup; but supper comes at last, the more welcome as it is in a short time succeeded by sleep.

Such, Mr. Adventurer, is the happiness, the hope of which seduced me from the duties and pleasures of a mercantile life. I shall be told by those who read my narrative, that there are many means of innocent amusement, and many schemes of useful employment, which I do not appear ever to have known; and that nature and art have provided pleasures, by which, without the drudgery of settled business, the active may be engaged, the solitary soothed, and the social entertained.

These arts, Sir, I have tried. When first I took possession of my estate, in conformity to the taste of my neighbours, I bought guns and nets, filled my kennel

---

[i] Johnson was too apt to destroy the *keeping* of character in his correspondences. A retired trader might desire a little more slumber, " a little folding of the hands to sleep;" but the lofty malignity of a fallen spirit sickening at the beams of day, would not be among the feelings of an ordinary mind. Some good remarks on this point may be seen in Miss Talbot's Letters to Mrs. Carter.

with dogs, and my stable with horses: but a little experience showed me, that these instruments of rural felicity would afford me few gratifications. I never shot but to miss the mark, and, to confess the truth, was afraid of the fire of my own gun. I could discover no musick in the cry of the dogs, nor could divest myself of pity for the animal whose peaceful and inoffensive life was sacrificed to our sport. I was not, indeed, always at leisure to reflect upon her danger; for my horse, who had been bred to the chase, did not always regard my choice either of speed or way, but leaped hedges and ditches at his own discretion, and hurried me along with the dogs, to the great diversion of my brother sportsmen. His eagerness of pursuit once incited him to swim a river; and I had leisure to resolve in the water, that I would never hazard my life again for the destruction of a hare.

I then ordered books to be procured, and by the direction of the vicar had in a few weeks a closet elegantly furnished. You will, perhaps, be surprised when I shall tell you, that when once I had ranged them according to their sizes, and piled them up in regular gradations, I had received all the pleasure which they could give me. I am not able to excite in myself any curiosity after events which have been long passed, and in which I can, therefore, have no interest; I am utterly unconcerned to know whether Tully or Demosthenes excelled in oratory, whether Hannibal lost Italy by his own negligence or the corruption of his countrymen. I have no skill in controversial learning, nor can conceive why so many volumes should have been written upon questions, which I have lived so long and so happily without understanding. I once resolved to go through the volumes relating to the office of justice of the peace, but found them so crabbed and intricate, that in less than a month I desisted in despair, and resolved to supply my deficiencies by paying a competent salary to a skilful clerk.

I am naturally inclined to hospitality, and for some time kept up a constant intercourse of visits with the neighbouring gentlemen ; but though they are easily brought about me by better wine than they can find at any other house, I am not much relieved by their conversation ; they have no skill in commerce or the stocks, and I have no knowledge of the history of families or the factions of the country ; so that when the first civilities are over, they usually talk to one another, and I am left alone in the midst of the company. Though I cannot drink myself, I am obliged to encourage the circulation of the glass ; their mirth grows more turbulent and obstreperous ; and before their merriment is at an end, I am sick with disgust, and, perhaps, reproached with my sobriety, or by some sly insinuations insulted as a cit.

Such, Mr. Adventurer, is the life to which I am condemned by a foolish endeavour to be happy by imitation ; such is the happiness to which I pleased myself with approaching, and which I considered as the chief end of my cares and my labours. I toiled year after year with cheerfulness, in expectation of the happy hour in which I might be idle : the privilege of idleness is attained, but has not brought with it the blessing of tranquillity.

I am yours, &c.
MERCATOR.

N°. 107. TUESDAY, NOVEMBER 13, 1753.

———Sub judice lis est.   Hor. De Ar. Poet. 78.

And of their vain disputings find no end.   FRANCIS.

IT has been sometimes asked by those who find the appearance of wisdom more easily attained by questions than solutions, how it comes to pass, that the world is divided by such difference of opinion ? and why men, equally reasonable, and equally lovers of truth, do not always think in the same manner ?

With regard to simple propositions, where the terms are understood, and the whole subject is comprehended at once, there is such an uniformity of sentiment among all human beings, that, for many ages, a very numerous set of notions were supposed to be innate, or necessarily co-existent with the faculty of reason: it being imagined, that universal agreement could proceed only from the invariable dictates of the universal parent.

In questions diffuse and compounded, this similarity of determination is no longer to be expected. At our first sally into the intellectual world, we all march together along one straight and open road; but as we proceed further, and wider prospects open to our view, every eye fixes upon a different scene; we divide into various paths, and, as we move forward, are still at a greater distance from each other. As a question becomes more compli-cated and involved, and extends to a greater number of relations, disagreement of opinion will always be multi-plied; not because we are irrational, but because we are finite beings, furnished with different kinds of knowledge, exerting different degrees of attention, one discovering consequences which escape another, none taking in the whole concatenation of causes and effects, and most com-prehending but a very small part, each comparing what he observes with a different criterion, and each referring it to a different purpose.

Where, then, is the wonder, that they who see only a small part should judge erroneously of the whole? or that they, who see different and dissimilar parts, should judge differently from each other?

Whatever has various respects, must have various ap-pearances of good and evil, beauty or deformity; thus, the gardener tears up as a weed, the plant which the physician gathers as a medicine; and "a general," says Sir Kenelm Digby, "will look with pleasure over a plain, as a fit place on which the fate of empires might be decided in battle, which the farmer will despise as bleak and barren, neither fruitful of pasturage, nor fit for tillage [k]."

Two men examining the same question proceed commonly like the physician and gardener in selecting herbs, or the farmer and hero looking on the plain; they bring minds impressed with different notions, and direct their inquiries to different ends; they form, therefore, contrary conclusions, and each wonders at the other's absurdity.

We have less reason to be surprised or offended when we find others differ from us in opinion, because we very often differ from ourselves. How often we alter our minds, we do not always remark; because the change is sometimes made imperceptibly and gradually, and the last conviction effaces all memory of the former: yet every man, accustomed from time to time to take a survey of his own notions, will by a slight retrospection be able to discover, that his mind has suffered many revolutions; that the same things have in the several parts of his life been condemned and approved, pursued and shunned: and that on many occasions, even when his practice has been steady, his mind has been wavering, and he has persisted in a scheme of action, rather because he feared the censure of inconstancy, than because he was always pleased with his own choice.

Of the different faces shown by the same objects, as they are viewed on opposite sides, and of the different inclinations which they must constantly raise in him that contemplates them, a more striking example cannot easily

---

[k] Livy has described the Achæan leader, Philopæmen, as actually so exercising his thoughts whilst he wandered among the rocky passes of the Morea, xxxv. 28. In the graphic page of the Roman historian, as in the stanzas of the " Ariosto of the North :"

> " From shingles grey the lances start,
> " The bracken bush sends forth the dart,
> " The rushes and the willow wand
> " Are bristling into axe and brand."
>
> Lady of the Lake. Canto v. 9.

be found than two Greek epigrammatists will afford us in their accounts of human life, which I shall lay before the reader in English prose.

Posidippus, a comick poet, utters this complaint: "Through which of the paths of life is it eligible to pass? In public assemblies are debates and troublesome affairs: domestick privacies are haunted with anxieties; in the country is labour; on the sea is terrour: in a foreign land, he that has money must live in fear, he that wants it must pine in distress: are you married? you are troubled with suspicions; are you single? you languish in solitude; children occasion toil, and a childless life is a state of destitution: the time of youth is a time of folly, and gray hairs are loaded with infirmity. This choice only, therefore, can be made, either never to receive being, or immediately to lose it[1]."

Such and so gloomy is the prospect, which Posidippus has laid before us. But we are not to acquiesce too hastily in his determination against the value of existence: for Metrodorus, a philosopher of Athens, has shown, that life has pleasures as well as pains; and having exhibited the present state of man in brighter colours, draws with equal appearance of reason, a contrary conclusion.

"You may pass well through any of the paths of life. In publick assemblies are honours and transactions of wisdom; in domestick privacy is stillness and quiet: in the country are the beauties of nature; on the sea is the hope of gain: in a foreign land, he that is rich is honoured, he that is poor may keep his poverty secret: are you married? you have a cheerful house; are you single? you

[1] " Count o'er the joys thine hours have seen,
" Count o'er thy days from anguish free,
" And know, whatever thou hast been,
" 'Tis something better not to be."

Lord Byron's Euthanasia.

Compare also the plaintive chorus in the Œdipus at Colonos, 1211. Among the tragedies of Sophocles this stands forth a mass of feeling. See Schlegel's remarks upon it in his Dramatic Literature.

are unincumbered; children are objects of affection, to be without children is to be without care: the time of youth is the time of vigour, and gray hairs are made venerable by piety. It will, therefore, never be a wise man's choice, either not to obtain existence, or to lose it; for every state of life has its felicity."

In these epigrams are included most of the questions which have engaged the speculations of the inquirers after happiness; and though they will not much assist our determinations, they may, perhaps, equally promote our quiet, by showing that no absolute determination ever can be formed.

Whether a publick station or private life be desirable, has always been debated. We see here both the allurements and discouragements of civil employments; on one side there is trouble, on the other honour; the management of affairs is vexatious and difficult, but it is the only duty in which wisdom can be conspicuously displayed: it must then still be left to every man to choose either ease or glory; nor can any general precept be given, since no man can be happy by the prescription of another.

Thus, what is said of children by Posidippus, "that they are occasions of fatigue," and by Metrodorus, "that they are objects of affection," is equally certain; but whether they will give most pain or pleasure, must depend on their future conduct and dispositions, on many causes over which the parent can have little influence: there is, therefore, room for all the caprices of imagination, and desire must be proportioned to the hope or fear that shall happen to predominate.

Such is the uncertainty in which we are always likely to remain with regard to questions wherein we have most interest, and which every day affords us fresh opportunity to examine: we may examine, indeed, but we never can decide, because our faculties are unequal to the subject; we see a little, and form an opinion; we see more, and change it.

This inconstancy and unsteadiness, to which we must so often-find ourselves liable, ought certainly to teach us moderation and forbearance towards those who cannot accommodate themselves to our sentiments: if they are deceived, we have no right to attribute their mistake to obstinacy or negligence, because we likewise have been mistaken; we may, perhaps, again change our own opinion: and what excuse shall we be able to find for aversion and malignity conceived against him, whom we shall then find to have committed no fault, and who offended us only by refusing to follow us into errour?

It may likewise contribute to soften that resentment which pride naturally raises against opposition, if we consider, that he who differs from us, does not always contradict us; he has one view of an object, and we have another; each describes what he sees with equal fidelity, and each regulates his steps by his own eyes: one man with Posidippus, looks on celibacy as a state of gloomy solitude, without a partner in joy, or a comforter in sorrow; the other considers it, with Metrodorus, as a state free from incumbrances, in which a man is at liberty to choose his own gratifications, to remove from place to place in quest of pleasure, and to think of nothing but merriment and diversion: full of these notions one hastens to choose a wife, and the other laughs at his rashness, or pities his ignorance; yet it is possible that each is right, but that each is right only for himself.

Life is not the object of science: we see a little, very little; and what is beyond we only can conjecture. If we inquire of those who have gone before us, we receive small satisfaction; some have travelled life without observation, and some willingly mislead us. The only thought, therefore, on which we can repose with comfort, is that which presents to us the care of Providence, whose eye takes in the whole of things, and under whose direction all involuntary errours will terminate in happiness.

N°. 108. SATURDAY, NOVEMBER 17, 1753.

Nobis, quum semel occidit brevis lux,
Nox est perpetua una dormienda.   Catullus. Lib. v. El. v.

When once the short-liv'd mortal dies,
A night eternal seals his eyes.   Addison.

IT may have been observed by every reader, that there
are certain topicks which never are exhausted. Of some
images and sentiments the mind of man may be said to be
enamoured ; it meets them, however often they occur, with
the same ardour which a lover feels at the sight of his mistress, and parts from them with the same regret when they
can no longer be enjoyed.

Of this kind are many descriptions which the poets have
transcribed from each other, and their successors will probably copy to the end of time ; which will continue to engage, or, as the French term it, to flatter the imagination,
as long as human nature shall remain the same.

When a poet mentions the spring, we know that the
zephyrs are about to whisper, that the groves are to recover their verdure, the linnets to warble forth their notes
of love, and the flocks and herds to frisk over vales painted
with flowers : yet, who is there so insensible of the beauties of nature, so little delighted with the renovation of the
world, as not to feel his heart bound at the mention of the
spring ?

When night overshadows a romantick scene, all is stillness, silence, and quiet ; the poets of the grove cease their
melody, the moon towers over the world in gentle majesty,
men forget their labours and their cares, and every passion
and pursuit is for a while suspended. All this we know
already, yet we hear it repeated without weariness ; because such is generally the life of man, that he is pleased
to think on the time when he shall pause from a sense of
his condition.

When a poetical grove invites us to its covert, we know
that we shall find what we have already seen, a limpid

brook murmuring over pebbles, a bank diversified with flowers, a green arch that excludes the sun, and a natural grot shaded with myrtles ; yet who can forbear to enter the pleasing gloom to enjoy coolness and privacy, and gratify himself once more by scenes with which nature has formed him to be delighted ?

Many moral sentiments likewise are so adapted to our state, that they find approbation whenever they solicit it, and are seldom read without exciting a gentle emotion in the mind: such is the comparison of the life of man with the duration of a flower, a thought which perhaps every nation has heard warbled in its own language, from the inspired poets of the Hebrews to our own times ; yet this comparion must always please, because every heart feels its justness, and every hour confirms it by example.

Such, likewise, is the precept that directs us to use the present hour, and refer nothing to a distant time, which we are uncertain whether we shall reach: this every moralist may venture to inculcate, because it will always be approved, and because it is always forgotten.

This rule is, indeed, every day enforced, by arguments more powerful than the dissertations of moralists: we see men pleasing themselves with future happiness, fixing a certain hour for the completion of their wishes, and perishing, some at a greater and some at a less distance from the happy time ; all complaining of their disappointments, and lamenting that they had suffered the years which heaven allowed them, to pass without improvement, and deferred the principal purpose of their lives to the time when life itself was to forsake them.

It is not only uncertain, whether, through all the casualties and dangers which beset the life of man, we shall be able to reach the time appointed for happiness or wisdom ; but it is likely, that whatever now hinders us from doing that which our reason and conscience declare necessary to be done, will equally obstruct us in times to come. It is easy for the imagination, operating on things not yet existing, to please itself with scenes of unmingled felicity, or plan out courses of uniform virtue; but good and evil are in real life inseparably united; habits grow stronger by indulgence; and reason loses her dignity, in proportion as she has oftener yielded to temptation: " he that cannot live well to-day," says Martial," will be less qualified to live well to-morrow."

Of the uncertainty of every human good, every human being seems to be convinced; yet this uncertainty is voluntarily increased by unnecessary delay, whether we respect external causes, or consider the nature of our own minds. He that now feels a desire to do right, and wishes to regulate his life according to his reason, is not sure that, at any future time assignable, he shall be able to rekindle the same ardour; he that has now an opportunity offered him of breaking loose from vice and folly, cannot know, but that he shall hereafter be more entangled, and struggle for freedom without obtaining it.

We are so unwilling to believe any thing to our own disadvantage, that we will always imagine the perspicacity of our judgment and the strength of our resolution more likely to increase than to grow less by time; and, therefore, conclude, that the will to pursue laudable purposes, will be always seconded by the power.

But, however we may be deceived in calculating the strength of our faculties, we cannot doubt the uncertainty of that life in which they must be employed: we see every day the unexpected death of our friends and our enemies, we see new graves hourly opened for men older and younger than ourselves, for the cautious and the careless, the dissolute and the temperate, for men who like us were providing to enjoy or improve hours now irreversibly cut off: we see all this, and yet, instead of living, let year glide after year in preparations to live.

Men are so frequently cut off in the midst of their projections, that sudden death causes little emotion in them that behold it, unless it be impressed upon the attention by uncommon circumstances. I, like every other man, have outlived multitudes, have seen ambition sink in its triumphs, and beauty perish in its bloom ; but have been seldom so much affected as by the fate of Euryalus, whom I lately lost as I began to love him.

Euryalus had for some time flourished in a lucrative profession ; but having suffered his imagination to be fired by an unextinguishable curiosity, he grew weary of the same dull round of life, resolved to harass himself no longer with the drudgery of getting money, but to quit his business and his profit, and enjoy for a few years the pleasures of travel. His friends heard him proclaim his resolution without suspecting that he intended to pursue it; but he was constant to his purpose, and with great expedition closed his accounts and sold his moveables, passed a few days in bidding farewell to his companions, and with all the eagerness of romantick chivalry crossed the sea in search of happiness. Whatever place was renowned in ancient or modern history, whatever region art or nature had distinguished, he determined to visit : full of design and hope he landed on the continent ; his friends expected accounts from him of the new scenes that opened in his progress, but were informed in a few days, that Euryalus was dead.

Such was the end of Euryalus. He is entered that state, whence none ever shall return ; and can now only benefit his friends, by remaining to their memories a permanent and efficacious instance of the blindness of desire, and the uncertainty of all terrestrial good. But perhaps, every man has like me lost an Euryalus, has known a friend die with happiness in his grasp ; and yet every man continues to think himself secure of life, and defers to some future time of leisure what he knows it will be fatal to have finally omitted.

It is, indeed, with this as with other frailties inherent in our nature ; the desire of deferring to another time, what cannot be done without endurance of some pain, or forbearance of some pleasure, will, perhaps, never be totally overcome or suppressed ; there will always be something that we shall wish to have finished, and be nevertheless unwilling to begin : but against this unwillingness it is our duty to struggle, and every conquest over our passions will make way for an easier conquest : custom is equally forcible to bad and good ; nature will always be at variance with reason, but will rebel more feebly as she is oftener subdued.

The common neglect of the present hour is more shameful and criminal, as no man is betrayed to it by errour, but admits it by negligence. Of the instability of life, the weakest understanding never thinks wrong, though the strongest often omits to think justly; reason and experience are always ready to inform us of our real state ; but we refuse to listen to their suggestions, because we feel our hearts unwilling to obey them : but, surely, nothing is more unworthy of a reasonable being, than to shut his eyes, when he sees the road which he is commanded to travel, that he may deviate with fewer reproaches from himself : nor could any motive to tenderness, except the consciousness that we have all been guilty of the same fault, dispose us to pity those who thus consign themselves to voluntary ruin.

N°. 111. TUESDAY, NOVEMBER 27, 1753.

——— *Quæ non fecimus ipsi,*
Vix ea nostra voco.   OVID.

The deeds of long descended ancestors
Are but by grace of imputation ours.   DRYDEN

THE evils inseparably annexed to the present condition of man, are so numerous and afflictive, that it has been, from age to age, the task of some to bewail, and of others to solace them ; and he, therefore, will be in danger of seeing a common enemy, who shall attempt to depreciate the few pleasures and felicities which nature has allowed us.

Yet I will confess, that I have sometimes employed my thoughts in examining the pretensions that are made to happiness, by the splendid and envied condition of life; and have not thought the hour unprofitably spent, when I have detected the imposture of counterfeit advantages, and found disquiet lurking under false appearances of gaiety and greatness.

It is asserted by a tragick poet, that *est miser nemo nisi comparatus*, " no man is miserable, but as he is compared with others happier than himself:" this position is not strictly and philosophically true. He might have said, with rigorous propriety, that no man is happy but as he is compared with the miserable; for such is the state of this world, that we find in it absolute misery, but happiness only comparative; we may incur as much pain as we can possibly endure, though we can never obtain as much happiness as we might possibly enjoy.

Yet it is certain, likewise, that many of our miseries are merely comparative: we are often made unhappy, not by the presence of any real evil, but by the absence of some fictitious good; of something which is not required by any real want of nature, which has not in itself any power of gratification, and which neither reason nor fancy would have prompted us to wish, did we not see it in the possession of others.

For a mind diseased with vain longings after unattainable advantages, no medicine can be prescribed, but an impartial inquiry into the real worth of that which is so ardently desired. It is well known, how much the mind, as well as the eye, is deceived by distance; and, perhaps, it will be found, that of many imagined blessings it may be doubted, whether he that wants or possesses them has more reason to be satisfied with his lot.

The dignity of high birth and long extraction, no man, to whom nature has denied it, can confer upon himself; and, therefore, it deserves to be considered, whether the want of that which can never be gained, may not easily be endured. It is true, that if we consider the triumph and delight with which most of those recount their ancestors, who have ancestors to recount, and the artifices by which some who have risen to unexpected fortune endeavour to insert themselves into an honourable stem, we shall be inclined to fancy that wisdom or virtue may be had by inheritance, or that all the excellencies of a line of progenitors are accumulated on their descendant. Reason, indeed, will soon inform us, that our estimation of birth is arbitrary and capricious, and that dead ancestors can have no influence but upon imagination; let it then be examined, whether one dream may not operate in the place of another; whether he that owes nothing to forefathers, may not receive equal pleasure from the consciousness of owing all to himself; whether he may not, with a little meditation, find it more honourable to found than to continue a family, and to gain dignity than transmit it; whether, if he receives no dignity from the virtues of his family, he does not likewise escape the danger of being disgraced by their crimes; and whether he that brings a new name into the world, has not the convenience of playing the game of life without a stake, and opportunity of winning much though he has nothing to lose.

There is another opinion concerning happiness, which approaches much more nearly to universality, but which may, perhaps, with equal reason be disputed. The pretensions to ancestral honours many of the sons of earth easily see to be ill-grounded; but all agree to celebrate the advantage of hereditary riches, and to consider those as the minions of fortune, who are wealthy from their cradles, whose estate is *res non parta labore, sed relicta;* " the acquisition of another, not of themselves ;" and whom a father's industry has dispensed from a laborious attention to arts or commerce, and left at liberty to dispose of life as fancy shall direct them.

If every man were wise and virtuous, capable to discern the best use of time, and resolute to practise it, it might be granted, I think, without hesitation, that total liberty would be a blessing; and that it would be desirable to be left at large to the exercise of religious and social duties, without the interruption of importunate avocations.

But, since felicity is relative, and that which is the means of happiness to one man may be to another the cause of misery, we are to consider, what state is best adapted to human nature in its present degeneracy and frailty. And, surely, to far the greater number it is highly expedient, that they should by some settled scheme of duties be rescued from the tyranny of caprice, that they should be driven on by necessity through the paths of life with their attention confined to a stated task, that they may be less at leisure to deviate into mischief at the call of folly.

When we observe the lives of those whom an ample inheritance has let loose to their own direction, what do we discover that can excite our envy? Their time seems not to pass with much applause from others, or satisfaction to themselves: many squander their exuberance of fortune in luxury and debauchery, and have no other use of money than to inflame their passions, and riot in a wide range of licentiousness; others, less criminal indeed, but surely not much to be praised, lie down to sleep, and rise up to trifle, are employed every morning in finding expedients to rid themselves of the day, chase pleasure through all the places of publick resort, fly from London to Bath, and from Bath to London, without any other reason for changing place, but that they go in quest of company as idle and as vagrant as themselves, always endeavouring to raise some new desire, that they may have something to pursue, to rekindle some hope which they know will be disappointed, changing one amusement for another which a few months will make equally insipid, or sinking into languor and disease for want of something to actuate their bodies or exhilarate their minds.

Whoever has frequented those places, where idlers assemble to escape from solitude, knows that this is generally the state of the wealthy; and from this state it is no great hardship to be debarred. No man can be happy in total idleness: he that should be condemned to lie torpid and motionless, " would fly for recreation," says South,

" to the mines and the galleys;" and it is well, when nature or fortune find employment for those, who would not have known how to procure it for themselves.

He, whose mind is engaged by the acquisition or improvement of a fortune, not only escapes the insipidity of indifference, and the tediousness of inactivity, but gains enjoyments wholly unknown to those, who live lazily on the toil of others; for life affords no higher pleasure than that of surmounting difficulties, passing from one step of success to another, forming new wishes, and seeing them gratified. He that labours in any great or laudable undertaking, has his fatigues first supported by hope, and afterwards rewarded by joy; he is always moving to a certain end, and when he has attained it, an end more distant invites him to a new pursuit.

It does not, indeed, always happen, that diligence is fortunate; the wisest schemes are broken by unexpected accidents; the most constant perseverance sometimes toils through life without a recompense; but labour, though unsuccessful, is more eligible than idleness; he that prosecutes a lawful purpose by lawful means, acts always with the approbation of his own reason; he is animated through the course of his endeavours by an expectation which, though not certain, he knows to be just; and is at last comforted in his disappointment, by the consciousness that he has not failed by his own fault.

That kind of life is most happy which affords us most opportunities of gaining our own esteem; and what can any man infer in his own favour from a condition to which, however prosperous, he contributed nothing, and which the vilest and weakest of the species would have obtained by the same right, had he happened to be the son of the same father?

To strive with difficulties, and to conquer them, is the highest human felicity; the next is, to strive, and deserve to conquer: but he whose life has passed without a contest, and who can boast neither success nor merit, can survey himself only as a useless filler of existence; and if he is content with his own character, must owe his satisfaction to insensibility.

Thus it appears that the satirist advised rightly, when he directed us to resign ourselves to the hands of Heaven, and to leave to superior powers the determination of our lot :

> Permittes ipsis expendere Numinibus, quid
> Conveniat nobis, rebusque sit utile nostris :——
> Carior est illis homo quam sibi.   Juv. Sat. x. 347.
> Intrust thy fortune to the Pow'rs above :
> Leave them to manage for thee, and to grant
> What their unerring wisdom sees the want.
> In goodness as in greatness they excel :
> Ah ! that we lov'd ourselves but half so well.   Dryden.

What state of life admits most happiness, is uncertain ; but that uncertainty ought to repress the petulance of comparison, and silence the murmurs of discontent.

Nº. 115.   TUESDAY, DECEMBER 11, 1753.

> Scribimus indocti doctique.   Hor. Lib. ii. Ep. i. 17.
> All dare to write, who can or cannot read.

THEY who have attentively considered the history of mankind, know that every age has its peculiar character. At one time, no desire is felt but for military honours ; every summer affords battles and sieges, and the world is filled with ravage, bloodshed, and devastation : this sanguinary fury at length subsides, and nations are divided into factions, by controversies about points that will never be decided. Men then grow weary of debate and altercation, and apply themselves to the arts of profit ; trading companies are formed, manufactures improved, and navigation extended ; and nothing is any longer thought on, but the increase and preservation of property, the artifices of getting money, and the pleasures of spending it.

The present age, if we consider chiefly the state of our own country, may be styled, with great propriety, *The Age of Authors*[m]; for, perhaps, there never was a time in which

---

[m] See Knox. Essay 50.

men of all degrees of ability, of every kind of education, of every profession and employment, were posting with ardour so general to the press. The province of writing was formerly left to those, who by study, or appearance of study, were supposed to have gained knowledge unattainable by the busy part of mankind; but in these enlightened days, every man is qualified to instruct every other man: and he that beats the anvil, or guides the plough, not content with supplying corporal necessities, amuses himself in the hours of leisure with providing intellectual pleasures for his countrymen.

It may be observed, that of this, as of other evils, complaints have been made by every generation: but though it may, perhaps, be true, that at all times more have been willing than have been able to write, yet there is no reason for believing, that the dogmatical legions of the present race were ever equalled in number by any former period: for so widely is spread the itch of literary praise, that almost every man is an author, either in act or in purpose: has either bestowed his favours on the publick, or withholds them, that they may be more seasonably offered, or made more worthy of acceptance.

In former times, the pen, like the sword, was considered as consigned by nature to the hands of men; the ladies contented themselves with private virtues and domestick excellence; and a female writer, like a female warrior, was considered as a kind of eccentrick being, that deviated, however illustriously, from her due sphere of motion, and was, therefore, rather to be gazed at with wonder, than countenanced by imitation. But as in the times past are said to have been a nation of Amazons, who drew the bow and wielded the battle-axe, formed encampments and wasted nations, the revolution of years has now produced a generation of Amazons of the pen, who with the spirit of their predecessors have set masculine tyranny at defiance, asserted their claim to the regions of science, and seem resolved to contest the usurpations of virility.

Some indeed there are, of both sexes, who are authors only in desire, but have not yet attained the power of executing their intentions ; whose performances have not arrived at bulk sufficient to form a volume, or who have not the confidence, however impatient of nameless obscurity, to solicit openly the assistance of the printer. Among these are the innumerable correspondents of publick papers, who are always offering assistance which no man will receive, and suggesting hints that are never taken ; and who complain loudly of the perverseness and arrogance of authors, lament their insensibility of their own interest, and fill the coffee-houses with dark stories of performances by eminent hands, which have been offered and rejected.

To what cause this universal eagerness of writing can be properly ascribed, I have not yet been able to discover. It is said, that every art is propagated in proportion to the rewards conferred upon it ; a position from which a stranger would naturally infer, that literature was now blessed with patronage far transcending the candour or munificence of the Augustan age, that the road to greatness was open to none but authors, and that by writing alone riches and honour were to be obtained.

But since it is true, that writers, like other competitors, are very little disposed to favour one another, it is not to be expected, that at a time when every man writes, any man will patronize ; and, accordingly, there is not one that I can recollect at present, who professes the least regard for the votaries of science, invites the addresses of learned men, or seems to hope for reputation from any pen but his own.

The cause, therefore, of this epidemical conspiracy for the destruction of paper, must remain a secret: nor can I discover, whether we owe it to the influences of the constellations, or the intemperature of seasons: whether the long continuance of the wind at any single point, or intoxicating vapours exhaled from the earth, have turned our nobles and our peasants, our soldiers and traders, our men and women, all into wits, philosophers, and writers.

It is, indeed, of more importance to search out the cure than the cause of this intellectual malady; and he would deserve well of this country, who, instead of amusing himself with conjectural speculations, should find means of persuading the peer to inspect his steward's accounts, or repair the rural mansion of his ancestors; who could replace the tradesman behind his counter, and send back the farmer to the mattock and the flail.

General irregularities are known in time to remédy themselves. By the constitution of ancient Egypt, the priesthood was continually increasing, till at length there was no people beside themselves; the establishment was then dissolved, and the number of priests was reduced and limited. Thus among us, writers will, perhaps, be multiplied, till no readers will be found, and then the ambition of writing must necessarily cease.

But as it will be long before the cure is thus gradually effected, and the evil should be stopped, if it be possible, before it rises to so great a height, I could wish that both sexes would fix their thoughts upon some salutary considerations, which might repress their ardour for that reputation, which not one of many thousands is fated to obtain.

Let it be deeply impressed, and frequently recollected, that he who has not obtained the proper qualifications of an author, can have no excuse for the arrogance of writing, but the power of imparting to mankind something necessary to be known. A man uneducated or unlettered may sometimes start a useful thought, or make a lucky discovery, or obtain by chance some secret of nature, or some intelligence of facts, of which the most enlightened mind may be ignorant, and which it is better to reveal, though by a rude and unskilful communication, than to lose for ever by suppressing it.

But few will be justified by this plea; for of the innumerable books and pamphlets that have overflowed the

nation, scarce one has made any addition to real knowledge, or contained more than a transposition of common
sentiments, and a repetition of common phrases.

It will be naturally inquired, when the man who feels
an inclination to write, may venture to suppose himself
properly qualified; and, since every man is inclined to
think well of his own intellect, by what test he may try
his abilities, without hazarding the contempt or resentment of the publick.

The first qualification of a writer is a perfect knowledge
of the subject which he undertakes to treat; since we
cannot teach what we do not know, nor can properly undertake to instruct others while we are ourselves in want
of instruction.   The next requisite is, that he be master
of the language in which he delivers his sentiments: if he
treats of science and demonstration, that he has attained a
style clear, pure, nervous, and expressive; if his topicks
be probable and persuasory, that he be able to recommend
them by the superaddition of elegance and imagery, to
display (the colours of varied diction,) and pour forth the
musick of modulated periods.

If it be again inquired, upon what principles any man
shall conclude that he wants those powers, it may be readily answered, that no end is attained but by the proper
means; he only can rationally presume that he understands a subject, who has read and compared the writers
that have hitherto discussed it, familiarized their arguments to himself by long meditation, consulted the foun-
dations of different systems, and separated truth from errour by a rigorous examination.

In like manner, he only has a right to suppose that he
can express his thoughts, whatever they are, with perspicuity or elegance, who has carefully perused the best authors, accurately noted their diversities of style, diligently
selected the best modes of diction, and familiarized them
by long habits of attentive practice.

No man is a rhetorician or philosopher by chance.   He
who knows that he undertakes to write on questions which

he has never studied, may without hesitation determine, that he is about to waste his own time and that of his reader, and expose himself to the derision of those whom he aspires to instruct: he that without forming his style by the study of the best models hastens to obtrude his compositions on the publick, may be certain, that whatever hope or flattery may suggest, he shall shock the learned ear with barbarisms, and contribute, wherever his work shall be received, to the depravation of taste and the corruption of language.

N°. 119. TUESDAY, DECEMBER 25, 1753.

Latius regnes, avidum domando
Spiritum, quam si Libyam remotis
Gadibus jungas, et uterque Pœnus
  Serviat uni.   Hor. Lib. ii. Ode ii. 9.

By virtue's precepts to controul
The thirsty cravings of the soul,
Is over wider realms to reign
Unenvied monarch, than if Spain
You could to distant Lybia join,
And both the Carthages were thine.   Francis.

WHEN Socrates was asked, "which of mortal men was to be accounted nearest to the *gods* in happiness?" he answered, "that man who is in want of the fewest things."

In this answer, Socrates left it to be guessed by his auditors, whether, by the exemption from want which was to constitute happiness, he meant amplitude of possessions or contraction of desire. And, indeed, there is so little difference between them, that Alexander the Great confessed the inhabitant of a tub the next man to the master of the world; and left a declaration to future ages, that if he was not Alexander he should wish to be Diogenes.

These two states, however, though they resemble each other in their consequence, differ widely with respect to the facility with which they may be attained. To make great acquisitions can happen to very few; and in the uncertainty of human affairs, to many it will be incident to labour without reward, and to lose what they already possess by endeavours to make it more : some will always want abilities, and others opportunities to accumulate wealth. It is therefore happy, that nature has allowed us a more certain and easy road to plenty; every man may grow rich by contracting his wishes, and by quiet acquiescence in what has been given him, supply the absence of more.

Yet so far is almost every man from emulating the happiness of the gods, by any other means than grasping at their power, that it seems to be the great business of life to create wants as fast as they are satisfied. It has been long observed by moralists, that every man squanders or loses a great part of that life, of which every man knows and deplores the shortness : and it may be remarked with equal justness, that though every man laments his own insufficiency to his happiness, and knows himself a necessitous and precarious being, incessantly soliciting the assistance of others, and feeling wants which his own art or strength cannot supply; yet there is no man, who does not, by the superaddition of unnatural cares, render himself still more dependent; who does not create an artificial poverty, and suffer himself to feel pain for the want of that, of which, when it is gained, he can have no enjoyment.

It must, indeed, be allowed, that as we lose part of our time because it steals away silent and invisible, and many an hour is passed before we recollect that it is passing; so unnatural desires insinuate themselves unobserved into the mind, and we do not perceive that they are gaining upon us, till the pain which they give us awakens us to notice. No man is sufficiently vigilant to take account of every minute of his life, or to watch every motion of his heart. Much of our time likewise is sacrificed to custom; we trifle, because we see others trifle; in the same manner we catch from example the contagion of desire; we see all about us busied in pursuit of imaginary good, and begin to bustle in the same chase, lest greater activity should triumph over us.

It is true, that to man as a member of society, many things become necessary, which, perhaps, in a state of nature are superfluous; and that many things, not absolutely necessary, are yet so useful and convenient, that they cannot easily be spared. I will make yet a more ample and liberal concession. In opulent states, and regular governments, the temptations to wealth and rank, and to the distinctions that follow them, are such as no force of understanding finds it easy to resist.

If, therefore, I saw the quiet of life disturbed only by endeavours after wealth and honour; by solicitude, which the world, whether justly or not, considered as important; I should scarcely have had courage to inculcate any precepts of moderation and forbearance. He that is engaged in a pursuit, in which all mankind profess to be his rivals, is supported by the authority of all mankind in the prosecution of his design, and will, therefore, scarcely stop to hear the lectures of a solitary philosopher. Nor am I certain, that the accumulation of honest gain ought to be hindered, or the ambition of just honours always to be repressed. Whatever can enable the possessor to confer any benefit upon others, may be desired upon virtuous principles; and we ought not too rashly to accuse any man of intending to confine the influence of his acquisitions to himself.

But if we look round upon mankind, whom shall we find among those that fortune permits to form their own manners, that is not tormenting himself with a wish for something, of which all the pleasure and all the benefit will cease at the moment of attainment? One man is beggaring his posterity to build a house, which when finished he never will inhabit; another is levelling mountains to open a prospect, which, when he has once enjoyed it, he can enjoy it no more; another is painting ceilings, carving wainscot, and filling his apartments with costly furniture, only that some neighbouring house may not be richer or finer than his own.

That splendour and elegance are not desirable, I am not

so abstracted from life to inculcate ; but if we inquire closely into the reason for which they are esteemed, we shall find them valued principally as evidences of wealth. Nothing, therefore, can show greater depravity of understanding, than to delight in the show when the reality is wanting ; or voluntarily to become poor, that strangers may for a time imagine us to be rich.

But there are yet minuter objects and more trifling anxieties. Men may be found, who are kept from sleep by the want of a shell particularly variegated ! who are wasting their lives, in stratagems to obtain a book in a language which they do not understand ; who pine with envy at the flowers of another man's parterre ; who hover like vultures round the owner of a fossil, in hopes to plunder his cabinet at his death ; and who would not much regret to see a street in flames, if a box of medals might be scattered in the tumult.

He that imagines me to speak of these sages in terms exaggerated and hyperbolical, has conversed but little with the race of virtuosos. A slight acquaintance with their studies, and a few visits to their assemblies, would inform him, that nothing is so worthless, but that prejudice and caprice can give it value ; nor any thing of so little use, but that by indulging an idle competition or unreasonable pride, a man may make it to himself one of the necessaries of life.

Desires like these, I may surely, without incurring the censure of moroseness, advise every man to repel when they invade his mind ; or if he admits them, never to allow them any greater influence than is necessary to give petty employments the power of pleasing, and diversify the day with slight amusements.

An ardent wish, whatever be its object, will always be able to interrupt tranquillity. What we believe ourselves to want, torments us not in proportion to its real value, but according to the estimation by which we have rated it in our own minds ; in some diseases, the patient has been observed to long for food, which scarce any extremity of hunger would in health have compelled him to swallow; but while his organs were thus depraved, the craving was irresistible, nor could any rest be obtained till it was appeased by compliance. Of the same nature are the irregular appetites of the mind; though they are often excited by trifles, they are equally disquieting with real wants: the Roman, who wept at the death of his lamprey, felt the same degree of sorrow that extorts tears on other occasions.

Inordinate desires, of whatever kind, ought to be repressed upon yet a higher consideration; they must be considered as enemies not only to happiness but to virtue. There are men, among those commonly reckoned the learned and the wise, who spare no stratagems to remove a competitor at an auction, who will sink the price of a rarity at the expense of truth, and whom it is not safe to trust alone in a library or cabinet. These are faults, which the fraternity seem to look upon as jocular mischiefs, or to think excused by the violence of the temptation: but I shall always fear that he, who accustoms himself to fraud in little things, wants only opportunity to practise it in greater; " he that has hardened himself by killing a sheep," says Pythagoras, " will with less reluctance shed the blood of a man."

To prize every thing according to its *real* use ought to be the aim of a rational being. There are few things which can much conduce to happiness, and, therefore, few things to be ardently desired. He that looks upon the business and bustle of the world, with the philosophy with which Socrates surveyed the fair at Athens, will turn away at last with his exclamation, " How many things are here which I do not want!"

Nº. 120. SATURDAY, DECEMBER 29, 1753.

————————*Ultima semper*
Expectanda dies homini : dicique beatus .
Ante obitum nemo supremaque funera debet.   Ovid. Met. Lib. iii. 135.

But no frail man, however great or high,
Can be concluded blest before he die.   ADDISON.

THE numerous miseries of human life have extorted in all
ages an universal complaint. The wisest of men terminated all his experiments in search of happiness, by the
mournful confession, that " all is vanity ;" and the ancient
patriarchs lamented, that " the days of their pilgrimage
were few and evil."

There is, indeed, no topick on which it is more superfluous to accumulate authorities, nor any assertion of which
our own eyes will more easily discover, or our sensations
more frequently impress the truth, than, that misery is the
lot of man, that our present state is a state of danger and
infelicity.

When we take the most distant prospect of life, what
does it present us but a chaos of unhappiness, a confused
and tumultuous scene of labour and contest, disappointment and defeat? If we view past ages in the reflection of
history, what do they offer to our meditation but crimes
and calamities? One year is distinguished by a famine,
another by an earthquake ; kingdoms are made desolate,
sometimes by wars, and sometimes by pestilence ; the peace
of the world is interrupted at one time by the caprices of
a tyrant, at another by the rage of the conqueror. The
memory is stored only with vicissitudes of evil ; and the
happiness, such as it is, of one part of mankind, is found to
arise commonly from sanguinary success, from victories
which confer upon them the power, not so much of improving life by any new enjoyment, as of inflicting misery
on others, and gratifying their own pride by comparative
greatness.

But by him that examines life with a more close attention, the happiness of the world will be found still less than it appears. In some intervals of publick prosperity, or to use terms more proper, in some intermissions of calamity, a general diffusion of happiness may seem to overspread a people; all is triumph and exultation, jollity and plenty; there are no publick fears and dangers, and "no complainings in the streets." But the condition of individuals is very little mended by this general calm : pain and malice and discontent still continue their havock; the silent depredation goes incessantly forward; and the grave continues to be filled by the victims of sorrow.

He that enters a gay assembly, beholds the cheerfulness displayed in every countenance, and finds all sitting vacant and disengaged, with no other attention than to give or to receive pleasure, would naturally imagine, that he had reached at last the metropolis of felicity, the place sacred to gladness of heart, from whence all fear and anxiety were irreversibly excluded. Such, indeed, we may often find to be the opinion of those, who from a lower station look up to the pomp and gaiety which they cannot reach : but who is there of those who frequent these luxurious assemblies, that will not confess his own uneasiness, or cannot recount the vexations and distresses that prey upon the lives of his gay companions?

The world, in its best state, is nothing more than a larger assembly of beings, combining to counterfeit happiness which they do not feel, employing every art and contrivance to embellish life, and to hide their real condition from the eyes of one another.

The species of happiness most obvious to the observation of others, is that which depends upon the goods of fortune; yet even this is often fictitious. There is in the world more poverty than is generally imagined; not only because many whose possessions are large have desires still larger, and many measure their wants by the gratifications which others enjoy; but great numbers are pressed by real necessities which it is their chief ambition to conceal, and are forced to purchase the appearance of competence and cheerfulness at the expense of many comforts and conveniencies of life.

Many, however, are confessedly rich, and many more are sufficiently removed from all danger of real poverty: but it has been long ago remarked, that money cannot purchase quiet; the highest of mankind can promise themselves no exemption from that discord or suspicion, by which the sweetness of domestick retirement is destroyed; and must always be even more exposed, in the same degree as they are elevated above others, to the treachery of dependants, the calumny of defamers and the violence of opponents.

Affliction is inseparable from our present state: it adheres to all the inhabitants of this world, in different proportions indeed, but with an allotment which seems very little regulated by our own conduct. It has been the boast of some swelling moralists, that every man's fortune was in his own power, that prudence supplied the place of all other divinities, and that happiness is the unfailing consequence of virtue. But, surely, the quiver of Omnipotence is stored with arrows, against which the shield of human virtue, however adamantine it has been boasted, is held up in vain: we do not always suffer by our crimes; we are not always protected by our innocence.

A good man is by no means exempt from the danger of suffering by the crimes of others; even his goodness may raise him enemies of implacable malice and restless perseverance: the good man has never been warranted by Heaven from the treachery of friends, the disobedience of children or the dishonesty of a wife; he may see his cares made useless by profusion, his instructions defeated by perverseness, and his kindness rejected by ingratitude; he may languish under the infamy of false accusations, or perish reproachfully by an unjust sentence.

A good man is subject, like other mortals, to all the influences of natural evil; his harvest is not spared by the tempest, nor his cattle by the murrain; his house flames like others in a conflagration; nor have his ships any peculiar power of resisting hurricanes: his mind, however elevated, inhabits a body subject to innumerable casualties, of which he must always share the dangers and the pains; he bears about him the seeds of disease, and may linger away a great part of his life under the tortures of the gout or stone; at one time groaning with insufferable anguish, at another dissolved in listlessness and languor.

From this general and indiscriminate distribution of misery, the moralists have always derived one of their strongest moral arguments for a future state; for since the common events of the present life happen alike to the good and bad, it follows from the justice of the Supreme Being, that there must be another state of existence, in which a just retribution shall be made, and every man shall be happy and miserable according to his works.

The miseries of life may, perhaps, afford some proof of a future state, compared as well with the mercy as the justice of God. It is scarcely to be imagined that Infinite Benevolence would create a being capable of enjoying so much more than is here to be enjoyed, and qualified by nature to prolong pain by remembrance, and anticipate it by terrour, if he was not designed for something nobler and better than a state, in which many of his faculties can serve only for his torment; in which he is to be importuned by desires that never can be satisfied, to feel many evils which he had no power to avoid, and to fear many which he shall never feel: there will surely come a time, when every capacity of happiness shall be filled, and none shall be wretched but by his own fault.

In the mean time, it is by affliction chiefly that the heart of man is purified, and that the thoughts are fixed upon a better state. Prosperity, allayed and imperfect as it is, has power to intoxicate the imagination, to fix the mind upon the present scene, to produce confidence and elation, and to make him who enjoys affluence and honours forget the hand by which they were bestowed. It is seldom that we are otherwise, than by affliction, awakened to a sense of our own imbecility, or taught to know how little all our acquisitions can conduce to safety or to quiet; and how justly we may ascribe to the superintendence of a higher Power, those blessings which in the wantonness of success we considered as the attainments of our policy or courage.

Nothing confers so much ability to resist the temptations that perpetually surround us, as an habitual consideration of the shortness of life, and the uncertainty of those pleasures that solicit our pursuit; and this consideration can be inculcated only by affliction. " O Death! how bitter · is the remembrance of thee, to a man that lives at ease in his possessions!" If our present state were one continued succession of delights, or one uniform flow of calmness and tranquillity, we should never willingly think upon its end ; death would then surely surprise us as " a thief in the night;" and our task of duty would remain unfinished, till " the night came when no man can work."

While affliction thus prepares us for felicity, we may console ourselves under its pressures, by remembering, that they are no particular marks of divine displeasure ; since all the distresses of persecution have been suffered by those, " of whom the world was not worthy ;" and the Redeemer of mankind himself was " a man of sorrows and acquainted with grief!"

Nº. 126. SATURDAY, JANUARY 19, 1754.

———*Steriles nec legit arenas*
Ut caneret paucis, mersitque hoc pulvere verum.   LUCAN.

Canst thou believe the vast eternal Mind
Was e'er to Syrts and Lybian sands confin'd?
That he would choose this waste, this barren ground,
To teach the thin inhabitants around,
And leave his truth in wilds and deserts drown'd?

THERE has always prevailed among that part of mankind that addict their minds to speculation, a propensity to talk much of the delights of retirement: and some of the most pleasing compositions produced in every age contain descriptions of the peace and happiness of a country life.

I know not whether those who thus ambitiously repeat the praises of solitude, have always considered, how much they depreciate mankind by declaring, that whatever is excellent or desirable is to be obtained by departing from them; that the assistance which we may derive from one another, is not equivalent to the evils which we have to fear; that the kindness of a few is overbalanced by the malice of many; and that the protection of society is too dearly purchased by encountering its dangers and enduring its oppressions.

These specious representations of solitary happiness, however opprobrious to human nature, have so far spread their influence over the world, that almost every man delights his imagination with the hopes of obtaining some time an opportunity of retreat. Many, indeed, who enjoy retreat only in imagination, content themselves with believing, that another year will transport them to rural tranquillity, and die while they talk of doing what, if they had lived longer, they would never have done. But many likewise there are, either of greater resolution or more credulity, who in earnest try the state which they have been taught to think thus secure from cares and dangers; and retire to privacy, either that they may improve their happiness, increase their knowledge, or exalt their virtue.

The greater part of the admirers of solitude, as of all other classes of mankind, have no higher or remoter view, than the present gratification of their passions. Of these, some, haughty and impetuous, fly from society only because they cannot bear to repay to others the regard which themselves exact; and think no state of life eligible, but that which places them out of the reach of censure or control, and affords them opportunities of living in a perpetual compliance with their own inclinations, without the necessity of regulating their actions by any other man's convenience or opinion.

There are others, of minds more delicate and tender,

easily offended by every deviation from rectitude, soon disgusted by ignorance or impertinence, and always expecting from the conversation of mankind more elegance, purity and truth, than the mingled mass of life will easily afford. Such men are in haste to retire from grossness, falsehood and brutality; and hope to find in private habitations at least a negative felicity, an exemption from the shocks and perturbations with which publick scenes are continually distressing them.

To neither of these votaries will solitude afford that content, which she has been taught so lavishly to promise. The man of arrogance will quickly discover, that by escaping from his opponents he has lost his flatterers, that greatness is nothing where it is not seen, and power nothing where it cannot be felt: and he, whose faculties are employed in too close an observation of failings and defects, will find his condition very little mended by transferring his attention from others to himself: he will probably soon come back in quest of new objects, and be glad to keep his captiousness employed on any character rather than his own.

Others are seduced into solitude merely by the authority of great names, and expect to find those charms in tranquillity which have allured statesmen and conquerors to the shades: these likewise are apt to wonder at their disappointment, for want of considering, that those whom they aspire to imitate carried with them to their country-seats minds full fraught with subjects of reflection, the consciousness of great merit, the memory of illustrious actions, the knowledge of important events, and the seeds of mighty designs to be ripened by future meditation. Solitude was to such men a release from fatigue, and an opportunity of usefulness. But what can retirement confer upon him, who having done nothing can receive no support from his own importance, who having known nothing can find no entertainment in reviewing the past, and who intending nothing can form no hopes from prospects of the future? He can, surely, take no wiser course than that of losing himself again in the crowd, and filling the vacuities of his mind with the news of the day.

Others consider solitude as the parent of philosophy, and retire in expectation of greater intimacies with science, as Numa repaired to the groves when he conferred with Egeria. These men have not always reason to repent. Some studies require a continued prosecution of the same train of thought, such as is too often interrupted by the petty avocations of common life : sometimes, likewise, it is necessary, that a multiplicity of objects be at once present to the mind ; and every thing, therefore, must be kept at a distance, which may perplex the memory or dissipate the attention.

But though learning may be conferred by solitude, its application must be attained by general converse. He has learned to no purpose, that is not able to teach ; and he will always teach unsuccessfully, who cannot recommend his sentiments by his diction or address.

Even the acquisition of knowledge is often much facilitated by the advantages of society : he that never compares his notions with those of others, readily acquiesces in his first thoughts, and very seldom discovers the objections which may be raised against his opinions ; he, therefore, often thinks himself in possession of truth, when he is only fondling an errour long since exploded. He that has neither companions nor rivals in his studies, will always applaud his own progress, and think highly of his performances, because he knows not that others have equalled or excelled him. And I am afraid it may be added, that the student who withdraws himself from the world, will soon feel that ardour extinguished which praise or emulation had enkindled, and take the advantage of secrecy to sleep, rather than to labour.

There remains yet another set of recluses, whose intention entitles them to higher respect, and whose motives deserve a more serious consideration. These retire from the world, not merely to bask in ease or gratify curiosity, but that, being disengaged from common cares, they may employ more time in the duties of religion; that they may regulate their actions with stricter vigilance, and purify their thoughts by more frequent meditation.

To men thus elevated above the mists of mortality, I am far from presuming myself qualified to give directions. On him that appears to " pass through things temporal," with no other care than not to " finally lose the things eternal," I look with such veneration as inclines me to approve his conduct in the whole, without a minute examination of its parts; yet I could never forbear to wish, that while vice is every day multiplying seducements, and stalking forth with more hardened effrontery, virtue would not withdraw the influence of her presence, or forbear to assert her natural dignity by open and undaunted perseverance in the right. Piety practised in solitude, like the flower that blooms in the desert, may give its fragrance to the winds of Heaven, and delight those unbodied spirits that survey the works of God and the actions of men; but it bestows no assistance upon earthly beings, and however free from taints of impurity, yet wants the sacred splendour of beneficence.

Our Maker, who, though he gave us such varieties of temper and such difference of powers, yet designed us all for happiness, undoubtedly intended that we should obtain that happiness by different means. Some are unable to resist the temptations of importunity, or the impetuosity of their own passions incited by the force of present temptations: of these it is undoubtedly the duty to fly from enemies which they cannot conquer, and cultivate, in the calm of solitude, that virtue which is too tender to endure the tempests of publick life. But there are others, whose passions grow more strong and irregular in privacy; and who cannot maintain an uniform tenour of virtue, but by exposing their manners to the publick eye, and assisting the admonitions of conscience with the fear of infamy: for such it is dangerous to exclude all witnesses of their conduct, till they have formed strong habits of virtue, and weakened their passions by frequent victories. But there is a higher order of men so inspired with ardour, and so fortified with resolution, that the world passes before them without influence or regard: these ought to consider themselves as appointed the guardians of mankind: they are placed in an evil world, to exhibit publick examples of good life; and may be said, when they withdraw to solitude, to desert the station which Providence assigned them.

Nᵒ. 128. SATURDAY, JANUARY 26, 1754.

Ille sinistrorsum, hic dextrorsum abit ; unus utrique
Error, sed variis illudit partibus.———— Hor. Lib. ii. Sat. iii. 50.
When in a wood we leave the certain way,
One error fools us, though we various stray,
Some to the left, and some to t'other side. Francis.

It is common among all the classes of mankind, to charge each other with trifling away life: every man looks on the occupation or amusement of his neighbour, as something below the dignity of our nature, and unworthy of the attention of a rational being.

A man who considers the paucity of the wants of nature, and who, being acquainted with the various means by which all manual occupations are now facilitated, observes what numbers are supported by the labour of a few, would, indeed, be inclined to wonder, how the multitudes who are exempted from the necessity of working, either for themselves or others, find business to fill up the vacuities of life. The greater part of mankind neither card the fleece, dig the mine, fell the wood, nor gather in the harvest; they neither tend herds nor build houses; in what then are they employed?

This is certainly a question, which a distant prospect of the world will not enable us to answer. We find all ranks and ages mingled together in a tumultuous confusion, with haste in their motions, and eagerness in their looks ; but what they have to pursue or avoid, a more minute observation must inform them.

When we analyze the crowd into individuals, it soon appears that the passions and imaginations of men will not easily suffer them to be idle : we see things coveted merely because they are rare, and pursued because they are fugitive; we see men conspire to fix an arbitrary value on that which is worthless in itself, and then contend for the possession.   One is a collector of fossils, of which he knows no other use than to show them ; and when he has stocked his own repository, grieves that the stones which he has left behind him should be picked up by another.   The florist nurses a tulip, and repines that his rival's beds enjoy the same showers and sunshine with his own.   This man is hurrying to a concert, only lest others should have heard the new musician before him ; another bursts from his company to the play, because he fancies himself the patron of an actress ; some spend the morning in consultations with their tailor, and some in directions to their cook ; some are forming parties for cards, and some laying wagers at a horse-race.

It cannot, I think, be denied, that some of these lives are passed in trifles, in occupations by which the busy neither benefit themselves nor others, and by which no man could be long engaged, who seriously considered what he was doing, or had knowledge enough to compare what he is, with what he might be made.   However, as people who have the same inclination generally flock together, every trifler is kept in countenance by the sight of others as unprofitably active as himself; by kindling the heat of competition, he in time thinks himself important, and by having his mind intensely engaged, he is secured from weariness of himself.

Some degree of self-approbation is always the reward of diligence ; and I cannot, therefore, but consider the laborious cultivation of petty pleasures, as a more happy and more virtuous disposition, than that universal con-

tempt and haughty negligence, which is sometimes associated with powerful faculties, but is often assumed by
indolence when it disowns its name, and aspires to the
appellation of greatness of mind.

It has been long observed, that drollery and ridicule
is the most easy kind of wit: let it be added that contempt and arrogance is the easiest philosophy. To find
some objection to every thing, and to dissolve in perpetual laziness under pretence that occasions are wanting to
call forth activity, to laugh at those who are ridiculously
busy without setting an example of more rational industry,
is no less in the power of the meanest than of the highest
intellects.

Our present state has placed us at once in such different relations, that every human employment, which is not
a visible and immediate act of goodness, will be in some
respect or other subject to contempt ; but it is true, likewise, that almost every act, which is not directly vicious,
is in some respect beneficial and laudable. "I often,"
says Bruyere, "observe from my window, two beings of
erect form and amiable countenance, endowed with the
powers of reason, able to clothe their thoughts in language, and convey their notions to each other. They
rise early in the morning, and are every day employed
till sunset in rubbing two smooth stones together, or, in
other terms, in polishing marble."

"If lions could paint," says the fable, "in the room of
those pictures which exhibit men vanquishing lions, we
should see lions feeding upon men." If the stone-cutter
could have written like Bruyere, what would he have
replied?

"I look up," says he, "every day from my shop, upon
a man whom the idlers, who stand still to gaze upon my
work, often celebrate as a wit and a philosopher. I often
perceive his face clouded with care, and am told that his
taper is sometimes burning at midnight. The sight of a
man who works so much harder than myself, excited my
curiosity. I heard no sound of tools in his apartment,

and, therefore, could not imagine what he was doing; but was told at last, that he was writing descriptions of mankind, who when he had described them would live just as they had lived before; that he sat up whole nights to change a sentence, because the sound of a letter was too often repeated: that he was often disquieted with doubts, about the propriety of a word which every body understood; that he would hesitate between two expressions equally proper, 'till he could not fix his choice but by consulting his friends; that he will run from one end of Paris to the other, for an opportunity of reading a period to a nice ear; that if a single line is heard with coldness and inattention, he returns home dejected and disconsolate; and that by all this care and labour, he hopes only to make a little book, which at last will teach no useful art, and which none who has it not will perceive himself to want. I have often wondered for what end such a being as this was sent into the world; and should be glad to see those who live thus foolishly, seized by an order of the government, and obliged to labour at some useful occupation."

Thus, by a partial and imperfect representation, may every thing be made equally ridiculous. He that gazed with contempt on human beings rubbing stones together, might have prolonged the same amusement by walking through the city, and seeing others with looks of importance heaping one brick upon another; or by rambling into the country, where he might observe other creatures of the same kind driving a piece of sharp iron into the clay, or, in the language of men less enlightened, ploughing the field.

As it is thus easy by a detail of minute circumstances to make every thing little, so it is not difficult by an aggregation of effects to make every thing great. The polisher of marble may be forming ornaments for the palaces of virtue, and the schools of science; or providing tables on which the actions of heroes and the discoveries of sages shall be recorded, for the incitement and instruction of future generations. The mason is exercising one of the principal arts by which reasoning beings are distinguished from the brute, the art to which life owes much of its safety and all its convenience, by which we are secured from the inclemency of the seasons, and fortified against the ravages of hostility; and the ploughman is changing the face of nature, diffusing plenty and happiness over kingdoms, and compelling the earth to give food to her inhabitants.

Greatness and littleness are terms merely comparative; and we err in our estimation of things, because we measure them by some wrong standard. The trifler proposes to himself only to equal or excel some other trifler, and is happy or miserable as he succeeds or miscarries: the man of sedentary desire and unactive ambition sits comparing his power with his wishes; and makes his inability to perform things impossible, an excuse to himself for performing nothing. Man can only form a just estimate of his own actions, by making his power the test of his performance, by comparing what he does with what he can do. Whoever steadily perseveres in the exertion of all his faculties, does what is great with respect to himself; and what will not be despised by Him, who has given to all created beings their different abilities: he faithfully performs the task of life, within whatever limits his labours may be confined, or how soon soever they may be forgotten.

We can conceive so much more than we can accomplish, that whoever tries his own actions by his imagination, may appear despicable in his own eyes. He that despises for its littleness any thing really useful, has no pretensions to applaud the grandeur of his conceptions; since nothing but narrowness of mind hinders him from seeing, that by pursuing the same principles every thing limited will appear contemptible.

He that neglects the care of his family, while his benevolence expands itself in scheming the happiness of imaginary kingdoms, might with equal reason sit on a throne dreaming of universal empire, and of the diffusion of blessings over all the globe : yet even this globe is little, compared with the system of matter within our view! and that system barely something more than nonentity, compared with the boundless regions of space, to which neither eye nor imagination can extend.

From conceptions, therefore, of what we might have been, and from wishes to be what we are not, conceptions that we know to be foolish, and wishes which we feel to be vain, we must necessarily descend to the consideration of what we are. We have powers very scanty in their utmost extent, but which in different men are differently proportioned. Suitably to these powers we have duties prescribed, which we must neither decline for the sake of delighting ourselves with easier amusements, nor overlook in idle contemplation of greater excellence or more extensive comprehension.

In order to the right conduct of our lives, we must remember, that we are not born to please ourselves. He that studies simply his own satisfaction, will always find the proper business of his station too hard or too easy for him. But if we bear continually in mind our relation to the Father of Being, by whom we are placed in the world, and who has allotted us the part which we are to bear in the general system of life, we shall be easily persuaded to resign our own inclinations to Unerring Wisdom, and do the work decreed for us with cheerfulness and diligence.

N°. 131. TUESDAY, FEBRUARY 5, 1754.

———————— *Misce*
Ergo aliquid nostris de moribus.   Juv. Sat. iv. 322.

·And mingle something of our times to please.   Dryden, Jun.

FONTENELLE, in his panegyrick on Sir Isaac Newton, closes a long enumeration of that great philosopher's virtues and attainments, with an observation, that "he was not distinguished from other men, by any singularity either natural or affected."

It is an eminent instance of Newton's superiority to the rest of mankind, that he was able to separate knowledge from those weaknesses by which knowledge is generally disgraced; that he was able to excel in science and wisdom without purchasing them by the neglect of little things; and that he stood alone, merely because he had left the rest of mankind behind him, not because he deviated from the beaten track.

Whoever, after the example of Plutarch, should compare the lives of illustrious men, might set this part of Newton's character to view with great advantage, by opposing it to that of Bacon, perhaps the only man, of later ages, who has any pretensions to dispute with him the palm of genius or science.

Bacon, after he had added to a long and careful contemplation of almost every other object of knowledge a curious inspection into common life, and after having surveyed nature as a philosopher, had examined " men's business and bosoms" as a statesman; yet failed so much in the conduct of domestick affairs, that, in the most lucrative post to which a great and wealthy kingdom could advance him, he felt all the miseries of distressful poverty, and committed all the crimes to which poverty incites. Such were at once his negligence and rapacity, that, as it is said, he would gain by unworthy practices that money, which, when so acquired, his servants might steal from one end of the table, while he sat studious and abstracted at the other.

As scarcely any man has reached the excellence, very few have sunk to the weakness of Bacon: but almost all the studious tribe, as they obtain any participation of his knowledge, feel likewise some contagion of his defects; and obstruct the veneration which learning would procure, by follies greater or less, to which only learning could betray them.

It has been formerly remarked by *The Guardian*, that

the world punishes with too great severity the errours of those, who imagine that the ignorance of little things may be compensated by the knowledge of great; for so it is, that as more can detect petty failings than can distinguish or esteem great qualifications, and as mankind is in general more easily disposed to censure than to admiration, contempt is often incurred by slight mistakes, which real virtue or usefulness cannot counterbalance.

Yet such mistakes and inadvertencies it is not easy for a man deeply immersed in study to avoid; no man can become qualified for the common intercourses of life, by private meditation: the manners of the world are not a regular system, planned by philosophers upon settled principles, in which every cause has a congruous effect, and one part has a just reference to another. Of the fashions prevalent in every country, a few have arisen, perhaps, from particular temperatures of the climate; a few more from the constitution of the government; but the greater part have grown up by chance; been started by caprice, been contrived by affectation, or borrowed without any just motives of choice from other countries.

Of all these, the savage that hunts his prey upon the mountains, and the sage that speculates in his closet, must necessarily live in equal ignorance: yet by the observation of those trifles it is, that the ranks of mankind are kept in order, that the address of one to another is regulated, and the general business of the world carried on with facility and method.

These things, therefore, though small in themselves, become great by their frequency: and he very much mistakes his own interest, who to the unavoidable unskilfulness of abstraction and retirement, adds a voluntary neglect of common forms, and increases the disadvantages of a studious course of life by an arrogant contempt of those practices, by which others endeavour to gain favour and multiply friendships.

A real and interior disdain of fashion and ceremony, is indeed, not very often to be found: much the greater part of those who pretend to laugh at foppery and formality, secretly wish to have possessed those qualifications which they pretend to despise; and because they find it difficult to wash away the tincture which they have so deeply imbibed, endeavour to harden themselves in a sullen approbation of their own colour. Neutrality is a state, into which the busy passions of man cannot easily subside; and he who is in danger of the pangs of envy, is generally forced to recreate his imagination with an effort of comfort.

Some, however, may be found, who, supported by the consciousness of great abilities, and elevated by a long course of reputation and applause, voluntarily consign themselves to singularity, affect to cross the roads of life because they know that they shall not be jostled, and indulge a boundless gratification of will because they perceive that they shall be quietly obeyed. Men of this kind are generally known by the name of Humourists, an appellation by which he that has obtained it, and can be contented to keep it, is set free at once from the shackles of fashion: and can go in or out, sit or stand, be talkative or silent, gloomy or merry, advance absurdities or oppose demonstration, without any other reprehension from mankind, than that it is his way, that he is an odd fellow, and must be let alone.

This seems to many an easy passport through the various factions of mankind; and those on whom it is bestowed, appear too frequently to consider the patience with which their caprices are suffered as an undoubted evidence of their own importance, of a genius to which submission is universally paid, and whose irregularities are only considered as consequences of its vigour. These peculiarities, however, are always found to spot a character, though they may not totally obscure it; and he who expects from mankind, that they should give up established customs in compliance with his single will, and exacts that deference which he does not pay, may be endured, but can never be approved.

Singularity is, I think, in its own nature universally and invariably displeasing. In whatever respect a man differs from others, he must be considered by them as either worse or better: by being better, it is well known that a man gains admiration oftener than love, since all approbation of his practice must necessarily condemn him that gives it; and though a man often pleases by inferiority, there are few who desire to give such pleasure. Yet the truth is, that singularity is almost always regarded as a brand of slight reproach; and where it is associated with acknowledged merit, serves as an abatement or an allay of excellence, by which weak eyes are reconciled to its lustre, and by which, though kindness is not gained, at least envy is averted.

But let no man be in haste to conclude his own merit so great or conspicuous, as to require or justify singularity: it is as hazardous for a moderate understanding to usurp the prerogatives of genius, as for a common form to play over the airs of uncontested beauty. The pride of men will not patiently endure to see one, whose understanding or attainments are but level with their own, break the rules by which they have consented to be bound, or forsake the direction which they submissively follow. All-violation of established practice implies in its own nature a rejection of the common opinion, a defiance of common censure, and an appeal from general laws to private judgment: he, therefore, who differs from others without apparent advantage, ought not to be angry if his arrogance is punished with ridicule; if those whose example he superciliously overlooks, point him out to derision, and hoot him back again into the common road.

The pride of singularity is often exerted in little things, where right and wrong are indeterminable, and where, therefore, vanity is without excuse. But there are occasions on which it is noble to dare to stand alone. To be pious among infidels, to be disinterested in a time of general venality, to lead a life of virtue and reason in the midst of sensualists, is a proof of a mind intent on nobler things than the praise or blame of men, of a soul fixed in the contemplation of the highest good, and superior to the tyranny of custom and example.

In moral and religious questions only, a wise man will hold no consultations with fashion, because these duties are constant and immutable, and depend not on the notions of men, but the commands of Heaven: yet even of these, the external mode is to be in some measure regulated by the prevailing taste of the age in which we live; for he is certainly no friend to virtue, who neglects to give it any lawful attraction, or suffers it to deceive the eye or alienate the affections for want of innocent compliance with fashionable decorations.

It is yet remembered of the learned and pious Nelson[n], that he was remarkably elegant in his manners, and splendid in his dress. He knew, that the eminence of his character drew many eyes upon him; and he was careful not to drive the young or the gay away from religion, by representing it as an enemy to any distinction or enjoyment in which human nature may innocently delight.

In this censure of singularity, I have, therefore, no intention to subject reason or conscience to custom or example. To comply with the notions and practices of mankind, is in some degree the duty of a social being; because by compliance only he can please, and by pleasing only he can become useful: but as the end is not to be lost for the sake of the means, we are not to give up virtue to complaisance; for the end of complaisance is only to gain the kindness of our fellow-beings, whose kindness is desirable only as instrumental to happiness, and happiness must be always lost by departure from virtue.

[n] The neglect of his writings must be considered as indicative of an increasing neglect of that apostolical establishment, whose Fasts and Festivals this author has illustrated with a raciness of style and sentiment worthy of a primitive father of the Church.

Nº. 137.   TUESDAY, FEBRUARY 26, 1754.

Τί δ' ἔρεξα;   PYTHAG.
What have I been doing?

As man is a being very sparingly furnished with the power of prescience, he can provide for the future only by considering the past; and as futurity is all in which he has any real interest, he ought very diligently to use the only means by which he can be enabled to enjoy it, and frequently to revolve the experiments which he has hitherto made upon life, that he may gain wisdom from his mistakes, and caution from his miscarriages.

Though I do not so exactly conform to the precepts of Pythagoras, as to practise every night this solemn recollection, yet I am not so lost in dissipation as wholly to omit it; nor can I forbear sometimes to inquire of myself, in what employment my life has passed away. Much of my time has sunk into nothing, and left no trace by which it can be distinguished; and of this I now only know, that it was once in my power, and might once have been improved.

Of other parts of life, memory can give some account; at some hours I have been gay, and at others serious; I have sometimes mingled in conversation, and sometimes meditated in solitude; one day has been spent in consulting the ancient sages, and another in writing *Adventurers*.

At the conclusion of any undertaking, it is usual to compute the loss and profit. As I shall soon cease to write *Adventurers*, I could not forbear lately to consider what has been the consequence of my labours; and whether I am to reckon the hours laid out in these compositions, as applied to a good and laudable purpose, or suffered to fume away in useless evaporations.

That I have intended well, I have the attestation of my own heart: but good intentions may be frustrated when they are executed without suitable skill, or directed to an end unattainable in itself.

Some there are, who leave writers very little room for self-congratulation; some who affirm, that books have no influence upon the publick, that no age was ever made better by its authors, and that to call upon mankind to correct their manners, is, like Xerxes, to scourge the wind, or shackle the torrent.

This opinion they pretend to support by unfailing experience. The world is full of fraud and corruption, rapine or malignity; interest is the ruling motive of mankind, and every one is endeavouring to increase his own stores of happiness by perpetual accumulation, without reflecting upon the numbers whom his superfluity condemns to want: in this state of things a book of morality is published, in which charity and benevolence are strongly enforced; and it is proved beyond opposition, that men are happy in proportion as they are virtuous, and rich as they are liberal. The book is applauded, and the author is preferred; he imagines his applause deserved, and receives less pleasure from the acquisition of reward than the consciousness of merit. Let us look again upon mankind: interest is still the ruling motive, and the world is yet full of fraud and corruption, malevolence and rapine.

The difficulty of confuting this assertion, arises merely from its generality and comprehension; to overthrow it by a detail of distinct facts, requires a wider survey of the world than human eyes can take; the progress of reformation is gradual and silent, as the extension of evening shadows; we know that they were short at noon, and are long at sunset, but our senses were not able to discern their increase: we know of every civil nation, that it was once savage, and how was it reclaimed but by precept and admonition?

Mankind are universally corrupt, but corrupt in different degrees; as they are universally ignorant, yet with greater or less irradiations of knowledge. How has knowledge or virtue been increased and preserved in one place beyond another, but by diligent inculcation and rational enforcement?

Books of morality are daily written, yet its influence is still little in the world; so the ground is annually ploughed, and yet multitudes are in want of bread. But, surely, neither the labours of the moralist nor of the husbandman are vain: let them for a while neglect their tasks, and their usefulness will be known; the wickedness that is now frequent will become universal, the bread that is now scarce would wholly fail.

The power, indeed, of every individual is small, and the consequence of his endeavours imperceptible, in a general prospect of the world. Providence has given no man ability to do much, that something might be left for every man to do. The business of life is carried on by a general co-operation; in which the part of any single man can be no more distinguished, than the effect of a particular drop when the meadows are floated by a summer shower: yet every drop increases the inundation, and every hand adds to the happiness or misery of mankind.

That a writer, however zealous or eloquent, seldom works a visible effect upon cities or nations, will readily be granted. The book which is read most, is read by few, compared with those that read it not; and of those few, the greater part peruse it with dispositions that very little favour their own improvement.

It is difficult to enumerate the several motives which procure to books the honour of perusal: spite, vanity, and curiosity, hope and fear, love and hatred, every passion which incites to any other action, serves at one time or other to stimulate a reader.

Some are fond to take a celebrated volume into their hands, because they hope to distinguish their penetration, by finding faults which have escaped the publick; others eagerly buy it in the first bloom of reputation, that they may join the chorus of praise, and not lag, as Falstaff terms it, in "the rearward of the fashion."

Some read for style, and some for argument: one has

little care about the sentiment, he observes only how it is expressed; another regards not the conclusion, but is diligent to mark how it is inferred: they read for other purposes than the attainment of practical knowledge; and are no more likely to grow wise by an examination of a treatise of moral prudence, than an architect to inflame his devotion by considering attentively the proportions of a temple.

Some read that they may embellish their conversation, or shine in dispute; some that they may not be detected in ignorance, or want the reputation of literary accomplishments: but the most general and prevalent reason of study is the impossibility of finding another amusement equally cheap or constant, equally independent on the hour or the weather. He that wants money to follow the chase of pleasure through her yearly circuit, and is left at home when the gay world rolls to Bath or Tunbridge; he whose gout compels him to hear from his chamber the rattle of chariots transporting happier beings to plays and assemblies, will be forced to seek in books a refuge from himself.

The author is not wholly useless, who provides innocent amusements for minds like these. There are, in the present state of things, so many more instigations to evil, than incitements to good, that he who keeps men in a neutral state, may be justly considered as a benefactor to life.

But, perhaps, it seldom happens, that study terminates in mere pastime. Books have always a secret influence on the understanding; we cannot, at pleasure, obliterate ideas: he that reads books of science, though without any fixed desire of improvement, will grow more knowing; he that entertains himself with moral or religious treatises, will imperceptibly advance in goodness; the ideas which are often offered to the mind, will at last find a lucky moment when it is disposed to receive them.

It is, therefore, urged without reason, as a discouragement to writers, that there are already books sufficient in the world; that all the topicks of persuasion have been discussed, and every important question clearly stated and justly decided; and that, therefore, there is no room to hope, that pigmies should conquer where heroes have been defeated, or that the petty copiers of the present time should advance the great work of reformation, which their predecessors were forced to leave unfinished.

Whatever be the present extent of human knowledge, it is not only finite, and therefore in its own nature capable of increase, but so narrow, that almost every understanding may, by a diligent application of its powers, hope to enlarge it. It is, however, not necessary that a man should forbear to write, till he has discovered some truth unknown before; he may be sufficiently useful, by only diversifying the surface of knowledge, and luring the mind by a new appearance to a second view of those beauties which it had passed over inattentively before. Every writer may find intellects correspondent to his own, to whom his expressions are familiar, and his thoughts congenial; and, perhaps, truth is often more successfully propagated by men of moderate abilities, who, adopting the opinions of others, have no care but to explain them clearly, than by subtle speculatists and curious searchers, who exact from their readers powers equal to their own, and if their fabricks of science be strong, take no care to render them accessible.

For my part, I do not regret the hours which I have laid out in these little compositions. That the world has grown apparently better, since the publication of the *Adventurer*, I have not observed; but am willing to think, that many have been affected by single sentiments, of which it is their business to renew the impression ; that many have caught hints of truth, which it is now their duty to pursue; and that those who have received no improvement, have wanted not opportunity but intention to improve.

No. 138. SATURDAY, MARCH 2, 1754.

Quid pure tranquillet ; honos, an dulce lucellum,
An secretum iter, et fallentis semita vitæ.   HOR. Lib. i. Ep. xviii. 102.

Whether the tranquil mind and pure,
Honours or wealth our bliss ensure :
Or down through life unknown to stray,
Where lonely leads the silent way.   FRANCIS.

HAVING considered the importance of authors to the wel-fare of the publick, I am led by a natural train of thought, to reflect on their condition with regard to themselves ; and to inquire what degree of happiness or vexation is annexed to the difficult and laborious employment of providing instruction or entertainment for mankind.

In estimating the pain or pleasure of any particular state, every man, indeed, draws his decisions from his own breast, and cannot with certainty determine whether other minds are affected by the same causes in the same manner. Yet by this criterion we must be content to judge, because no other can be obtained ; and, indeed, we have no reason to think it very fallacious, for excepting here and there an anomalous mind, which either does not feel like others, or dissembles its sensibility, we find men unanimously concur in attributing happiness or misery to particular conditions, as they agree in acknowledging the cold of winter and the heat of autumn.

If we apply to authors themselves for an account of their state, it will appear very little to deserve envy ; for they have in all ages been addicted to complaint. The neglect of learning, the ingratitude of the present age, and the absurd preference by which ignorance and dulness often obtain favour and rewards, have been from age to age topicks of invective ; and few have left their names to posterity, without some appeal to future candour from the perverseness and malice of their own times.

I have, nevertheless, been often inclined to doubt, whether authors, however querulous, are in reality more miserable than their fellow mortals.   The present life is to all a state of infelicity; every man, like an author, believes himself to merit more than he obtains, and solaces the present with the prospect of the future; others, indeed, suffer those disappointments in silence, of which the writer complains, to show how well he has learnt the art of lamentation.

There is at least one gleam of felicity, of which few writers have missed the enjoyment: he whose hopes have so far overpowered his fears, as that he has resolved to stand forth a candidate for fame, seldom fails to amuse himself, before his appearance, with pleasing scenes of affluence or honour: while his fortune is yet under the regulation of fancy, he easily models it to his wish, suffers no thoughts of criticks or rivals to intrude upon his mind, but counts over the bounties of patronage, or listens to the voice of praise.

Some there are, that talk very luxuriously of the second period of an author's happiness, and tell of the tumultuous raptures of invention, when the mind riots in imagery, and the choice stands suspended between different sentiments.

These pleasures, I believe, may sometimes be indulged to those, who come to a subject of disquisition with minds full of ideas, and with fancies so vigorous, as easily to excite, select, and arrange them.   To write is, indeed, no unpleasing employment, when one sentiment readily produces another, and both ideas and expressions present themselves at the first summons; but such happiness, the greatest genius does not always obtain; and common writers know it only to such a degree, as to credit its possibility.   Composition is, for the most part, an effort of slow diligence and steady perseverance, to which the mind is dragged by necessity or resolution, and from which the attention is every moment starting to more delightful amusements.

It frequently happens, that a design which, when considered at a distance, gave flattering hopes of facility, mocks us in the execution with unexpected difficulties;

the mind which, while it considered it in the gross, imagined itself amply furnished with materials, finds sometimes an unexpected barrenness and vacuity, and wonders whither all those ideas are vanished, which a little before seemed struggling for emission.

Sometimes many thoughts present themselves ; but so confused and unconnected, that they are not without difficulty reduced to method, or concatenated in a regular and dependent series ; the mind falls at once into a labyrinth, of which neither the beginning nor end can be discovered, and toils and struggles without progress or extrication.

It is asserted by Horace, that, " if matter be once got together, words will be found with very little difficulty ;" a position which, though sufficiently plausible to be inserted in poetical precepts, is by no means strictly and philosophically true. If words were naturally and necessarily consequential to sentiments, it would always follow, that he who has most knowledge must have most eloquence, and that every man would clearly express what he fully understood : yet we find, that to think, and discourse, are often the qualities of different persons : and many books might surely be produced, where just and noble sentiments are degraded and obscured by unsuitable diction.

Words, therefore, as well as things, claim the care of an author. Indeed of many authors, and those not useless or contemptible, words are almost the only care : many make it their study, not so much to strike out new sentiments, as to recommend those which are already known to more favourable notice by fairer decorations ; but every man, whether he copies or invents, whether he delivers his own thoughts or those of another, has often found himself deficient in the power of expression, big with ideas which he could not utter, obliged to ransack his memory for terms adequate to his conceptions, and at last unable to impress upon his reader the image existing in his own mind.

It is one of the common distresses of a writer, to be

within a word of a happy period, to want only a single epithet to give amplification its full force, to require only a correspondent term in order to finish a paragraph with elegance, and make one of its members answer to the other; but these deficiencies cannot always be supplied: and after a long study and vexation, the passage is turned anew, and the web unwoven that was so nearly finished.

But when thoughts and words are collected and adjusted, and the whole composition at last concluded, it seldom gratifies the author, when he comes coolly and deliberately to review it, with the hopes which had been excited in the fury of the performance: novelty always captivates the mind; as our thoughts rise fresh upon us, we readily believe them just and original, which, when the pleasure of production is over, we find to be mean and common, or borrowed from the works of others, and supplied by memory rather than invention.

But though it should happen that the writer finds no such faults in his performance, he is still to remember, that he looks upon it with partial eyes: and when he considers, how much men, who could judge of others with great exactness, have often failed of judging of themselves, he will be afraid of deciding too hastily in his own favour, or of allowing himself to contemplate with too much complacence, treasure that has not yet been brought to the test, nor passed the only trial that can stamp its value.

From the publick, and only from the publick, is he to await a confirmation of his claim, and a final justification of self-esteem; but the publick is not easily persuaded to favour an author. If mankind were left to judge for themselves, it is reasonable to imagine, that of such writings, at least, as describe the movements of the human passions, and of which every man carries the archetype within him, a just opinion would be formed; but whoever has remarked the fate of books, must have found it governed by other causes than general consent arising from general conviction. If a new performance happens not to fall into the hands of some who have courage to tell, and authority to propagate their opinion, it often remains long in obscurity, and perishes unknown and unexamined. A few, a very few, commonly constitute the taste of the time; the judgment which they have once pronounced, some are too lazy to discuss, and some too timorous to contradict; it may however be, I think, observed, that their power is greater to depress than exalt, as mankind are more credulous of censure than of praise.

This perversion of the publick judgment is not to be rashly numbered amongst the miseries of an author; since it commonly serves, after miscarriage, to reconcile him to himself. Because the world has sometimes passed an unjust sentence, he readily concludes the sentence unjust by which his performance is condemned; because some have been exalted above their merits by partiality, he is sure to ascribe the success of a rival, not to the merit of his work, but the zeal of his patrons. Upon the whole, as the author seems to share all the common miseries of life, he appears to partake likewise of its lenitives and abatements[o].

[o] See a pamphlet entitled " The Case of Authors by Profession," 8vo. 1758. It is the production of Mr. James Ralph, who knew from painful experience the bitter evils incident to an employment which yielded a bare maintenance to Johnson himself. For anecdotes of Ralph, and the work alluded to, see Dr. Drake's Essays on Rambler, &c. vol. i. p. 96.

THE IDLER.

ADVERTISEMENT.

————

THE IDLER having omitted to distinguish the essays of his correspondents by any particular signature, thinks it necessary to inform his readers, that from the ninth, the fifteenth, thirty-third, forty-second, fifty-fourth, sixty-seventh, seventy-sixth, seventy-ninth, eighty-second, ninety-third, ninety-sixth, and ninety-eighth papers, he claims no other praise than that of having given them to the publick *.

* The names of the Authors of these Papers, as far as known, will be given in the course of the present edition.

IDLER.

—

N°. 1. SATURDAY, APRIL 15, 1758.

———

——Vacui sub umbra
Lusimus.——　　　　　Hor. Lib. i. Ode xxxii. 1.

THOSE who attempt periodical essays seem to be often stopped in the beginning, by the difficulty of finding a proper title. Two writers, since the time of the Spectator, have assumed his name [a], without any pretensions to lawful inheritance; an effort was once made to revive the Tatler [b], and the strange appellations, by which other papers have been called, show that the authors were distressed, like the natives of America, who come to the Europeans to beg a name.

It will be easily believed of the Idler, that if his title had required any search, he never would have found it. Every mode of life has its conveniencies. The Idler, who habituates himself to be satisfied with what he can most easily obtain, not only escapes labours which are often fruitless, but sometimes succeeds better than those who

---

[a] The Universal Spectator in 1728, by the celebrated antiquary William Oldys.

The Female Spectator in 1744, by Eliza Haywood.

These were followed by the New Spectator in 1784; and lastly, by the Country Spectator in 1792. This last is a production of very considerable merit.

[b] This attempt was made in 1750, under the title of the Tatler Revived. After a short trial it completely failed.

despise all that is within their reach, and think every thing more valuable as it is harder to be acquired.

If similitude of manners be a motive to kindness, the Idler may flatter himself with universal patronage. There is no single character under which such numbers are comprised. Every man is, or hopes to be, an Idler. Even those who seem to differ most from us are hastening to increase our fraternity; as peace is the end of war, so to be idle is the ultimate purpose of the busy.

There is perhaps no appellation by which a writer can better denote his kindred to the human species. It has been found hard to describe man by an adequate definition. Some philosophers have called him a reasonable animal; but others have considered reason as a quality of which many creatures partake. He has been termed likewise a laughing animal; but it is said that some men have never laughed. Perhaps man may be more properly distinguished as an idle animal; for there is no man who is not sometimes idle. It is at least a definition from which none that shall find it in this paper can be excepted; for who can be more idle than the reader of the Idler?

That the definition may be complete, idleness must be not only the general, but the peculiar characteristick of man; and perhaps man is the only being that can properly be called idle, that does by others what he might do himself, or sacrifices duty or pleasure to the love of ease.

Scarcely any name can be imagined from which less envy or competition is to be dreaded. The Idler has no rivals or enemies. The man of business forgets him; the man of enterprise despises him; and though such as tread the same track of life fall commonly into jealousy and discord, Idlers are always found to associate in peace; and he who is most famed for doing nothing, is glad to meet another as idle as himself.

What is to be expected from this paper, whether it will be uniform or various, learned or familiar, serious or gay, political or moral, continued or interrupted, it is hoped that no reader will inquire. That the Idler has some scheme, cannot be doubted, for to form schemes is the Idler's privilege. But though he has many projects in his head, he is now grown sparing of communication, having observed, that his hearers are apt to remember what he forgets himself; that his tardiness of execution exposes him to the encroachments of those who catch a hint and fall to work; and that very specious plans, after long contrivance and pompous displays, have subsided in weariness without a trial, and without miscarriage have been blasted by derision.

Something the Idler's character may be supposed to promise. Those that are curious after diminutive history, who watch the revolutions of families, and the rise and fall of characters either male or female, will hope to be gratified by this paper; for the Idler is always inquisitive and seldom retentive. He that delights in obloquy and satire, and wishes to see clouds gathering over any reputation that dazzles him with its brightness, will snatch up the Idler's essays with a beating heart. The Idler is naturally censorious; those who attempt nothing themselves, think every thing easily performed, and consider the unsuccessful always as criminal.

I think it necessary to give notice, that I make no contract, nor incur any obligation. If those who depend on the Idler for intelligence and entertainment, should suffer the disappointment which commonly follows ill-placed expectations, they are to lay the blame only on themselves.

Yet hope is not wholly to be cast away. The Idler, though sluggish, is yet alive, and may sometimes be stimulated to vigour and activity. He may descend into profoundness, or tower into sublimity; for the diligence of an Idler is rapid and impetuous, as ponderous bodies forced into velocity move with violence proportionate to their weight.

But these vehement exertions of intellect cannot be frequent, and he will therefore gladly receive help from any correspondent, who shall enable him to please without his own labour. He excludes no style, he prohibits no subject; only let him that writes to the Idler remember, that his letters must not be long; no words are to be squandered in declarations of esteem, or confessions of inability; conscious dulness has little right to be prolix, and praise is not so welcome to the Idler as quiet.

N°. 2. SATURDAY, APRIL 22, 1758.

———*Toto non quater anno*
Membranam.———   Hor. Lib. ii. Sat. iii. 1.

MANY positions are often on the tongue, and seldom in the mind; there are many truths which every human being acknowledges and forgets. It is generally known, that he who expects much will be often disappointed; yet disappointment seldom cures us of expectation, or has any other effect than that of producing a moral sentence, or peevish exclamation. He that embarks in the voyage of life, will always wish to advance rather by the impulse of the wind, than the strokes of the oar; and many founder in the passage, while they lie waiting for the gale that is to waft them to their wish.

It will naturally be suspected that the Idler has lately suffered some disappointment, and that he does not talk thus gravely for nothing. No man is required to betray his own secrets. I will however, confess, that I have now been a writer almost a week, and have not yet heard a single word of praise, nor received one hint from any correspondent.

Whence this negligence proceeds I am not able to discover. Many of my predecessors have thought themselves obliged to return their acknowledgments in the second paper, for the kind reception of the first; and in a short time, apologies have become necessary to those ingenious gentlemen and ladies, whose performances, though in the highest degree elegant and learned, have been un-avoidably delayed.

What then will be thought of me, who, having expe-rienced no kindness, have no thanks to return; whom no gentleman or lady has yet enabled to give any cause of discontent, and who have therefore no opportunity of showing how skilfully I can pacify resentment, extenuate negligence, or palliate rejection.

I have long known that splendour of reputation is not to be counted among the necessaries of life, and therefore shall not much repine if praise be withheld till it is better deserved. But surely I may be allowed to complain, that, in a nation of authors, not one has thought me worthy of notice after so fair an invitation.

At the time when the rage of writing has seized the old and young, when the cook warbles her lyricks in the kitchen, and the thrasher vociferates his heroicks in the barn; when our traders deal out knowledge in bulky vo-lumes, and our girls forsake their samplers to teach king-doms wisdom; it may seem very unnecessary to draw any more from their proper occupations, by affording new op-portunities of literary fame[c].

I should be indeed unwilling to find that, for the sake of corresponding with the Idler, the smith's iron had cooled on the anvil, or the spinster's distaff stood unemployed. I solicit only the contributions of those who have already devoted themselves to literature, or, without any deter-minate intention, wander at large through the expanse of life, and wear out the day in hearing at one place what they utter at another.

Of these, a great part are already writers. One has a friend in the country upon whom he exercises his powers; whose passions he raises and depresses; whose under-standing he perplexes with paradoxes, or strengthens by argument; whose admiration he courts, whose praises he enjoys; and who serves him instead of a senate or a

---

[c] See Knox's Essays. Number 50.

theatre; as the young soldiers in the Roman camp learned
the use of their weapons by fencing against a post in the
place of an enemy.

Another has his pockets filled with essays and epigrams,
which he reads from house to house, to select parties; and
which his acquaintances are daily entreating him to withhold no longer from the impatience of the publick.

If among these any one is persuaded, that, by such pre-
ludes of composition, he has qualified himself to appear in
the open world, and is yet afraid of those censures which
they who have already written, and they who cannot write,
are equally ready to fulminate against publick pretenders
to fame, he may, by transmitting his performances to the
Idler, make a cheap experiment of his abilities, and enjoy
the pleasure of success, without the hazard of miscarriage.

Many advantages not generally known arise from this
method of stealing on the publick. The standing author
of the paper is always the object of critical malignity.
Whatever is mean will be imputed to him, and whatever
is excellent be ascribed to his assistants. It does not
much alter the event, that the author and his correspondents are equally unknown; for the author, whoever
he be, is an individual, of whom every reader has some
fixed idea, and whom he is therefore unwilling to gratify
with applause; but the praises given to his correspondents
are scattered in the air, none can tell on whom they will
light, and therefore none are unwilling to bestow them.

He that is known to contribute to a periodical work,
needs no other caution than not to tell what particular
pieces are his own; such secrecy is indeed very difficult;
but if it can be maintained, it is scarcely to be imagined
at how small an expense he may grow considerable.

A person of quality, by a single paper, may engross the
honour of a volume. Fame is indeed dealt with a hand
less and less bounteous through the subordinate ranks, till
it descends to the professed author, who will find it very
difficult to get more than he deserves; but every man who
does not want it, or who needs not value it, may have

liberal allowances ; and, for five letters in the year sent to
the Idler, of which perhaps only two are printed, will be
promoted to the first rank of writers by those who are
weary of the present race of wits, and wish to sink them
into obscurity before the lustre of a name not yet known
enough to be detested.

<hr>

N°. 3. SATURDAY, APRIL 29, 1758.

——*Otia vitæ*
Solamur cantu.   STAT.

IT has long been the complaint of those who frequent the
theatres, that all the dramatick art has been long exhausted, and that the vicissitudes of fortune, and accidents of life, have been shown in every possible combination, till the first scene informs us of the last, and the
play no sooner opens, than every auditor knows how it
will conclude. When a conspiracy is formed in a tragedy,
we guess by whom it will be detected ; when a letter is
dropt in a comedy, we can tell by whom it will be found.
Nothing is now left for the poet but character and sentiment, which are to make their way as they can, without
the soft anxiety of suspense, or the enlivening agitation of
surprise.

A new paper lies under the same disadvantages as a
new play. There is danger lest it be new without novelty. My earlier predecessors had their choice of vices
and follies, and selected such as were most likely to raise
merriment or attract attention ; they had the whole field
of life before them, untrodden and unsurveyed ; characters of every kind shot up in their way, and those of the
most luxuriant growth, or most conspicuous colours, were
naturally cropt by the first sickle. They that follow are
forced to peep into neglected corners, to note the casual
varieties of the same species, and to recommend them-

selves by minute industry and distinctions too subtle for common eyes.

Sometimes it may happen, that the haste or negligence of the first inquirers has left enough behind to reward another search; sometimes new objects start up under the eye, and he that is looking for one kind of matter, is amply gratified by the discovery of another. But still it must be allowed, that, as more is taken, less can remain; and every truth brought newly to light impoverishes the mine, from which succeeding intellects are to dig their treasures.

Many philosophers imagine, that the elements themselves may be in time exhausted; that the sun, by shining long, will effuse all its light; and that, by the continual waste of aqueous particles, the whole earth will at last become a sandy desert.

I would not advise my readers to disturb themselves by contriving how they shall live without light and water. For the days of universal thirst and perpetual darkness are at a great distance. The ocean and the sun will last our time, and we may leave posterity to shift for themselves.

But if the stores of nature are limited, much more narrow bounds must be set to the modes of life; and mankind may want a moral or amusing paper, many years before they shall be deprived of drink or day-light. This want, which to the busy and the inventive may seem easily remediable by some substitute or other, the whole race of Idlers will feel with all the sensibility that such torpid animals can suffer.

When I consider the innumerable multitudes that, having no motive of desire, or determination of will, lie freezing in perpetual inactivity, till some external impulse puts them in motion; who awake in the morning, vacant of thought, with minds gaping for the intellectual food, which some kind essayist has been accustomed to supply; I am moved by the commiseration with which all human beings ought to behold the distresses of each other, to try some expedients for their relief, and to inquire by what methods the listless may be actuated, and the empty be replenished.

There are said to be pleasures in madness known only to madmen. There are certainly miseries in idleness, which the Idler only can conceive. These miseries I have often felt and often bewailed. I know by experience, how welcome is every avocation that summons the thoughts to a new image; and how much languor and lassitude are relieved by that officiousness which offers a momentary amusement to him who is unable to find it for himself.

It is naturally indifferent to this race of men what entertainment they receive, so they are but entertained. They catch, with equal eagerness, at a moral lecture, or the memoirs of a robber; a prediction of the appearance of a comet, or the calculation of the chances of a lottery.

They might therefore easily be pleased, if they consulted only their own minds; but those who will not take the trouble to think for themselves, have always somebody to think for them; and the difficulty in writing is to please those from whom others learn to be pleased.

Much mischief is done in the world with very little interest or design. He that assumes the character of a critick, and justifies his claim by perpetual censure, imagines that he is hurting none but the author, and him he considers as a pestilent animal, whom every other being has a right to persecute; little does he think how many harmless men he involves in his own guilt, by teaching them to be noxious without malignity, and to repeat objections which they do not understand; or how many honest minds he debars from pleasure, by exciting an artificial fastidiousness, and making them too wise to concur with their own sensations. He who is taught by a critick to dislike that which pleased him in his natural state, has the same reason to complain of his instructer, as the madman to rail at his doctor, who, when he thought himself master of Peru, physicked him to poverty.

If men will struggle against their own advantage, they

are not to expect that the Idler will take much pains upon them; he has himself to please as well as them, and has long learned, or endeavoured to learn, not to make the ˙ pleasure of others too necessary to his own.

N°. 4.   SATURDAY, MAY 6, 1758.

Πάντας γὰρ φιλέεσκε.   Hom.

CHARITY, or tenderness for the poor, which is now justly considered, by a great part of mankind, as inseparable from piety, and in which almost all the goodness of the present age consists, is, I think, known only to those who enjoy, either immediately or by transmission, the light of revelation.

Those ancient nations who have given us the wisest models of government, and the brightest examples of patriotism, whose institutions have been transcribed by all succeeding legislatures, and whose history is studied by every candidate for political or military reputation, have yet left behind them no mention of alms-houses or hospitals, or places where age might repose, or sickness be relieved.

The Roman emperours, indeed, gave large donatives to the citizens and soldiers, but these distributions were always reckoned rather popular than virtuous: nothing more was intended than an ostentation of liberality, nor was any recompense expected, but suffrages and acclamations.

Their beneficence was merely occasional; he that ceased to need the favour of the people, ceased likewise to court it; and, therefore, no man thought it either necessary or wise to make any standing provision for the needy, to look forwards to the wants of posterity, or to secure successions of charity, for successions of distress.

Compassion is by some reasoners, on whom the name of philosophers has been too easily conferred, resolved into an affection merely selfish, an involuntary perception of pain at the involuntary sight of a being like ourselves languishing in misery. But this sensation, if ever it be felt at all from the brute instinct of uninstructed nature, will only produce effects desultory and transient; it will never settle into a principle of action, or extend relief to calamities unseen, in generations not yet in being.

The devotion of life or fortune to the succour of the poor, is a height of virtue, to which humanity has never risen by its own power. The charity of the Mahometans is a precept which their teacher evidently transplanted from the doctrines of Christianity; and the care with which some of the Oriental sects attend, as is said, to the necessities of the diseased and indigent, may be added to the other arguments, which prove Zoroaster to have borrowed his institutions from the law of Moses.

The present age, though not likely to shine hereafter among the most splendid periods of history, has yet given examples of charity, which may be very properly recommended to imitation. The equal distribution of wealth, which long commerce has produced, does not enable any single hand to raise edifices of piety like fortified cities, to appropriate manors to religious uses, or deal out such large and lasting beneficence as was scattered over the land in ancient times, by those who possessed counties or provinces. But no sooner is a new species of misery brought to view, and a design of relieving it professed, than every hand is open to contribute something, every tongue is busied in solicitation, and every art of pleasure is employed for a time in the interest of virtue.

The most apparent and pressing miseries incident to man, have now their peculiar houses of reception and relief; and there are few among us, raised however little above the danger of poverty, who may not justly claim, what is implored by the Mahometans in their most ardent benedictions, the prayers of the poor.

Among those actions which the mind can most securely review with unabated pleasure, is that of having contributed to an hospital for the sick. Of some kinds of cha-

rity the consequences are dubious : some evils which beneficence has been busy to remedy, are not certainly known
to be very grievous to the sufferer, or detrimental to the
community ; but no man can question whether wounds
and sickness are not really painful ; whether it be not
worthy of a good man's care to restore those to ease and
usefulness, from whose labour infants and women expect
their bread, and who, by a casual hurt, or lingering disease, lie pining in want and anguish, burthensome to
others, and weary of themselves.

Yet as the hospitals of the present time subsist only by
gifts bestowed at pleasure, without any solid fund of support, there is danger lest the blaze of charity, which now
burns with so much heat and splendour, should die away
for want of lasting fuel ; lest fashion should suddenly withdraw her smile, and inconstancy transfer the publick attention to something which may appear more eligible, because it will be new.

Whatever is left in the hands of chance must be subject
to vicissitude ; and when any establishment is found to be
useful, it ought to be the next care to make it permanent.

But man is a transitory being, and his designs must
partake of the imperfections of their author. To confer
duration is not always in our power. We must snatch the
present moment, and employ it well, without too much
solicitude for the future, and content ourselves with reflecting that our part is performed. He that waits for an
opportunity to do much at once, may breathe out his life
in idle wishes, and regret, in the last hour, his useless intentions, and barren zeal.

The most active promoters of the present schemes of
charity cannot be cleared from some instances of misconduct, which may awaken contempt or censure, and hasten
that neglect which is likely to come too soon of itself.
The open competitions between different hospitals, and
the animosity with which their patrons oppose one another,
may prejudice weak minds against them all. For it will
not be easily believed, that any man can, for good reasons,

wish to exclude another from doing good. The spirit of charity can only be continued by a reconciliation of these ridiculous feuds; and therefore, instead of contentions who shall be the only benefactors to the needy, let there be no other struggle than who shall be the first.

N°. 5.   SATURDAY, MAY 13, 1758.

———Κάλλος
'Ἀντ' ἐγχέων ἁπάντων
'Ἀντ' ἀσπίδων ἁπασῶν.   ANAC.

OUR military operations are at last begun; our troops are marching in all the pomp of war, and a camp is marked out on the Isle of Wight; the heart of every Englishman now swells with confidence, though somewhat softened by generous compassion for the consternation and distresses of our enemies.

This formidable armament and splendid march produce different effects upon different minds, according to the boundless diversities of temper, occupation, and habits of thought.

Many a tender maiden considers her lover as already lost, because he cannot reach the camp but by crossing the sea; men of a more political understanding are persuaded that we shall now see, in a few days, the ambassadours of France supplicating for pity. Some are hoping for a bloody battle, because a bloody battle makes a vendible narrative; some are composing songs of victory; some planning arches of triumph; and some are mixing fireworks for the celebration of a peace.

Of all extensive and complicated objects, different parts are selected by different eyes; and minds are variously affected, as they vary their attention. The care of the publick is now fixed upon our soldiers, who are leaving their native country to wander, none can tell how long, in the pathless deserts of the Isle of Wight. The tender sigh for their sufferings, and the gay drink to their success.   I, who look, or believe myself to look, with more philosophick eyes on human affairs, must confess, that I saw the troops march with little emotion ; my thoughts were fixed upon other scenes, and the tear stole into my eyes, not for those who were going away, but for those who were left behind.

We have no reason to doubt but our troops will proceed with proper caution ; there are men among them who can take care of themselves.   But how shall the ladies endure without them?   By what arts can they, who have long had no joy but from the civilities of a soldier, now amuse their hours, and solace their separation ?

Of fifty thousand men, now destined to different stations, if we allow each to have been occasionally necessary only to four women, a short computation will inform us, that two hundred thousand ladies are left to languish in distress ; two hundred thousand ladies, who must run to sales and auctions without an attendant ; sit at the play, without a critick to direct their opinion ; buy their fans by their own judgment ; dispose shells by their own invention ; walk in the Mall without a gallant ; go to the gardens without a protector ; and shuffle cards with vain impatience, for want of a fourth to complete the party.

Of these ladies, some, I hope, have lap-dogs, and some monkeys ; but they are unsatisfactory companions.   Many useful offices are performed by men of scarlet, to which neither dog nor monkey has adequate abilities.   A parrot, indeed, is as fine as a colonel, and, if he has been much used to good company, is not wholly without conversation ; but a parrot, after all, is a poor little creature, and has neither sword nor shoulder-knot, can neither dance nor play at cards.

Since the soldiers must obey the call of their duty, and go to that side of the kingdom which faces France, I know not why the ladies, who cannot live without them, should not follow them.   The prejudices and pride of man have long presumed the sword and spindle made for different hands, and denied the other sex to partake the grandeur of military glory. This notion may be consistently enough received in France, where the salick law excludes females from the throne; but we, who allow them to be sovereigns, may surely suppose them capable to be soldiers.

It were to be wished that some man, whose experience and authority might enforce regard, would propose that our encampments for the present year should comprise an equal number of men and women, who should march and fight in mingled bodies. If proper colonels were once appointed, and the drums ordered to beat for female volunteers, our regiments would soon be filled without the reproach or cruelty of an impress.

Of these heroines, some might serve on foot under the denomination of the *Female Buffs,* and some on horseback, with the title of *Lady Hussars.*

What objections can be made to this scheme I have endeavoured maturely to consider; and cannot find that a modern soldier has any duties, except that of obedience, which a lady cannot perform. If the hair has lost its powder, a lady has a puff; if a coat be spotted, a lady has a brush. Strength is of less importance since fire-arms have been used; blows of the hand are now seldom exchanged; and what is there to be done in the charge or the retreat beyond the powers of a sprightly maiden?

Our masculine squadrons will not suppose themselves disgraced by their auxiliaries, till they have done something which women could not have done. The troops of Braddock never saw their enemies, and perhaps were defeated by women. If our American general had headed an army of girls, he might still have built a fort and taken it. Had Minorca been defended by a female garrison, it might have been surrendered, as it was, without a breach; and I cannot but think, that seven thousand women might have ventured to look at Rochfort, sack a village, rob a vineyard, and return in safety.

N°. 6. SATURDAY, MAY 20, 1758.

Ταμείον ἀρετῆς γενναία γυνή.   GR. PRO.

THE lady who had undertaken to ride on one horse a thousand miles in a thousand hours, has completed her journey in little more than two-thirds of the time stipulated, and was conducted through the last mile with triumphal honours. Acclamation shouted before her, and all the flowers of the spring were scattered in her way.

Every heart ought to rejoice when true merit is distinguished with publick notice. I am far from wishing either to the amazon or her horse any diminution of happiness or fame, and cannot but lament that they were not more amply and suitably rewarded.

There was once a time when wreaths of bays or oak were considered as recompenses equal to the most wearisome labours and terrifick dangers, and when the miseries of long marches and stormy seas were at once driven from the remembrance by the fragrance of a garland.

If this heroine had been born in ancient times, she might perhaps have been delighted with the simplicity of ancient gratitude; or if any thing was wanting to full satisfaction, she might have supplied the deficiency with the hope of deification, and anticipated the altars that would be raised, and the vows that would be made, by future candidates for equestrian glory, to the patroness of the race and the goddess of the stable.

But fate reserved her for a more enlightened age, which has discovered leaves and flowers to be transitory things; which considers profit as the end of honour; and rates the event of every undertaking only by the money that is gained or lost. In these days, to strew the road with daisies and lilies, is to mock merit, and delude hope. The toyman will not give his jewels, nor the mercer measure out his silks, for vegetable coin. A primrose, though picked up under the feet of the most renowned courser, will neither be received as a stake at cards, nor procure a seat at an opera, nor buy candles for a rout, nor lace for a livery. And though there are many virtuosos, whose sole ambition is to possess something which can be found in no other hand, yet some are more accustomed to store their cabinets by theft than purchase, and none of them would either steal or buy one of the flowers of gratulation till he knows that all the rest are totally destroyed.

Little therefore did it avail this wonderful lady to be received, however joyfully, with such obsolete and barren ceremonies of praise. Had the way been covered with guineas, though but for the tenth part of the last mile, she would have considered her skill and diligence as not wholly lost; and might have rejoiced in the speed and perseverance which had left her such superfluity of time, that she could at leisure gather her reward without the danger of Atalanta's miscarriage.

So much ground could not indeed have been paved with gold but at a large expense, and we are at present engaged in a war, which demands and enforces frugality. But common rules are made only for common life, and some deviation from general policy may be allowed in favour of a lady that rode a thousand miles in a thousand hours.

Since the spirit of antiquity so much prevails amongst us, that even on this great occasion we have given flowers instead of money, let us at least complete our imitation of the ancients, and endeavour to transmit to posterity the memory of that virtue, which we consider as superior to pecuniary recompense. Let an equestrian statue of this heroine be erected, near the starting-post on the heath of Newmarket, to fill kindred souls with emulation, and tell the grand-daughters of our grand-daughters what an English maiden has once performed.

As events, however illustrious, are soon obscured if they are intrusted to tradition, I think it necessary, that the pedestal should be inscribed with a concise account of this great performance. The composition of this narrative ought not to be committed rashly to improper hands. If the rhetoricians of Newmarket, who may be supposed likely to conceive in its full strength the dignity of the subject, should undertake to express it, there is danger lest they admit some phrases which, though well understood at present, may be ambiguous in another century. If posterity should read on a publick monument, that *the lady carried her horse a thousand miles in a thousand hours*, they may think that the statue and inscription are at variance, because one will represent the horse as carrying his lady, and the other tell that the lady carried her horse.

Some doubts likewise may be raised by speculatists, and some controversies be agitated among historians, concerning the motive as well as the manner of the action. As it will be known, that this wonder was performed in a time of war, some will suppose that the lady was frighted by invaders, and fled to preserve her life or her chastity: others will conjecture, that she was thus honoured for some intelligence carried of the enemy's designs: some will think that she brought news of a victory; others, that she was commissioned to tell of a conspiracy; and some will congratulate themselves on their acuter penetration, and find, that all these notions of patriotism and publick spirit are improbable and chimerical; they will confidently tell, that she only ran away from her guardians, and that the true causes of her speed were fear and love.

Let it therefore be carefully mentioned, that by this performance *she won her wager*; and, lest this should, by any change of manners, seem an inadequate or incredible incitement, let it be added, that at this time the original motives of human actions had lost their influence; that the love of praise was extinct; the fear of infamy was become ridiculous; and the only wish of an Englishman was, *to win his wager* [d].

[d] The incident, so pleasingly ridiculed in this paper, happened in 1758; and the newspapers of the time gave it due importance.

ONE of the principal amusements of the *Idler* is to read the works of those minute historians the writers of news, who, though contemptuously overlooked by the composers of bulky volumes, are yet necessary in a nation where much wealth produces much leisure, and one part of the people has nothing to do but to observe the lives and fortunes of the other.

To us, who are regaled every morning and evening with intelligence, and are supplied from day to day with materials for conversation, it is difficult to conceive how man can subsist without a newspaper, or to what entertainment companies can assemble, in those wide regions of the earth that have neither *Chronicles* nor *Magazines*, neither *Gazettes* nor *Advertisers*, neither *Journals* nor *Evening Posts*.

There are never great numbers in any nation, whose reason or invention can find employment for their tongues, who can raise a pleasing discourse from their own stock of sentiments and images; and those few who have qualified themselves by speculation for general disquisitions are soon left without an audience. The common talk of men must relate to facts in which the talkers have, or think they have, an interest; and where such facts cannot be known, the pleasures of society will be merely sensual. Thus the natives of the Mahometan empires, who approach most nearly to European civility, have no higher pleasure at their convivial assemblies than to hear a piper, or gaze upon a tumbler; and no company can keep together longer than they are diverted by sounds or shows.

All foreigners remark, that the knowledge of the common people of England is greater than that of any other vulgar. This superiority we undoubtedly owe to the rivulets of intelligence, which are continually trickling among us, which every one may catch, and of which every one partakes[e].

This universal diffusion of instruction is, perhaps, not wholly without its inconveniencies; it certainly fills the nation with superficial disputants; enables those to talk who were born to work; and affords information sufficient to elate vanity, and stiffen obstinacy, but too little to enlarge the mind into complete skill for full comprehension.

Whatever is found to gratify the publick, will be multiplied by the emulation of venders beyond necessity or use. This plenty indeed produces cheapness, but cheapness always ends in negligence and depravation.

The compilation of newspapers is often committed to narrow and mercenary minds, not qualified for the task of delighting or instructing; who are content to fill their paper, with whatever matter, without industry to gather, or discernment to select.

Thus journals are daily multiplied without increase of knowledge. The tale of the morning paper is told again in the evening, and the narratives of the evening are bought again in the morning. These repetitions, indeed, waste time, but they do not shorten it. The most eager peruser of news is tired before he has completed his labour; and many a man, who enters the coffee-house in his nightgown and slippers, is called away to his shop, or his dinner, before he has well considered the state of Europe.

[e] For some pleasing remarks on this subject see De Lolme on the constitution of England, chap. 12. We cannot refrain from quoting here the speech of Sir James Mackintosh in the well known Peltier cause. "A sort of prophetic instinct, if I may so speak, seems to have revealed to her (Queen Elizabeth) the importance of that great instrument, for rousing and guiding the minds of men, of the effects of which she had no experience; which, since her time, has changed the condition of the world; but which few modern statesmen have thoroughly understood, or wisely employed; which is no doubt connected with many ridiculous and degrading details; which has produced, and may again produce, terrible mischiefs; but of which the influence must after all be considered as the most certain effect of the most efficacious cause of civilization; and which, whether it be a blessing or a curse, is the most powerful engine that a politician can move—I mean the Press. It is a curious fact, that in the year of the Armada, Queen Elizabeth caused to be printed the first Gazettes that ever appeared in England."

It is discovered by Reaumur, that spiders might make silk, if they could be persuaded to live in peace together. The writers of news, if they could be confederated, might give more pleasure to the publick. The morning and evening authors might divide an event between them; a single action, and that not of much importance, might be gradually discovered, so as to vary a whole week with joy, anxiety, and conjecture.

We know that a French ship of war was lately taken by a ship of England; but this event was suffered to burst upon us all at once, and then what we knew already was echoed from day to day, and from week to week.

Let us suppose these spiders of literature to spin together, and inquire to what an extensive web such another event might be regularly drawn, and how six morning and six evening writers might agree to retail their articles.

On *Monday Morning* the Captain of a ship might arrive, who left the *Friseur* of *France*, and the *Bull-dog,* Captain *Grim*, in sight of one another, so that an engagement seemed unavoidable.

Monday Evening. A sound of cannon was heard off Cape Finisterre, supposed to be those of the Bull-dog and Friseur.

Tuesday Morning. It was this morning reported that the Bull-dog engaged the Friseur, yard-arm and yard-arm, three glasses and a half, but was obliged to sheer off for want of powder. It is hoped that inquiry will be made into this affair in a proper place.

Tuesday Evening. The account of the engagement between the Bull-dog and Friseur was premature.

Wednesday Morning. Another express is arrived, which brings news, that the Friseur had lost all her masts, and three hundred of her men, in the late engagement; and that Captain Grim is come into harbour much shattered.

Wednesday Evening. We hear that the brave Captain Grim, having expended his powder, proposed to enter the

Friseur sword in hand; but that his lieutenant, the nephew of a certain nobleman, remonstrated against it.

Thursday Morning. We wait impatiently for a full account of the late engagement between the Bull-dog and Friseur.

Thursday Evening. It is said the order of the Bath will be sent to Captain Grim.

Friday Morning. A certain Lord of the Admiralty has been heard to say of a certain Captain, that if he had done his duty, a certain French ship might have been taken. It was not thus that merit was rewarded in the days of Cromwell.

Friday Evening. There is certain information at the Admiralty, that the Friseur is taken, after a resistance of two hours.

Saturday Morning. A letter from one of the gunners of the Bull-dog mentions the taking of the Friseur, and attributes their success wholly to the bravery and resolution of Captain Grim, who never owed any of his advancement to borough-jobbers, or any other corrupters of the people.

Saturday Evening. Captain Grim arrived at the Admiralty, with an account that he engaged the Friseur, a ship of equal force with his own, off Cape Finisterre, and took her after an obstinate resistance, having killed one hundred and fifty of the French, with the loss of ninety-five of his own men.

Nᵒ. 8. SATURDAY, JUNE 3, 1758.

TO THE IDLER.

SIR,

IN the time of publick danger, it is every man's duty to withdraw his thoughts in some measure from his private interest, and employ part of his time for the general welfare. National conduct ought to be the result of national wisdom, a plan formed by mature consideration and diligent selection out of all the schemes which may be offered, and all the information which can be procured.

In a battle, every man should fight as if he was the single champion; in preparations for war, every man should think, as if the last event depended on his counsel. None can tell what discoveries are within his reach, or how much he may contribute to the publick safety.

Full of these considerations, I have carefully reviewed the process of the war, and find, what every other man has found, that we have hitherto added nothing to our military reputation : that at one time we have been beaten by enemies whom we did not see ; and, at another, have avoided the sight of enemies lest we should be beaten.

Whether our troops are defective in discipline or in courage, is not very useful to inquire ; they evidently want something necessary to success ; and he that shall supply that want will deserve well of his country.

To learn of an enemy has always been accounted politick and honourable ; and therefore I hope it will raise no prejudices against my project, to confess that I borrowed it from a Frenchman.

When the Isle of Rhodes was, many centuries ago, in the hands of that military order now called the Knights of Malta, it was ravaged by a dragon, who inhabited a den under a rock, from which he issued forth when he was hungry or wanton, and without fear or mercy devoured men and beasts as they came in his way. Many councils were held, and many devices offered, for his destruction; but as his back was armed with impenetrable scales, none would venture to attack him. At last Dudon, a French knight, undertook the deliverance of the island. From some place of security, he took a view of the dragon, or, as a modern soldier would say, *reconnoitred* him, and observed that his belly was naked and vulnerable. He then returned home to make his *arrangements;* and, by a very exact imitation of nature, made a dragon of pasteboard, in

the belly of which he put beef and mutton, and accustomed
two sturdy mastiffs to feed themselves by tearing their
way to the concealed flesh. When his dogs were well
practised in this method of plunder, he marched out with
them at his heels, and showed them the dragon; they
rushed upon him in quest of their dinner; Dudon battered
his scull, while they lacerated his belly; and neither his
sting nor claws were able to defend him.

Something like this might be practised in our present
state. Let a fortification be raised on Salisbury Plain,
resembling Brest, or Toulon, or Paris itself, with all the
usual preparation for defence; let the inclosure be filled
with beef and ale: let the soldiers, from some proper
eminence, see shirts waving upon lines, and here and there
a plump landlady hurrying about with pots in her hands.
When they are sufficiently animated to advance, lead
them in exact order, with fife and drum, to that side
whence the wind blows, till they come within the scent of
roast meat and tobacco. Contrive that they may approach
the place fasting about an hour after dinner-time, assure
them that there is no danger, and command an attack.

If nobody within either moves or speaks, it is not unlikely that they may carry the place by storm; but if a
panick should seize them, it will be proper to defer the
enterprise to a more hungry hour. When they have
entered, let them fill their bellies and return to the camp.

On the next day let the same place be shown them
again, but with some additions of strength or terrour. I
cannot pretend to inform our generals through what gradations of danger they should train their men to fortitude.
They best know what the soldiers and what themselves can
bear. It will be proper that the war should every day vary
its appearance. Sometimes, as they mount the rampart, a
cook may throw fat upon the fire, to accustom them to a
sudden blaze; and sometimes, by the clatter of empty
.pots, they may be inured to formidable noises. But let it
never be forgotten, that victory must repose with a full
belly.

In time it will be proper to bring our French prisoners from the coast, and place them upon the walls in martial order. At their first appearance their hands must be tied, but they may be allowed to grin. In a month they may guard the place with their hands loosed, provided that on pain of death they be forbidden to strike.

By this method our army will soon be brought to look an enemy in the face. But it has been lately observed, that fear is received by the ear as well as the eyes ; and the Indian war-cry is represented as too dreadful to be endured ; as a sound that will force the bravest veteran to drop his weapon, and desert his rank ; that will deafen his ear, and chill his breast ; that will neither suffer him to hear orders or to feel shame, or retain any sensibility but the dread of death.

That the savage clamours of naked barbarians should thus terrify troops disciplined to war, and ranged in array with arms in their hands, is surely strange. But this is no time to reason. I am of opinion, that by a proper mixture of asses, bulls, turkeys, geese, and tragedians, a noise might be procured equally horrid with the war-cry. When our men have been encouraged by frequent victories, nothing will remain but to qualify them for extreme danger, by a sudden concert of terrifick vociferation. When they have endured this last trial, let them be led to action, as men who are no longer to be frightened ; as men who can bear at once the grimaces of the Gauls, and the howl of the Americans.

Nº. 9. SATURDAY, JUNE 10, 1758.

TO THE IDLER.

SIR,

   I HAVE read you ; that is a favour few authors can boast of having received from me besides yourself. My intention in telling you of it is to inform you, that you have both pleased and angered me. Never did writer

appear so delightful to me as you did when you adopted
the name of the *Idler*.   But what a falling off was there
when your first production was brought to light! A natural
irresistible attachment to that favourable passion, *idling*,
had led me to hope for indulgence from the *Idler*, but I
find him a stranger to the title.

What rules has he proposed totally to unbrace the
slackened nerve ; to shade the heavy eye of inattention ;
to give the smooth feature and the uncontracted muscle ;
or procure insensibility to the whole animal composition ?

These were some of the placid blessings I promised myself the enjoyment of, when I committed violence upon
myself by mustering up all my strength to set about reading you ; but I am disappointed in them all, and the stroke
of eleven in the morning is still as terrible to me as before,
and I find putting on my clothes still as painful and laborious.   Oh that our climate would permit that original
nakedness which the thrice happy Indians to this day
enjoy! How many unsolicitous hours should I bask away,
warmed in bed by the sun's glorious beams, could I, like
them, tumble from thence in a moment, when necessity
obliges me to endure the torment of getting upon my legs !

But wherefore do I talk to you upon subjects of this
delicate nature? you who seem ignorant of the inexpres-
sible charms of the elbow-chair, attended with a soft stool
for the elevation of the feet ! Thus, vacant of thought, do
I indulge the live-long day.

You may define happiness as you please ; I embrace
that opinion which makes it consist in the absence of pain.
To reflect is pain ; to stir is pain ; therefore I never reflect
or stir but when I cannot help it.   Perhaps you will call
my scheme of life indolence, and therefore think the *Idler*
excused from taking any notice of me ; but I have always
looked upon indolence and idleness as the same ; and so
desire you will now and then, while you profess yourself
of our fraternity, take some notice of me, and others in my
situation, who think they have a right to your assistance ;
or relinquish the name.

You may publish, burn, or destroy this, just as you are in the humour; it is ten to one but I forget that I wrote it, before it reaches you. I believe you may find a motto for it in Horace, but I cannot reach him without getting out of my chair; that is a sufficient reason for my not af-fixing any.—And being obliged to sit upright to ring the bell for my servant to convey this to the penny-post, if I slip the opportunity of his being now in the room, makes me break off abruptly[f].

This correspondent, whoever he be, is not to be dismis-sed without some tokens of regard. There is no mark more certain of a genuine Idler, than uneasiness without molestation, and complaint without a grievance.

Yet my gratitude to the contributor of half a paper shall not wholly overpower my sincerity. I must inform him, that, with all his pretensions, he that calls for directions to be idle, is yet but in the rudiments of idleness, and has attained neither the practice nor theory of wasting life. The true nature of idleness he will know in time, by con-tinuing to be idle. Virgil tells us of an impetuous and rapid being, that acquires strength by motion. The Idler acquires weight by lying still.

The *vis inertiæ*, the quality of resisting all external im-pulses, is hourly increasing; the restless and troublesome faculties of attention and distinction, reflection on the past, and solicitude for the future, by a long indulgence of idle-ness, will, like tapers in unelastick air, be gradually ex-tinguished; and the officious lover, the vigilant soldier, the busy trader, may, by a judicious composure of his mind, sink into a state approaching to that of brute matter; in which he shall retain the consciousness of his own exis-tence, only by an obtuse languor and drowsy discontent.

This is the lowest stage to which the favourites of idle-ness can descend; these regions of undelighted quiet can be entered by few. Of those that are prepared to sink

---

[f] By an unknown correspondent.

down into their shade, some are roused into action by avarice or ambition, some are awakened by the voice of fame, some allured by the smile of beauty, and many withheld by the importunities of want. Of all the enemies of idleness, want is the most formidable. Fame is soon found to be a sound, and love a dream; avarice and ambition may be justly suspected of privy confederacies with idleness; for, when they have for a while protected their votaries, they often deliver them up to end their lives under her dominion. Want always struggles against idleness, but want herself is often overcome; and every hour shows the careful observer those who had rather live in ease than in plenty.

So wide is the region of Idleness, and so powerful her influence. But she does not immediately confer all her gifts. My correspondent, who seems, with all his errours, worthy of advice, must be told, that he is calling too hastily for the last effusion of total insensibility. Whatever he may have been taught by unskilful Idlers to believe, labour is necessary in his initiation to idleness. He that never labours may know the pains of idleness, but not the pleasure. The comfort is, that if he devotes himself to insensibility, he will daily lengthen the intervals of idleness, and shorten those of labour, till at last he will lie down to rest, and no longer disturb the world or himself by bustle or competition.

Thus I have endeavoured to give him that information which, perhaps, after all, he did not want; for a true Idler often calls for that which he knows is never to be had, and asks questions which he does not desire ever to be answered.

N°. 10. SATURDAY, JUNE 17, 1758.

CREDULITY, or confidence of opinion too great for the evidence from which opinion is derived, we find to be a general weakness imputed by every sect and party to all others, and indeed by every man to every other man.

Of all kinds of credulity, the most obstinate and wonderful is that of political zealots; of men, who being numbered, they know not how or why, in any of the parties that divide a state, resign the use of their own eyes and ears, and resolve to believe nothing that does not favour those whom they profess to follow.

The bigot of philosophy is seduced by authorities which he has not always opportunities to examine, is entangled in systems by which truth and falsehood are inextricably complicated, or undertakes to talk on subjects which nature did not form him able to comprehend.

The Cartesian, who denies that his horse feels the spur, or that the hare is afraid when the hounds approach her; the disciple of Malbranche, who maintains that the man was not hurt by the bullet, which, according to vulgar apprehension, swept away his legs; the follower of Berkeley, who while he sits writing at his table, declares that he has neither table, paper, nor fingers; have all the honour at least of being deceived by fallacies not easily detected, and may plead that they did not forsake truth, but for appearances which they were not able to distinguish from it.

But the man who engages in a party has seldom to do with any thing remote or abstruse. The present state of things is before his eyes; and, if he cannot be satisfied without retrospection, yet he seldom extends his views beyond the historical events of the last century. All the knowledge that he can want is within his attainment, and most of the arguments which he can hear are within his capacity.

Yet so it is, that an Idler meets every hour of his life with men who have different opinions upon every thing past, present, and future; who deny the most notorious facts, contradict the most cogent truths, and persist in asserting to-day what they asserted yesterday, in defiance of evidence, and contempt of confutation.

Two of my companions, who are grown old in idleness, are Tom Tempest and Jack Sneaker. Both of them consider themselves as neglected by their parties, and therefore entitled to credit; for why should they favour ingratitude? They are both men of integrity, where no factious interest is to be promoted; and both lovers of truth, when they are not heated with political debate.

Tom Tempest is a steady friend to the house of Stuart. He can recount the prodigies that have appeared in the sky, and the calamities that have afflicted the nation every year from the Revolution; and is of opinion, that, if the exiled family had continued to reign, there would have neither been worms in our ships nor caterpillars in our trees. He wonders that the nation was not awakened by the hard frost to a revocation of the true king, and is hourly afraid that the whole island will be lost in the sea. He believes that king William burned Whitehall that he might steal the furniture; and that Tillotson died an atheist. Of queen Anne he speaks with more tenderness, owns that she meant well, and can tell by whom and why she was poisoned. In the succeeding reigns all has been corruption, malice, and design. He believes that nothing ill has ever happened for these forty years by chance or errour; he holds that the battle of Dettingen was won by mistake, and that of Fontenoy lost by contract; that the Victory was sunk by a private order; that Cornhill was fired by emissaries from the council; and the arch of Westminster-bridge was so contrived as to sink on purpose that the nation might be put to charge. He considers the new road to Islington as an encroachment on liberty, and often asserts that *broad wheels* will be the ruin of England.

Tom is generally vehement and noisy, but nevertheless has some secrets which he always communicates in a whisper. Many and many a time has Tom told me, in a corner, that our miseries were almost at an end, and that we should see, in a month, another monarch on the throne; the time elapses without a revolution; Tom meets me again with new intelligence, the whole scheme is now settled, and we shall see great events in another month.

Jack Sneaker is a hearty adherent to the present establishment; he has known those who saw the bed into which the Pretender was conveyed in a warming-pan. He often rejoices that the nation was not enslaved by the Irish. He believes that king William never lost a battle, and that if he had lived one year longer he would have conquered France. He holds that Charles the First was a Papist. He allows there were some good men in the reign of queen Anne, but the peace of Utrecht brought a blast upon the nation, and has been the cause of all the evil that we have suffered to the present hour. He believes that the scheme of the South Sea was well intended, but that it miscarried by the influence of France. He considers a standing army as the bulwark of liberty, thinks us secured from corruption by septennial parliaments, relates how we are enriched and strengthened by the electoral dominions, and declares that the publick debt is a blessing to the nation.

Yet, amidst all this prosperity, poor Jack is hourly disturbed by the dread of Popery. He wonders that some stricter laws are not made against Papists, and is sometimes afraid that they are busy with French gold among the bishops and judges.

He cannot believe that the Nonjurors are so quiet for nothing, they must certainly be forming some plot for the establishment of Popery; he does not think the present oaths sufficiently binding, and wishes that some better security could be found for the succession of Hanover. He is zealous for the naturalization of foreign Protestants, and rejoiced at the admission of the Jews to the English privileges, because he thought a Jew would never be a Papist.

N°. 11. SATURDAY, JUNE 24, 1758.

———Nec te quæsiveris extra.   PERS.

IT is commonly observed, that when two Englishmen meet, their first talk is of the weather; they are in haste to tell each other, what each must already know, that it is hot or cold, bright or cloudy, windy or calm.

There are, among the numerous lovers of subtilties and paradoxes, some who derive the civil institutions of every country from its climate, who impute freedom and slavery to the temperature of the air, can fix the meridian of vice and virtue, and tell at what degree of latitude we are to expect courage or timidity, knowledge or ignorance.

From these dreams of idle speculation, a slight survey of life, and a little knowledge of history, are sufficient to awaken any inquirer, whose ambition of distinction has not overpowered his love of truth. Forms of government are seldom the result of much deliberation; they are framed by chance in popular assemblies, or in conquered countries, by despotick authority. Laws are often occasional, often capricious, made always by a few, and sometimes by a single voice. Nations have changed their characters; slavery is now no where more patiently endured, than in countries once inhabited by the zealots of liberty.

But national customs can arise only from general agreement; they are not imposed, but chosen, and are continued only by the continuance of their cause. An Englishman's notice of the weather is the natural consequence of changeable skies and uncertain seasons. In many parts of the world, wet weather and dry are regularly expected at certain periods; but in our island every man goes to sleep, unable to guess whether he shall behold in the morning a bright or cloudy atmosphere, whether his rest shall be lulled by a shower, or broken by a tempest. We therefore rejoice mutually at good weather, as at an escape from something that we feared; and mutually complain of bad, as of the loss of something that we hoped.

Such is the reason of our practice; and who shall treat it with contempt? Surely not the attendant on a court, whose business is to watch the looks of a being weak and foolish as himself, and whose vanity is to recount the names of men, who might drop into nothing, and leave no vacuity; nor the proprietor of funds, who stops his acquaintance in the street to tell him of the loss of half-a-crown; nor the inquirer after news, who fills his head with foreign events, and talks of skirmishes and sieges, of which no consequence will ever reach his hearers or himself. The weather is a nobler and more interesting subject; it is the present state of the skies and of the earth, on which plenty and famine are suspended, on which millions depend for the necessaries of life.

The weather is frequently mentioned for another reason, less honourable to my dear countrymen. Our dispositions too frequently change with the colour of the sky; and when we find ourselves cheerful and good-natured, we naturally pay our acknowledgments to the powers of sunshine; or, if we sink into dulness and peevishness, look round the horizon for an excuse, and charge our discontent upon an easterly wind or a cloudy day.

Surely nothing is more reproachful to a being endowed with reason, than to resign its powers to the influence of the air, and live in dependence on the weather and the wind, for the only blessings which nature has put into our power, tranquillity and benevolence. To look up to the sky for the nutriment of our bodies, is the condition of nature; to call upon the sun for peace and gaiety, or deprecate the clouds lest sorrow should overwhelm us, is the cowardice of idleness, and the idolatry of folly.

Yet even in this age of inquiry and knowledge, when superstition is driven away, and omens and prodigies have lost their terrours, we find this folly countenanced by frequent examples. Those that laugh at the portentous glare of a comet, and hear a crow with equal tranquillity from the right or left, will yet talk of times and situations proper for intellectual performances, will imagine the fancy exalted by vernal breezes, and the reason invigorated by a bright calm.

If men who have given up themselves to fanciful credulity would confine their conceits in their own minds, they might regulate their lives by the barometer, with inconvenience only to themselves; but to fill the world with accounts of intellects subject to ebb and flow, of one genius that awakened in the spring, and another that ripened in the autumn, of one mind expanded in the summer, and of another concentrated in the winter, is no less dangerous than to tell children of bugbears and goblins. Fear will find every house haunted; and idleness will wait for ever for the moment of illumination.

This distinction of seasons is produced only by imagination operating on luxury. To temperance every day is bright, and every hour is propitious to diligence. He that shall resolutely excite his faculties, or exert his virtues, will soon make himself superior to the seasons, and may set at defiance the morning mist, and the evening damp, the blasts of the east, and the clouds of the south.

It was the boast of the Stoick philosophy, to make man unshaken by calamity, and unelated by success, incorruptible by pleasure, and invulnerable by pain; these are heights of wisdom which none ever attained, and to which few can aspire; but there are lower degrees of constancy necessary to common virtue; and every man, however he may distrust himself in the extremes of good or evil, might at least struggle against the tyranny of the climate, and refuse to enslave his virtue or his reason to the most variable of all variations, the changes of the weather.

No. 12. SATURDAY, JULY 1, 1758.

THAT every man is important in his own eyes, is a position of which we all either voluntarily or unwarily at least once an hour confess the truth; and it will unavoidably follow, that every man believes himself important to the publick.

The right which this importance gives us to general notice and visible distinction, is one of those disputable privileges which we have not always courage to assert; and which we therefore suffer to lie dormant till some elation of mind, or vicissitude of fortune, incites us to declare our pretensions and enforce our demands. And hopeless as the claim of vulgar characters may seem to the supercilious and severe, there are few who do not at one time or other endeavour to step forward beyond their rank; who do not make some struggles for fame, and show that they think all other conveniencies and delights imperfectly enjoyed without a name.

To get a name, can happen but to few. A name, even in the most commercial nation, is one of the few things which cannot be bought. It is the free gift of mankind, which must be deserved before it will be granted, and is at last unwillingly bestowed. But this unwillingness only increases desire in him who believes his merit sufficient to overcome it.

There is a particular period of life, in which this fondness for a name seems principally to predominate in both sexes. Scarce any couple comes together but the nuptials are declared in the newspapers with encomiums on each party. Many an eye, ranging over the page with eager curiosity in quest of statesmen and heroes, is stopped by a marriage celebrated between Mr. Buckram, an eminent salesman in Threadneedle-street, and Miss Dolly Juniper, the only daughter of an eminent distiller, of the parish of St. Giles's in the Fields, a young lady adorned with every accomplishment that can give happiness to the married state. Or we are told, amidst our impatience for the event of a battle, that on a certain day Mr. Winker, a tide-waiter at Yarmouth, was married to Mrs. Cackle, a widow lady of great accomplishments, and that as soon as the ceremony was performed they set out in a post-chaise for Yarmouth.

Many are the inquiries which such intelligence must undoubtedly raise, but nothing in this world is lasting. When the reader has contemplated with envy, or with gladness, the felicity of Mr. Buckram and Mr. Winker, and ransacked his memory for the names of Juniper and Cackle, his attention is diverted to other thoughts, by finding that Mirza will nòt cover this season; or that a spaniel has been lost or stolen, that answers to the name of Ranger.

Whence it arises that on the day of marriage all agree to call thus openly for honours, I am not able to discover. Some, perhaps, think it kind, by a publick declaration, to put an end to the hopes of rivalry and the fears of jealousy, to let parents know that they may set their daughters at liberty whom they have locked up for fear of the bridegroom, or to dismiss to their counters and their offices the amorous youths that had been used to hover round the dwelling of the bride.

These connubial praises may have another cause. It may be the intention of the husband and wife to dignify themselves in the eyes of each other, and, according to their different tempers or expectations, to win affection, or enforce respect.

It was said of the family of Lucas, that it was *noble*, for *all the brothers were valiant, and all the sisters were virtuous.* What would a stranger say of the *English* nation, in which on the day of marriage all the men are *eminent*, and all the women *beautiful, accomplished,* and *rich?*

How long the wife will be persuaded of the eminence of her husband, or the husband continue to believe that his wife has the qualities required to make marriage happy, may reasonably be questioned. I am afraid that much time seldom passes before each is convinced that praises are fallacious, and particularly those praises which we confer upon ourselves.

I should therefore think, that this custom might be omitted without any loss to the community; and that the sons and daughters of lanes and alleys might go hereafter to the next church, with no witnesses of their worth or happiness but their parents and their friends; but if they cannot be happy on the bridal day without some gratification of their vanity, I hope they will be willing to encourage a friend of mine who proposes to devote his powers to their service.

Mr. Settle, a man whose *eminence* was once allowed by the *eminent,* and whose *accomplishments* were confessed by the *accomplished,* in the latter part of a long life supported himself by an uncommon expedient. He had a standing elegy and epithalamium, of which only the first and last were leaves varied occasionally, and the intermediate pages were, by general terms, left applicable alike to every character. When any marriage became known, Settle ran to the bridegroom with his epithalamium; and when he heard of any death, ran to the heir with his elegy.

Who can think himself disgraced by a trade that was practised so long by the rival of Dryden, by the poet whose "Empress of Morocco" was played before princes by ladies of the court?

My friend purposes to open an office in the Fleet for matrimonial panegyricks, and will accommodate all with praise who think their own powers of expression inadequate to their merit. He will sell any man or woman the virtue or qualification which is most fashionable or most desired; but desires his customers to remember, that he sets beauty at the highest price, and riches at the next, and, if he be well paid, throws in virtue for nothing.

Nº. 13.   SATURDAY, JULY 8, 1758.

TO THE IDLER.

DEAR MR. IDLER,

THOUGH few men of prudence are much inclined to interpose in disputes between man and wife, who commonly make peace at the expense of the arbitrator; yet I

will venture to lay before you a controversy, by which the
quiet of my house has been long disturbed, and which,
unless you can decide it, is likely to produce lasting evils,
and embitter those hours which nature seems to have appropriated to tenderness and repose.

I married a wife with no great fortune, but of a family
remarkable for domestick prudence, and elegant frugality.
I lived with her at ease, if not with happiness, and seldom
had any reason of complaint. The house was always clean,
the servants were active and regular, dinner was on the
table every day at the same minute, and the ladies of the
neighbourhood were frightened when I invited their husbands, lest their own economy should be less esteemed.

During this gentle lapse of life, my dear brought me
three daughters. I wished for a son, to continue the
family; but my wife often tells me, that boys are dirty
things, and are always troublesome in a house; and declares that she has hated the sight of them ever since she
saw lady Fondle's eldest son ride over a carpet with his
hobby-horse all mire.

I did not much attend to her opinion, but knew that
girls could not be made boys; and therefore composed
myself to bear what I could not remedy, and resolved to
bestow that care on my daughters, to which only the sons
are commonly thought entitled.

But my wife's notions of education differ widely from
mine. She is an irreconcilable enemy to idleness, and
considers every state of life as idleness, in which the hands
are not employed, or some art acquired, by which she thinks
money may be got or saved.

In pursuance of this principle, she calls up her daughters at a certain hour, and appoints them a task of needle-
work to be performed before breakfast. They are confined
in a garret, which has its window in the roof, both because
work is best done at a sky-light, and because children are
apt to lose time by looking about them.

They bring down their work to breakfast, and as they
deserve are commended or reproved; they are then sent

up with a new task till dinner ; if no company is expected, their mother sits with them the whole afternoon, to direct their operations, and to draw patterns, and is sometimes denied to her nearest relations when she is engaged in teaching them a new stitch.

By this continual exercise of their diligence, she has obtained a very considerable number of laborious performances. We have twice as many fire-skreens as chimneys, and three flourished quilts for every bed. Half the rooms are adorned with a kind of *sutile pictures*, which imitate tapestry. But all their work is not set out to show ; she has boxes filled with knit garters and braided shoes. She has twenty covers for side-saddles embroidered with silver flowers, and has curtains wrought with gold in various figures, which she resolves some time or other to hang up. All these she displays to her company whenever she is elate with merit, and eager for praise ; and amidst the praises which her friends and herself bestow upon her merit, she never fails to turn to me, and ask what all these would cost, if I had been to buy them.

I sometimes venture to tell her, that many of the ornaments are superfluous ; that what is done with so much labour might have been supplied by a very easy purchase ; that the work is not always worth the materials ; and that I know not why the children should be persecuted with useless tasks, or obliged to make shoes that are never worn. She answers with a look of contempt, that men never care how money goes, and proceeds to tell of a dozen new chairs for which she is contriving covers, and of a couch which she intends to stand as a monument of needle-work.

In the mean time, the girls grow up in total ignorance of every thing past, present, and future. Molly asked me the other day, whether Ireland was in France, and was ordered by her mother to mend her hem. Kitty knows not, at sixteen, the difference between a Protestant and a Papist, because she has been employed three years in filling the side of a closet with a hanging that is to represent Cranmer in the flames. And Dolly, my eldest girl, is now unable to read a chapter in the Bible, having spent all the time, which other children pass at school, in working the interview between Solomon and the queen of Sheba.

About a month ago, Tent and Turkey-stitch seemed at a stand; my wife knew not what new work to introduce; I ventured to propose that the girls should now learn to read and write, and mentioned the necessity of a little arithmetick; but, unhappily, my wife has discovered that linen wears out, and has bought the girls three little wheels, that they may spin huckaback for the servants' table. I remonstrated, that with larger wheels they might despatch in an hour what must now cost them a day; but she told me, with irresistible authority, that any business is better than idleness; that when these wheels are set upon a table, with mats under them, they will turn without noise, and keep the girls upright; that great wheels are not fit for gentlewomen; and that with these, small as they are, she does not doubt but that the three girls, if they are kept close, will spin every year as much cloth as would cost five pounds if one were to buy it.

~~~~~~~~~~~~~~~~~~~~~

. N° 14.   SATURDAY, JULY 15, 1758.

———

WHEN Diogenes received a visit in his tub from Alexander the Great, and was asked, according to the ancient forms of royal courtesy, what petition he had to offer; " I have nothing," said he, " to ask, but that you would remove to the other side, that you may not, by intercepting the sunshine, take from me what you cannot give me."

Such was the demand of Diogenes from the greatest monarch of the earth, which those, who have less power than Alexander, may, with yet more propriety, apply to themselves. He that does much good, may be allowed to do sometimes a little' harm. But if the opportunities of beneficence be denied by fortune, innocence should at least be vigilantly preserved.

It is well known, that time once passed never returns; and that the moment which is lost, is lost for ever. Time therefore ought, above all other kinds of property, to be free from invasion; and yet there is no man who does not claim the power of wasting that time which is the right of others.

This usurpation is so general, that a very small part of the year is spent by choice; scarcely any thing is done when it is intended, or obtained when it is desired. Life is continually ravaged by invaders; one steals away an hour, and another a day; one conceals the robbery by hurrying us into business, another by lulling us with amusement; the depredation is continued through a thousand vicissitudes of tumult and tranquillity, till, having lost all, we can lose no more.

This waste of the lives of men has been very frequently charged upon the Great, whose followers linger from year to year in expectations, and die at last with petitions in their hands. Those who raise envy will easily incur censure. I know not whether statesmen and patrons do not suffer more reproaches than they deserve, and may not rather themselves complain, that they are given up a prey to pretensions without merit, and to importunity without shame.

The truth is, that the inconveniencies of attendance are more lamented than felt. To the greater number solicitation is its own reward. To be seen in good company, to talk of familiarities with men of power, to be able to tell the freshest news, to gratify an inferior circle with predictions of increase or decline of favour, and to be regarded as a candidate for high offices, are compensations more than equivalent to the delay of favours, which, perhaps, he that begs them has hardly confidence to expect.

A man conspicuous in a high station, who multiplies hopes that he may multiply dependants, may be considered as a beast of prey, justly dreaded, but easily avoided; his den is known, and they who would not be devoured, need not approach it. The great danger of the waste of time is from caterpillars and moths, who are not resisted, because they are not feared, and who work on with unheeded mischiefs, and invisible encroachments.

He, whose rank or merit procures him the notice of mankind, must give up himself, in a great measure, to the convenience or humour of those who surround him. Every man, who is sick of himself, will fly to him for relief; he that wants to speak will require him to hear; and he that wants to hear will expect him to speak. Hour passes after hour, the noon succeeds to morning, and the evening to noon, while a thousand objects are forced upon his attention, which he rejects as fast as they are offered, but which the custom of the world requires to be received with appearance of regard.

If we will have the kindness of others, we must endure their follies. He who cannot persuade himself to withdraw from society, must be content to pay a tribute of his time to a multitude of tyrants; to the loiterer, who makes appointments which he never keeps; to the consulter, who asks advice which he never takes; to the boaster, who blusters only to be praised; to the complainer, who whines only to be pitied; to the projector, whose happiness is to entertain his friends with expectations which all but himself know to be vain; to the economist, who tells of bargains and settlements; to the politician, who predicts the fate of battles and breach of alliances; to the usurer, who compares the different funds; and to the talker, who talks only because he loves to be talking.

To put every man in possession of his own time, and rescue the day from this succession of usurpers, is beyond my power, and beyond my hope. Yet, perhaps, some stop might be put to this unmerciful persecution, if all would seriously reflect, that whoever pays a visit that is not desired, or talks longer than the hearer is willing to attend, is guilty of an injury which he cannot repair, and takes away that which he cannot give.

~~~~~~~~~~~~~~~~~~~~~~~~~

N°. 15.   SATURDAY, JULY 22, 1758.

TO THE IDLER.

SIR,

I HAVE the misfortune to be a man of business; that, you will say, is a most grievous one; but what makes it the more so to me, is, that my wife has nothing to do: at least she had too good an education, and the prospect of too good a fortune in reversion when I married her, to think of employing herself either in my shop-affairs, or the management of my family.

Her time, you know, as well as my own, must be filled up some way or other. For my part, I have enough to mind in weighing my goods out, and waiting on my customers: but my wife, though she could be of as much use as a shopman to me, if she would put her hand to it, is now only in my way. She walks all the morning sauntering about the shop with her arms through her pocket-holes or stands gaping at the door-sill, and looking at every person that passes by. She is continually asking me a thousand frivolous questions about every customer that comes in and goes out; and all the while that I am entering any thing in my day-book, she is lolling over the counter, and staring at it, as if I was only scribbling or drawing figures for her amusement. Sometimes, indeed, she will take a needle; but as she always works at the door, or in the middle of the shop, she has so many interruptions, that she is longer hemming a towel, or darning a stocking, than I am in breaking forty loaves of sugar, and making it up into pounds.

In the afternoons I am sure likewise to have her company, except she is called upon by some of her acquaintance : and then, as we let out all the upper part of our house, and have only a little room backwards for ourselves, they either keep such a chattering, or else are calling out every moment to me, that I cannot mind my business for them.

My wife, I am sure, might do all the little matters our family requires ; and I could wish that she would employ herself in them ; but, instead of that, we have a girl to do the work, and look after a little boy about two years old, which, I may fairly say, is the mother's own child. The brat must be humoured in every thing : he is therefore suffered constantly to play in the shop, pull all the goods about, and clamber up the shelves to get at the plums and sugar. I dare not correct him ; because, if I did, I should have wife and maid both upon me at once. As to the latter, she is as lazy and sluttish as her mistress ; and because she complains she has too much work, we can scarcely get her to do any thing at all : nay, what is worse than that, I am afraid she is hardly honest ; and as she is intrusted to buy-in all our provisions, the jade, I am sure, makes a market-penny out of every article.

But to return to my deary.—The evenings are the only time, when it is fine weather, that I am left to myself ; for then she generally takes the child out to give it milk in the Park. When she comes home again, she is so fatigued with walking, that she cannot stir from her chair : and it is an hour, after shop is shut, before I can get a bit of supper, while the maid is taken up in undressing and putting the child to bed.

But you will pity me much more, when I tell you the manner in which we generally pass our Sundays. In the morning she is commonly too ill to dress herself to go to church ; she therefore never gets up till noon ; and, what is still more vexatious, keeps me in bed with her, when I ought to be busily engaged in better employment. It is well if she can get her things on by dinner-time ; and, when that is over, I am sure to be dragged out by her either to Georgia, or Hornsey Wood, or the White Con-

duit House.   Yet even these near excursions are so very
fatiguing to her, that, besides what it costs me in tea and
hot rolls, and sillabubs, and cakes for the boy, I am frequently forced to take a hackney-coach, or drive them out
in a one-horse chair.   At other times, as my wife is rather
of the fattest, and a very poor walker, besides bearing her
whole weight upon my arm, I am obliged to carry the
child myself.

Thus, Sir, does she constantly drawl out her time, without either profit or satisfaction; and, while I see my
neighbours' wives helping in the shop, and almost earning
as much as their husbands, I have the mortification to find
that mine is nothing but a dead weight upon me.   In
short, I do not know any greater misfortune can happen
to a plain hard-working tradesman, as I am, than to be
joined to such a woman, who is rather a clog than a help-
mate to him.

I am, Sir,

Your humble servant,

ZACHARY TREACLE.[s]

N°. 16.   SATURDAY, JULY 29, 1758.

I PAID a visit yesterday to my old friend Ned Drugget,
at his country-lodgings.   Ned began trade with a very
small fortune; he took a small house in an obscure street,
and for some years dealt only in remnants.   Knowing that
light gains make a heavy purse, he was content with moderate profit: having observed or heard the effects of civility, he bowed down to the counter-edge at the entrance
and departure of every customer, listened without impatience to the objections of the ignorant, and refused without resentment the offers of the penurious.   His only recreation was to stand at his own door and look into the

[s] An unknown correspondent.

street.   His dinner was sent him from a neighbouring alehouse, and he opened and shut the shop at a certain hour
with his own hands.

His reputation soon extended from one end of the street
to the other; and Mr. Drugget's exemplary conduct was
recommended by every master to his apprentice, and by
every father to his son.   Ned was not only considered as
a thriving trader, but as a man of elegance and politeness,
for he was remarkably neat in his dress, and would wear
his coat threadbare without spotting it; his hat was always brushed, his shoes glossy, his wig nicely curled, and
his stockings without a wrinkle.   With such qualifications
it was not very difficult for him to gain the heart of Miss
Comfit, the only daughter of Mr. Comfit the confectioner.

Ned is one of those whose happiness marriage has increased.   His wife had the same disposition with himself;
and his method of life was very little changed, except that
he dismissed the lodgers from the first floor, and took the
whole house into his own hands.

He had already, by his parsimony, accumulated a considerable sum, to which the fortune of his wife was now
added.   From this time he began to grasp at greater acquisitions, and was always ready, with money in his hand,
to pick up the refuse of a sale, or to buy the stock of a
trader who retired from business.   He soon added his
parlour to his shop, and was obliged a few months afterwards to hire a warehouse.

He had now a shop splendidly and copiously furnished
with every thing that time had injured, or fashion had degraded, with fragments of tissues, odd yards of brocade,
vast bales of faded silk, and innumerable boxes of anti-
quated ribbons.   His shop was soon celebrated through
all quarters of the town, and frequented by every form of
ostentatious poverty.   Every maid, whose misfortune it
was to be taller than her lady, matched her gown at Mr.
Drugget's; and many a maiden, who had passed a winter
with her aunt in London, dazzled the rusticks, at her return, with cheap finery which Drugget had supplied.   His

shop was often visited in a morning by ladies who left their coaches in the next street, and crept through the alley in linen gowns. Drugget knows the rank of his customers by their bashfulness; and, when he finds them unwilling to be seen, invites them up stairs, or retires with them to the back window.

I rejoiced at the increasing prosperity of my friend, and imagined that, as he grew rich, he was growing happy. His mind has partaken the enlargement of his fortune. When I stepped in for the first five years, I was welcomed only with a shake of the hand; in the next period of his life, he beckoned across the way for a pot of beer; but for six years past, he invites me to dinner; and, if he bespeaks me the day before, never fails to regale me with a fillet of veal.

His riches neither made him uncivil nor negligent; he rose at the same hour, attended with the same assiduity, and bowed with the same gentleness. But for some years he has been much inclined to talk of the fatigues of business, and the confinement of a shop, and to wish that he had been so happy as to have renewed his uncle's lease of a farm, that he might have lived without noise and hurry, in a pure air, in the artless society of honest villagers, and the contemplation of the works of nature.

I soon discovered the cause of my friend's philosophy. He thought himself grown rich enough to have a lodging in the country, like the mercers on Ludgate-hill, and was resolved to enjoy himself in the decline of life. This was a revolution not to be made suddenly. He talked three years of the pleasures of the country, but passed every night over his own shop. But at last he resolved to be happy, and hired a lodging in the country, that he may steal some hours in the week from business; for, says he, *when a man advances in life, he loves to entertain himself sometimes with his own thoughts.*

I was invited to this seat of quiet and contemplation, among those whom Mr. Drugget considers as his most reputable friends, and desires to make the first witnesses of his elevation to the highest dignities of a shopkeeper. I found him at Islington, in a room which overlooked the high road, amusing himself with looking through the window, which the clouds of dust would not suffer him to open. He embraced me, told me I was welcome into the country, and asked me if I did not feel myself refreshed. He then desired that dinner might be hastened, for fresh air always sharpened his appetite, and ordered me a toast and a glass of wine after my walk. He told me much of the pleasures he found in retirement, and wondered what had kept him so long out of the country. After dinner company came in, and Mr. Drugget again repeated the praises of the country, recommended the pleasures of meditation, and told them that he had been all the morning. at the window, counting the carriages as they passed before him.

N°. 17.   SATURDAY, AUGUST 5, 1758.

Surge tandem Carnifes [h].   ~~MECCALLED AUGUSTUS.~~

THE rainy weather, which has continued the last month, is said to have given great disturbance to the inspectors of barometers. The oraculous glasses have deceived their votaries; shower has succeeded shower, though they predicted sunshine and dry skies ; and, by fatal confidence in these fallacious promises, many coats have lost their gloss, and many curls been moistened to flaccidity.

This is one of the distresses to which mortals subject themselves by the pride of speculation. I had no part in this learned disappointment, who am content to credit my senses, and to believe that rain will fall when the air blackens, and that the weather will be dry when the sun is bright. My caution, indeed, does not always preserve me

[h] Dr. Johnson gave this, among other mottos, to Mrs Piozzi. They will be inserted in this Edition in their proper places, and indicated by an asterisk. See Mrs Piozzi's Anecdotes, and Chalmers' British Essayists, vol. 33.

from a shower. To be wet may happen to the genuine
Idler; but to be wet in opposition to theory, can befall
only the Idler that pretends to be busy. ' Of those that
spin out life in trifles and die without a memorial, many
flatter themselves with high opinions of their own importance, and imagine that they are every day adding some
improvement to human life. To be idle and to be poor
have always been reproaches, and therefore every man endeavours, with his utmost care, to hide his poverty from
others, and his idleness from himself.

Among those whom I never could persuade to rank
themselves with Idlers, and who speak with indignation of
my morning sleeps and nocturnal rambles; one passes the
day in catching spiders, that he may count their eyes with
a microscope; another erects his head, and exhibits the
dust of a marigold separated from the flower with a dexterity worthy of Leuwenhœck himself. Some turn the
wheel of electricity; some suspend rings to a load-stone,
and find that what they did yesterday they can do again
to-day. Some register the changes of the wind, and die
fully convinced that the wind is changeable.

There are men yet more profound, who have heard that
two colourless liquors may produce a colour by union,
and that two cold bodies will grow hot if they are mingled;
they mingle them, and produce the effect expected, say it
is strange, and mingle them again.

The Idlers that sport only with inanimate nature may
claim some indulgence; if they are useless, they are still
innocent: but there are others, whom I know not how to
mention without more emotion than my love of quiet willingly admits. Among the inferior professors of medical
knowledge, is a race of wretches, whose lives are only
varied by varieties of cruelty; whose favourite amusement is to nail dogs to tables and open them alive; to try
how long life may be continued in various degrees of mutilation, or with the excision or laceration of the vital
parts; to examine whether burning irons are felt more
acutely by the bone or tendon; and whether the more

lasting agonies are produced by poison forced into the mouth, or injected into the veins.

It is not without reluctance that I offend the sensibility of the tender mind with images like these. If such cruelties were not practised, it were to be desired that they should not be conceived; but, since they are published every day with ostentation, let me be allowed once to mention them, since I mention them with abhorrence.

Mead has invidiously remarked of Woodward, that he gathered shells and stones, and would pass for a philosopher. With pretensions much less reasonable, the anatomical novice tears out the living bowels of an animal, and styles himself physician, prepares himself by familiar cruelty for that profession which he is to exercise upon the tender and the helpless, upon feeble bodies and broken minds, and by which he has opportunities to extend his arts of torture, and continue those experiments upon infancy and age, which he has hitherto tried upon cats and dogs.

What is alleged in defence of these hateful practices, every one knows; but the truth is, that by knives, fire, and poison, knowledge is not always sought, and is very seldom attained. The experiments that have been tried, are tried again; he that burned an animal with irons yesterday, will be willing to amuse himself with burning another to-morrow. I know not, that by living dissections any discovery has been made by which a single malady is more easily cured. And if the knowledge of physiology has been somewhat increased, he surely buys knowledge dear, who learns the use of the lacteals at the expense of his humanity. It is time that universal resentment should arise against these horrid operations, which tend to harden the heart, extinguish those sensations which give man confidence in man, and make the physician more dreadful than the gout or stone.

Nº. 18. SATURDAY, AUGUST 12, 1758.

TO THE IDLER.

SIR,

IT commonly happens to him who endeavours to obtain distinction by ridicule or censure, that he teaches others to practise his own arts against himself; and that, after a short enjoyment of the applause paid to his sagacity, or of the mirth excited by his wit, he is doomed to suffer the same severities of scrutiny, to hear inquiry detecting his faults, and exaggeration sporting with his failings.

The natural discontent of inferiority will seldom fail to operate in some degree of malice against him who professes to superintend the conduct of others, especially if he seats himself uncalled in the chair of judicature, and exercises authority by his own commission.

You cannot, therefore, wonder that your observations on human folly, if they produce laughter at one time, awaken criticism at another; and that among the numbers whom you have taught to scoff at the retirement of Drugget, there is one who offers his apology.

The mistake of your old friend is by no means peculiar. The publick pleasures of far the greater part of mankind are counterfeit. Very few carry their philosophy to places of diversion, or are very careful to analyze their enjoyments. The general condition of life is so full of misery, that we are glad to catch delight without inquiring whence it comes, or by what power it is bestowed.

The mind is seldom quickened to very vigorous operations but by pain, or the dread of pain. We do not disturb ourselves with the detection of fallacies which do us no harm, nor willingly decline a pleasing effect to investigate its cause. He that is happy, by whatever means, desires nothing but the continuance of happiness, and is no more solicitous to distribute his sensations into their proper species, than the common gazer on the beauties of the spring to separate light into its original rays.

Pleasure is therefore seldom such as it appears to others, nor often such as we represent it to ourselves. Of the ladies that sparkle at a musical performance, a very small number has any quick sensibility of harmonious sounds. But every one that goes has her pleasure. She has the pleasure of wearing fine clothes, and of showing them, of outshining those whom she suspects to envy her ; she has the pleasure of appearing among other ladies in a place whither the race of meaner mortals seldom intrudes, and of reflecting that, in the conversations of the next morning, her name will be mentioned among those that sat in the first row ; she has the pleasure of returning courtesies, or refusing to return them, of receiving compliments with civility, or rejecting them with disdain. She has the pleasure of meeting some of her acquaintance, of guessing why the rest are absent, and of telling them that she saw the opera, on pretence of inquiring why they would miss it. She has the pleasure of being supposed to be pleased with a refined amusement, and of hoping to be numbered among the votaresses of harmony. She has the pleasure of escaping for two hours the superiority of a sister, or the control of a husband ; and from all these pleasures she concludes, that heavenly musick is the balm of life.

All assemblies of gaiety are brought together by motives of the same kind. The theatre is not filled with those that know or regard the skill of the actor, nor the ball-room by those who dance, or attend to the dancers. To all places of general resort, where the standard of pleasure is erected, we run with equal eagerness, or appearance of eagerness, for very different reasons. One goes that he may say he has been there, another because he never misses. This man goes to try what he can find, and that to discover what others find. Whatever diversion is costly will be frequented by those who desire to be thought rich; and whatever has, by any accident, become fashionable, easily continues its reputation, because every one is ashamed of not partaking it.

To every place of entertainment we go with expectation and desire of being pleased; we meet others who are brought by the same motives; no one will be the first to own the disappointment; one face reflects the smile of another, till each believes the rest delighted, and endeavours to catch and transmit the circulating rapture. In time all are deceived by the cheat to which all contribute. The fiction of happiness is propagated by every tongue, and confirmed by every look, till at last all profess the joy which they do not feel, consent to yield to the general delusion; and when the voluntary dream is at an end, lament that bliss is of so short a duration.

If Drugget pretended to pleasures of which he had no perception, or boasted of one amusement where he was indulging another, what did he which is not done by all those who read his story? of whom some pretend delight in conversation, only because they dare not be alone; some praise the quiet of solitude, because they are envious of sense, and impatient of folly; and some gratify their pride, by writing characters which expose the vanity of life.

I am, Sir,

Your humble servant.

Nᵒ. 19. SATURDAY, AUGUST 19, 1758.

SOME of those ancient sages that have exercised their abilities in the inquiry after the *supreme good*, have been of opinion, that the highest degree of earthly happiness is quiet; a calm repose both of mind and body, undisturbed by the sight of folly or the noise of business, the tumults of publick commotion, or the agitations of private interest: a state in which the mind has no other employment, but to observe and regulate her own motions, to trace thought from thought, combine one image with another, raise systems of science, and form theories of virtue.

To the scheme of these solitary speculatists, it has been justly objected, that if they are happy, they are happy only by being useless. That mankind is one vast republick, where every individual receives many benefits from the labours of others, which, by labouring in his turn for others, he is obliged to repay ; and that where the united efforts of all are not able to exempt all from misery, none have a right to withdraw from their task of vigilance, or to be indulged in idle wisdom or solitary pleasures.

It is common for controvertists, in the heat of disputation, to add one position to another till they reach the extremities of knowledge, where truth and falsehood lose their distinction. Their admirers follow them to the brink of absurdity, and then start back from each side towards the middle point. So it has happened in this great disquisition. Many perceive alike the force of the contrary arguments, find quiet shameful, and business dangerous, and therefore pass their lives between them, in bustle without business, and negligence without quiet.

Among the principal names of this moderate set is that great philosopher Jack Whirler, whose business keeps him in perpetual motion, and whose motion always eludes his business ; who is always to do what he never does, who cannot stand still because he is wanted in another place, and who is wanted in many places because he stays in none.

Jack has more business than he can conveniently transact in one house; he has therefore one habitation near Bow-church, and another about a mile distant. By this ingenious distribution of himself between two houses, Jack has contrived to be found at neither. Jack's trade is extensive, and he has many dealers ; his conversation is sprightly, and he has many companions ; his disposition is kind, and he has many friends. Jack neither forbears pleasure for business, nor omits business for pleasure, but is equally invisible to his friends and his customers ; to him that comes with an invitation to a club, and to him that waits to settle an account.

When you call at his house, his clerk tells you that Mr. Whirler has just stept out, but will be at home exactly at two; you wait at a coffee-house till two, and then find that he has been at home, and is gone out again, but left word that he should be at the Half-moon tavern at seven, where he hopes to meet you. At seven you go to the tavern. At eight in comes Mr. Whirler to tell you that he is glad to see you, and only begs leave to run for a few minutes to a gentleman that lives near the Exchange, from whom he will return before supper can be ready. Away he runs to the Exchange, to tell those who are waiting for him that he must beg them to defer the business till to-morrow, because his time is come at the Half-moon.

Jack's cheerfulness and civility rank him among those whose presence never gives pain, and whom all receive with fondness and caresses. He calls often on his friends, to tell them that he will come again to-morrow; on the morrow he comes again, to tell them how an unexpected summons hurries him away.—When he enters a house, his first declaration is, that he cannot sit down; and so short are his visits, that he seldom appears to have come for any other reason, but to say, He must go.

The dogs of Egypt, when thirst brings them to the Nile, are said to run as they drink for fear of the crocodiles. Jack Whirler always dines at full speed. He enters, finds the family at table, sits familiarly down, and fills his plate; but while the first morsel is in his mouth, hears the clock strike, and rises; then goes to another house, sits down again, recollects another engagement, has only time to taste the soup, makes a short excuse to the company, and continues through another street his desultory dinner.

But, overwhelmed as he is with business, his chief desire is to have still more. Every new proposal takes possession of his thoughts; he soon balances probabilities, engages in the project, brings it almost to completion, and then forsakes it for another, which he catches with the same alacrity, urges with the same vehemence, and abandons with the same coldness.

Every man may be observed to have a certain strain of lamentation, some peculiar theme of complaint, on which he dwells in his moments of dejection. Jack's topick of sorrow is the want of time. Many an excellent design languishes in empty theory for want of time. For the omission of any civilities, want of time is his plea to others; for the neglect of any affairs, want of time is his excuse to himself. That he wants time, he sincerely believes; for he once pined away many months with a lingering distemper, for want of time to attend to his health.

Thus Jack Whirler lives in perpetual fatigue without proportionate advantage, because he does not consider that no man can see all with his own eyes, or do all with his own hands; that whoever is engaged in multiplicity of business, must transact much by substitution, and leave something to hazard; and that he who attempts to do all, will waste his life in doing little.

N°. 20. SATURDAY, AUGUST 26, 1758.

THERE is no crime more infamous than the violation of truth. It is apparent that men can be social beings no longer than they believe each other. When speech is employed only as the vehicle of falsehood, every man must disunite himself from others, inhabit his own cave, and seek prey only for himself.

Yet the law of truth, thus sacred and necessary, is broken without punishment, without censure, in compliance with inveterate prejudice and prevailing passions. Men are willing to credit what they wish, and encourage rather those who gratify them with pleasure, than those that instruct them with fidelity.

For this reason every historian discovers his country; and it is impossible to read the different accounts of any great event, without a wish that truth had more power over partiality.

Amidst the joy of my countrymen for the acquisition of Louisbourg, I could not forbear to consider how differently this revolution of American power is not only now mentioned by the contending nations, but will be represented by the writers of another century.

The English historian will imagine himself barely doing justice to English virtue, when he relates the capture of Louisbourg in the following manner:

" The English had hitherto seen, with great indignation, their attempts baffled and their force defied by an enemy, whom they considered themselves as entitled to conquer by the right of prescription, and whom many ages of hereditary superiority had taught them to despise. Their fleets were more numerous, and their seamen braver, than those of France; yet they only floated useless on the ocean, and the French derided them from their ports. Misfortunes, as is usual, produced discontent; the people murmured at the ministers, and the ministers censured the commanders.

" In the summer of this year, the English began to find their success answerable to their cause. A fleet and an army were sent to America to dislodge the enemies from the settlements which they had so perfidiously made, and so insolently maintained, and to repress that power which was growing more every day by the association of the Indians, with whom these degenerate Europeans intermarried, and whom they secured to their party by presents and promises.

" In the beginning of June the ships of war and vessels containing the land-forces appeared before Louisbourg, a place so secured by nature that art was almost superfluous, and yet fortified by art as if nature had left it open. The French boasted that it was impregnable, and spoke with scorn of all attempts that could be made against it. The garrison was numerous, the stores equal to the longest siege, and their engineers and commanders high in reputation. The mouth of the harbour was so narrow, that three ships within might easily defend it against all attacks from the sea. The French had, with that caution which cowards borrow from fear, and attribute to policy, eluded our fleets, and sent into that port five great ships and six smaller, of which they sunk four in the mouth of the passage, having raised batteries and posted troops at all the places where they thought it possible to make a descent. The English, however, had more to dread from the roughness of the sea, than from the skill or bravery of the defendants. Some days passed before the surges, which rise very high round that island, would suffer them to land. At last their impatience could be restrained no longer; they got possession of the shore with little loss by the sea, and with less by the enemy. In a few days the artillery was landed, the batteries were raised, and the French had no other hope than to escape from one post to another. A shot from the batteries fired the powder in one of their largest ships, the flame spread to the two next, and all three were destroyed; the English admiral sent his boats against the two large ships yet remaining, took them without resistance, and terrified the garrison to an immediate capitulation."

Let us now oppose to this English narrative the relation which will be produced, about the same time, by the writer of the age of Louis XV.

" About this time the English admitted to the conduct of affairs a man who undertook to save from destruction that ferocious and turbulent people, who, from the mean insolence of wealthy traders, and the lawless confidence of successful robbers, were now sunk in despair and stupified with horrour. He called in the ships which had been dispersed over the ocean to guard their merchants, and sent a fleet and an army, in which almost the whole strength of England was comprised, to secure their possessions in America, which were endangered alike by the French arms and the French virtue. We had taken the English fortresses by force, and gained the Indian nations by humanity. The English, wherever they come, are sure to have the natives for their enemies; for the only motive of their settlements is avarice, and the only consequence of their success is oppression. In this war they acted like other barbarians; and, with a degree of outrageous cruelty, which the gentleness of our manners scarcely suffers us to conceive, offered rewards by open proclamation to those who should bring-in the scalps of Indian women and children. A trader always makes war with the cruelty of a pirate.

·" They had long looked with envy and with terrour upon the influence which the French exerted over all the northern regions of America by the possession of Louisbourg, a place naturally strong, and new-fortified with some slight outworks. They hoped to surprise the garrison unprovided; but that sluggishness, which always defeats their malice, gave us time to send supplies, and to station ships for the defence of the harbour. They came before Louisbourg in June, and were for some time in doubt whether they should land. But the commanders, who had lately seen an admiral shot for not having done what he had not power to do, durst not leave the place unassaulted. An Englishman has no ardour for honour, nor zeal for duty; he neither values glory nor loves his king, but balances one danger with another, and will fight rather than be hanged. They therefore landed, but with great loss their engineers had, in the last war with the French, learned something of the military science, and made their approaches with sufficient skill; but all their efforts had been without effect, had not a ball unfortunately fallen into the powder of one of our ships, which communicated the fire to the rest, and, by opening the passage of the harbour, obliged the garrison to capitulate. Thus was Louisbourg lost, and our troops marched out with the admiration of their enemies, who durst hardly think themselves masters of the place."

N°. 21. SATURDAY, SEPTEMBER 2, 1758.

TO THE IDLER.

DEAR MR. IDLER,

THERE is a species of misery, or of disease, for which our language is commonly supposed to be without a name, but which I think is emphatically enough denominated *listlessness,* and which is commonly termed a want of something to do.

Of the unhappiness of this state I do not expect all your readers to have an adequate idea. Many are overburdened with business, and can imagine no comfort but in rest; many have minds so placid, as willingly to indulge a voluntary lethargy; or so narrow, as easily to be filled to their utmost capacity. By these I shall not be understood, and therefore cannot be pitied. Those only will sympathize with my complaint, whose imagination is active, and resolution weak, whose desires are ardent, and whose choice is delicate; who cannot satisfy themselves with standing still, and yet cannot find a motive to direct their course.

I was the second son of a gentleman, whose estate was barely sufficient to support himself and his heir in the dignity of killing game. He therefore made use of the interest which the alliances of his family afforded him, to procure me a post in the army. I passed some years in the most contemptible of all human stations, that of a soldier in time of peace. I wandered with the regiment as the quarters were changed, without opportunity for business, taste for knowledge, or money for pleasure. Wherever I came, I was for some time a stranger without curiosity, and afterwards an acquaintance without friendship. Having nothing to hope in these places of fortuitous residence, I resigned my conduct to chance; I had no intention to offend, I had no ambition to delight.

I suppose every man is shocked when he hears how frequently soldiers are wishing for war. The wish is not always sincere; the greater part are content with sleep and lace, and counterfeit an ardour which they do not feel; but those who desire it most are neither prompted by malevolence nor patriotism; they neither pant for laurels, nor delight in blood; but long to be delivered from the tyranny of idleness, and restored to the dignity of active beings.

I never imagined myself to have more courage than other men, yet was often involuntarily wishing for a war, but of a war, at that time, I had no prospect; and being enabled, by the death of an uncle, to live without my pay, I quitted the army, and resolved to regulate my own motions.

I was pleased, for a while, with the novelty of independence, and imagined that I had now found what every man desires. My time was in my own power, and my habitation was wherever my choice should fix it. I amused myself for two years in passing from place to place, and comparing one convenience with another; but being at last ashamed of inquiry, and weary of uncertainty, I purchased a house, and established my family.

I now expected to begin to be happy, and was happy for a short time with that expectation. But I soon perceived my spirits to subside, and my imagination to grow dark. The gloom thickened every day round me. I wondered by what malignant power my peace was blasted, till I discovered at last that I had nothing to do.

Time, with all its celerity, moves slowly to him whose whole employment is to watch its flight. I am forced upon a thousand shifts to enable me to endure the tediousness of the day. I rise when I can sleep no longer, and take my morning-walk; I see what I have seen before, and return. I sit down, and persuade myself that I sit down to think; find it impossible to think without a subject, rise up to inquire after news, and endeavour to kindle in myself an artificial impatience for intelligence of events, which will never extend any consequence to me, but that, a few minutes, they abstract me from myself.

When I have heard any thing that may gratify curiosity, I am busied for a while in running to relate it. I hasten from one place of concourse to another, delighted with my own importance, and proud to think that I am doing something, though I know that another hour would spare my labour.

I had once a round of visits, which I paid very regularly; but I have now tired most of my friends. When I have sat down I forget to rise, and have more than once overheard one asking another, when I would be gone. I perceive the company tired, I observe the mistress of the family whispering to her servants, I find orders given to put off business till to-morrow, I see the watches frequently inspected, and yet cannot withdraw to the vacuity of solitude, or venture myself in my own company.

Thus burdensome to myself and others, I form many schemes of employment which may make my life useful or agreeable, and exempt me from the ignominy of living by sufferance. This new course I have long designed, but have not yet begun. The present moment is never proper for the change, but there is always a time in view when all obstacles will be removed, and I shall surprise all that know me with a new distribution of my time. Twenty years have past since I have resolved a complete amendment, and twenty years have been lost in delays. Age is coming upon me; and I should look back with rage and despair upon the waste of life, but that I am now beginning in earnest to begin a reformation.

I am, Sir,

Your humble servant,

DICK LINGER.

N°. 22. SATURDAY, SEPTEMBER 16, 1758.

* Oh nomen dulce libertatis! Oh jus eximium nostræ civitatis! CICERO.

TO THE IDLER.

SIR,

As I was passing lately under one of the gates of this city, I was struck with horrour by a rueful cry, which summoned me *to remember the poor debtors.*

The wisdom and justice of the English laws are, by Englishmen at least, loudly celebrated: but scarcely the most zealous admirers of our institutions can think that law wise, which, when men are capable of work, obliges them to beg; or just, which exposes the liberty of one to the passions of another.

The prosperity of a people is proportionate to the number of hands and minds usefully employed. To the community, sedition is a fever, corruption is a gangrene, and idleness an atrophy. Whatever body, and whatever society, wastes more than it acquires, must gradually decay; and every being that continues to be fed, and ceases to labour, takes away something from the publick stock.

The confinement, therefore, of any man in the sloth and darkness of a prison, is a loss to the nation, and no gain to the creditor. For of the multitudes who are pining in those cells of misery, a very small part is suspected of any fraudulent act by which they retain what belongs to others. The rest are imprisoned by the wantonness of pride, the malignity of revenge, or the acrimony of disappointed expectation.

If those, who thus rigorously exercise the power which the law has put into their hands, be asked, why they continue to imprison those whom they know to be unable to pay them; one will answer, that his debtor once lived better than himself; another, that his wife looked above her neighbours, and his children went in silk clothes to the dancing-school; and another, that he pretended to be a joker and a wit. Some will reply, that if they were in debt, they should meet with the same treatment; some, that they owe no more than they can pay, and need therefore give no account of their actions. Some will confess their resolution, that their debtors shall rot in jail; and some will discover, that they hope, by cruelty, to wring the payment from their friends.

The end of all civil regulations is to secure private happiness from private malignity; to keep individuals from the power of one another; but this end is apparently neglected, when a man, irritated with loss, is allowed to be the judge of his own cause, and to assign the punishment of his own pain; when the distinction between guilt and happiness, between casualty and design, is intrusted to eyes blind with interest, to understandings depraved by resentment.

Since poverty is punished among us as a crime, it ought at least to be treated with the same lenity as other crimes; the offender ought not to languish at the will of him whom he has offended, but to be allowed some appeal to the justice of his country. There can be no reason why any debtor should be imprisoned, but that he may be compelled to payment; and a term should therefore be fixed, in which the creditor should exhibit his accusation of concealed property. If such property can be discovered, let it be given to the creditor; if the charge is not offered, or cannot be proved, let the prisoner be dismissed.

Those who made the laws have apparently supposed, that every deficiency of payment is the crime of the debtor. But the truth is, that the creditor always shares the act, and often more than shares the guilt, of improper trust. It seldom happens that any man imprisons another but for debts which he suffered to be contracted in hope of advantage to himself, and for bargains in which he proportioned his profit to his own opinion of the hazard; and there is no reason why one should punish the other for a contract in which both concurred.

Many of the inhabitants of prisons may justly complain

of harder treatment. He that once owes more than he can pay, is often obliged to bribe his creditor to patience, by increasing his debt. Worse and worse commodities, at a higher and higher price, are forced upon him; he is impoverished by compulsive traffick, and at last overwhelmed, in the common receptacles of misery, by debts, which, without his own consent, were accumulated on his head. To the relief of this distress, no other objection can be made, but that by an easy dissolution of debts fraud will be left without punishment, and imprudence without awe; and that when insolvency should be no longer punishable, credit will cease.

The motive to credit is the hope of advantage. Commerce can never be at a stop, while one man wants what another can supply; and credit will never be denied, while it is likely to be repaid with profit. He that trusts one whom he designs to sue, is criminal by the act of trust: the cessation of such insidious traffick is to be desired, and no reason can be given why a change of the law should impair any other.

We see nation trade with nation, where no payment can be compelled. Mutual convenience produces mutual confidence; and the merchants continue to satisfy the demands of each other, though they have nothing to dread but the loss of trade.

It is vain to continue an institution, which experience shows to be ineffectual. We have now imprisoned one generation of debtors after another, but we do not find that their numbers lessen. We have now learned that rashness and imprudence will not be deterred from taking credit; let us try whether fraud and avarice may be more easily restrained from giving it[1].

I am, Sir, &c.

---

[1] This number was substituted, for some reason not ascertained, for the keenly satirical original, which is reprinted at the end of this volume.

The observations of the present paper are such as would naturally suggest themselves to an honest and benevolent mind like Johnson's; but their political correctness may reasonably be questioned. An attempt has been made, since

N°. 23. SATURDAY, SEPTEMBER 23, 1758.

LIFE has no pleasure higher or nobler than that of friendship. It is painful to consider, that this sublime enjoyment may be impaired or destroyed by innumerable causes, and that there is no human possession of which the duration is less certain.

Many have talked, in very exalted language, of the perpetuity of friendship, of invincible constancy, and unalienable kindness; and some examples have been seen of men who have continued faithful to their earliest choice, and whose affection has predominated over changes of fortune, and contrariety of opinion.

But these instances are memorable, because they are rare. The friendship which is to be practised or expected by common mortals, must take its rise from mutual pleasure, and must end when the power ceases of delighting each other.

Many accidents therefore may happen, by which the ardour of kindness will be abated, without criminal baseness or contemptible inconstancy on either part. To give pleasure is not always in our power; and little does he know himself, who believes that he can be always able to receive it.

Those who would gladly pass their days together may be separated by the different course of their affairs; and friendship, like love, is destroyed by long absence, though it may be increased by short intermissions. What we have missed long enough to want it, we value more when it is regained; but that which has been lost till it is forgotten, will be found at last with little gladness, and with

his day, to provide a humane protection for the unfortunate debtor. But has it not, at the same time, exposed the confiding tradesman to deception and to consequent ruin, by destroying all adequate punishment, and therefore removing every check upon vice and prodigality? In a *Dictionnaire des Gens du Monde*, insolvency has been, not unaptly, defined, a mode of getting rich by infallible rules! See Idler 38, and Note.

still less if a substitute has supplied the place. A man deprived of the companion to whom he used to open his bosom, and with whom he shared.the hours of leisure and merriment, feels the day at first hanging heavy on him; his difficulties oppress, and his doubts distract him; he sees time come and go without his wonted gratification, and all is sadness within, and solitude about him. But this uneasiness never lasts long; necessity produces expedients, new amusements are discovered, and new conversation is admitted.

No expectation is more frequently disappointed, than that which naturally arises in the mind from the prospect of meeting an old friend after long separation. We expect the attraction to be revived, and the coalition to be renewed; no man considers how much alteration time has made in himself, and very few inquire what effect it has had upon others. The first hour convinces them that the pleasure, which they had formerly enjoyed, is for ever at an end; different scenes have made different impressions; the opinions of both are changed; and that similitude of manners and sentiment is lost, which confirmed them both in the approbation of themselves.

Friendship is often destroyed by opposition of interest, not only by the ponderous and visible interest which the desire of wealth and greatness forms and maintains, but by a thousand secret and slight competitions, scarcely known to the mind upon which they operate. There is scarcely any man without some favourite trifle which he values above greater attainments, some desire of petty praise which he cannot patiently suffer to be frustrated. This minute ambition is sometimes crossed before it is known, and sometimes defeated by wanton petulance; but such attacks are seldom made without the loss of friendship; for whoever has once found the vulnerable part will always be feared, and the resentment will burn on in secret, of which shame hinders the discovery.

This, however, is a slow malignity, which a wise man will obviate as inconsistent with quiet, and a good man will repress as contrary to virtue; but human happiness is sometimes violated by some more sudden strokes.

A dispute begun in jest upon a subject which, a moment before, was on both parts regarded with careless indifference, is continued by the desire of conquest, till vanity kindles into rage, and opposition rankles into enmity. Against this hasty mischief, I know not what security can be obtained: men will be sometimes surprised into quarrels; and though they might both hasten to reconciliation, as soon as their tumult had subsided, yet two minds will seldom be found together, which can at once subdue their discontent, or immediately enjoy the sweets of peace, without remembering the wounds of the conflict.

Friendship has other enemies. Suspicion is always hardening the cautious, and disgust repelling the delicate. Very slender differences will sometimes part those whom long reciprocation of civility or beneficence has united. Lonelove and Ranger retired into the country to enjoy the company of each other, and returned in six weeks cold and petulant; Ranger's pleasure was to walk in the fields, and Lonelove's to sit in a bower; each had complied with the other in his turn, and each was angry that compliance had been exacted.

The most fatal disease of friendship is gradual decay, or dislike hourly increased by causes too slender for complaint, and too numerous for removal.—Those who are angry may be reconciled; those who have been injured may receive a recompense: but when the desire of pleasing and willingness to be pleased is silently diminished, the renovation of friendship is hopeless; as, when the vital powers sink into languor, there is no longer any use of the physician.

Nᵒ. 24. SATURDAY, SEPTEMBER 30, 1758.

WHEN man sees one of the inferior creatures perched upon a tree, or basking in the sunshine, without any apparent endeavour or pursuit, he often asks himself, or his companion, *On what that animal can be supposed to be thinking?*

Of this question, since neither bird nor beast can answer it, we must be content to live without the resolution. We know not how much the brutes recollect of the past, or anticipate of the future; what power they have of comparing and preferring; or whether their faculties may not rest in motionless indifference, till they are moved by the presence of their proper object, or stimulated to act by corporal sensations.

I am the less inclined to these superfluous inquiries, because I have always been able to find sufficient matter for curiosity in my own species. It is useless to go far in quest of that which may be found at home; a very narrow circle of observation will supply a sufficient number of men and women, who might be asked, with equal propriety, *On what they can be thinking?*

It is reasonable to believe, that thought, like every thing else, has its causes and effects; that it must proceed from something known, done, or suffered; and must produce some action or event. Yet how great is the number of those in whose minds no source of thought has ever been opened, in whose life no consequence of thought is ever discovered; who have learned nothing upon which they can reflect; who have neither seen nor felt any thing which could leave its traces on the memory; who neither foresee nor desire any change in their condition, and have therefore neither fear, hope, nor design, and yet are supposed to be thinking beings.

To every act a subject is required. He that thinks must think upon something. But tell me, ye that pierce deepest into nature, ye that take the widest surveys of life, inform me, kind shades of Malbranche and of Locke, what that something can be, which excites and continues thought in maiden aunts with small fortunes; in younger brothers that live upon annuities; in traders retired from business; in soldiers absent from their regiments; or in widows that have no children?

Life is commonly considered as either active or contemplative; but surely this division, how long soever it has been received, is inadequate and fallacious. There are mortals whose life is certainly not active, for they do neither good nor evil; and whose life cannot be properly called contemplative, for they never attend either to the conduct of men, or the works of nature, but rise in the morning, look round them till night in careless stupidity, go to bed and sleep, and rise again in the morning.

It has been lately a celebrated question in the schools of philosophy, *Whether the soul always thinks?* Some have defined the soul to be the *power of thinking;* concluded that its essence consists in act; that, if it should cease to act, it would cease to be; and that cessation of thought is but another name for extinction of mind. This argument is subtle, but not conclusive; because it supposes what cannot be proved, that the nature of mind is properly defined. Others affect to disdain subtilty, when subtilty will not serve their purpose, and appeal to daily experience. We spend many hours, they say, in sleep, without the least remembrance of any thoughts which then passed in our minds; and since we can only by our own consciousness be sure that we think, why should we imagine that we have had thought of which no consciousness remains?

This argument, which appeals to experience, may from experience be confuted. We every day do something which we forget when it is done, and know to have been done only by consequence. The waking hours are not denied to have been passed in thought; yet he that shall endeavour to recollect on one day the ideas of the former, will only turn the eye of reflection upon vacancy; he will find that the greater part is irrevocably vanished, and wonder how the moments could come and go, and leave so little behind them.

To discover only that the arguments on both sides are defective, and to throw back the tenet into its former uncertainty, is the sport of wanton or malevolent skepticism, delighting to see the sons of philosophy at work upon a task which never can be decided. I shall suggest an argument hitherto overlooked, which may perhaps determine the controversy.

If it be impossible to think without materials, there must necessarily be minds that do not always think ; and whence shall we furnish materials for the meditation of the glutton between his meals, of the sportsman in a rainy month, of the annuitant between the days of quarterly payment, of the politician when the mails are detained by contrary winds?

But how frequent soever may be the examples of existence without thought, it is certainly a state not much to be desired. He that lives in torpid insensibility, wants nothing of a carcass but putrefaction. It is the part of every inhabitant of the earth to partake the pains and pleasures of his fellow-beings ; and, as in a road through a country desert and uniform, the traveller languishes for want of amusement, so the passage of life will be tedious and irksome to him who does not beguile it by diversified ideas.

N°. 25. SATURDAY, OCTOBER 7, 1758.

TO THE IDLER.

SIR,

I AM a very constant frequenter of the playhouse, a place to which I suppose the *Idler* not much a stranger, since he can have no where else so much entertainment with so little concurrence of his own endeavour. At all other assemblies, he that comes to receive delight, will be expected to give it; but in the theatre nothing is necessary to the amusement of two hours, but to sit down and be willing to be pleased.

The last week has offered two new actors to the town. The appearance and retirement of actors are the great events of the theatrical world; and their first performances fill the pit with conjecture and prognostication, as the first actions of a new monarch agitate nations with hope or fear.

What opinion I have formed of the future excellence of these candidates for dramatick glory, it is not necessary to declare. Their entrance gave me a higher and nobler pleasure than any borrowed character can afford. I saw the ranks of the theatre emulating each other in candour and humanity, and contending who should most effectually assist the struggles of endeavour, dissipate the blush of diffidence, and still the flutter of timidity.

This behaviour is such as becomes a people, too tender to repress those who wish to please, too generous to insult those who can make no resistance. A publick performer is so much in the power of spectators, that all unnecessary severity is restrained by that general law of humanity, which forbids us to be cruel where there is nothing to be feared.

In every new performer something must be pardoned. No man ean, by any force of resolution, secure to himself the full possession of his own powers under the eye of a large assembly. Variation of gesture, and flexion of voice, are to be obtained only by experience.

There is nothing for which such numbers think themselves qualified as for theatrical exhibition. Every human being has an action graceful to his own eye, a voice musical to his own ear, and a sensibility which nature forbids him to know that any other bosom can excel. An art in which such numbers fancy themselves excellent, and which the publick liberally rewards, will excite many competitors, and in many attempts there must be many miscarriages.

The care of the critick should be to distinguish errour from inability, faults of inexperience from defects of nature.   Action irregular and turbulent may be reclaimed; vociferation vehement and confused may be restrained and modulated; the stalk of the tyrant may become the gait of the man; the yell of inarticulate distress may be reduced to human lamentation.   All these faults should be for a time overlooked, and afterwards censured with gentleness and candour.   But if in an actor there appears an utter vacancy of meaning, a frigid equality, a stupid languor, a torpid apathy, the greatest kindness that can be shown him is a speedy sentence of expulsion.

I am, Sir, &c.

THE plea which my correspondent has offered for young actors, I am very far from wishing to invalidate.   I always considered those combinations which are sometimes formed in the playhouse, as acts of fraud or of cruelty; he that applauds him who does not deserve praise, is endeavouring to deceive the publick; he that hisses in malice or sport, is an oppressor and a robber.

But surely this laudable forbearance might be justly extended to young poets.   The art of the writer, like that of the player, is attained by slow degrees.   The power of distinguishing and discriminating comick characters, or of filling tragedy with poetical images, must be the gift of nature, which no instruction nor labour can supply; but the art of dramatick disposition, the contexture of the scenes, the opposition of characters, the involution of the plot, the expedients of suspension, and the stratagems of surprise, are to be learned by practice; and it is cruel to discourage a poet for ever, because he has not from genius what only experience can bestow.

Life is a stage.   Let me likewise solicit candour for the young actor on the stage of life.   They that enter into the world are too often treated with unreasonable rigour by those that were once as ignorant and heady as themselves; and distinction is not always made between the faults which require speedy and violent eradication, and those that will gradually drop away in the progression of life. Vicious solicitations of appetite, if not checked, will grow more importunate; and mean arts of profit or ambition will gather strength in the mind, if they are not early suppressed. But mistaken notions of superiority, desires of useless show, pride of little accomplishments, and all the train of vanity, will be brushed away by the wing of time,

Reproof should not exhaust its power upon petty failings; let it watch diligently against the incursion of vice, and leave foppery and futility to die of themselves.

N°. 26. SATURDAY, OCTOBER 14, 1758.

MR. IDLER,

I NEVER thought that I should write any thing to be printed; but having lately seen your first essay, which was sent down into the kitchen, with a great bundle of gazettes and useless papers, I find that you are willing to admit any correspondent, and therefore hope you will not reject me. If you publish my letter, it may encourage others, in the same condition with myself, to tell their stories, which may be, perhaps, as useful as those of great ladies.

I am a poor girl. I was bred in the country at a charity-school, maintained by the contributions of wealthy neighbours. The ladies, or patronesses, visited us from time to time, examined how we were taught, and saw that our clothes were clean. We lived happily enough, and were instructed to be thankful to those at whose cost we were educated. I was always the favourite of my mistress; she used to call me to read and show my copy-book to all strangers, who never dismissed me without commendation, and very seldom without a shilling.

At last the chief of our subscribers, having passed a winter in London, came down full of an opinion new and

strange to the whole country.   She held it little less than
criminal to teach poor girls to read and write.   They who
are born to poverty, she said, are born to ignorance, and
will work the harder the less they know.   She told her
friends, that London was in confusion by the insolence of
servants; that scarcely a wench was to be got for *all work*,
since education had made such numbers of fine ladies;
that nobody would now accept a lower title than that of a
waiting-maid, or something that might qualify her to wear
laced shoes and long ruffles, and to sit at work in the
parlour window.   But she was resolved, for her part, to
spoil no more girls; those, who were to live by their hands,
should neither read nor write out of her pocket; the world
was bad enough already, and she would have no part in
making it worse.

She was for a short time warmly opposed; but she
persevered in her notions, and withdrew her subscription.
Few listen without a desire of conviction to those who
advise them to spare their money.   Her example and her
arguments gained ground daily; and in less than a year
the whole parish was convinced, that the nation would be
ruined, if the children of the poor were taught to read and
write.

Our school was now dissolved: my mistress kissed me
when we parted, and told me, that, being old and helpless, she could not assist me; advised me to seek a service,
and charged me not to forget what I had learned.

My reputation for scholarship, which had hitherto recommended me to favour, was, by the adherents to the
new opinion, considered as a crime; and, when I offered
myself to any mistress, I had no other answer than,
" Sure, child, you would not work! hard work is not fit
for a pen-woman; a scrubbing-brush would spoil your
hand, child!"

I could not live at home; and while I was considering
to what I should betake me, one of the girls, who had
gone from our school to London, came down in a silk
gown, and told her acquaintance how well she lived, what

fine things she saw, and what great wages she received.
I resolved to try my fortune, and took my passage in the
next week's waggon to London.   I had no snares laid for
me at my arrival, but came safe to a sister of my mistress,
who undertook to get me a place.   She knew only the
families of mean tradesmen; and I, having no high opinion
of my own qualifications, was willing to accept the first
offer.

My first mistress was wife of a working watch-maker,
who earned more than was sufficient to keep his family in decency and plenty; but it was their constant
practice to hire a chaise on Sunday, and spend half the
wages of the week on Richmond Hill; of Monday he
commonly lay half in bed, and spent the other half in
merriment; Tuesday and Wednesday consumed the rest
of his money; and three days every week were passed in
extremity of want by us who were left at home, while my
master lived on trust at an alehouse.   You may be sure,
that of the sufferers, the maid suffered most; and I left
them, after three months, rather than be starved.

I was then maid to a hatter's wife.   There was no
want to be dreaded, for they lived in perpetual luxury.
My mistress was a diligent woman, and rose early in the
morning to set the journeymen to work; my master was
a man much beloved by his neighbours, and sat at one
club or other every night.   I was obliged to wait on my
master at night, and on my mistress in the morning.   He
seldom came home before two, and she rose at five.   I
could no more live without sleep than without food, and
therefore entreated them to look out for another servant.

My next removal was to a linen-draper's, who had six
children.   My mistress, when I first entered the house,
informed me, that I must never contradict the children,
nor suffer them to cry.   I had no desire to offend, and
readily promised to do my best.   But when I gave them
their breakfast, I could not help all first; when I was
playing with one in my lap, I was forced to keep the rest
in expectation.   That which was not gratified, always re-

sented the injury with a loud outcry, which put my mistress in a fury at me, and procured sugar-plums to the child. I could not keep six children quiet, who were bribed to be clamorous; and was therefore dismissed, as a girl honest, but not good-natured.

I then lived with a couple that kept a petty shop of remnants and cheap linen. I was qualified to make a bill, or keep a book; and being therefore often called, at a busy time, to serve the customers, expected that I should now be happy, in proportion as I was useful. But my mistress appropriated every day part of the profit to some private use, and, as she grew bolder in her thefts, at last deducted such sums, that my master began to wonder how he sold so much, and gained so little. She pretended to assist his inquiries, and began, very gravely, to hope that "Betty was honest, and yet those sharp girls were apt to be light-fingered." You will believe that I did not stay there much longer.

The rest of my story I will tell you in another letter; and only beg to be informed, in some paper, for which of my places, except perhaps the last, I was disqualified by my skill in reading and writing.

I am, Sir,

Your very humble servant,

BETTY BROOM.

***

No. 27.   SATURDAY, OCTOBER 21, 1758.

IT has been the endeavour of all those whom the world has reverenced for superior wisdom, to persuade man to be acquainted with himself, to learn his own powers and his own weakness, to observe by what evils he is most dangerously beset, and by what temptations most easily overcome.

This counsel has been often given with serious dignity, and often received with appearance of conviction; but, as very few can search deep into their own minds without meeting what they wish to hide from themselves, scarcely any man persists in cultivating such disagreeable acquaintance, but draws the veil again between his eyes and his heart, leaves his passions and appetites as he found them, and advises others to look into themselves.

This is the common result of inquiry even among those that endeavour to grow wiser or better: but this endeavour is far enough from frequency; the greater part of the multitudes that swarm upon the earth have never been disturbed by such uneasy curiosity, but deliver themselves up to business or to pleasure, plunge into the current of life, whether placid or turbulent, and pass on from one point or prospect to another, attentive rather to any thing than the state of their minds; satisfied, at an easy rate, with an opinion, that they are no worse than others, that every man must mind his own interest, or that their pleasures hurt only themselves, and are therefore no proper subjects of censure.

Some, however, there are, whom the intrusion of scruples, the recollection of better notions, or the latent reprehension of good examples, will not suffer to live entirely contented with their own conduct; these are forced to pacify the mutiny of reason with fair promises, and quiet their thoughts with designs of calling all their actions to review, and planning a new scheme for the time to come.

There is nothing which we estimate so fallaciously as the force of our own resolutions, nor any fallacy which we so unwillingly and tardily detect. He that has resolved a thousand times, and a thousand times deserted his own purpose, yet suffers no abatement of his confidence, but still believes himself his own master; and able, by innate vigour of soul, to press forward to his end, through all the obstructions that inconveniencies or delights can put in his way.

That this mistake should prevail for a time, is very natural. When conviction is present, and temptation out of sight, we do not easily conceive how any reasonable being can deviate from his true interest. What ought to be done, while it yet hangs only on speculation, is so plain and certain, that there is no place for doubt; the whole soul yields itself to the predominance of truth, and readily determines to do what, when the time of action comes, will be at last omitted.

I believe most men may review all the lives that have passed within their observation, without remembering one efficacious resolution, or being able to tell a single instance of a course of practice suddenly changed in consequence of a change of opinion, or an establishment of determination. Many, indeed, alter their conduct, and are not at fifty what they were at thirty; but they commonly varied imperceptibly from themselves, followed the train of external causes, and rather suffered reformation than made it.

It is not uncommon to charge the difference between promise and performance, between profession and reality, upon deep design and studied deceit; but the truth is, that there is very little hypocrisy in the world; we do not so often endeavour or wish to impose on others, as on ourselves; we resolve to do right, we hope to keep our resolutions, we declare them to confirm our own hope, and fix our own inconstancy by calling witnesses of our actions; but at last habit prevails, and those whom we invited to our triumph laugh at our defeat.

Custom is commonly too strong for the most resolute resolver, though furnished for the assault with all the weapons of philosophy. "He that endeavours to free himself from an ill habit," says Bacon, "must not change too much at a time, lest he should be discouraged by difficulty; nor too little, for then he will make but slow advances." This is a precept which may be applauded in a book, but will fail in the trial, in which every change will be found too great or too little. Those who have been able to conquer habit, are like those that are fabled to have returned from the realms of Pluto:

> ————" Pauci, quos æquus ámavit
> Jupiter, atque ardens evexit ad æthera virtus,"

They are sufficient to give hope, but not security; to animate the contest, but not to promise victory.

Those who are in the power of evil habits must conquer them as they can; and conquered they must be, or neither wisdom nor happiness can be attained; but those who are not yet subject to their influence may, by timely caution, preserve their freedom; they may effectually resolve to escape the tyrant, whom they will very vainly resolve to conquer.

N°. 28. SATURDAY, OCTOBER 28, 1758.

TO THE IDLER.

SIR,

IT is very easy for a man who sits idle at home, and has nobody to please but himself, to ridicule or to censure the common practices of mankind; and those who have no present temptation to break the rules of propriety, may applaud his judgment, and join in his merriment; but let the author or his readers mingle with common life, they will find themselves irresistibly borne away by the stream of custom, and must submit, after they have laughed at others, to give others the same opportunity of laughing at them.

There is no paper published by the Idler which I have read with more approbation than that which censures the practice of recording vulgar marriages in the newspapers. I carried it about in my pocket, and read it to all those whom I suspected of having published their nuptials, or of being inclined to publish them, and sent transcripts of it to all the couples that transgressed your precepts for the next fortnight. I hoped that they were all vexed, and pleased myself with imagining their misery..

But short is the triumph of malignity. I was married last week to Miss Mohair, the daughter of a salesman; and, at my first appearance after the wedding night, was

-asked, by my wife's mother, whether I had sent our marriage to the Advertiser? I endeavoured to show how unfit
it was to demand the attention of the publick to our domestick affairs; but she told me, with great vehemence,
" That she would not have it thought to be a stolen
match; that the blood of the Mohairs should never be disgraced; that her husband had served all the parish offices
but one; that she had lived five-and-thirty years at the same
house, had paid every body twenty shillings in the pound,
and would have me know, though she was not as fine and
as flaunting as Mrs. Gingham, the deputy's wife, she was
not ashamed to tell her name, and would show her face with
the best of them; and since I had married her daughter——"
At this instant entered my father-in-law, a grave man,
from whom I expected succour; but upon hearing the
case, he told me, " That it would be very imprudent to
miss such an opportunity of advertising my shop; and that
when notice was given of my marriage, many of my wife's
friends would think themselves obliged to be my customers." I was subdued by clamour on one side, and
gravity on the other, and shall be obliged to tell the town,
that " three days ago Timothy Mushroom, an eminent
oilman in Seacoal-lane, was married to Miss Polly Mohair of Lothbury, a beautiful young lady, with a large
fortune."

I am, Sir, &c.

SIR,

        I AM the unfortunate wife of the grocer whose
letter you published about ten weeks ago, in which he
complains, like a sorry fellow, that I loiter in the shop with
my needle-work in my hand, and that I oblige him to take
me out on Sundays, and keep a girl to look after the child.
Sweet Mr. Idler, if you did but know all, you would give
no encouragement to such an unreasonable grumbler. I
brought him three hundred pounds, which set him up in a
shop, and bought-in a stock, on which, with good management, we might live comfortably; but now I have given

him a shop, I am forced to watch him and the shop too.
I will tell you, Mr. Idler, how it is. There is an alehouse
over the way, with a ninepin alley, to which he is sure to
run when I turn my back, and there he loses his money, for
he plays at ninepins as he does every thing else. While
he is at this favourite sport, he sets a dirty boy to watch
his door, and call him to his customers; but he is so long
in coming, and so rude when he comes, that our custom
falls off every day.

Those who cannot govern themselves, must be governed. I have resolved to keep him for the future behind his counter, and let him bounce at his customers if he
dares. I cannot be above stairs and below at the same
time, and have therefore taken a girl to look after the
child, and dress the dinner; and, after all, pray who is to
blame?

On a Sunday, it is true, I make him walk abroad, and
sometimes carry the child; I wonder who should carry it!
But I never take him out till after church-time, nor would
do it then, but that, if he is left alone, he will be upon
the bed. On a Sunday, if he stays at home, he has six
meals, and, when he can eat no longer, has twenty stratagems to escape from me to the alehouse; but I commonly
keep the door locked, till Monday produces something for
him to do.

This is the true state of the case, and these are the pro-
vocations for which he has written his letter to you. I
hope you will write a paper to show, that, if a wife must
spend her whole time in watching her husband, she cannot
conveniently tend her child, or sit at her needle.

I am, Sir, &c.

SIR,

THERE is in this town a species of oppression
which the law has not hitherto prevented or redressed.

I am a chairman. You know, Sir, we come when we
are called, and are expected to carry all who require our
assistance. It is common for men of the most unwieldy

corpulence to crowd themselves into a chair, and demand to be carried for a shilling as far as an airy young lady whom we scarcely feel upon our poles. Surely we ought to be paid, like all other mortals, in proportion to our labour. Engines should be fixed in proper places to weigh chairs as they weigh waggons; and those, whom ease and plenty have made unable to carry themselves, should give part of their superfluities to those who carry them.

I am, Sir, &c.

N°. 29. SATURDAY, NOVEMBER 4, 1758.

TO THE IDLER.

SIR,

I HAVE often observed, that friends are lost by discontinuance of intercourse without any offence on either part, and have long known, that it is more dangerous to be forgotten than to be blamed; I therefore make haste to send you the rest of my story, lest, by the delay of another fortnight, the name of Betty Broom might be no longer remembered by you or your readers.

Having left the last place in haste, to avoid the charge or the suspicion of theft, I had not secured another service, and was forced to take a lodging in a back-street. I had now got good clothes. The woman who lived in the garret opposite to mine was very officious, and offered to take care of my room and clean it, while I went round to my acquaintance to inquire for a mistress. I knew not why she was so kind, nor how I could recompense her; but in a few days I missed some of my linen, went to another lodging, and resolved not to have another friend in the next garret.

In six weeks I became under-maid at the house of a mercer in Cornhill, whose son was his apprentice. The young gentleman used to sit late at the tavern, without the knowledge of his father; and I was ordered by my mistress to let him in silently to his bed under the counter, and to be very careful to take away his candle. The hours which I was obliged to watch, whilst the rest of the family was in bed, I considered as supernumerary, and, having no business assigned for them, thought myself at liberty to spend them my own way: I kept myself awake with a book, and for some time liked my state the better for this opportunity of reading. At last, the upper-maid found my book, and showed it to my mistress, who told me, that wenches like me might spend their time better; that she never knew any of the readers that had good designs in their heads; that she could always find something else to do with her time, than to puzzle over books; and did not like that such a fine lady should sit up for her young master.

This was the first time that I found it thought criminal or dangerous to know how to read. I was dismissed decently, lest I should tell tales, and had a small gratuity above my wages.

I then lived with a gentlewoman of a small fortune. This was the only happy part of my life. My mistress, for whom publick diversions were too expensive, spent her time with books, and was pleased to find a maid who could partake her amusements. I rose early in the morning, that I might have time in the afternoon to read or listen, and was suffered to tell my opinion, or express my delight. Thus fifteen months stole away, in which I did not repine that I was born to servitude. But a burning fever seized my mistress, of whom I shall say no more, than that her servant wept upon her grave.

I had lived in a kind of luxury, which made me very unfit for another place; and was rather too delicate for the conversation of a kitchen; so that when I was hired in the family of an East-India director, my behaviour was so different, as they said, from that of a common servant, that they concluded me a gentlewoman in disguise, and turned me out in three weeks, on suspicion of some design which they could not comprehend.

I then fled for refuge to the other end of the town, where I hoped to find no obstruction from my new accomplishments, and was hired under the housekeeper in a splendid family. Here I was too wise for the maids, and too nice for the footmen; yet I might have lived on without much uneasiness, had not my mistress, the housekeeper, who used to employ me in buying necessaries for the family, found a bill which I had made of one day's expense. I suppose it did not quite agree with her own book, for she fiercely declared her resolution, that there should be no pen and ink in that kitchen but her own.

She had the justice, or the prudence, not to injure my reputation; and I was easily admitted into another house in the neighbourhood, where my business was to sweep the rooms and make the beds. Here I was, for some time, the favourite of Mrs. Simper, my lady's woman, who could not bear the vulgar girls, and was happy in the attendance of a young woman of some education. Mrs. Simper loved a novel, though she could not read hard words, and therefore, when her lady was abroad, we always laid hold on her books. At last, my abilities became so much celebrated, that the house-steward used to employ me in keeping his accounts. Mrs. Simper then found out, that my sauciness was grown to such a height that nobody could endure it, and told my lady, that there never had been a room well swept, since Betty Broom came into the house.

I was then hired by a consumptive lady, who wanted a maid that could read and write. I attended her four years, and though she was never pleased, yet when I declared my resolution to leave her, she burst into tears, and told me that I must bear the peevishness of a sick bed, and I should find myself remembered in her will. I complied, and a codicil was added in my favour; but in less than a week, when I set her gruel before her, I laid the spoon on the left side, and she threw her will into the fire. In two days she made another, which she burnt in the same manner, because she could not eat her chicken. A third was made, and destroyed because she heard a mouse within the wainscot, and was sure that I should suffer her to be carried away alive. After this I was for some time out of favour, but as her illness grew upon her, resentment and sullenness gave way to kinder sentiments. She died, and left me five hundred pounds; with this fortune I am going to settle in my native parish, where I resolve to spend some hours every day in teaching poor girls to read and write[h].

I am, Sir,

Your humble servant,

BETTY BROOM.

N°. 30. SATURDAY, NOVEMBER 11, 1758.

THE desires of man increase with his acquisitions; every step which he advances brings something within his view, which he did not see before, and which, as soon as he sees it, he begins to want. Where necessity ends, curiosity begins; and no sooner are we supplied with every thing that nature can demand, than we sit down to contrive artificial appetites.

By this restlessness of mind, every populous and wealthy city is filled with innumerable employments, for which the greater part of mankind is without a name; with artificers, whose labour is exerted in producing such petty conveniencies, that many shops are furnished with instruments, of which the use can hardly be found without inquiry, but which he that once knows them quickly learns to number among necessary things.

Such is the diligence with which, in countries completely civilized, one part of mankind labours for another, that wants are supplied faster than they can be formed,

[h] Mrs. Gardiner, a pious, sensible, and charitable woman, for whom Johnson entertained a high respect, is said to have afforded a hint for the story of Betty Broom, from her zealous support of a Ladies' Charity-school, confined to females. Boswell, vol. iv.

and the idle and luxurious find life stagnate for want of some desire to keep it in motion. This species of distress furnishes a new set of occupations; and multitudes are busied, from day to day, in finding the rich and the fortunate something to do.

It is very common to reproach those artists as useless, who produce only such superfluities as neither accommodate the body, nor improve the mind; and of which no other effect can be imagined, than that they are the occasions of spending money, and consuming time.

But this censure will be mitigated, when it is seriously considered, that money and time are the heaviest burdens of life, and that the unhappiest of all mortals are those who have more of either than they know how to use. To set himself free from these incumbrances, one hurries to Newmarket; another travels over Europe; one pulls down his house and calls architects about him; another buys a seat in the country, and follows his hounds over hedges and through rivers; one makes collections of shells; and another searches the world for tulips and carnations.

He is surely a publick benefactor who finds employment for those to whom it is thus difficult to find it for themselves. It is true, that this is seldom done merely from generosity or compassion; almost every man seeks his own advantage in helping others, and therefore it is too common for mercenary officiousness to consider rather what is grateful, than what is right.

We all know that it is more profitable to be loved than esteemed; and ministers of pleasure will always be found, who study to make themselves necessary, and to supplant those who are practising the same arts.

One of the amusements of idleness is reading without the fatigue of close attention, and the world therefore swarms with writers whose wish is not to be studied, but to be read.

No species of literary men has lately been so much multiplied as the writers of news. Not many years ago the nation was content with one gazette; but now we have

not only in the metropolis papers for every morning and
every evening, but almost every large town has its weekly
historian, who regularly circulates his periodical intelligence, and fills the villages of his district with conjectures
on the events of war, and with debates on the true interest
of Europe.

To write news in its perfection requires such a combination of qualities, that a man completely fitted for the task
is not always to be found. In Sir Henry Wotton's jocular
definition, *An ambassador* is said to be *a man of virtue
sent abroad to tell lies for the advantage of his country* ;
a news-writer is *a man without virtue, who writes lies at
home for his own profit*. To these compositions is required
neither genius nor knowledge, neither industry nor sprightliness ; but contempt of shame and indifference to truth
are absolutely necessary. He who by a long familiarity
with infamy has obtained these qualities, may confidently
tell to-day what he intends to contradict to-morrow ; he
may affirm fearlessly what he knows that he shall be obliged to recant, and may write letters from Amsterdam or
Dresden to himself.

In a time of war the nation is always of one mind, eager
to hear something good of themselves and ill of the enemy.
At this time the task of news-writers is easy: they have
nothing to do but to tell that a battle is expected, and
afterwards that a battle has been fought, in which we and
our friends, whether conquering or conquered, did all, and
our enemies did nothing.

Scarcely any thing awakens attention like a tale of
cruelty. The writer of news never fails in the intermission of action to tell how the enemies murdered children
and ravished virgins ; and, if the scene of action be somewhat distant, scalps half the inhabitants of a province.

Among the calamities of war may be justly numbered
the diminution of the love of truth, by the falsehoods
which interest dictates, and credulity encourages. A
peace will equally leave the warriour and relater of wars
destitute of employment ; and I know not whether more

is to be dreaded from streets filled with soldiers accustomed to plunder, or from garrets filled with scribblers accustomed to lie.

<hr />

Nᵒ. 31. · SATURDAY, NOVEMBER 18, 1758.

MANY moralists have remarked, that pride has of all human vices the widest dominion, appears in the greatest multiplicity of forms, and lies hid under the greatest variety of disguises ; of disguises, which, like the moon's *veil of brightness*, are both its *lustre and its shade*, and betray it to others, though they hide it from ourselves.

It is not my intention to degrade pride from this preeminence of mischief; yet I know not whether idleness may not maintain a very doubtful and obstinate competition.

There are some that profess idleness in its full dignity, who call themselves the *Idle*, as Busiris in the play calls himself the *Proud*; who boast that they do nothing, and thank their stars that they have nothing to do ; who sleep every night till they can sleep no longer, and rise only that exercise may enable them to sleep again; who prolong the reign of darkness by double curtains, and never see the sun but to *tell him how they hate his beams;* whose whole labour is to vary the posture of indolence, and whose day differs from their night, but as a couch or chair differs from a bed.

These are the true and open votaries of idleness, for whom she weaves the garlands of poppies, and into whose cup she pours the waters of oblivion ; who exist in a state of unruffled stupidity, forgetting and forgotten ; who have long ceased to live, and at whose death the survivors can only say, that they have ceased to breathe.

But idleness predominates in many lives where it is not suspected; for, being a vice which terminates in itself, it may be enjoyed without injury to others ; and it is therefore not watched like fraud, which endangers property ; or like pride, which naturally seeks its gratifications in another's inferiority.   Idleness is a silent and peaceful quality, that neither raises envy by ostentation, nor hatred by opposition ; and therefore nobody is busy to censure or detect it.

As pride sometimes is hid under humility, idleness is often covered by turbulence and hurry.   He that neglects his known duty and real employment, naturally endeavours to crowd his mind with something that may bar out the remembrance of his own folly, and does any thing but what he ought to do with eager diligence, that he may keep himself in his own favour.

Some are always in a state of preparation, occupied in previous measures, forming plans, accumulating materials, and providing for the main affair.   These are certainly under the secret power of idleness.   Nothing is to be expected from the workman whose tools are for ever to be sought.   I was once told by a great master, that no man ever excelled in painting, who was eminently curious about pencils and colours.

There are others to whom idleness dictates another expedient, by which life may be passed unprofitably away without the tediousness of many vacant hours.   The art is, to fill the day with petty business, to have always something in hand which may raise curiosity, but not solicitude, and keep the mind in a state of action, but not of labour.

This art has for many years been practised by my old friend Sober with wonderful success.   Sober is a man of strong desires and quick imagination, so exactly balanced by the love of ease, that they can seldom stimulate him to any difficult undertaking; they have, however, so much power, that they will not suffer him to lie quite at rest; and though they do not make him sufficiently useful to others, they make him at least weary of himself.

Mr. Sober's chief pleasure is conversation; there is no end of his talk or his attention; to speak or to hear is equally pleasing; for he still fancies that he is teaching or learning something, and is free for the time from his own reproaches.

But there is one time at night when he must go home, that his friends may sleep; and another time in the morning, when all the world agrees to shut out interruption. These are the moments of which poor Sober trembles at the thought. But the misery of these tiresome intervals he has many means of alleviating. He has persuaded himself that the manual arts are undeservedly overlooked; he has observed in many trades the effects of close thought, and just ratiocination. From speculation he proceeded to practice, and supplied himself with the tools of a carpenter, with which he mended his coal-box very successfully, and which he still continues to employ, as he finds occasion.

He has attempted at other times the crafts of the shoemaker, tinman, plumber, and potter; in all these arts he has failed, and resolves to qualify himself for them by better information. But his daily amusement is chymistry. He has a small furnace, which he employs in distillation, and which has long been the solace of his life. He draws oils and waters, and essences and spirits, which he knows to be of no use; sits and counts the drops, as they come from his retort, and forgets that, whilst a drop is falling, a moment flies away.

Poor Sober! I have often teased him with reproof, and he has often promised reformation; for no man is so much open to conviction as the Idler, but there is none on whom it operates so little. What will be the effect of this paper I know not; perhaps, he will read it and laugh, and light the fire in his furnace; but my hope is, that he will quit his trifles, and betake himself to rational and useful diligence[1].

[1] In Mr. Sober, we may recognise traits of Dr. Johnson's own character. No. 67 of the Idler is another portrait of him.

N°. 32. SATURDAY, NOVEMBER 25, 1758.

AMONG the innumerable mortifications that waylay human arrogance on every side, may well be reckoned our ignorance of the most common objects and effects, a defect of which we become more sensible, by every attempt to supply it. Vulgar and inactive minds confound familiarity with knowledge, and conceive themselves informed of the whole nature of things when they are shown their form or told their use; but the speculatist, who is not content with superficial views, harasses himself with fruitless curiosity, and still as he inquires more, perceives only that he knows less.

Sleep is a state in which a great part of every life is passed. No animal has been yet discovered, whose existence is not varied with intervals of insensibility; and some late philosophers have extended the empire of sleep over the vegetable world.

Yet of this change, so frequent, so great, so general, and so necessary, no searcher has yet found either the efficient or final cause; or can tell by what power the mind and body are thus chained down in irresistible stupefaction; or what benefits the animal receives from this alternate suspension of its active powers.

Whatever may be the multiplicity or contrariety of opinions upon this subject, nature has taken sufficient care that theory shall have little influence on practice. The most diligent inquirer is not able long to keep his eyes open; the most eager disputant will begin about midnight to desert his argument; and, once in four-and-twenty hours, the gay and the gloomy, the witty and the dull, the clamorous and the silent, the busy and the idle, are all overpowered by the gentle tyrant, and all lie down in the equality of sleep.

Philosophy has often attempted to repress insolence, by asserting, that all conditions are levelled by death; a position which, however it may deject the happy, will seldom afford much comfort to the wretched. It is far more pleasing to consider, that sleep is equally a leveller with death; that the time is never at a great distance, when the balm of rest shall be diffused alike upon every head, when the diversities of life shall stop their operation, and the high and the low shall lie down together [m].

It is somewhere recorded of Alexander, that in the pride of conquests, and intoxication of flattery, he declared that he only perceived himself to be a man by the necessity of sleep. Whether he considered sleep as necessary to his mind or body, it was indeed a sufficient evidence of human infirmity; the body which required such frequency of renovation, gave but faint promises of immortality; and the mind which, from time to time, sunk gladly into insensibility, had made no very near approaches to the felicity of the supreme and self-sufficient nature.

I know not what can tend more to repress all the passions, that disturb the peace of the world, than the consideration that there is no height of happiness or honour, from which man does not eagerly descend to a state of unconscious repose; that the best condition of life is such, that we contentedly quit its good to be disentangled from its evils; that in a few hours splendour fades before the eye, and praise itself deadens in the ear; the senses withdraw from their objects, and reason favours the retreat.

What then are the hopes and prospects of covetousness, ambition, and rapacity? Let him that desires most have all his desires gratified, he never shall attain a state which he can, for a day and a night, contemplate with satisfaction, or from which, if he had the power of perpetual vigilance, he would not long for periodical separations.

All envy would be extinguished, if it were universally known that there are none to be envied, and surely none

---

m " For half their life," says Aristotle, " the happy differ not from the wretched."—Nichom. Ethic. i. 13.

Ὕπν᾽ ὀδύνας ἀδαὴς, Ὕπνε δ᾽ ἀλγέων
Εὐαὴς ἡμῖν ἔλθοις,
Εὐαίων, εὐαίων ἄναξ. Soph. Philoct. 827.

can be much envied who are not pleased with themselves. There is reason to suspect, that the distinctions of mankind have more show than value, when it is found that all agree to be weary alike of pleasures and of cares; that the powerful and the weak, the celebrated and obscure, join in one common wish, and implore from nature's hand the nectar of oblivion.

Such is our desire of abstraction from ourselves, that very few are satisfied with the quantity of stupefaction which the needs of the body force upon the mind. Alexander himself added intemperance to sleep, and solaced with the fumes of wine the sovereignty of the world: and almost every man has some art by which he steals his thoughts away from his present state.

It is not much of life that is spent in close attention to any important duty. Many hours of every day are suffered to fly away without any traces left upon the intellects. We suffer phantoms to rise up before us, and amuse ourselves with the dance of airy images, which, after a time, we dismiss for ever, and know not how we have been busied.

Many have no happier moments than those that they pass in solitude, abandoned to their own imagination, which sometimes puts sceptres in their hands or mitres on their heads, shifts the scene of pleasure with endless variety, bids all the forms of beauty sparkle before them, and gluts them with every change of visionary luxury.

It is easy in these semi-slumbers to collect all the possibilities of happiness, to alter the course of the sun, to bring back the past, and anticipate the future, to unite all the beauties of all seasons, and all the blessings of all climates, to receive and bestow felicity, and forget that misery is the lot of man. All this is a voluntary dream, a temporary recession from the realities of life to airy fictions; and habitual subjection of reason to fancy.

Others are afraid to be alone, and amuse themselves by a perpetual succession of companions: but the difference is not great; in solitude we have our dreams to ourselves, and in company we agree to dream in concert. The end sought in both is forgetfulness of ourselves.

Nº. 33. SATURDAY, DECEMBER 2, 1758.

net

[I hope the author of the following letter[n] will excuse the omission of some parts, and allow me to remark, that the Journal of the Citizen in the Spectator has almost precluded the attempt of any future writer.]

———— *Non ita Romuli*
Præscriptum, et intonsi Catonis
Auspiciis, veterumque normá. HOR. Lib. ii. Ode xv. 10.

SIR,

YOU have often solicited correspondence. I have sent you the Journal of a Senior Fellow, or Genuine Idler, just transmitted from Cambridge by a facetious correspondent, and warranted to have been transcribed from the common-place book of the journalist.

Monday, Nine o'Clock. Turned off my bed-maker for waking me at eight. Weather rainy. Consulted my weather-glass. No hopes of a ride before dinner.

Ditto, Ten. After breakfast, transcribed half a sermon from Dr. Hickman. N. B. Never to transcribe any more from Calamy; Mrs. Pilcocks, at my curacy, having one volume of that author lying in her parlour-window.

Ditto, Eleven. Went down into my cellar. Mem. My Mountain will be fit to drink in a month's time. N. B. To remove the five-year old port into the new bin on the left hand.

Ditto, Twelve. Mended a pen. Looked at my weather-glass again. Quicksilver very low. Shaved. Barber's hand shakes.

Ditto, One. Dined alone in my room on a sole. N. B. The shrimp-sauce not so good as Mr. H. of Peterhouse and I used to eat in London last winter at the Mitre in Fleet-street. Sat down to a pint of Madeira. Mr. H. surprised me over it. We finished two bottles of port

———
[a] Mr. Thomas Warton.

together, and were very cheerful. Mem. To dine with Mr. H. at Peterhouse next Wednesday. One of the dishes a leg of pork and pease, by my desire.

Ditto, Six. Newspaper in the common room.

Ditto, Seven. Returned to my room. Made a tiff of warm punch, and to bed before nine; did not fall asleep till ten, a young fellow commoner being very noisy over my head.

Tuesday, Nine. Rose squeamish. A fine morning. Weather-glass very high.

Ditto, Ten. Ordered my horse, and rode to the five-mile stone on the Newmarket road. Appetite gets better. A pack of hounds, in full cry, crossed the road, and startled my horse.

Ditto, Twelve. Drest. Found a letter on my table to be in London the 19th inst. Bespoke a new wig.

Ditto, One. At dinner in the hall. Too much water in the soup. Dr. Dry always orders the beef to be salted too much for me.

Ditto, Two. In the common room. Dr. Dry gave us an instance of a gentleman who kept the gout out of his stomach by drinking old Madeira. Conversation chiefly on the expeditions. Company broke up at four. Dr. Dry and myself played at backgammon for a brace of snipes. Won.

Ditto, Five. At the coffee-house. Met Mr. H. there. Could not get a sight of the Monitor.

Ditto, Seven. Returned home, and stirred my fire. Went to the common room, and supped on the snipes with Dr. Dry.

Ditto, Eight. Began the evening in the common room. Dr. Dry told several stories. Were very merry. Our new fellow, that studies physick, very talkative toward twelve. Pretends he will bring the youngest Miss —— to drink tea with me soon. Impertinent blockhead!

Wednesday, Nine. Alarmed with a pain in my ankle. Q. The gout? Fear I can't dine at Peterhouse; but I

hope a ride will set all to rights. Weather-glass below
Fair.

. Ditto, Ten. Mounted my horse, though the weather
suspicious. Pain in my ankle entirely gone. Caught in
a shower coming back. Convinced that my weather-glass
is the best in Cambridge.

' Ditto, Twelve. Drest. Sauntered up to the Fish-
monger's hill. Met Mr. H. and went with him to Peterhouse. Cook made us wait thirty-six minutes beyond the
time. The company, some of my Emmanuel friends. For
dinner, a pair of soles, a leg of pork and pease, among
other things. Mem. Pease-pudding not boiled enough.
Cook reprimanded and sconced in my presence.

. Ditto, after Dinner. Pain in my ankle returns. Dull
all the afternoon. Rallied for being no company. Mr.
H.'s account of the accommodations on the road in his Bath
journey.

Ditto, Six. Got into spirits. Never was more chatty.
We sat late at whist. Mr. H. and self agreed at parting
to take a gentle ride, and dine at the old house on the
London road to-morrow.

Thursday, Nine. My sempstress. She has lost the
measure of my wrist. Forced to be measured again. The
baggage has got a trick of smiling.

Ditto, Ten to Eleven. Made some rappee snuff. Read
the magazines. Received a present of pickles from Miss
Pilcocks. Mem. To send in return some collared eel,
which I know both the old lady and miss are fond of.

Ditto, Eleven. Glass very high. Mounted at the gate
with Mr. H. Horse skittish, and wants exercise. Arrive
at the old house. All the provisions bespoke by some
rakish fellow-commoner in the next room, who had been
on a scheme to Newmarket. Could get nothing but mut-
ton-chops off the worst end. Port very new. Agree to
try some other house to-morrow.

Here the journal breaks off: for the next morning, as
my friend informs me, our genial academick was waked
with a severe fit of the gout; and, at present, enjoys all

the dignity of that disease. But I believe we have lost
nothing by this interruption: since a continuation of the
remainder of the journal, through the remainder of the
week, would most probably have exhibited nothing more
than a repeated relation of the same circumstances of
idling and luxury.

I hope it will not be concluded, from this specimen of
academick life, that I have attempted to decry our universities. If literature is not the essential requisite of
the modern academick, I am yet persuaded, that Cambridge and Oxford, however degenerated, surpass the
fashionable *academies* of our metropolis, and the *gymnasia*
of foreign countries. The number of learned persons in
these celebrated seats is still considerable, and more conveniencies and opportunities for study still subsist in them,
than in any other place. There is at least one very powerful incentive to learning; I mean the GENIUS *of the
place.* It is a sort of inspiring deity, which every youth
of quick sensibility and ingenious disposition creates to
himself, by reflecting, that he is placed under those venerable walls, where a HOOKER and a HAMMOND, a BA-
CON and a NEWTON, once pursued the same course of
science, and from whence they soared to the most elevated heights of literary fame. This is that incitement
which Tully, according to his own testimony, experienced
at Athens, when he contemplated the porticos where Socrates sat, and the laurel-groves where Plato disputed[o].
But there are other circumstances, and of the highest importance, which render our colleges superior to all other
places of education. Their institutions, although somewhat fallen from their primæval simplicity, are such as influence, in a particular manner, the moral conduct of their
youth; and in this general depravity of manners and laxity
of principles, pure religion is no where more strongly inculcated. The *academies*, as they are presumptuously styled,

---

[o] A rich assemblage of examples of the " influence of perceptible objects in
reviving former thoughts and former feelings," is collected in Dr. Brown's Philosophy of the Human Mind, vol. 2. Lecture 38.

are too low to be mentioned ; and foreign seminaries are
likely to prejudice the unwary mind with Calvinism. But
English universities render their students virtuous, at least
by excluding all opportunities of vice ; and, by teaching
them the principles of the Church of England, confirm
them in those of true Christianity.

N°. 34. SATURDAY, DECEMBER 9, 1758.

To illustrate one thing by its resemblance to another, has
been always the most popular and efficacious art of instruction.   There is indeed no other method· of teaching
that of which any one is ignorant, but by means of something already known ; and a mind so enlarged by contemplation, and inquiry, that it has always many objects within
its view, will seldom be long without some near and familiar
image through which an easy transition may be made to
truths more distant and obscure.

Of the parallels which have been drawn by wit and curiosity, some are literal and real, as between poetry and
painting, two arts which pursue the same end, by the operation of the same mental faculties, and which differ only as
the one represents things by marks permanent and natural,
the other by signs accidental and arbitrary.   The one,
therefore, is more easily and generally understood, since similitude of form is immediately perceived ; the other is
capable of conveying more ideas, for men have thought
and spoken of many things which they do not see.

Other parallels are fortuitous and fanciful, yet these
have sometimes been extended to many particulars of re·
semblance by a lucky concurrence of diligence and chance.
The animal body is composed of many members, united
under the direction of one mind: any number of individuals, connected for some common purpose, is therefore
called a body.   From this participation of the same appellation arose the comparison of the body natural and body

politick, of which, how far soever it has been deduced, no end has hitherto been found.

In these imaginary similitudes, the same word is used at once in its primitive and metaphorical sense. Thus health, ascribed to the body natural, is opposed to sickness; but attributed to the body politick stands as contrary to adversity. These parallels therefore have more of genius, but less of truth; they often please, but they never convince.

Of this kind is a curious speculation frequently indulged by a philosopher of my acquaintance, who had discovered, that the qualities requisite to conversation are very exactly represented by a bowl of punch.

Punch, says this profound investigator, is a liquor compounded of spirit and acid juices, sugar and water. The spirit, volatile and fiery, is the proper emblem of vivacity and wit; the acidity of the lemon will very aptly figure pungency of raillery, and acrimony of censure; sugar is the natural representative of luscious adulation and gentle complaisance; and water is the proper hieroglyphick of easy prattle, innocent and tasteless.

Spirit alone is too powerful for use. It will produce madness rather than merriment; and instead of quenching thirst will inflame the blood. Thus wit, too copiously poured out, agitates the hearer with emotions rather violent than pleasing; every one shrinks from the force of its oppression, the company sits entranced and overpowered; all are astonished, but nobody is pleased.

The acid juices give this genial liquor all its power of stimulating the palate. Conversation would become dull and vapid, if negligence were not sometimes roused, and sluggishness quickened, by due severity of reprehension. But acids unmixed will distort the face and torture the palate; and he that has no other qualities than penetration and asperity, he whose constant employment is detection and censure, who looks only to find faults, and speaks only to punish them, will soon be dreaded, hated and avoided.

The taste of sugar is generally pleasing, but it cannot long be eaten by itself. Thus meekness and courtesy will always recommend the first address, but soon pall and nauseate, unless they are associated with more sprightly qualities. The chief use of sugar is to temper the taste of other substances; and softness of behaviour, in the same manner, mitigates the roughness of contradiction, and allays the bitterness of unwelcome truth.

Water is the universal vehicle by which are conveyed the particles necessary to sustenance and growth, by which thirst is quenched, and all the wants of life and nature are supplied. Thus all the business of the world is transacted by artless and easy talk, neither sublimed by fancy, nor discoloured by affectation, without either the harshness of satire, or the lusciousness of flattery. By this limpid vein of language, curiosity is gratified, and all the knowledge is conveyed which one man is required to impart for the safety or convenience of another. Water is the only ingredient in punch which can be used alone, and with which man is content till fancy has framed an artificial want. Thus while we only desire to have our ignorance informed, we are most delighted with the plainest diction; and it is only in the moments of idleness or pride, that we call for the gratifications of wit or flattery.

He only will please long, who, by tempering the acidity of satire with the sugar of civility, and allaying the heat of wit with the frigidity of humble chat, can make the true punch of conversation; and, as that punch can be drunk in the greatest quantity which has the largest proportion of water, so that companion will be oftenest welcome, whose talk flows out with inoffensive copiousness, and unenvied insipidity.

N°. 35.　SATURDAY, DECEMBER 16, 1758.

TO THE IDLER.

MR. IDLER,

If it be difficult to persuade the idle to be busy, it is likewise, as experience has taught me, not easy to convince the busy that it is better to be idle. When you shall despair of stimulating sluggishness to motion, I hope you will turn your thoughts towards the means of stilling the bustle of pernicious activity.

I am the unfortunate husband of a *buyer of bargains*. My wife has somewhere heard, that a good housewife *never* has any thing to *purchase when it is wanted*. This maxim is. often in her mouth, and always in her head. She is not one of those philosophical talkers that speculate without practice; and learn sentences of wisdom only to repeat them: she is always making additions to her stores; she never looks into a broker's shop, but she spies something that may be wanted some time; and it is impossible to make her pass the door of a house where she hears *goods selling by auction*.

Whatever she thinks cheap, she holds it the duty of an economist to buy; in consequence of this maxim, we are encumbered on every side with useless lumber. The servants can scarcely creep to their beds through the chests and boxes that surround them. The carpenter is employed once a week in building closets, fixing cupboards, and fastening shelves; and my house has the appearance of a ship stored for a voyage to the colonies.

I had often observed that advertisements set her on fire; and therefore, pretending to emulate her laudable frugality, I forbade the newspaper to be taken any longer; but my precaution is vain; I know not by what fatality, or by what confederacy, every catalogue of *genuine furniture* comes to her hand, every advertisement of a warehouse newly opened, is in her pocketbook, and she knows before any of her neighbours when the stock of any man *leaving off trade* is to be *sold cheap for ready money*.

Such intelligence is to my dear-one the Syren's song. No engagement, no duty, no interest, can withhold her from a sale, from which she always returns congratulating herself upon her dexterity at a bargain; the porter lays down his burden in the hall; she displays her new acquisitions, and spends the rest of the day in contriving where they shall be put.

As she cannot bear to have any thing uncomplete, one purchase necessitates another; she has twenty feather-beds more than she can use, and a late sale has supplied her with a proportionable number of Witney blankets, a large roll of linen for sheets, and five quilts for every bed, which she bought because the seller told her, that if she would clear his hands he would let her have a bargain.

Thus by hourly encroachments my habitation is made narrower and narrower; the dining-room is so crowded with tables, that dinner scarcely can be served; the parlour is decorated with so many piles of china, that I dare not step within the door; at every turn of the stairs I have a clock, and half the windows of the upper floors are darkened, that shelves may be set before them.

This, however, might be borne, if she would gratify her own inclinations without opposing mine. But I, who am idle, am luxurious, and she condemns me to live upon salt provisions. She knows the loss of buying in small quantities, we have, therefore, whole hogs and quarters of oxen. Part of our meat is tainted before it is eaten, and part is thrown away because it is spoiled; but she persists in her system, and will never buy any thing by single penny-worths.

The common vice of those who are still grasping at more, is to neglect that which they already possess; but from this failing my charmer is free. It is the great care of her life that the pieces of beef should be boiled in the order in which they are bought; that the second bag of pease should not be opened till the first be eaten; that every feather-bed should be lain on in its turn; that the carpets should be taken out of the chests once a month and brushed, and the rolls of linen opened now and then before the fire. She is daily inquiring after the best traps for mice, and keeps the rooms always scented by fumigations to destroy the moths. She employs workmen, from time to time, to adjust six clocks that never go, and clean five jacks that rust in the garret; and a woman in the next alley lives by scouring the brass and pewter, which are only laid up to tarnish again.

She is always imagining some distant time, in which she shall use whatever she accumulates: she has four looking-glasses which she cannot hang up in her house, but which will be handsome in more lofty rooms; and pays rent for the place of a vast copper in some warehouse, because, when we live in the country, we shall brew our own beer.

Of this life I have long been weary, but know not how to change it: all the married men whom I consult advise me to have patience; but some old bachelors are of opinion that, since she loves sales so well, she should have a sale of her own; and I have, I think, resolved to open her hoards, and advertise an auction.

I am, Sir,

Your very humble servant,

PETER PLENTY.

<hr>

N°. 36.   SATURDAY, DECEMBER 23, 1758.

THE great differences that disturb the peace of mankind are not about ends, but means. We have all the same general desires, but how those desires shall be accomplished will for ever be disputed. The ultimate purpose of government is temporal, and that of religion is eternal

happiness.   Hitherto we agree; but here we must part,
to try, according to the endless varieties of passion and
understanding)combined with one another, every possible
form of government, and every imaginable tenet of religion.

We are told by Cumberland that *rectitude*, applied to
action or contemplation, is merely metaphorical; and that
as a *right* line describes the shortest passage from point to
point, so a *right* action effects a good design by the fewest
means; and so likewise a *right* opinion is that which con-
nects distant truths by the shortest train of intermediate
propositions.

To find the nearest way from truth to truth, or from
purpose to effect, not to use more instruments where
fewer will be sufficient; not to move by wheels and levers
what will give way to the naked hand, is the great proof
of a healthful and vigorous mind, neither feeble with helpless ignorance, nor overburdened with unwieldy knowledge.

But there are men who seem to think nothing so much
the characteristick of a genius, as to do common things in
an uncommon manner; like Hudibras, to *tell the clock by
algebra*; or like the lady in Dr. Young's satires, *to drink
tea by stratagem*; to quit the beaten track, only because
it is known, and take a new path, however crooked or
rough, because the straight was found out before.

Every man speaks and writes with intent to be understood; and it can seldom happen but he that understands
himself, might convey his notions to another, if, content to
be understood, he did not seek to be admired; but when
once he begins to contrive how his sentiments may be received, not with most ease to his reader, but with most
advantage to himself, he then transfers his consideration
from words to sounds, from sentences to periods, and as he
grows more elegant becomes less intelligible.

It is difficult to enumerate every species of authors
whose labours counteract themselves; the man of exuberance and copiousness, who diffuses every thought through

so many diversities of expression, that it is lost like water in a mist; the ponderous dictator of sentences, whose no-tions are delivered in the lump, and are, like uncoined bullion, of more weight than use; the liberal illustrator, who shows by examples and comparisons what was clearly seen when it was first proposed; and the stately son of de-monstration, who proves with mathematical formality what no man has yet pretended to doubt.

There is a mode of style for which I know not that the masters of oratory have yet found a name; a style by which the most evident truths are so obscured that they can no longer be perceived, and the most familiar propo-sitions so disguised that they cannot be known. Every other kind of eloquence is the dress of sense; but this is the mask by which a true master of his art will so effec-tually conceal it, that a man will as easily mistake his own positions, if he meets them thus transformed, as he may pass in a masquerade his nearest acquaintance.

This style may be called the *terrifick*, for its chief in-tention is to terrify and amaze; it may be termed the *re-pulsive*, for its natural effect is to drive away the reader; or it may be distinguished, in plain English, by the deno-mination of the *bugbear style*, for it has more terrour than danger, and will appear less formidable as it is more nearly approached.

A mother tells her infant, that *two and two make four*; the child remembers the proposition, and is able to count four to all the purposes of life, till the course of his edu-cation brings him among philosophers, who fright him from his former knowledge, by telling him, that four is a certain aggregate of units; that all numbers being only the repe-tition of an unit, which, though not a number itself, is the parent, root, or original of all number, *four* is the deno-mination assigned to a certain number of such repetitions. The only danger is, lest, when he first hears these dreadful sounds, the pupil should run away; if he has but the cou-rage to stay till the conclusion, he will find that, when spe-culation has done its worst, two and two still make four.

An illustrious example of this species of eloquence may be found in " Letters concerning Mind." The author begins by declaring, that " the sorts of things are things that now are, have been, and shall be, and the things that strictly *are*." In this position, except the last clause, in which he uses something of the scholastick language, there is nothing but what every man has heard, and imagines himself to know. But who would not believe that some wonderful novelty is presented to his intellect, when he is afterwards told, in the true bugbear style, that " the *ares*, in the former sense, are things that lie between the *have-beens* and *shall-bes*. The *have-beens* are things that are past; the *shall-bes* are things that are to come; and the things that *are*, in the latter sense, are things that have not been, nor shall be, nor stand in the midst of such as are before them, or shall be after them. The things that *have been*, and *shall be*, have respect to present, past, and future. Those likewise that now *are* have moreover place; that, for instance, which is here, that which is to the east, that which is to the west."

All this, my dear reader, is very strange; but though it be strange, it is not new; survey these wonderful sentences again, and they will be found to contain nothing more than very plain truths, which, till this author arose, had always been delivered in plain language[p].

[p] These " Letters on Mind" were written by a Mr. Petvin, who after some years again astounded the literary public by sending forth, in diction equally terrific, another tract entitled a " Summary of the Soul's Perceptive Faculties," 1768. He was at that time compared to Duns Scotus, the subtle Doctor, who, in the weakness of old age, wept because he could not understand the subtleties of his earlier writings.

N°. 37.   SATURDAY, DECEMBER 30, 1758.

THOSE who are skilled in the extraction and preparation
of metals declare, that iron is every where to be found;
and that not only its proper ore is copiously treasured in
the caverns of the earth, but that its particles are dispersed
throughout all other bodies.

If the extent of the human view could comprehend the
whole frame of the universe, I believe it would be found
invariably true, that Providence has given that in greatest
plenty, which the condition of life makes of greatest use;
and that nothing is penuriously imparted, or placed far from
the reach of man, of which a more liberal distribution, or
more easy acquisition, would increase real and rational
felicity.

Iron is common, and gold is rare. Iron contributes so
much to supply the wants of nature, that its use constitutes much of the difference between savage and polished
life, between the state of him that slumbers in European
palaces, and him that shelters himself in the cavities of a
rock from the chilness of the night, or the violence of the
storm. Gold can never be hardened into saws or axes;
it can neither furnish instruments of manufacture, utensils
of agriculture, nor weapons of defence; its only quality is
to shine, and the value of its lustre arises from its scarcity.

Throughout the whole circle, both of natural and moral
life, necessaries are as iron, and superfluities as gold.
What we really need we may readily obtain; so readily,
that far the greater part of mankind has, in the wantonness
of abundance, confounded natural with artificial desires,
and invented necessities for the sake of employment; because the mind is impatient of inaction, and life is sustained
with so little labour, that the tediousness of idle time cannot otherwise be supported.

Thus plenty is the original cause of many of our needs;
and even the poverty, which is so frequent and distressful
in civilized nations, proceeds often from that change of

manners which opulence has produced. Nature makes us
poor only when we want necessaries; but custom gives
the name of poverty to the want of superfluities.

When Socrates passed through shops of toys and ornaments, he cried out, "How many things are here which
I do not need!" And the same exclamation may every
man make who surveys the common accommodations of
life.

Superfluity and difficulty begin together. To dress food
for the stomach is easy, the art is to irritate the palate
when the stomach is sufficed. A rude hand may build
walls, form roofs, and lay floors, and provide all that
warmth and security require; we only call the nicer artificers to carve the cornice, or to paint the ceilings. Such
dress as may enable the body to endure the different seasons, the most unenlightened nations have been able to
procure; but the work of science begins in the ambition
of distinction, in variations of fashion, and emulation of
elegance. Corn grows with easy culture; the gardener's
experiments are only employed to exalt the flavours of
fruits, and brighten the colours of flowers.

Even of knowledge, those parts are most easy which are
generally necessary. The intercourse of society is maintained without the elegancies of language. Figures, cri-
ticisms, and refinements, are the work of those whom idleness makes weary of themselves. The commerce of the
world is carried on by easy methods of computation. Subtilty and study are required only when questions are invented merely to puzzle, and calculations are extended to
show the skill of the calculator. The light of the sun is
equally beneficial to him whose eyes tell him that it moves,
and to him whose reason persuades him that it stands still;
and plants grow with the same luxuriance, whether we
suppose earth or water the parent of vegetation.

If we raise our thoughts to nobler inquiries, we shall
still find facility concurring with usefulness. No man
needs stay to be virtuous, till the moralists have determined
the essence of virtue; our duty is made apparent by its

proximate consequences, though the general and ultimate reason should never be discovered. Religion may
regulate the life of him to whom the Scotists and Thomists
are alike unknown ; and the assertors of fate and free-will,
however different in their talk, agree to act in the same
manner.

It is not my intention to depreciate the politer arts or
abstruser studies. That curiosity which always succeeds
ease and plenty, was undoubtedly given us as a proof of
capacity which our present state is not able to fill, as a
preparative for some better mode of existence, which shall
furnish employment for the whole soul, and where pleasure shall be adequate to our powers of fruition. In the
mean time, let us gratefully acknowledge that goodness
which grants us ease at a cheap rate, which changes the
seasons where the nature of heat and cold has not been
yet examined, and gives the vicissitudes of day and night
to those who never marked the tropicks, or numbered the
constellations.

N°. 38. SATURDAY, JANUARY 6, 1759.

SINCE the publication of the letter concerning the condition of those who are confined in gaols by their creditors,
an inquiry is said to have been made, by which it appears
that more than twenty thousand¹ are at this time prisoners
for debt.

We often look with indifference on the successive parts
of that, which, if the whole were seen together, would
shake us with emotion. A debtor is dragged to prison,
pitied for a moment, and then forgotten ; another follows
him, and is lost alike in the caverns of oblivion ; but when
the whole mass of calamity rises up at once, when twenty
thousand reasonable beings are heard all groaning in un-

q This number was, at that time, confidently published ; but the author has
since found reason to question the calculation.

necessary misery, not by the infirmity of nature, but the mistake or negligence of policy. who can forbear to pity and lament, to wonder and abhor?

There is here no need of declamatory vehemence: we live in an age of commerce and computation; let us, therefore, coolly inquire what is the sum of evil which the imprisonment of debtors brings upon our country.

It seems to be the opinion of the later computists, that the inhabitants of England do not exceed six millions, of which twenty thousand is the three-hundredth part. What shall we say of the humanity or the wisdom of a nation, that voluntarily sacrifices one in every three hundred to lingering destruction?

The misfortunes of an individual do not extend their influence to many; yet, if we consider the effects of consanguinity and friendship, and the general reciprocation of wants and benefits, which make one man dear or necessary to another, it may reasonably be supposed, that every man languishing in prison gives trouble of some kind to two others who love or need him. By this multiplication of misery we see distress extended to the hundredth part of the whole society.

If we estimate at a shilling a day what is lost by the inaction, and consumed in the support of each man thus chained down to involuntary idleness, the publick loss will rise in one year to three hundred thousand pounds; in ten years to more than a sixth part of our circulating coin.

I am afraid that those who are best acquainted with the state of our prisons will confess that my conjecture is too near the truth, when I suppose that the corrosion of resentment, the heaviness of sorrow, the corruption of confined air, the want of exercise, and sometimes of food, the contagion of diseases, from which there is no retreat, and the severity of tyrants, against whom there can be no resistance, and all the complicated horrours of a prison, put an end every year to the life of one in four of those that are shut up from the common comforts of human life.

Thus perish yearly five thousand men overborne with sorrow, consumed by famine, or putrefied by filth; many of them in the most vigorous and useful part of life; for the thoughtless and imprudent are commonly young, and the active and busy are seldom old.

According to the rule generally received, which supposes that one in thirty dies yearly, the race of man may be said to be renewed at the end of thirty years. Who would have believed till now, that of every English generation, a hundred and fifty thousand perish in our gaols? that in every century, a nation eminent for science, studious of commerce, ambitious of empire, should willingly lose, in noisome dungeons, five hundred thousand of its inhabitants; a number greater than has ever been destroyed in the same time by pestilence and the sword?

A very late occurrence may show us the value of the number which we thus condemn to be useless; in the re-establishment of the trained bands, thirty thousand are considered as a force sufficient against all exigencies. While, therefore, we detain twenty thousand in prison, we shut up in darkness and uselessness two-thirds of an army which ourselves judge equal to the defence of our country.

The monastick institutions have been often blamed, as tending to retard the increase of mankind. And, perhaps, retirement ought rarely to be permitted, except to those whose employment is consistent with abstraction, and who, though solitary, will not be idle; to those whom infirmity makes useless to the commonwealth, or to those who have paid their due proportion to society, and who, having lived for others, may be honourably dismissed to live for themselves. But whatever be the evil or the folly of these retreats, those have no right to censure them whose prisons contain greater numbers than the monasteries of other countries. It is, surely, less foolish and less criminal to permit inaction than compel it; to comply with doubtful opinions of happiness, than condemn to certain and apparent misery; to indulge the extravagancies of erroneous piety, than to multiply and enforce temptations to wickedness.

The misery of gaols is not half their evil: they are filled with every corruption which poverty and wickedness can generate between them; with all the shameless and profligate enormities that can be produced by the impudence of ignominy, the rage of want, and the malignity of despair. In a prison the awe of the publick eye is lost, and the power of the law is spent; there are few fears, there are no blushes. The lewd inflame the lewd, the audacious harden the audacious. Every one fortifies himself as he can against his own sensibility, endeavours to practise on others the arts which are practised on himself; and gains the kindness of his associates by similitude of manners.

Thus some sink amidst their misery, and others survive only to propagate villany. It may be hoped, that our lawgivers will at length take away from us this power of starving and depraving one another; but, if there be any reason why this inveterate evil should not be removed in our age, which true policy has enlightened beyond any former time, let those, whose writings form the opinions and the practices of their contemporaries, endeavour to transfer the reproach of such imprisonment from the debtor to the creditor, till universal infamy shall pursue the wretch whose wantonness of power, or revenge of disappointment, condemns another to torture and to ruin; till he shall be hunted through the world as an enemy to man, and find in riches no shelter from contempt.

Surely, he whose debtor has perished in prison, although he may acquit himself of deliberate murder, must at least have his mind clouded with discontent, when he considers how much another has suffered from him; when he thinks on the wife bewailing her husband, or the children begging the bread which their father would have earned. If there are any made so obdurate by avarice or cruelty, as to revolve these consequences without dread or pity, I must leave them to be awakened by some other power, for I write only to human beings[r].

---

[r] A series of Essays, entitled the Farrago, was published in 1792, for the benefit of the society for the discharge and relief of persons imprisoned for small debts. See Dr. Drake's Essays on the Rambler, &c. vol. ii. p. 427. The Congress of the United States passed a law in 1824, abolishing arrest and imprisonment for debt. The measure has yet to stand the test of practice and experience. See Idler 22. and note.

N°. 39. SATURDAY, JANUARY 13, 1759.

---

*   Nec genus ornatus unum est: quod quamque decebit,
Eligat————   OVID. Ars. Am. iii. 135.

TO THE IDLER.

SIR,

As none look more diligently about them than those who have nothing to do, or who do nothing, I suppose it has not escaped your observation, that the bracelet, an ornament of great antiquity, has been for some years revived among the English ladies.

The genius of our nation is said, I know not for what reason, to appear rather in improvement than invention. The bracelet was known in the earliest ages; but it was formerly only a hoop of gold, or a cluster of jewels, and showed nothing but the wealth or vanity of the wearer, till our ladies, by carrying pictures on their wrists, made their ornaments works of fancy and exercises of judgment.

This addition of art to luxury is one of the innumerable proofs that might be given of the late increase of female erudition; and I have often congratulated myself that my life has happened at a time when those, on whom so much of human felicity depends, have learned to think as well as speak, and when respect takes possession of the ear, while love is entering at the eye.

I have observed, that, even by the suffrages of their own sex, those ladies are accounted wisest, who do not yet disdain to be taught; and, therefore, I shall offer a few hints for the completion of the bracelet, without any dread of the fate of Orpheus.

To the ladies, who wear the pictures of their husbands or children, or any other relations, I can offer nothing more decent or more proper. It is reasonable to believe that she intends at least to perform her duty, who carries a perpetual excitement to recollection and caution, whose own ornaments must upbraid her with every failure, and who, by an open violation of her engagements, must for ever forfeit her bracelet.

Yet I know not whether it is the interest of the husband to solicit very earnestly a place on the bracelet. If his image be not in the heart, it is of small avail to hang it on the hand. A husband encircled with diamonds and rubies may gain some esteem, but will never excite love. He that thinks himself most secure of his wife, should be fearful of persecuting her continually with his presence. The joy of life is variety; the tenderest love requires to be rekindled by intervals of absence; and Fidelity herself will be wearied with transferring her eye only from the same man to the same picture.

In many countries the condition of every woman is known by her dress. Marriage is rewarded with some honourable distinction, which celibacy is forbidden to usurp. Some such information a bracelet might afford. The ladies might enrol themselves in distinct classes, and carry in open view the emblems of their order. The bracelet of the authoress may exhibit the Muses in a grove of laurel; the housewife may show Penelope with her web; the votaress of a single life may carry Ursula with her troop of virgins; the gamester may have Fortune with her wheel; and those women *that have no character at all* may display a field of white enamel, as imploring help to fill up the vacuity.

There is a set of ladies who have outlived most animal pleasures, and, having nothing rational to put in their place, solace with cards the loss of what time has taken away, and the want of what wisdom, having never been courted, has never given. For these I know not how to provide a proper decoration. They cannot be numbered among the gamesters; for though they are always at play, they play for nothing, and never rise to the dignity of hazard or the reputation of skill. They neither love nor are loved, and cannot be supposed to contemplate any human image with delight. Yet, though they despair to please, they always wish to be fine, and, therefore, cannot be without a bracelet. To this sisterhood I can recommend nothing more likely to please them than the king of clubs, a personage very comely and majestick, who will never meet their eyes without reviving the thought of some past or future party, and who may be displayed, in the act of dealing, with grace and propriety.

But the bracelet which might be most easily introduced into general use is a small convex mirror, in which the lady may see herself whenever she shall lift her hand. This will be a perpetual source of delight. Other ornaments are of use only in publick, but this will furnish gratifications to solitude. This will show a face that must always please; she who is followed by admirers will carry about her a perpetual justification of the publick voice; and she who passes without notice may appeal from prejudice to her own eyes.

But I know not why the privilege of the bracelet should be confined to women; it was in former ages worn by heroes in battle; and, as modern soldiers are always distinguished by splendour of dress, I should rejoice to see the bracelet added to the cockade.

In hope of this ornamental innovation, I have spent some thoughts upon military bracelets. There is no passion more heroick than love; and, therefore, I should be glad to see the sons of England marching in the field, every man with the picture of a woman of honour bound upon his hand. But since in the army, as every where else, there will always be men who love nobody but themselves, or whom no woman of honour will permit to love her, there is a necessity of some other distinctions and devices.

I have read of a prince who, having lost a town, ordered the name of it to be every morning shouted in his ear till it should be recovered. For the same purpose I think the prospect of Minorca might be properly worn on the hands of some of our generals: others might delight their countrymen, and dignify themselves, with a view of Rochfort as it appeared to them at sea: and those that shall return from the conquest of America, may exhibit the warehouse of Frontenac, with an inscription denoting, that it was taken in less than three years by less than twenty thousand men.

I am, Sir, &c.

Tom Toy.

N°. 40. SATURDAY, JANUARY 20, 1759.

THE practice of appending to the narratives of publick transactions more minute and domestick intelligence, and filling the newspapers with advertisements, has grown up by slow degrees to its present state.

Genius is shown only by invention. The man who first took advantage of the general curiosity that was excited by a siege or battle, to betray the readers of news into the knowledge of the shop where the best puffs and powder were to be sold, was undoubtedly a man of great sagacity, and profound skill in the nature of man. But when he had once shown the way, it was easy to follow him; and every man now knows a ready method of informing the publick of all that he desires to buy or sell; whether his wares be material or intellectual; whether he makes clothes, or teaches the mathematicks; whether he be a tutor that wants a pupil, or a pupil that wants a tutor.

Whatever is common is despised. Advertisements are now so numerous that they are very negligently perused, and it is, therefore, become necessary to gain attention by magnificence of promises, and by eloquence sometimes sublime and sometimes pathetick.

Promise, large promise, is the soul of an advertisement. I remember a *wash-ball* that had a quality truly wonderful—it gave *an exquisite edge to the razor*. And there are now to be sold, *for ready money only*, some *duvets for bed-coverings, of down, beyond comparison superior to what is called otter-down*, and indeed such, that its *many excellencies cannot be here set forth*. With one excellence we are made acquainted—*it is warmer than four or five blankets, and lighter than one*.

There are some, however, that know the prejudice of mankind in favour of modest sincerity. The vender of the *beautifying fluid* sells a lotion that repels pimples, washes away freckles, smooths the skin, and plumps the flesh ; and yet, with a generous abhorrence of osteutation, confesses, that it will not *restore the bloom of fifteen to a lady of fifty.*

The true pathos of advertisements must have sunk deep into the heart of every man that remembers the zeal shown by the seller of the *anodyne necklace*, for the ease and safety *of poor teething infants*, and the affection with which he warned every mother, that *she would never forgive herself*, if her infant should perish without a necklace.

I cannot but remark to the celebrated author who gave, in his notifications of the camel and dromedary, so many specimens of the genuine sublime, that there is now arrived another subject yet more worthy of his pen. *A famous Mohawk Indian warrior, who took* Dieskaw *the French general prisoner, dressed in the same manner with the native Indians when they go to war, with his face and body painted, with his scalping-knife, tom-axe, and all other implements of war ! a sight worthy the curiosity of every true Briton !* This is a very powerful description ; but a critick of great refinement would say, that it conveys rather *horrour* than *terrour.* An Indian, dressed as he goes to war, may bring company together ; but if he carries the scalping-knife and tom-axe, there are many true Britons that will never be persuaded to see him but through a grate.

It has been remarked by the severer judges, that the salutary sorrow of tragick scenes is too soon effaced by the merriment of the epilogue ; the same inconvenience arises from the improper disposition of advertisements. The noblest objects may be so associated as to be made ridiculous. The camel and dromedary themselves might have lost much of their dignity between *the true flower of mustard* and the *original Daffy's elixir;* and I could not but feel some indignation when I found this illustrious Indian warrior immediately succeeded by *a fresh parcel of Dublin butter*.

The trade of advertising is now so near to perfection, that it is not easy to propose any improvement. But as every art ought to be exercised in due subordination to the publick good, I cannot but propose it as a moral question to these masters of the publick ear, Whether they do not sometimes play too wantonly with our passions, as when the registrar of lottery-tickets invites us to his shop by an account of the prize which he sold last year; and whether the advertising controvertists do not indulge asperity of language without any adequate provocation; as in the dispute about *straps for razors*, now happily subsided, and in the altercation which at present subsists concerning *eau de luce?*

In an advertisement it is allowed to every man to speak well of himself, but I know not why he should assume the privilege of censuring his neighbour. He may proclaim his own virtue or skill, but ought not to exclude others from the same pretensions.

Every man 'that advertises his own excellence should write with some consciousness of a character which dares to call the attention of the publick. He should remember that his name is to stand in the same paper with those of the king of Prussia and the emperour of Germany, and endeavour to make himself worthy of such association.

Some regard is likewise to be paid to posterity. There are men of diligence and curiosity who treasure up the papers of the day merely because others neglect them, and in time they will be scarce. When these collections shall be read in another century, how will numberless contradictions be reconciled? and how shall fame be possibly distributed among the tailors and bodice-makers of the present age?

Surely these things deserve consideration. It is enough for me to have hinted my desire that these abuses may be rectified; but such is the state of nature, that what all

have the right of doing, many will attempt without sufficient care or due qualifications[a].

<hr>

N°. 41. SATURDAY, JANUARY 27, 1759.

THE following letter relates to an affliction perhaps not
necessary to be imparted to the publick; but I could not
persuade myself to suppress it, because I think, I know
the sentiments to be sincere, and I feel no disposition to
provide for this day any other entertainment.

> *At, tu quisquis eris, miseri qui cruda poetæ*
> *Credideris fletu funera digna tuo,*
> *Hæc postrema tibi sit flendi causa, fluatque*
> *Lenis inoffenso vitaque morsque gradu.*   OVID.

MR. IDLER,

NOTWITHSTANDING the warnings of philosophers,
and the daily examples of losses and misfortunes which
life forces upon our observation, such is the absorption of
our thoughts in the business of the present day, such the
resignation of our reason to empty hopes of future felicity,
or such our unwillingness to foresee what we dread, that
every calamity comes suddenly upon us, and not only
presses us as a burden, but crushes as a blow.

.There are evils which happen out of the common course
of nature, against which it is no reproach not to be provided. A flash of lightning intercepts the traveller in his
way. The concussion of an earthquake heaps the ruins of
cities upon their inhabitants. But other miseries time
brings, though silently yet visibly, forward by its even
lapse, which yet approach us unseen, because we turn our
eyes away, and seize us unresisted, because we could not
arm ourselves against them but by setting them before
us.

[a] A history of newspapers, more diffuse than the chronological series in
Nichols' Literary Anecdotes, Vol. iv. is desirable. See Preface.

That it is vain to shrink from what cannot be avoided, and to hide that from ourselves which must some time be found, is a truth which we all know, but which all neglect, and, perhaps, none more than the speculative reasoner, whose thoughts are always from home, whose eye wanders over life, whose fancy dances after meteors of happiness kindled by itself, and who examines every thing rather than his own state.

Nothing is more evident than that the decays of age must terminate in death; yet there is no man, says Tully, who does not believe that he may yet live another year; and there is none who does not, upon the same principle, hope another year for his parent or his friend: but the fallacy will be in time detected; the last year, the last day, must come. It has come, and is past. The life which made my own life pleasant is at an end, and the gates of death are shut upon my prospects.

The loss of a friend upon whom the heart was fixed, to whom every wish and endeavour tended, is a state of dreary desolation, in which the mind looks abroad impatient of itself, and finds nothing but emptiness and horrour. The blameless life, the artless tenderness, the pious simplicity, the modest resignation, the patient sickness, and the quiet death, are remembered only to add value to the loss, to aggravate regret for what cannot be amended, to deepen sorrow for what cannot be recalled.

These are the calamities by which Providence gradually disengages us from the love of life. Other evils fortitude may repel, or hope may mitigate; but irreparable privation leaves nothing to exercise resolution or flatter expectation. The dead cannot return, and nothing is left us here but languishment and grief.

Yet such is the course of nature, that whoever lives long must outlive those whom he loves and honours. Such is the condition of our present existence, that life must one time lose its associations, and every inhabitant of the earth must walk downward to the grave alone and unregarded, without any partner of his joy or grief, without any interested witness of his misfortunes or success.

Misfortune, indeed, he may yet feel; for where is the bottom of the misery of man? But what is success to him that has none to enjoy it? Happiness is not found in self-contemplation; it is perceived only when it is reflected from another.

We know little of the state of departed souls, because such knowledge is not necessary to a good life. Reason deserts us at the brink of the grave, and can give no further intelligence. Revelation is not wholly silent. " There is joy in the angels of Heaven over one sinner that repenteth;" and, surely, this joy is not incommunicable to souls disentangled from the body, and made like angels.

Let hope therefore dictate, what revelation does not confute, that the union of souls may still remain; and that we who are struggling with sin, sorrow, and infirmities, may have our part in the attention and kindness of those who have finished their course, and are now receiving their reward.

These are the great occasions which <u>force the</u> mind to take refuge in religion: when we have no help in ourselves, what can remain but that we look up to a higher and a greater Power? and to what hope may we not raise our eyes and hearts, when we consider that the greatest POWER is the BEST?

Surely there is no man who, thus afflicted, does not seek succour in the *gospel,* which has brought *life and immortality to light.* The precepts of Epicurus, who teaches us to endure what the laws of the universe make necessary, may silence, but not content us. The dictates of Zeno, who commands us to look with indifference on external things, may dispose us to conceal our sorrow, but cannot assuage it. Real alleviation of the loss of friends, and rational tranquillity, in the prospect of our own dissolution, can be received only from the promises of Him in whose hands are life and death, and from the assurance of another and better state, in which all tears will be wiped from the eyes, and the whole soul shall be filled with joy. Philosophy may infuse stubbornness, but Religion only can give patience [‘].

I am, &c.

Nº. 42. SATURDAY, FEBRUARY   1759.

THE subject of the following letter is not wholly unmentioned by the Rambler. The Spectator has also a letter containing a case not much different. I hope my correspondent's performance is more an effort of genius, than an effusion of the passions; and that she hath rather attempted to paint some possible distress, than really feels the evils which she has described.

TO THE IDLER.

SIR,

THERE is a cause of misery, which, though certainly known both to you and your predecessors, has been little taken notice of in your papers; I mean the snares that the bad behaviour of parents extends over the paths of life which their children are to tread after them; and as I make no doubt but the Idler holds the shield for virtue, as well as the glass for folly; that he will employ his leisure hours as much to his own satisfaction in warning his readers against a danger, as in laughing them out of a fashion: for this reason I am tempted to ask admittance for my story in your paper, though it has nothing to recommend it but truth, and the honest wish of warning others to shun the track which, I am afraid, may lead me at last to ruin.

I am the child of a father, who, having always lived in one spot in the country where he was born, and having had no genteel education himself, thought no qualifications in the world desirable but as they led up to fortune; and no

[‘] See Preface.

learning necessary to happiness but such as might most
effectually teach me to make the best market of myself. I
was unfortunately born a beauty, to a full sense of which
my father took care to flatter me; and having, when very
young, put me to a school in the country, afterwards transplanted me to another in town, at the instigation of his
friends, where his ill-judged fondness let me remain no
longer than to learn just enough experience to convince
me of the sordidness of his views, to give me an idea of
perfections which my present situation will never suffer
me to reach, and to teach me sufficient morals to dare to
despise what is bad, though it be in a father.

Thus equipped (as he thought completely) for life, I was
carried back into the country, and lived with him and my
mother in a small village, within a few miles of the county
town; where I mixed, at first with reluctance, among company which, though I never despised, I could not approve,
as they were brought up with other inclinations, and narrower views than my own. My father took great pains to
show me every where, both at his own house, and at such
publick diversions as the country afforded : he frequently
told the people all he had was for his daughter; took care
to repeat the civilities I had received from all his friends
in London; told how much I was admired, and all his little
ambition could suggest to set me in a stronger light.

Thus have I continued tricked out for sale, as I may
call it, and doomed, by parental authority, to a state little
better than that of prostitution. I look on myself as growing cheaper every hour, and am losing all that honest
pride, that modest confidence, in which the virgin dignity
consists. Nor does my misfortune stop here : though
many would be too generous to impute the follies of a
father to a child whose heart has set her above them; yet
I am afraid the most charitable of them will hardly think
it possible for me to be a daily spectatress of his vices
without tacitly allowing them, and at last consenting to
them, as the eye of the frightened infant is, by degrees,
reconciled to the darkness of which at first it was afraid.

It is a common opinion, he himself must very well know, that vices, like diseases, are often hereditary; and that the property of the one is to infect the manners, as the other poisons the springs of life.

Yet this, though bad, is not the worst; my father deceives himself in the hopes of the very child he has brought into the world; he suffers his house to be the seat of drunkenness, riot, and irreligion, who seduces, almost in my sight, the menial servant, converses with the prostitute, and corrupts the wife! Thus I, who from my earliest dawn of reason was taught to think that at my approach every eye sparkled with pleasure, or was dejected as conscious of superior charms, am excluded from society, through fear lest I should partake, if not of my father's crimes, at least of his reproach. Is a parent, who is so little solicitous for the welfare of a child, better than a pirate who turns a wretch adrift in a boat at sea, without a star to steer by, or an anchor to hold it fast? Am I not to lay all my miseries at those doors which ought to have been opened only for my protection? And if doomed to add at last one more to the number of those wretches whom neither the world nor its law befriends, may I not justly say that I have been awed by a parent into ruin? But though a parent's power is screened from insult and violation by the very words of Heaven, yet surely no laws, divine or human, forbid me to remove myself from the malignant shade of a plant that poisons all around it, blasts the bloom of youth, checks its improvements, and makes all its flowrets fade; but to whom can the wretched, can the dependant fly? For me to fly a father's house, is to be a beggar: I have only one comfort amidst my anxieties, a pious relation, who bids me appeal to Heaven for a witness to my just intentions, fly as a deserted wretch to its protection; and, being asked who my father is, point, like the ancient philosopher, with my finger to the heavens.

The hope in which I write this is, that you will give it a place in your paper; and, as your essays sometimes find their way into the country, that my father may read my story there ; and, if not for his own sake, yet for mine, spare to perpetuate that worst of calamities to me, the loss of character, from which all his dissimulation has not been able to rescue himself. Tell the world, Sir, that it is possible for virtue to keep its throne unshaken without any other guard than itself; that it is possible to maintain that purity of thought so necessary to the completion of human excellence, even in the midst of temptations; when they have no friend within, nor are assisted by the voluntary indulgence of vicious thoughts.

If the insertion of a story like this does not break in on the plan of your paper, you have it in your power to be a better friend than her father to

PERDITA[a].

N°. 43. SATURDAY, FEBRUARY 10, 1759.

THE natural advantages which arise from the position of the earth which we inhabit with respect to the other planets, afford much employment to mathematical speculation; by which it has been discovered, that no other conformation of the system could have given such commodious distributions of light and heat, or imparted fertility and pleasure to so great a part of a revolving sphere.

It may be, perhaps, observed by the moralist, with equal reason, that our globe seems particularly fitted for the residence of a being, placed here only for a short time, whose task is to advance himself to a higher and happier state of existence, by unremitted vigilance of caution, and activity of virtue.

The duties required of man are such as human nature does not willingly perform, and such as those are inclined to delay who yet intend some time to fulfil them. It was, therefore, necessary that this universal reluctance should be

[a] From an unknown correspondent.

counteracted, and the drowsiness of hesitation wakened into resolve; that the danger of procrastination should be always in view, and the fallacies of security be hourly detected.

To this end all the appearances of nature uniformly conspire. Whatever we see on every side reminds us of the lapse of time and the flux of life. The day and night succeed each other, the rotation of seasons diversifies the year, the sun rises, attains the meridian, declines, and sets; and the moon every night changes its form.

The day has been considered as an image of the year, and the year as the representation of life. The morning answers to the spring, and the spring to childhood and youth; the noon corresponds to the summer, and the summer to the strength of manhood. The evening is an emblem of autumn, and autumn of declining life. The night with its silence and darkness shows the winter, in which all the powers of vegetation are benumbed; and the winter points out the time when life shall cease, with its hopes and pleasures.

He that is carried forward, however swiftly, by a motion equable and easy, perceives not the change of place but by the variation of objects. If the wheel of life, which rolls thus silently along, passed on through undistinguishable uniformity, we should never mark its approaches to the end of the course. If one hour were like another; if the passage of the sun did not show that the day is wasting; if the change of seasons did not impress upon us the flight of the year; quantities of duration equal to days and years would glide unobserved. If the parts of time were not variously coloured, we should never discern their departure or succession, but should live thoughtless of the past, and careless of the future, without will, and perhaps without power, to compute the periods of life, or to compare the time which is already lost with that which may probably remain.

But the course of time is so visibly marked, that it is observed even by the birds of passage, and by nations who have raised their minds very little above animal instinct: there are human beings whose language does not supply them with words by which they can number five, but I have read of none, that have not names for day and night, for summer and winter.

Yet it is certain, that these admonitions of nature, however forcible, however importunate, are too often vain; and that many who mark with such accuracy the course of time, appear to have little sensibility of the decline of life. Every man has something to do which he neglects; every man has faults to conquer which he delays to combat.

So little do we accustom ourselves to consider the effects of time, that things necessary and certain often surprise us like unexpected contingencies. We leave the beauty in her bloom, and, after an absence of twenty years, wonder, at our return, to find her faded. We meet those whom we left children, and can scarcely persuade ourselves to treat them as men. The traveller visits in age those countries through which he rambled in his youth, and hopes for merriment at the old place. The man of business, wearied with unsatisfactory prosperity, retires to the town of his nativity, and expects to play away the last years with the companions of his childhood, and recover youth in the fields, where he once was young.

From this inattention, so general and so mischievous, let it be every man's study to exempt himself. Let him that desires to see others happy make haste to give, while his gift can be enjoyed, and remember that every moment of delay takes away something from the value of his benefaction. And let him, who purposes his own happiness, reflect, that while he forms his purpose the day rolls on, and *the night cometh when no man can work*.

N°. 44. SATURDAY, FEBRUARY 17, 1759.

MEMORY is, among the faculties of the human mind, that of which we make the most frequent use, or rather that of which the agency is incessant, or perpetual. Memory is the primary and fundamental power, without which there could be no other intellectual operation. Judgment and ratiocination suppose something already known, and draw their decisions only from experience. Imagination selects ideas from the treasures of remembrance, and produces novelty only by varied combinations. We do not even form conjectures of distant, or anticipations of future events, but by concluding what is possible from what is past.

The two offices of memory are collection and distribution; by one images are accumulated, and by the other produced for use. Collection is always the employment of our first years; and distribution commonly that of our advanced age.

To collect and reposite the various forms of things, is far the most pleasing part of mental occupation. We are naturally delighted with novelty, and there is a time when all that we see is new. When first we enter into the world, whithersoever we turn our eyes, they meet knowledge with pleasure at her side; every diversity of nature pours ideas in upon the soul; neither search nor labour are necessary; we have nothing more to do than to open our eyes, and curiosity is gratified.

Much of the pleasure which the first survey of the world affords, is exhausted before we are conscious of our own felicity, or able to compare our condition with some other possible state. We have, therefore, few traces of the joy of our earliest discoveries; yet we all remember a time, when nature had so many untasted gratifications, that every excursion gave delight which can now be found no longer, when the noise of a torrent, the rustle of a wood, the song of birds, or the play of lambs, had power to fill the attention, and suspend all perception of the course of time.

But these easy pleasures are soon at an end ; we have seen in a very little time so much, that we call out for new objects of observation, and endeavour to find variety in books and life.   But study is laborious, and not always satisfactory; and conversation has its pains as well pleasures; we are willing to learn, but not willing to be taught ; we are pained by ignorance, but pained yet more by another's knowledge.

From the vexation of pupilage men commonly set themselves free about the middle of life, by shutting up the avenues of intelligence, and resolving to rest in their present state.; and they, whose ardour of inquiry continues longer, find themselves insensibly forsaken by their instructors.   As every man advances in life, the proportion between those that are younger and that are older than himself is continually changing ; and he that has lived half a century finds few that do not require from him that information which he once expected from those that went before him.

Then it is, that the magazines of memory are opened, and the stores of accumulated knowledge are displayed by vanity or benevolence, or in honest commerce of mutual interest.   Every man wants others, and is, therefore, glad when he is wanted by them.   And as few men will endure the labour of intense meditation without necessity, he that has learned enough for his profit or his honour, seldom endeavours after further acquisitions.

The pleasure of recollecting speculative notions would not be much less than that of gaining them, if they could be kept pure and unmingled with the passages of life; but such is the necessary concatenation of our thoughts, that good and evil are linked together, and no pleasure recurs but associated with pain.   Every revived idea reminds us of a time when something was enjoyed that is now lost, when some hope was not yet blasted, when some purpose had yet not languished into sluggishness or indifference.

Whether it be, that life has more vexations than comforts, or, what is in the event just the same, that evil makes deeper impression than good, it is certain that few can review the time past without heaviness of heart.   He remembers many calamities incurred by folly, many opportunities lost by negligence.   The shades of the dead rise up before him; and he laments the companions of his youth, the partners of his amusements, the assistants of his labours, whom the hand of death has snatched away.

, When an offer was made to Themistocles of teaching him the art of memory, he answered, that he would rather wish for the art of forgetfulness.   He felt his imagination haunted by phantoms of misery which he was unable to suppress, and would gladly have calmed his thoughts with some *oblivious antidote*.   In this we all resemble one another; the hero and the sage are, like vulgar mortals, overburdened by the weight of life; all shrink from recollection, and all wish for an art of forgetfulness[x].

N°. 45. SATURDAY, FEBRUARY 24, 1759.

THERE is in many minds a kind of vanity exerted to the disadvantage of themselves; a desire to be praised for superior acuteness discovered only in the degradation of their species, or censure of their country.

Defamation is sufficiently copious.   The general lampooner of mankind may find long exercise for his zeal or wit, in the defects of nature, the vexations of life, the follies of opinion, and the corruptions of practice.   But fiction is easier than discernment; and most of these writers spare themselves the labour of inquiry, and exhaust their virulence upon imaginary crimes, which, as they never existed, can never be amended.

That the painters find no encouragement among the

---

[x] Read the sublime story of Sadak in search of the waters of oblivion in the Tales of the Genii. Those who have seen Martin's picture on the subject, have failed almost to recognise the respective limits of poetry and of painting.

English for many other works than portraits, has been imputed to national selfishness. 'Tis vain, says the satirist, to set before any Englishman the scenes of landscape, or the heroes of history; nature and antiquity are nothing in his eye; he has no value but for himself, nor desires any copy but of his own form.

Whoever is delighted with his own picture must derive his pleasure from the pleasure of another. Every man is always present to himself, and has, therefore, little need of his own resemblance, nor can desire it, but for the sake of those whom he loves, and by whom he hopes to be remembered. This use of the art is a natural and reasonable consequence of affection; and though, like other human actions, it is often complicated with pride, yet even such pride is more laudable than that by which palaces are covered with pictures, that, however excellent, neither imply the owner's virtue, nor excite it.

Genius is chiefly exerted in historical pictures; and the art of the painter of portraits is often lost in the obscurity of his subject. But it is in painting as in life; what is greatest is not always best. I should grieve to see Reynolds transfer to heroes and to goddesses, to empty splendour and to airy fiction, that art which is now employed in diffusing friendship, in reviving tenderness, in quickening the affections of the absent, and continuing the presence of the dead[y].

Yet in a nation great and opulent there is room, and ought to be patronage, for an art like that of painting through all its diversities; and it is to be wished, that the reward now offered for an historical picture may excite an honest emulation, and give beginning to an English school.

---

[y] Some judicious remarks on portrait painting may be found in Chalmers' Preface to Idler, Brit. Ess. 33.

The difference between the French and English schools, in this department of the Art well proves that mind has scope for its powers in portrait, and that genius alone can so generalize the details " as to identify the individual man with the dignity of his thinking powers."

It is not very easy to find an action or event that can be efficaciously represented by a painter.

He must have an action not successive but instantaneous; for the time of a picture is a single moment. For this reason, the death of Hercules cannot well be painted, though, at the first view, it flatters the imagination with very glittering ideas: the gloomy mountain, overhanging the sea, and covered with trees, some bending to the wind, and some torn from their roots by the raging hero; the violence with which he rends from his shoulders the envenomed garment; the propriety with which his muscular nakedness may be displayed; the death of Lycas whirled from the promontory; the gigantick presence of Philoctetes; the blaze of the fatal pile, which the deities behold with grief and terrour from the sky.

All these images fill the mind, but will not compose a picture, because they cannot be united in a single moment[z]. Hercules must have rent his flesh at one time, and tossed Lycas into the air at another; he must first tear up the trees, and then lie down upon the pile.

The action must be circumstantial and distinct. There is a passage in the Iliad which cannot be read without strong emotions. A Trojan prince, seized by Achilles in the battle, falls at his feet, and in moving terms supplicates for life. "How can a wretch like thee," says the haughty Greek, "intreat to live, when thou knowest that the time must come when Achilles is to die?" This cannot be painted, because no peculiarity of attitude or disposition can so supply the place of language as to impress the sentiment.

The event painted must be such as excites passion, and different passions in the several actors, or a tumult of contending passions in the chief.

Perhaps the discovery of Ulysses by his nurse is of this

---

[z] Has that picture, which is considered the finest in the world, the transfiguration, this requisite? Could any human eye, at one and the same moment, - have beheld the apostles baffled with the stubborn spirit which they had not faith to quell, and the glories on the Mount?

kind. The surprise of the nurse mingled with joy ; that of Ulysses checked by prudence, and clouded by solicitude; and the distinctness of the action by which the scar is found; all concur to complete the subject. But the picture, having only two figures, will want variety.

A much nobler assemblage may be furnished by the death of Epaminondas. The mixture of gladness and grief in the face of the messenger who brings his dying general an account of the victory; the various passions of the attendants; the sublimity of composure in the hero, while the dart is by his own command drawn from his side, and the faint gleam of satisfaction that diffuses itself over the languor of death; are worthy of that pencil which yet I do not wish to see employed upon them.

If the design were not too multifarious and extensive, I should wish that our painters would attempt the dissolution of the parliament by Cromwell*. The point of time may be chosen when Cromwell, looking round the Pandæmonium with contempt, ordered the bauble to be taken away; and Harrison laid hands on the Speaker to drag him from the chair.

The various appearances which rage, and terrour, and astonishment, and guilt, might exhibit in the faces of that hateful assembly, of whom the principal persons may be faithfully drawn from portraits or prints; the irresolute repugnance of some, the hypocritical submissions of others, the ferocious insolence of Cromwell, the rugged brutality of Harrison, and the general trepidation of fear and wickedness, would, if some proper disposition could be contrived, make a picture of unexampled variety, and irresistible instruction.

---

* This subject has now been most successfully handled by West. Hall's exquisite engraving has rendered the picture familiar.

Nº. 46.   SATURDAY, MARCH 3, 1759.

---

* Fugit ad salices, sed se cupit ante videri.   VIRGIL.

MR. IDLER,

I AM encouraged, by the notice you have taken of Betty Broom, to represent the miseries which I suffer from a species of tyranny, which, I believe, is not very uncommon, though perhaps it may have escaped the observation of those who converse little with fine ladies, or see them only in their publick characters.

To this method of venting my vexation I am the more inclined, because if I do not complain to you, I must burst in silence; for my mistress has teased me and teased me till I can hold no longer, and yet I must not tell her of her tricks. The girls that live in common services can quarrel, and give warning, and find other places; but we that live with great ladies, if we once offend them, have nothing left but to return into the country.

I am waiting-maid to a lady who keeps the best company, and is seen at every place of fashionable resort. I am envied by all the maids in the square, for few countesses leave off so many clothes as my mistress, and nobody shares with me: so that I supply two families in the country with finery for the assizes and horse-races, besides what I wear myself. The steward and housekeeper have joined against me to procure my removal, that they may advance a relation of their own; but their designs are found out by my lady, who says I need not fear them, for she will never have dowdies about her.

You would think, Mr. Idler, like others, that I am very happy, and may well be contented with my lot. But I will tell you. My lady has an odd humour. She never orders any thing in direct words, for she loves a sharp girl that can take a hint.

I would not have you suspect that she has any thing to hint

which she is ashamed to speak at length; for none can have greater purity of sentiment, or rectitude of intention. She has nothing to hide, yet nothing will she tell. She always gives her directions obliquely and allusively, by the mention of something relative or consequential, without any other purpose than to exercise my acuteness and her own.

It is impossible to give a notion of this style otherwise than by examples. One night, when she had sat writing letters till it was time to be dressed, *Molly,* said she, *the Ladies are all to be at Court to-night in white aprons.* When she means that I should send to order the chair, she says, *I think the streets are clean, I may venture to walk.* When she would have something put into its place, she bids me *lay it on the floor.* If she would have me snuff the candles, she asks *whether I think her eyes are like a cat's?* If she thinks her chocolate delayed, she talks of *the benefit of abstinence.* If any needle-work is forgotten, she supposes *that I have heard of the lady who died by pricking her finger.*

She always imagines that I can recall every thing past from a single word. If she wants her head from the milliner, she only says, *Molly, you know Mrs. Tape.* If she would have the mantua-maker sent for, she remarks *that Mr. Taffety, the mercer, was here last week.* She ordered, a fortnight ago, that the first time she was abroad all day I should choose her a new set of coffee-cups at the china-shop: of this she reminded me yesterday, as she was going down stairs, by saying, *You can't find your way now to Pall-mall.*

All this would never vex me, if, by increasing my trouble, she spared her own; but, dear Mr. Idler, is it not as easy to say *coffee-cups,* as *Pall-mall?* and to tell me in plain words what I am to do, and when it is to be done, as to torment her own head with the labour of finding hints, and mine with that of understanding them?

When first I came to this lady, I had nothing like the learning that I have now; for she has many books, and I have much time to read; so that of late I seldom have missed her meaning: but when she first took me I was an ignorant girl; and she, who, as is very common, confounded want of knowledge with want of understanding, began once to despair of bringing me to any thing, because, when I came into her chamber at the call of her bell, she asked me, *Whether we lived in Zembla*; and I did not guess the meaning of her inquiry, but modestly answered, that *I could not tell*. She had happened to ring once when I did not hear her, and meant to put me in mind of that country where sounds are said to be congealed by the frost.

Another time, as I was dressing her head, she began to talk on a sudden of *Medusa*, and *snakes*, and *men turned into stone, and maids that, if they were not watched, would let their mistresses be Gorgons*. I looked round me half frightened, and quite bewildered; till at last, finding that her literature was thrown away upon me, she bid me with great vehemence, reach the curling-irons.

It is not without some indignation, Mr. Idler, that I discover, in these artifices of vexation, something worse than foppery or caprice; a mean delight in superiority, which knows itself in no danger of reproof or opposition; a cruel pleasure in seeing the perplexity of a mind obliged to find what is studiously concealed, and a mean indulgence of petty malevolence, in the sharp censure of involuntary, and very often of inevitable, failings. When, beyond her expectation, I hit upon her meaning, I can perceive a sudden cloud of disappointment spread over her face; and have sometimes been afraid, lest I should lose her favour by understanding her when she means to puzzle me.

This day, however, she has conquered my sagacity. When she went out of her dressing-room, she said nothing, but, *Molly, you know*, and hastened to her chariot. What I am to know is yet a secret; but if I do not know before she comes back, what I yet have no means of discovering, she will make my dullness a pretence for a fortnight's ill humour, treat me as a creature devoid of the faculties necessary to the common duties of life, and perhaps give the next gown to the housekeeper.

I am, Sir,
Your humble servant,
MOLLY QUICK.

N°. 47. SATURDAY, MARCH 10, 1759.

TO THE IDLER.

MR. IDLER,

I AM the unfortunate wife of a city wit, and cannot but think that my case may deserve equal compassion with any of those which have been represented in your paper.

I married my husband within three months after the expiration of his apprenticeship; we put our money together, and furnished a large and splendid shop, in which he was for five years and a half diligent and civil. The notice which curiosity or kindness commonly bestows on beginners, was continued by confidence and esteem; one customer, pleased with his treatment and his bargain, recommended another; and we were busy behind the counter from morning to night.

Thus every day increased our wealth and our reputation. My husband was often invited to dinner openly on the Exchange by hundred thousand pounds men; and whenever I went to any of the halls, the wives of the aldermen made me low courtesies. We always took up our notes before the day, and made all considerable payments by draughts upon our banker.

You will easily believe that I was well enough pleased with my condition; for what happiness can be greater than that of growing every day richer and richer? I will not deny, that, imagining myself likely to be in a short time the sheriff's lady, I broke off my acquaintance with some of my neighbours; and advised my husband to keep good

company, and not to be seen with men that were worth
nothing.

In time he found that ale disagreed with his constitution,
and went every night to drink his pint at a tavern, where
he met with a set of criticks, who disputed upon the merit
of the different theatrical performers. By these idle fellows he was taken to the play, which at first he did not
seem much to heed; for he owned, that he very seldom
knew what they were doing, and that, while his companions would let him alone, he was commonly thinking on
his last bargain.

Having once gone, however, he went again and again,
though I often told him that three shillings were thrown
away: at last he grew uneasy if he missed a night, and
importuned me to go with him. I went to a tragedy,
which they called Macbeth; and, when I came home, told
him, that I could not bear to see men and women make
themselves such fools, by pretending to be witches and
ghosts, generals and kings, and to walk in their sleep when
they were as much awake, as those that looked at them.
He told me that I must get higher notions, and that a
play was the most rational of all entertainments, and most
proper to relax the mind after the business of the day.

By degrees he gained knowledge of some of the players:
and, when the play was over, very frequently treated them
with suppers; for which he was admitted to stand behind
the scenes

He soon began to lose some of his morning hours in the
same folly, and was for one winter very diligent in his attendance on the rehearsals; but of this species of idleness
he grew weary, and said, that the play was nothing without
the company.

His ardour for the diversion of the evening increased;
he bought a sword, and paid five shillings a night to sit in
the boxes; he went sometimes into a place which he calls
the green-room, where all the wits of the age assemble
and, when he had been there, could do nothing, for two or
three days, but repeat their jests, or tell their disputes.

He has now lost his regard for every thing but the play-house; he invites, three times a week, one or other to drink claret, and talk of the drama. His first care in the morning is to read the play-bills; and, if he remembers any lines of the tragedy which is to be represented, walks about the shop, repeating them so loud, and with such strange gestures, that the passengers gather round the door.

His greatest pleasure, when I married him, was to hear the situation of his shop commended, and to be told how many estates have been got in it by the same trade; but of late he grows peevish at any mention of business, and delights in nothing so much as to be told that he speaks like Mossop.

Among his new associates he has learned another language, and speaks in such a strain that his neighbours cannot understand him. If a customer talks longer than he is willing to bear, he will complain that he has been excruciated with unmeaning verbosity; he laughs at the letters of his friends for their tameness of expression, and often declares himself weary of attending to the minutiæ of a shop.

It is well for me that I know how to keep a book, for of late he is scarcely ever in the way. Since one of his friends told him that he had a genius for tragick poetry, he has locked himself in an upper room six or seven hours a day; and, when I carry him any paper to be read or signed, I hear him talking vehemently to himself, sometimes of love and beauty, sometimes of friendship and virtue, but more frequently of liberty and his country.

I would gladly, Mr. Idler, be informed what to think of a shopkeeper, who is incessantly talking about liberty; a word, which, since his acquaintance with polite life, my husband has always in his mouth: he is, on all occasions, afraid of our liberty, and declares his resolution to hazard all for liberty. What can the man mean? I am sure he has liberty enough; it were better for him and me if his liberty was lessened.

He has a friend, whom he calls a critick, that comes twice a week to read what he is writing. This critick tells him that his piece is a little irregular, but that some detached scenes will shine prodigiously, and that in the character of Bombulus he is wonderfully great. My scribbler then squeezes his hand, calls him the best of friends, thanks him for his sincerity, and tells him that he hates to be flattered. I have reason to believe that he seldom parts with his dear friend without lending him two guineas, and am afraid that he gave bail for him three days ago.

By this course of life our credit as traders is lessened; and I cannot forbear to suspect, that my husband's honour as a wit is not much advanced, for he seems to be always the lowest of the company, and is afraid to tell his opinion till the rest have spoken. When he was behind his counter, he used to be brisk, active, and jocular, like a man that knew what he was doing, and did not fear to look another in the face; but among wits and criticks he is timorous and awkward, and hangs down his head at his own table. Dear Mr. Idler, persuade him, if you can, to return once more to his native element. Tell him, that wit will never make him rich, but that there are places where riches will always make a wit.

I am, Sir, &c.

DEBORAH GINGER.

Nº. 48. SATURDAY, MARCH 17, 1759.

THERE is no kind of idleness, by which we are so easily seduced, as that which dignifies itself by the appearance of business; and, by making the loiterer imagine that he has something to do which must not be neglected, keeps him in perpetual agitation, and hurries him rapidly from place to place.

He that sits still, or reposes himself upon a couch, no more deceives himself than he deceives others; he knows that he is doing nothing, and has no other solace of his insignificance than the resolution, which the lazy hourly make, of changing his mode of life.

To do nothing every man is ashamed; and to do much almost every man is unwilling or afraid. Innumerable expedients have, therefore, been invented to produce motion without labour, and employment without solicitude. The greater part of those, whom the kindness of fortune has left to their own direction, and whom want does not keep chained to the counter or the plough, play throughout life with the shadows of business, and know not at last what they have been doing.

These imitators of action are of all denominations. Some are seen at every auction without intention to purchase; others appear punctually at the Exchange, though they are known there only by their faces: some are always making parties to visit collections for which they have no taste; and some neglect every pleasure and every duty to hear questions, in which they have no interest, debated in parliament.

These men never appear more ridiculous than in the distress which they imagine themselves to feel from some accidental interruption of those empty pursuits. A tiger newly imprisoned is indeed more formidable, but not more angry, than Jack Tulip, withheld from a florist's feast, or Tom Distich, hindered from seeing the first representation of a play.

As political affairs are the highest and most extensive of temporal concerns, the mimick of a politician is more busy and important than any other trifler. Monsieur le Noir, a man who, without property or importance in any corner of the earth, has, in the present confusion of the world, declared himself a steady adherent to the French, is made miserable by a wind that keeps back the packet-boat, and still more miserable by every account of a Malouin privateer caught in his cruise; he knows well that nothing can be done or said by him which can produce any effect but that of laughter, that he can neither hasten nor retard good or evil, that his joys and sorrows have scarcely any partakers; yet such is his zeal, and such his curiosity, that he would run barefooted to Gravesend, for the sake of knowing first that the English had lost a tender, and would ride out to meet every mail from the continent, if he might be permitted to open it.

Learning is generally confessed to be desirable, and there are some who fancy themselves always busy in acquiring it. Of these ambulatory students, one of the most busy is my friend Tom Restless.

Tom has long had a mind to be a man of knowledge, but he does not care to spend much time among authors; for he is of opinion that few books deserve the labour of perusal, that they give the mind an unfashionable cast, and destroy that freedom of thought, and easiness of manners, indispensably requisite to acceptance in the world. Tom has, therefore, found another way to wisdom. When he rises he goes into a coffee-house, where he creeps so near to men whom he takes to be reasoners, as to hear their discourse, and endeavours to remember something which, when it has been strained through Tom's head, is so near to nothing, that what it once was cannot be discovered. This he carries round from friend to friend through a circle of visits, till, hearing what each says upon the question, he becomes able at dinner to say a little himself; and, as every great genius relaxes himself among his inferiors, meets with some who wonder how so young a man can talk so wisely.

At night he has a new feast prepared for his intellects; he always runs to a disputing society, or a speaking club, where he half hears what, if he had heard the whole, he would but half understand; goes home pleased with the consciousness of a day well spent, lies down full of ideas, and rises in the morning empty as before.

N°. 49. SATURDAY, MARCH 24, 1759.

I SUPPED three nights ago with my friend Will Marvel. His affairs obliged him lately to take a journey into Devonshire, from which he has just returned. He knows me to be a very patient hearer, and was glad of my company, as it gave him an opportunity of disburdening himself, by a minute relation of the casualties of his expedition.

Will is not one of those who go out and return with nothing to tell. He has a story of his travels, which will strike a home-bred citizen with horrour, and has in ten days suffered so often the extremes of terrour and joy, that he is in doubt whether he shall ever again expose either his body or mind to such danger and fatigue.

When he left London the morning was bright, and a fair day was promised. But Will is born to struggle with difficulties. That happened to him, which has sometimes, perhaps, happened to others. Before he had gone more than ten miles, it began to rain. What course was to be taken? His soul disdained' to turn back. He did what the King of Prussia might have done; he flapped his hat, buttoned up his cape, and went forwards, fortifying his mind by the stoical consolation, that whatever is violent will be short.

His constancy was not long tried; at the distance of about half a mile he saw an inn, which he entered wet and weary, and found civil treatment and proper refreshment. After a respite of about two hours, he looked abroad, and seeing the sky clear, called for his horse, and passed the first stage without any other memorable accident.

Will considered, that labour must be relieved by pleasure, and that the strength which great undertakings require must be maintained by copious nutriment; he, therefore, ordered himself an elegant supper, drank two bottles of claret, and passed the beginning of the night in sound sleep; but, waking before light, was forewarned of the troubles of the next day, by a shower beating against his windows with such violence, as to threaten the dissolution of nature. When he arose, he found what he expected, that the country was under water. He joined himself, however, to a company that was travelling the same way, and came safely to the place of dinner, though every step of his horse dashed the mud into the air.

In the afternoon, having parted from his company, he set forward alone, and passed many collections of water, of which it was impossible to guess the depth, and which he now cannot review without some censure of his own rashness; but what a man undertakes he must perform, and Marvel hates a coward at his heart.

Few that lie warm in their beds think what others undergo, who have, perhaps, been as tenderly educated, and have as acute sensations as themselves. My friend was now to lodge the second night almost fifty miles from home, in a house which he never had seen before, among people to whom he was totally a stranger, not knowing whether the next man he should meet would prove good or bad; but seeing an inn of a good appearance, he rode resolutely into the yard; and knowing that respect is often paid in proportion as it is claimed, delivered his injunctions to the ostler with spirit, and entering the house, called vigorously about him.

On the third day up rose the sun and Mr. Marvel. His troubles and his dangers were now such as he wishes no other man ever to encounter. The ways were less frequented, and the country more thinly inhabited. He rode many a lonely hour through mire and water, and met not a single soul for two miles together, with whom he could exchange a word. He cannot deny that, looking round upon the dreary region, and seeing nothing but bleak fields and naked trees, hills obscured by fogs, and flats covered with inundations, he did, for some time, suffer melancholy to prevail upon him, and wished himself again safe at home. One comfort he had, which was, to consider that none of his friends were in the same distress, for whom, if they had been with him, he should have suffered more

than for himself; he could not forbear sometimes to consider how happily the Idler is settled in an easier condition,
who, surrounded like him with terrours, could have done
nothing but lie down and die.

Amidst these reflections he came to a town, and found
a dinner which disposed him to more cheerful sentiments:
but the joys of life are short, and its miseries are long; he
mounted and travelled fifteen miles more through dirt and
desolation.

At last the sun set, and all the horrours of darkness came
upon him. He then repented the weak indulgence in
which he had gratified himself at noon with too long an interval of rest: yet he went forward along a path which he
could no longer see, sometimes rushing suddenly into water,
and sometimes incumbered with stiff clay, ignorant whither
he was going, and uncertain whether his next step might
not be the last.

In this dismal gloom of nocturnal peregrination his horse
unexpectedly stood still. Marvel had heard many relations of the instinct of horses, and was in doubt what
danger might be at hand. Sometimes he fancied that he
was on the bank of a river still and deep, and sometimes
that a dead body lay across the track. He sat still awhile
to recollect his thoughts; and as he was about to alight
and explore the darkness, out stepped a man with a lantern,
and opened the turnpike. He hired a guide to the town,
arrived in safety, and slept in quiet.

The rest of his journey was nothing but danger. He
climbed and descended precipices on which vulgar mortals tremble to look; he passed marshes like the *Serbonian*
bog, where armies whole have sunk; he forded rivers
where the current roared like the Egre or the Severn; or
ventured himself on bridges that trembled under him,
from which he looked down on foaming whirlpools, or
dreadful abysses; he wandered over houseless heaths,
amidst all the rage of the elements, with the snow driving in
his face, and the tempest howling in his ears.

Such are the colours in which Marvel paints his adventures. He has accustomed himself to sounding words and hyperbolical images, till he has lost the power of true description. In a road, through which the heaviest carriages pass without difficulty, and the post-boy every day and night goes and returns, he meets with hardships like those which are endured in Siberian deserts, and misses nothing of romantick danger but a giant and a dragon. When his dreadful story is told in proper terms, it is only that the way was dirty in winter, and that he experienced the common vicissitudes of rain and sunshine.

Nº. 50. SATURDAY, MARCH 31, 1759.

THE character of Mr. Marvel has raised the merriment of some and the contempt of others, who do not sufficiently consider how often they hear and practise the same arts of exaggerated narration.

There is not, perhaps, among the multitudes of all conditions that swarm upon the earth, a single man who does not believe that he has something extraordinary to relate of himself; and who does not, at one time or other, summon the attention of his friends to the casualties of his adventures and the vicissitudes of his fortune; casualties and vicissitudes that happen alike in lives uniform and diversified; to the commander of armies and the writer at a desk; to the sailor who resigns himself to the wind and water, and the farmer whose longest journey is to the market.

In the present state of the world man may pass through Shakespeare's seven stages of life, and meet nothing singular or wonderful. But such is every man's attention to himself, that what is common and unheeded, when it is only seen, becomes remarkable and peculiar when we happen to feel it.

It is well enough known to be according to the usual process of nature, that men should sicken and recover, that some designs should succeed and others miscarry, that friends should be separated and meet again, that some should be made angry by endeavours to please them, and some be pleased when no care has been used to gain their approbation; that men and women should at first come together by chance, like each other so well as to commence acquaintance, improve acquaintance into fondness, increase or extinguish fondness by marriage, and have children of different degrees of intellects and virtue, some of whom die before their parents, and others survive them.

Yet let any man tell his own story, and nothing of all this has ever befallen him according to the common order of things; something has always discriminated his case; some unusual concurrence of events has appeared, which made him more happy or more miserable than other mortals; for in pleasures or calamities, however common, every one has comforts and afflictions of his own.

It is certain that without some artificial augmentations, many of the pleasures of life, and almost all its embellishments, would fall to the ground. If no man was to express more delight than he felt, those who felt most would raise little envy. If travellers were to describe the most laboured performances of art with the same coldness as they survey them, all expectations of happiness from change of place would cease. The pictures of Raphaël would hang without spectators, and the gardens of Versailles might be inhabited by hermits. All the pleasure that is received ends in an opportunity of splendid falsehood, in the power of gaining notice by the display of beauties which the eye was weary of beholding, and a history of happy moments, of which, in reality, the most happy was the last.

The ambition of superior sensibility and superior eloquence disposes the lovers of arts to receive rapture at one time, and communicate it at another; and each labours first to impose upon himself, and then to propagate the imposture.

Pain is less subject than pleasure to caprices of expres-

sion. The torments of disease, and the grief for irremediable misfortunes, sometimes are such as no words can declare, and can only be signified by groans, or sobs, or inarticulate ejaculations. Man has from nature a mode of
utterance peculiar to pain, but he has none peculiar to
pleasure, because he never has pleasure but in such degrees as the ordinary use of language may equal or surpass.

It is nevertheless certain, that many pains, as well as
pleasures, are heightened by rhetorical affectation, and
that the picture is, for the most part, bigger than the life.

When we describe our sensations of another's sorrows,
either in friendly or ceremonious condolence, the customs
of the world scarcely admit of rigid veracity. Perhaps,
the fondest friendship would enrage oftener than comfort,
were the tongue on such occasions faithfully to represent
the sentiments of the heart; and I think the strictest
moralists allow forms of address to be used without much
regard to their literal acceptation, when either respect or
tenderness requires them; because they are universally
known to denote not the degree but the species of our
sentiments.

But the same indulgence cannot be allowed to him who
aggravates dangers incurred, or sorrow endured, by himself, because he darkens the prospect of futurity, and
multiplies the pains of our condition by useless terrour.
Those who magnify their delights are less criminal de-
ceivers, yet they raise hopes which are sure to be disappointed. It would be undoubtedly best, if we could see
and hear every thing as it is, that nothing might be too
anxiously dreaded, or too ardently pursued.

N°. 51. SATURDAY, APRIL 7, 1759.

IT has been commonly remarked, that eminent men are
least eminent at home, that bright characters lose much of
their splendour at a nearer view, and many, who fill the

world with their fame, excite very little reverence among
those that surround them in their domestick privacies.

To blame or suspect is easy and natural. When the
fact is evident, and the cause doubtful, some accusation is
always engendered between idleness and malignity. This
disparity of general and familiar esteem is, therefore, imputed to hidden vices, and to practices indulged in secret,
but carefully covered from the publick eye.

Vice will indeed always produce contempt. The dignity
of Alexander, though nations fell prostrate before him,
was certainly held in little veneration by the partakers of
his midnight revels, who had seen him, in the madness of
wine, murder his friend, or set fire to the Persian palace
at the instigation of a harlot; and it is well remembered
among us, that the avarice of Marlborough kept him in
subjection to his wife, while he was dreaded by France as
her conqueror, and honoured by the emperour as his de-
liverer.

But though, where there is vice there must be want of
reverence, it is not reciprocally true, that where there is
want of reverence there is always vice. That awe which
great actions or abilities impress will be inevitably diminished by acquaintance, though nothing either mean or
criminal should be found.

Of men, as of every thing else, we must judge according to our knowledge. When we see of a hero only his
battles, or of a writer only his books, we have nothing to
allay our ideas of their greatness. We consider the one
only as the guardian of his country, and the other only as
the instructer of mankind. We have neither opportunity
nor motive to examine the minuter parts of their lives, or
the less apparent peculiarities of their characters; we
name them with habitual respect, and forget, what we still
continue to know, that they are men like other mortals.

But such is the constitution of the world, that much of
life must be spent in the same manner by the wise and the
ignorant, the exalted and the low. Men, however distinguished by external accidents or intrinsick qualities, have

all the same wants, the same pains, and, as far as the
senses are consulted, the same pleasures. The petty cares
and petty duties are the same in every station to every understanding, and every hour brings some occasion on which
we all sink to the common level. We are all naked till
we are dressed, and hungry till we are fed ; and the general's triumph, and sage's disputation, end, like the humble
labours of the smith or ploughman, in a dinner or in sleep.

Those notions which are to be collected by reason, in
opposition to the senses, will seldom stand forward in the
mind, but lie treasured in the remoter repositories of memory, to be found only when they are sought. Whatever
any man may have written or done, his precepts or his valour will scarcely overbalance the unimportant uniformity
which runs through his time. We do not easily consider
him as great, whom our own eyes show us to be little ; nor
labour to keep present to our thoughts the latent excellencies of him, who shares with us all our weaknesses and
many of our follies ; who, like us, is delighted with slight
amusements, busied with trifling employments, and disturbed by little vexations.

Great powers cannot be exerted, but when great exigencies make them necessary. Great exigencies can happen but seldom, and, therefore, those qualities which have
a claim to the veneration of mankind, lie hid, for the most
part, like subterranean treasures, over which the foot
passes as on common ground, till necessity breaks open
the golden cavern.

In the ancient celebration of victory, a slave was placed
on the triumphal car, by the side of the general, who reminded him by a short sentence, that he was a man[h].
Whatever danger there might be lest a leader, in his passage to the capitol, should forget the frailties of his nature, there was surely no need of such an admonition; the
intoxication could not have continued long ; he would

---

[h] ———————————— Sibi Consul

Ne placeat, curru servus portatur eodem.   Juv. Sat. x. 41.

have been at home but a few hours, before some of his dependants would have forgot his greatness, and shown him, that, notwithstanding his laurels, he was yet a man.

There are some who try to escape this domestick degradation, by labouring to appear always wise or always great; but he that strives against nature, will for ever strive in vain. To be grave of mien and slow of utterrance; to look with solicitude and speak with hesitation, is attainable at will; but the show of wisdom is ridiculous when there is nothing to cause doubt, as that of valour where there is nothing to be feared.

A man who has duly considered the condition of his being, will contentedly yield to the course of things; he will not pant for distinction where distinction would imply no merit; but though on great occasions he may wish to be greater than others, he will be satisfied in common occurrences not to be less.

N° 52. SATURDAY, APRIL 14, 1759.

Responsare cupidinibus.——   Hor. Lib. ii. Sat. vii. 85.

THE practice of self-denial, or the forbearance of lawful pleasure, has been considered by almost every nation, from the remotest ages, as the highest exaltation of human virtue; and all have agreed to pay respect and veneration to those who abstained from the delights of life, even when they did not censure those who enjoy them.

The general voice of mankind, civil and barbarous, confesses that the mind and body are at variance, and that neither can be made happy by its proper gratifications, but at the expense of the other; that a pampered body will darken the mind, and an enlightened mind will macerate the body. And none have failed to confer their esteem on those who prefer intellect to sense, who control their lower by their higher faculties, and forget the wants and desires of animal life for rational disquisitions or pious contemplations.

The earth has scarcely a country, so far advanced towards political regularity as to divide the inhabitants into classes, where some orders of men or women are not distinguished by voluntary severities, and where the reputation of their sanctity is not increased in proportion to the rigour of their rules, and the exactness of their performance.

When an opinion to which there is no temptation of interest spreads wide, and continues long, it may be reasonably presumed to have been infused by nature or dictated by reason. It has been often observed that the fictions of imposture, and illusions of fancy, soon give way to time and experience; and that nothing keeps its ground but truth, which gains every day new influence by new confirmation.

But truth, when it is reduced to practice, easily becomes subject to caprice and imagination; and many particular acts will be wrong, though their general principle be right. It cannot be denied that a just conviction of the restraint necessary to be laid upon the appetites has produced extravagant and unnatural modes of mortification, and institutions, which, however favourably considered, will be found to violate nature without promoting piety[c].

But the doctrine of self-denial is not weakened in itself by the errours of those who misinterpret or misapply it; the encroachment of the appetites upon the understanding is hourly perceived; and the state of those, whom sensuality has enslaved, is known to be in the highest degree despicable and wretched.

The dread of such shameful captivity may justly raise alarms, and wisdom will endeavour to keep danger at a distance. By timely caution and suspicious vigilance those desires may be repressed, to which indulgence would soon give absolute dominion; those enemies may be over-

---

[c] See Rambler 110 and Note. Read also the splendid passage on monastic seclusion in Adventurer 127. The recluses of the Certosa and Chartreuse forsook the world for abodes lordly as those of princes.

come, which, when they have been a while accustomed to victory, can no longer be resisted.

Nothing is more fatal to happiness or virtue, than that confidence which flatters us with an opinion of our own strength, and, by assuring us of the power of retreat, precipitates us into hazard. Some may safely venture farther than others into the regions of delight, lay themselves more open to the golden shafts of pleasure, and advance nearer to the residence of the Syrens; but he that is best armed with constancy and reason is yet vulnerable in one part or other, and to every man there is a point fixed, beyond which, if he passes, he will not easily return. It is certainly most wise; as it is most safe, to stop before he touches the utmost limit, since every step of advance will more and more entice him to go forward, till he shall at last enter into the recesses of voluptuousness, and sloth and despondency close the passage behind him.

To deny early and inflexibly, is the only art of checking the importunity of desire, and of preserving quiet and innocence. Innocent gratifications must be sometimes withheld; he that complies with all lawful desires will certainly lose his empire over himself, and, in time, either submit his reason to his wishes, and think all his desires lawful, or dismiss his reason as troublesome and intrusive, and resolve to snatch what he may happen to wish, without inquiring about right and wrong.

No man, whose appetites are his masters, can perform the duties of his nature with strictness and regularity; he that would be superior to external influences must first become superior to his own passions.

When the Roman general, sitting at supper with a plate of turnips before him, was solicited by large presents to betray his trust, he asked the messengers whether he that could sup on turnips was a man likely to sell his own country. Upon him who has reduced his senses to obedience, temptation has lost its power; he is able to attend impartially to virtue, and execute her commands without hesitation.

To set the mind above the appetites is the end of abstinence, which one of the Fathers observes to be not a virtue, but the ground-work of virtue. By forbearing to do what may innocently be done, we may add hourly new vigour to resolution, and secure the power of resistance when pleasure or interest shall lend their charms to guilt.

Nº. 53. SATURDAY, APRIL 21, 1759.

TO THE IDLER.

SIR,

I HAVE a wife that keeps good company. You know that the word *good* varies its meaning according to the value set upon different qualities in different places. To be a good man in a college, is to be learned; in a camp, to be brave; and in the city, to be rich. By good company in the place which I have the misfortune to inhabit, we understand not only those from whom any good can be learned, whether wisdom or virtue; or by whom any good can be conferred, whether profit or reputation: —good company is the company of those whose birth is high, and whose riches are great; or of those whom the rich and noble admit to familiarity.

I am a gentleman of a fortune by no means exuberant, but more than equal to the wants of my family, and for some years equal to our desires. My wife, who had never been accustomèd to splendour, joined her endeavours to mine in the superintendence of our economy; we lived in decent plenty, and were not excluded from moderate pleasures.

But slight causes produce great effects. All my happiness has been destroyed by change of place: virtue is too often merely local; in some situations the air diseases the body, and in others poisons the mind. Being obliged to remove my habitation, I was led by my evil genius to a convenient house in a street where many of the nobility reside. We had scarcely ranged our furniture, and aired our rooms, when my wife began to grow discontented, and to wonder what the neighbours would think, when they saw so few chairs and chariots at her door.

Her acquaintance, who came to see her from the quarter that we had left, mortified her without design, by continual inquiries about the ladies whose houses they viewed from our windows. She was ashamed to confess that she had no intercourse with them, and sheltered her distress under general answers, which always tended to raise suspicion that she knew more than she would tell; but she was often reduced to difficulties, when the course of talk introduced questions about the furniture or ornaments of their houses, which, when she could get no intelligence, she was forced to pass slightly over, as things which she saw so often that she never minded them.

To all these vexations she was resolved to put an end, and redoubled her visits to those few of her friends who visited those who kept good company; and, if ever she met a lady of quality, forced herself into notice by respect and assiduity. Her advances were generally rejected; and she heard them, as they went down stairs, talk how some creatures put themselves forward.

She was not discouraged, but crept forward from one to another; and, as perseverance will do great things, sapped her way unperceived, till, unexpectedly, she appeared at the card-table of lady Biddy Porpoise, a lethargick virgin of seventy-six, whom all the families in the next square visited very punctually when she was not at home.

This was the first step of that elevation to which my wife has since ascended. For five months she had no name in her mouth but that of lady Biddy, who, let the world say what it would, had a fine understanding, and such a command of her temper, that, whether she won or lost, she slept over her cards.

At lady Biddy's she met with lady Tawdry, whose favour she gained by estimating her ear-rings, which were counterfeit, at twice the value of real diamonds. When she had once entered two houses of distinction, she was easily admitted into more, and in ten weeks had all her time anticipated by parties and engagements. Every morning she is bespoke, in the summer, for the gardens, in the winter, for a sale; every afternoon she has visits to pay, and every night brings an inviolable appointment, or an assembly in which the best company in the town are to appear.

You will easily imagine that much of my domestick comfort is withdrawn. I never see my wife but in the hurry of preparation, or the languor of weariness. To dress and to undress is almost her whole business in private, and the servants take advantage of her negligence to increase expense. But I can supply her omissions by my own diligence, and should not much regret this new course of life, if it did nothing more than transfer to me the care of our accounts. The changes which it has made are more vexatious. My wife has no longer the use of her understanding. She has no rule of action but the fashion. She has no opinion but that of the people of quality. She has no language but the dialect of her own set of company. She hates and admires in humble imitation; and echoes the words *charming* and *detestable* without consulting her own perceptions.

If for a few minutes we sit down together, she entertains me with the repartees of lady Cackle, or the conversation of lord Whiffler and Miss Quick, and wonders to find me receiving with indifference sayings which put all the company into laughter.

By her old friends she is no longer very willing to be seen, but she must not rid herself of them all at once; and is sometimes surprised by her best visitants in company which she would not show, and cannot hide; but from the moment that a countess enters, she takes care neither to hear nor see them: they soon find themselves neglected, and retire; and she tells her ladyship that they are somehow related at a great distance, and that, as they are a good sort of people, she cannot be rude to them.

As by this ambitious union with those that are above her, she is always forced upon disadvantageous comparisons of her condition with theirs, <u>she has a constant source of misery within</u>; and never returns from glittering assemblies and magnificent apartments but she growls out her discontent, and wonders why she was doomed to so indigent a state. When she attends the duchess to a sale, she always sees something that she cannot buy; and, that she may not seem wholly insignificant, she will sometimes venture to bid, and often make acquisitions which she did not want at prices which she cannot afford.

What adds to all this uneasiness is, that this expense is without use, and this vanity without honour; she forsakes houses where she might be courted, for those where she is only suffered; her equals are daily made her enemies, and her superiors will never be her friends.

I am, Sir, yours, &c.

N°. 54. SATURDAY, APRIL 28, 1759.

TO THE IDLER.

SIR,

You have lately entertained your admirers with the case of an unfortunate husband, and, thereby, given a demonstrative proof you are not averse even to hear appeals and terminate differences between man and wife; I, therefore, take the liberty to present you with the case of an injured lady, which, as it chiefly relates to what I think the lawyers call a point of law, I shall do in as juridical a manner as I am capable, and submit it to the consideration of the learned gentlemen of that profession.

Imprimis. In the style of my marriage articles, a marriage was *had and solemnized* about six months ago, between me and Mr. Savecharges, a gentleman possessed of a plentiful fortune of his own, and one who, I was persuaded, would improve, and not spend, mine.

Before our marriage, Mr. Savecharges had all along preferred the salutary exercise of walking on foot to the distempered ease, as he terms it, of lolling in a chariot; but, notwithstanding his fine panegyricks on walking, the great advantages the infantry were in the sole possession of, and the many dreadful dangers they escaped, he found I had very different notions of an equipage, and was not easily to be converted, or gained over to his party.

An equipage I was determined to have, whenever I married. I too well knew the disposition of my intended consort to leave the providing one entirely to his honour, and flatter myself Mr. Savecharges has, in the articles made previous to our marriage, *agreed to keep me a coach*; but lest I should be mistaken, or the attorneys should not have done me justice in methodizing or legalizing these half-dozen words, I will set about and transcribe that part of the agreement, which will explain the matter to you much better than can be done by one who is so deeply interested in the event; and show on what foundation I build my hopes of being soon under the transporting, delightful denomination of a fashionable lady, who enjoys the exalted and much-envied felicity of bowling about in her own coach.

"And further the said Solomon Savecharges, for divers good causes and considerations him hereunto moving, hath agreed, and doth hereby agree, that the said Solomon Savecharges shall and will, so soon as conveniently may be after the solemnization of the said intended marriage, at his own proper cost and charges, find and provide a *certain vehicle, or four-wheel-carriage, commonly called or known by the name of a coach;* which said vehicle, or wheel-carriage, so called or known by the name of a coach, shall be *used and enjoyed* by the said Sukey Modish, his intended wife," [pray mind that, Mr. Idler,] "at such times and in such manner as she, the said Sukey Modish, shall think fit and convenient."

Such, Mr. Idler, is the agreement my passionate admirer entered into; and what the dear, frugal husband calls

a performance of it, remains to be described.   Soon after
the ceremony of signing and sealing was over, our wed-
ding-clothes being sent home, and, in short, every thing in
readiness except the coach, my own shadow was scarcely
more constant than my passionate lover in his attendance
on me: wearied by his perpetual importunities for what he
called a completion of his bliss, I consented to make him
happy; in a few days I gave him my hand, and, attended
by Hymen in his saffron robes, retired to a country-seat of
my husband's, where the honey-moon flew over our heads
ere we had time to recollect ourselves, or think of our engagements in town.   Well, to town we came, and you
may be sure, Sir, I expected to step into my coach on my
arrival here; but, what was my surprise and disappointment, when, instead of this, he began to sound in my ears?
" that the interest of money was low, very low; and what
a terrible thing it was to be encumbered with a little regiment of servants in these hard times!"   I could easily perceive what all this tended to, but would not seem to understand him; which made it highly necessary for Mr.
Savecharges to explain himself more intelligibly; to harp
upon and protest he dreaded the expense of keeping a
coach.   And truly, for his part, he could not conceive how
the pleasure resulting from such a convenience could be
any way adequate to the heavy expense attending it.   I
now thought it high time to speak with equal plainness,
and told him, as the fortune I brought fairly entitled me
to ride in my own coach, and as I was sensible his circumstances would very well afford it, he must pardon me if I
insisted on a performance of his agreement.

I appeal to you, Mr. Idler, whether any thing could be
more civil, more complaisant, than this? And, would you
believe it, the creature in return, a few days after, accosted me, in an offended tone, with, " Madam, I can now
tell you, your coach is ready; and since you are so pas-
sionately fond of one, I intend you the honour of keeping
a pair of horses.—You insisted upon having an article of
pin-money, and horses are no part of my agreement." Base,

designing wretch!—I beg your pardon, Mr. Idler, the very recital of such mean, ungentleman-like behaviour fires my blood, and lights up a flame within me. But hence, thou worst of monsters, ill-timed Rage! and let me not spoil my cause for want of temper.

Now, though I am convinced I might make a worse use of part of the pin-money, than by extending my bounty to-wards the support of so useful a part of the brute creation; yet, like a true-born Englishwoman, I am so tenacious of my rights and privileges, and moreover so good a friend to the gentlemen of the law, that I protest, Mr. Idler, sooner than tamely give up the point, and be quibbled out of my right, I will receive my pin-money, as it were, with one hand, and pay it to them with the other; provided they will give me, or, which is the same thing, my trustees, encouragement to commence a suit against this dear, fru-gal husband of mine.

And of this I can't have the least shadow of doubt, in-asmuch as I have been told by very good authority, it is somewhere or other laid down as a rule " *That when-ever* the law doth give any thing to one, it giveth im-pliedly whatever is necessary for taking and enjoying the same [d]." Now, I would gladly know what enjoy-ment I, or any lady in the kingdom, can have of a coach without horses? The answer is obvious—None at all! For, as Serjeant Catlyne very wisely observes, " though a coach has wheels, to the end it may thereby and by virtue thereof be enabled to move; yet in point of utility it may as well have none, if they are not put in motion by means of its vital parts, that is, the horses."

And, therefore, Sir, I humbly hope you and the learned in the law will be of opinion, that two certain animals, or quadruped creatures, commonly called or known by the name of horses, ought to be annexed to, and go along with, the coach. 　　　SUKEY SAVECHARGES [e]

---

[d] Quando lex aliquid alicui concedit, concedere videtur et id, sine quo res ipsa esse non potest. Coke on Littleton, 56. a. ED.

[e] An unknown correspondent.

No. 55.   SATURDAY, MAY 5, 1759.

TO THE IDLER.

MR. IDLER,

I HAVE taken the liberty of laying before you my complaint, and of desiring advice or consolation with the greater confidence, because I believe many other writers have suffered the same indignities with myself, and hope my quarrel will be regarded by you and your readers as the common cause of literature.

Having been long a student, I thought myself qualified in time to become an author. My inquiries have been much diversified and far extended, and not finding my genius directing me by irresistible impulse to any particular subject, I deliberated three years which part of knowledge to illustrate by my labours. Choice is more often determined by accident than by reason : I walked abroad one morning with a curious lady, and, by her inquiries and observations, was incited to write the natural history of the country in which I reside.

Natural history is no work for one that loves his chair or his bed. Speculation may be pursued on a soft couch, but nature must be observed in the open air. I have collected materials with indefatigable pertinacity. I have gathered glow-worms in the evening, and snails in the morning; I have seen the daisy close and open, I have heard the owl shriek at midnight, and hunted insects in the heat of noon.

Seven years I was employed in collecting animals and vegetables, and then found that my design was yet imperfect. The subterranean treasures of the place had been passed unobserved, and another year was to be spent in mines and coal-pits. What I had already done supplied a sufficient motive to do more. I acquainted myself with the black inhabitants of metallick caverns, and, in defiance of damps and floods, wandered through the gloomy labyrinths, and gathered fossils from every fissure.

At last I began to write, and as I finished any section of my book, read it to such of my friends, as were most skilful in the matter which it treated. None of them were satisfied; one disliked the disposition of the parts, another the colours of the style; one advised me to enlarge, another to abridge. I resolved to read no more, but to take my own way and write on, for by consultation I only perplexed my thoughts and retarded my work.

The book was at last finished, and I did not doubt but my labour would be repaid by profit, and my ambition satisfied with honours. I considered that natural history is neither temporary nor local, and that though I limited my inquiries to my own country, yet every part of the earth has productions common to all the rest. Civil history may be partially studied, the revolutions of one nation may be neglected by another; but after that in which all have an interest, all must be inquisitive. No man can have sunk so far into stupidity as not to consider the properties of the ground on which he walks, of the plants on which he feeds, or the animals that delight his ear, or amuse his eye; and, therefore, I computed that universal curiosity would call for many editions of my book, and that in five years I should gain fifteen thousand pounds by the sale of thirty thousand copies.

When I began to write, I insured the house; and suffered the utmost solicitude when I entrusted my book to the carrier, though I had secured it against mischances by lodging two transcripts in different places. At my arrival, I expected that the patrons of learning would contend for the honour of a dedication, and resolved to maintain the dignity of letters, by a haughty contempt of pecuniary solicitations.

I took my lodgings near the house of the Royal Society, and expected every morning a visit from the president. I walked in the Park, and wondered that I overheard no mention of the great naturalist. At last I visited a noble earl, and told him of my work: he answered, that he was under an engagement never to subscribe. I was angry to have that refused which I did not mean to ask, and concealed my design of making him immortal. I went next day to another, and, in resentment of my late affront, offered to prefix his name to my new book. He said, coldly, that *he did not understand those things*; another thought, *there were too many books*; and another would *talk with me when the races were over.*

Being amazed to find a man of learning so indecently slighted, I resolved to indulge the philosophical pride of retirement and independence. I then sent to some of the principal booksellers the plan of my book, and bespoke a large room in the next tavern, that I might more commodiously see them together, and enjoy the contest, while they were outbidding one another. I drank my coffee, and yet nobody was come; at last I received a note from one, to tell me that he was going out of town; and from another, that natural history was out of his way. At last there came a grave man, who desired to see the work, and, without opening it, told me, that a book of that size *would never do.*

I then condescended to step into shops, and mentioned my work to the masters. Some never dealt with authors; others had their hands full; some never had known such a dead time; others had lost by all that they had published for the last twelvemonth. One offered to print my work, if I could procure subscriptions for five hundred, and would allow me two hundred copies for my property. I lost my patience, and gave him a kick; for which he has indicted me.

I can easily perceive, that there is a combination among them to defeat my expectations; and I find it so general, that I am sure it must have been long concerted. I suppose some of my friends, to whom I read the first part, gave notice of my design, and, perhaps, sold the treacherous intelligence at a higher price than the fraudulence of trade will now allow me for my book.

Inform me, Mr. Idler, what I must do; where must knowledge and industry find their recompense, thus ne-

glected by the high, and cheated by the low? I sometimes resolve to print my book at my own expense, and,
like the Sibyl, double the price; and sometimes am
tempted, in emulation of Raleigh, to throw it into the
fire, and leave this sordid generation to the curses of
posterity. Tell me, dear Idler, what I shall do.

I am, Sir, &c.

Nᵒ. 56. SATURDAY, MAY 12, 1759.

THERE is such difference between the pursuits of men,
that one part of the inhabitants of a great city lives to
little other purpose than to wonder at the rest. Some
have hopes and fears, wishes and aversions, which never
enter into the thoughts of others, and inquiry is laboriously
exerted to gain that which those who possess it are ready
to throw away.

To those who are accustomed to value every thing by
its use, and have no such superfluity of time or money, as
may prompt them to unnatural wants or capricious emula-
tions, nothing appears more improbable or extravagant
than the love of curiosities, or that desire of accumulating
trifles, which distinguishes many by whom no other distinction could have ever been obtained.

He that has lived without knowing to what height desire may be raised by vanity, with what rapture baubles
are snatched out of the hands of rival collectors, how the
eagerness of one raises eagerness in another, and one
worthless purchase makes a second necessary, may, by
passing a few hours at an auction, learn more than can be
shown by many volumes of maxims or essays.

The advertisement of a sale is a signal which, at once,
puts a thousand hearts in motion, and brings contenders
from every part to the scene of distribution. He that
had resolved to buy no more, feels his constancy subdued;
there is now something in the catalogue which completes

his cabinet, and which he was never before able to find. He whose sober reflections inform him, that of adding collection to collection there is no end, and that it is wise to leave early that which must be left imperfect at last, yet cannot withhold himself from coming to see what it is that brings so many together, and when he comes is soon overpowered by his habitual passion; he is attracted by rarity, seduced by example, and inflamed by competition.

While the stores of pride and happiness are surveyed, one looks with longing eyes and gloomy countenance on that which he despairs to gain from a richer bidder; another keeps his eye with care from settling too long on that which he most earnestly desires; and another, with more art than virtue, depreciates that which he values most, in hope to have it at an easy rate.

The novice is often surprised to see what minute and unimportant discriminations increase or diminish value. An irregular contortion of a turbinated shell, which common eyes pass unregarded, will ten times treble its price in the imagination of philosophers. Beauty is far from operating upon collectors as upon low and vulgar minds, even where beauty might be thought the only quality that could deserve notice. Among the shells that please by their variety of colours, if one can be found accidentally deformed by a cloudy spot, it is boasted as the pride of the collection. China is sometimes purchased for little less than its weight in gold, only because it is old, though neither less brittle, nor better painted, than the modern; and brown china is caught up with ecstasy, though no reason can be imagined for which it should be preferred to common vessels of common clay.

The fate of prints and coins is equally inexplicable. Some prints are treasured up as inestimably valuable, because the impression was made before the plate was finished. Of coins the price rises not from the purity of the metal, the excellence of the workmanship, the elegance of the legend, or the chronological use. A piece, of which neither the inscription can be read, nor the face distinguished, if there remain of it but enough to show that it is rare, will be sought by contending nations, and dignify the treasury in which it shall be shown.

Whether this curiosity, so barren of immediate advantage, and so liable to depravation, does more harm or good, is not easily decided. Its harm is apparent at first view. It fills the mind with trifling ambition; fixes the attention upon things which have seldom any tendency towards virtue or wisdom; employs in idle inquiries the time that is given for better purposes; and often ends in mean and dishonest practices, when desire increases by indulgence beyond the power of honest gratification.

These are the effects of curiosity in excess; but what passion in excess will not become vicious? All indifferent qualities and practices are bad, if they are compared with those which are good, and good, if they are opposed to those that are bad. The pride or the pleasure of making collections, if it be restrained by prudence and morality, produces a pleasing remission after more laborious studies; furnishes an amusement not wholly unprofitable for that part of life, the greater part of many lives, which would otherwise be lost in idleness or vice; it produces an useful traffick between the industry of indigence and the curiosity of wealth; it brings many things to notice that would be neglected, and, by fixing the thoughts upon intellectual pleasures, resists the natural encroachments of sensuality, and maintains the mind in her lawful superiority.

N°. 57. SATURDAY, MAY 19, 1759.

PRUDENCE is of more frequent use than any other intellectual quality; it is exerted on slight occasions, and called into act by the cursory business of common life.

Whatever is universally necessary, has been granted to mankind on easy terms. Prudence, as it is always wanted, is without great difficulty obtained. It requires neither extensive view nor profound search, but forces itself, by spontaneous impulse, upon a mind neither great nor busy, neither engrossed by vast designs, nor distracted by multiplicity of attention.

Prudence operates on life in the same manner as rules on composition: it produces vigilance rather than elevation, rather prevents loss than procures advantage; and often escapes miscarriages, but seldom reaches either power or honour. It quenches that ardour of enterprise, by which every thing is done that can claim praise or admiration; and represses that generous temerity which often fails, and often succeeds. Rules may obviate faults, but can never confer beauties; and prudence keeps life safe, but does not often make it happy. The world is not amazed with prodigies of excellence, but when wit tramples upon rules, and magnanimity breaks the chains of prudence.

One of the most prudent of all that have fallen within my observation, is my old companion Sophron, who has passed through the world in quiet, by perpetual adherence to a few plain maxims, and wonders how contention and distress can so often happen.

The first principle of Sophron is, *to run no hazards.* Though he loves money, he is of opinion that frugality is a more certain source of riches than industry. It is to no purpose that any prospect of large profit is set before him; he believes little about futurity, and does not love to trust his money out of his sight, for *nobody knows what may happen.* He has a small estate, which he lets at the old rent, because *it is better to have a little than nothing;* but he rigorously demands payment on the stated day, for *he that cannot pay one quarter cannot pay two.* If he is told of any improvements in agriculture, he likes the old way, has observed that changes very seldom answer expectation, is of opinion that our forefathers knew how to till the ground as well as we; and concludes with an argument that nothing can overpower, that the expense of planting and fencing is immediate, and the advantage distant, and that *he is no wise man who will quit a certainty for an uncertainty.*

Another of Sophron's rules is, *to mind no business but his own.* In the state, he is of no party; but hears and speaks of publick affairs with the same coldness as of the administration of some ancient republick. If any flagrant act of fraud or oppression is mentioned, he hopes that *all is not true that is told:* if misconduct or corruption puts the nation in a flame, he hopes *every man means well.* At elections he leaves his dependants to their own choice, and declines to vote himself, for every candidate is a good man, whom he is unwilling to oppose or offend.

If disputes happen among his neighbours, he observes an invariable and cold neutrality. His punctuality has gained him the reputation of honesty, and his caution that of wisdom; and few would refuse to refer their claims to his award. He might have prevented many expensive law-suits, and quenched many a feud in its first smoke; but always refuses the office of arbitration, because he must decide against one or the other.

With the affairs of other families he is always unacquainted. He sees estates bought and sold, squandered and increased, without praising the economist, or censuring the spendthrift. He never courts the rising, lest they should fall; nor insults the fallen, lest they should rise again. His caution has the appearance of virtue, and all who do not want his help praise his benevolence; but, if any man solicits his assistance, he has just sent away all his money; and, when the petitioner is gone, declares to his family that he is sorry for his misfortunes, has always looked upon him with particular kindness, and, therefore, could not lend him money, lest he should destroy their friendship by the necessity of enforcing payment.

Of domestick misfortunes he has never heard. When he is told the hundredth time of a gentleman's daughter who has married the coachman, he lifts up his hands with astonishment, for he always thought her a sober girl.

When nuptial quarrels, after having filled the country with talk and laughter, at last end in separation, he never can conceive how it happened, for he looked upon them as a happy couple.

If his advice is asked, he never gives any particular direction, because events are uncertain, and he will bring no blame upon himself; but he takes the consulter tenderly by the hand, tells him he makes his case his own, and advises him not to act rashly, but to weigh the reasons on both sides; observes, that a man may be as easily too hasty as too slow; and that as many fail by doing too much as too little; that *a wise man has two ears and one tongue;* and that *little said is soon mended;* that he could tell him this and that, but that after all every man is the best judge of his own affairs.

With this some are satisfied, and go home with great reverence of Sophron's wisdom; and none are offended, because every one is left in full possession of his own opinion.

Sophron gives no characters. It is equally vain to tell him of vice and virtue; for he has remarked, that no man likes to be censured, and that very few are delighted with the praises of another. He has a few terms which he uses to all alike. With respect to fortune, he believes every one to be in good circumstances; he never exalts any understanding by lavish praise, yet he meets with none but very sensible people. Every man is honest and hearty; and every woman is a good creature.

Thus Sophron creeps along, neither loved nor hated, neither favoured nor opposed; he has never attempted to grow rich, for fear of growing poor; and has raised no friends, for fear of making enemies.

Nᵒ. 58. SATURDAY, MAY 26, 1759.

PLEASURE is very seldom found where it is sought. Our brightest blazes of gladness are commonly kindled by unexpected sparks. The flowers which scatter their odours, from time to time, in the paths of life, grow up without culture from seeds scattered by chance.

Nothing is more hopeless than a scheme of merriment. Wits and humourists are brought together from distant quarters by preconcerted invitations; they come, attended by their admirers, prepared to laugh and to applaud; they gaze awhile on each other, ashamed to be silent, and afraid to speak; every man is discontented with himself, grows angry with those that give him pain, and resolves that he will contribute nothing to the merriment of such worthless company. Wine inflames the general malignity, and changes sullenness to petulance, till at last none can bear any longer the presence of the rest. They retire to vent their indignation in safer places, where they are heard with attention; their importance is restored, they recover their good humour, and gladden the night with wit and jocularity.

Merriment is always the effect of a sudden impression. The jest which is expected is already destroyed. The most active imagination will be sometimes torpid, under the frigid influence of melancholy, and sometimes occasions will be wanting to tempt the mind, however volatile, to sallies and excursions. Nothing was ever said with uncommon felicity, but by the co-operation of chance; and, therefore, wit, as well as valour, must be content to share its honours with fortune.

All other pleasures are equally uncertain; the general remedy of uneasiness is change of place; almost every one has some journey of pleasure in his mind, with which he flatters his expectation. He that travels in theory has no inconvenience; he has shade and sunshine at his disposal, and wherever he alights finds tables of plenty and looks of gaiety. These ideas are indulged till the day of departure arrives, the chaise is called, and the progress of happiness begins.

A few miles teach him the fallacies of imagination. The road is dusty, the air is sultry, the horses are sluggish, and the postillion brutal. He longs for the time of dinner, that he may eat and rest. The inn is crowded, his orders are neglected, and nothing remains but that he devour in haste what the cook has spoiled, and drive on in quest of better entertainment. He finds at night a more commodious house, but the best is always worse than he expected.

He at last enters his native province, and resolves to feast his mind with the conversation of his old friends, and the recollection of juvenile frolicks. He stops at the house of his friend, whom he designs to overpower with pleasure by the unexpected interview. He is not known till he tells his name, and revives the memory of himself by a gradual explanation. He is then coldly received, and ceremoniously feasted. He hastes away to another, whom his affairs have called to a distant place, and, having seen the empty house, goes away disgusted by a disappointment which could not be intended, because it could not be foreseen. At the next house he finds every face clouded with misfortune, and is regarded with malevolence as an unreasonable intruder, who comes not to visit but to insult them.

It is seldom that we find either men or places such as we expect them. He that has pictured a prospect upon his fancy, will receive little pleasure from his eyes; he that has anticipated the conversation of a wit, will wonder to what prejudice he owes his reputation. Yet it is necessary to hope, though hope should always be deluded; for hope itself is happiness, and its frustrations, however frequent, are less dreadful than its extinction.

Nº. 59. SATURDAY, JUNE 2, 1759.

In the common enjoyments of life, we cannot very liberally indulge the present hour, but by anticipating part of the pleasure which might have relieved the tediousness of another day; and any uncommon exertion of strength, or perseverance in labour, is succeeded by a long interval of languor and weariness. Whatever advantage we snatch beyond the certain portion allotted us by nature, is like money spent before it is due, which, at the time of regular payment, will be missed and regretted.

Fame, like all other things which are supposed to give or to increase happiness, is dispensed with the same equality of distribution. He that is loudly praised will be clamorously censured; he that rises hastily into fame will be in danger of sinking suddenly into oblivion.

Of many writers who filled their age with wonder, and whose names we find celebrated in the books of their contemporaries, the works are now no longer to be seen, or are seen only amidst the lumber of libraries which are seldom visited, where they lie only to show the deceitfulness of hope, and the uncertainty of honour.

Of the decline of reputation many causes may be assigned. It is commonly lost because it never was deserved; and was conferred at first, not by the suffrage of criticism, but by the fondness of friendship, or servility of flattery. The great and popular are very freely applauded; but all soon grow weary of echoing to each other a name which has no other claim to notice, but that many mouths are pronouncing it at once.

But many have lost the final reward of their labours, because they were too hasty to enjoy it. They have laid hold on recent occurrences, and eminent names, and delighted their readers with allusions and remarks, in which all were interested, and to which all, therefore, were attentive. But the effect ceased with its cause; the time quickly came when new events drove the former from memory,

when the vicissitudes of the world brought new hopes and
fears, transferred the love and hatred of the publick to
other agents; and the writer, whose works were no longer
assisted by gratitude or resentment, was left to the cold
regard of idle curiosity.

He that writes upon general principles, or delivers universal truths, may hope to be often read, because his work
will be equally useful at all times and in every country;
but he cannot expect it to be received with eagerness, or
to spread with rapidity, because desire can have no particular stimulation: that which is to be loved long, must be
loved with reason rather than with passion. He that lays
his labours out upon temporary subjects, easily finds readers, and quickly loses them; for what should make the
book valued when the subject is no more?

These observations will show the reason why the poem
of Hudibras is almost forgotten, however embellished with
sentiments and diversified with allusions, however bright
with wit, and however solid with truth. The hypocrisy
which it detected, and the folly which it ridiculed, have
long vanished from publick notice. Those who had felt the
mischief of discord, and the tyranny of usurpation, read it
with rapture; for every line brought back to memory something known, and gratified resentment by the just censure
of something hated. But the book, which was once quoted
by princes, and which supplied conversation to all the assemblies of the gay and witty, is now seldom mentioned,
and even by those that affect to mention it, is seldom read.
So vainly is wit lavished upon fugitive topicks; so little
can architecture secure duration when the ground is false.

N°. 60. SATURDAY, JUNE 9, 1759.

CRITICISM is a study by which men grow important and formidable at a very small expense. The power of invention has been conferred by nature upon few, and the labour of learning those sciences, which may by mere labour be obtained, is too great to be willingly endured; but every man can exert such judgment as he has upon the works of others; and he whom nature has made weak, and idleness keeps ignorant, may yet support his vanity by the name of a Critick.

I hope it will give comfort to great numbers who are passing through the world in obscurity, when I inform them how easily distinction may be obtained. All the other powers of literature are coy and haughty, they must be long courted, and at last are not always gained; but Criticism is a goddess easy of access and forward of advance, who will meet the slow, and encourage the timorous; the want of meaning she supplies with words, and the want of spirit she recompenses with malignity.

This profession has one recommendation peculiar to itself, that it gives vent to malignity without real mischief. No genius was ever blasted by the breath of criticks. The poison which, if confined, would have burst the heart, fumes away in empty hisses, and malice is set at ease with very little danger to merit. The critick is the only man whose triumph is without another's pain, and whose greatness does not rise upon another's ruin.

To a study at once so easy and so reputable, so malicious and so harmless, it cannot be necessary to invite my readers by a long or laboured exhortation; it is sufficient, since all would be criticks if they could, to show, by one eminent example, that all can be criticks if they will.

Dick Minim, after the common course of puerile studies, in which he was no great proficient, was put an apprentice to a brewer, with whom he had lived two years, when his uncle died in the city, and left him a large fortune in the

stocks. Dick had for six months before used the company of the lower players, of whom he had learned to
scorn a trade, and, being now at liberty to follow his genius, he resolved to be a man of wit and humour. That
he might be properly initiated in his new character, he frequented the coffee-houses near the theatres, where he
listened very diligently, day after day, to those who talked
of language and sentiments, and unities and catastrophes,
till, by slow degrees, he began to think that he understood
something of the stage, and hoped in time to talk himself.

But he did not trust so much to natural sagacity as
wholly to neglect the help of books. When the theatres
were shut, he retired to Richmond with a few select writers,
whose opinions he impressed upon his memory by unwearied diligence; and, when he returned with other wits
to the town, was able to tell, in very proper phrases, that
the chief business of art is to copy nature; that a perfect
writer is not to be expected, because genius decays as
judgment increases; that the great art is the art of blot-
ting; and that, according to the rule of Horace, every
piece should be kept nine years.

Of the great authors he now began to display the characters, laying down as an universal position, that all had
beauties and defects. His opinion was, that Shakespeare,
committing himself wholly to the impulse of nature, wanted
that correctness which learning would have given him;
and that Jonson, trusting to learning, did not sufficiently
cast his eyes on nature. He blamed the stanzas of Spenser,
and could not bear the hexameters of Sidney. Denham
and Waller he held the first reformers of English numbers; and thought that if Waller could have obtained the
strength of Denham, or Denham the sweetness of Waller,
there had been nothing wanting to complete a poet. He
often expressed his commiseration of Dryden's poverty,
and his indignation at the age which suffered him to write
for bread; he repeated with rapture the first lines of All
for Love, but wondered at the corruption of taste which
could bear any thing so unnatural as rhyming tragedies.

In Otway he found uncommon powers of moving the passions, but was disgusted by his general negligence, and blamed him for making a conspirator his hero; and never concluded his disquisition, without remarking how happily the sound of the clock is made to alarm the audience. Southern would have been his favourite, but that he mixes comick with tragick scenes, intercepts the natural course of the passions, and fills the mind with a wild confusion of mirth and melancholy. The versification of Rowe he thought too melodious for the stage, and too little varied in different passions. He made it the great fault of Congreve, that all his persons were wits, and that he always wrote with more art than nature. He considered Cato rather as a poem than a play, and allowed Addison to be the complete master of allegory and grave humour, but paid no great deference to him as a critick. He thought the chief merit of Prior was in his easy tales and lighter poems, though he allowed that his Solomon had many noble sentiments elegantly expressed. In Swift he discovered an inimitable vein of irony, and an easiness which all would hope and few would attain. Pope he was inclined to degrade from a poet to a versifier, and thought his numbers rather luscious than sweet. He often lamented the neglect of Phædra and Hippolytus, and wished to see the stage under better regulations.

These assertions passed commonly uncontradicted; and if now and then an opponent started up, he was quickly repressed by the suffrages of the company, and Minim went away from every dispute with elation of heart and increase of confidence.

He now grew conscious of his abilities, and began to talk of the present state of dramatick poetry; wondered what had become of the comick genius which supplied our ancestors with wit and pleasantry, and why no writer could be found that durst now venture beyond a farce. He saw no reason for thinking that the vein of humour was exhausted, since we live in a country, where liberty suffers every character to spread itself to its utmost bulk, and which, therefore, produces more originals than all the rest of the world together. Of tragedy he concluded business to be the soul, and yet often hinted that love predominates too much upon the modern stage.

He was now an acknowledged critick, and had his own seat in a coffee-house, and headed a party in the pit. Minim has more vanity than ill-nature, and seldom desires to do much mischief; he will, perhaps, murmur a little in the ear of him that sits next him, but endeavours to influence the audience to favour, by clapping when an actor exclaims, *Ye gods!* or laments the misery of his country.

By degrees he was admitted to rehearsals; and many of his friends are of opinion, that our present poets are indebted to him for their happiest thoughts; by his contrivance the bell was rung twice in Barbarossa, and by his persuasion the author of Cleone concluded his play without a couplet; for what can be more absurd, said Minim, than that part of a play should be rhymed, and part written in blank verse? and by what acquisition of faculties is the speaker, who never could find rhymes before, enabled to rhyme at the conclusion of an act?

He is the great investigator of hidden beauties, and is particularly delighted when he finds "the sound an echo to the sense." He has read all our poets, with particular attention to this delicacy of versification, and wonders at the supineness with which their works have been hitherto perused, so that no man has found the sound of a drum in this distich:

> " When pulpit, drum ecclesiastic,
> Was beat with fist instead of a stick;"

and that the wonderful lines upon honour and a bubble have hitherto passed without notice:

> " Honour is like the glassy bubble,
> Which costs philosophers such trouble;
> Where, one part crack'd, the whole does fly,
> And wits are crack'd to find out why."

In these verses, says Minim, we have two striking accommodations of the sound to the sense. It is impossible to utter the first two lines emphatically without an act like that which they describe; *bubble* and *trouble* causing a momentary inflation of the cheeks by the retention of the breath, which is afterwards forcibly emitted, as in the practice of *blowing bubbles*.   But the greatest excellence is in the third line, which is *crack'd* in the middle to express a crack, and then shivers into monosyllables.   Yet has this diamond lain neglected with common stones, and among the innumerable admirers of Hudibras the observation of·this superlative passage has been reserved for the sagacity of Minim.

<hr>

N°. 61. SATURDAY, JUNE 15, 1759.

MR. MINIM had now advanced himself to the zenith of critical reputation; when he was in the pit, every eye in the boxes was fixed upon him; when he entered his coffee-house, he was surrounded by circles of candidates, who passed their noviciate of literature under his tuition : his opinion was asked by all who had no opinion of their own, and yet loved to debate and decide ; and no composition was supposed to pass in safety to posterity, till it had been secured by Minim's approbation.

Minim professes great admiration of the wisdom and munificence by which the academies of the continent were raised; and often wishes for some standard of taste, for some tribunal, to which· merit may appeal from caprice, prejudice and malignity.   He has formed a plan for an academy of criticism, where every work of imagination may be read before it is printed, and which shall authoritatively direct the theatres what pieces to receive or reject, to exclude or to revive.

Such an institution would, in Dick's opinion, spread the fame of English literature over Europe, and make London the metropolis of elegance and politeness, the place to which the learned and ingenious of all countries would repair for instruction and improvement, and where nothing would any longer be applauded or endured that was not conformed to the nicest rules, and finished with the highest elegance.

Till some happy conjunction of the planets shall dispose our princes or ministers to make themselves immortal by such an academy, Minim contents himself to preside four nights in a week in a critical society selected by himself, where he is heard without contradiction, and whence his judgment is disseminated through the great vulgar and the small.

When he is placed in the chair of criticism, he declares loudly for the noble simplicity of our ancestors, in opposition to the petty refinements, and ornamental luxuriance. Sometimes he is sunk in despair, and perceives false delicacy daily gaining ground, and sometimes brightens his countenance with a gleam of hope, and predicts the revival of the true sublime. He then fulminates his loudest censures against the monkish barbarity of rhyme; wonders how beings that pretend to reason can be pleased with one line always ending like another; tells how unjustly and unnaturally sense is sacrificed to sound; how often the best thoughts are mangled by the necessity of confining or extending them to the dimensions of a couplet; and rejoices that genius has, in our days, shaken off the shackles which had encumbered it so long. Yet he allows that rhyme may sometimes be borne, if the lines be often broken, and the pauses judiciously diversified.

From blank verse he makes an easy transition to Milton, whom he produces as an example of the slow advance of lasting reputation. Milton is the only writer in whose books Minim can read for ever without weariness. What cause it is that exempts this pleasure from satiety he has long and diligently inquired, and believes it to consist in the perpetual variation of the numbers, by which the ear is gratified and the attention awakened. The lines that are commonly thought rugged and unmusical, he conceives

to have been written to temper the melodious luxury of
the rest, or to express things by a proper cadence : for he
scarcely finds a verse that has not this favourite beauty ;
he declares that he could shiver in a hot-house when he
reads that

> " the ground
> " Burns frore, and cold performs th' effect of fire ;"

and that, when Milton bewails his blindness, the verse,

> " So thick a drop serene has quench'd these orbs,"

has, he knows not how, something that strikes him with an
obscure sensation like that which he fancies would be felt
from the sound of darkness.

Minim is not so confident of his rules of judgment as
not very eagerly to catch new light from the name of the
author. He is commonly so prudent as to spare those
whom he cannot resist, unless, as will sometimes happen,
he finds the publick combined against them. But a fresh
pretender to fame he is strongly inclined to censure, till
his own honour requires that he commend him. Till he
knows the success of a composition, he intrenches himself
in general terms ; there are some new thoughts and beautiful passages, but there is likewise much which he would
have advised the author to expunge. He has several favourite epithets, of which he has never settled the meaning,
but which are very commodiously applied to books which
he has not read, or cannot understand. One is *manly*,
another is *dry*, another *stiff*, and another *flimsy* ; sometimes he discovers delicacy of style, and sometimes meets
with *strange expressions*.

He is never so great, or so happy, as when a youth of
promising parts is brought to receive his directions for the
prosecution of his studies. He then puts on a very serious air ; he advises the pupil to read none but the best
authors ; and when he finds one congenial to his own mind,
to study his beauties, but avoid his faults ; and, when he
sits down to write, to consider how his favourite author

would think at the present time on the present occasion. He exhorts him to catch those moments when he finds his thoughts expanded and his genius exalted, but to take care lest imagination hurry him beyond the bounds of nature. He holds diligence the mother of success; yet enjoins him, with great earnestness, not to read more than he can digest, and not to confuse his mind by pursuing studies of contrary tendencies. He tells him, that every man has his genius, and that Cicero could never be a poet. The boy retires illuminated, resolves to follow his genius, and to think how Milton would have thought: and Minim feasts upon his own beneficence till another day brings another pupil.

N°. 62. SATURDAY, JUNE 23, 1759.

*   *Quid faciam, præscribe. Quiescas.——*
                              HOR. Lib. ii. Sat. i. 5.

TO THE IDLER.

SIR,

AN opinion prevails almost universally in the world, that he who has money has every thing. This is not a modern paradox, or the tenet of a small and obscure sect, but a persuasion which appears to have operated upon most minds in all ages, and which is supported by authorities so numerous and so cogent, that nothing but long experience could have given me confidence to question its truth.

But experience is the test by which all the philosophers of the present age agree, that speculation must be tried; and I may be, therefore, allowed to doubt the power of money, since I have been a long time rich, and have not yet found that riches can make me happy.

My father was a farmer neither wealthy nor indigent, who gave me a better education than was suitable to my birth, because my uncle in the city designed me for his heir, and desired that I might be bred a gentleman. My uncle's wealth was the perpetual subject of conversation in the house; and when any little misfortune befell us, or any mortification dejected us, my father always exhorted me to hold up my head, for my uncle would never marry.

My uncle, indeed, kept his promise. Having his mind completely busied between his warehouse and the 'Change, he felt no tediousness of life, nor any want of domestick amusements. When my father died, he received me kindly; but, after a few months, finding no great pleasure in the conversation of each other, we parted; and he remitted me a small annuity, on which I lived a quiet and studious life, without any wish to grow great by the death of my benefactor.

But though I never suffered any malignant impatience to take hold on my mind, I could not forbear sometimes to imagine to myself the pleasure of being rich; and, when I read of diversions and magnificence, resolved to try, when time should put the trial in my power, what pleasure they could afford.

My uncle, in the latter spring of his life, when his ruddy cheek and his firm nerves promised him a long and healthy age, died of an apoplexy. His death gave me neither joy nor sorrow. He did me good, and I regarded him with gratitude; but I could not please him, and, therefore, could not love him.

He had the policy of little minds, who love to surprise; and, having always represented his fortune as less than it was, had, I suppose, often gratified himself with thinking, how I should be delighted to find myself twice as rich as I expected. My wealth was such as exceeded all the schemes of expense which I had formed; and I soon began to expand my thoughts, and look round for some purchase of felicity.

The most striking effect of riches is the splendour of dress, which every man has observed to enforce respect, and facilitate reception; and my first desire was to be fine. I sent for a tailor who was employed by the nobility, and ordered such a suit of clothes as I had often looked on with involuntary submission, and am ashamed to remember with what flutters of expectation I waited for the hour, when I should issue forth in all the splendour of embroidery. The clothes were brought, and for three days I observed many eyes turned towards me as I passed: but I felt myself obstructed in the common intercourse of civility by an uneasy consciousness of my new appearance; as I thought myself more observed, I was more anxious about my mien and behaviour; and the mien which is formed by care is commonly ridiculous. A short time accustomed me to myself, and my dress was without pain, and without pleasure.

For a little while I tried to be a rake, but I began too late; and having by nature no turn for a frolick, was in great danger of ending in a drunkard. A fever, in which not one of my companions paid me a visit, gave me time for reflection. I found that there was no great pleasure in breaking windows and lying in the round-house; and resolved to associate no longer with those whom, though I had treated and bailed them, I could not make friends.

I then changed my measures, kept running horses, and had the comfort of seeing my name very often in the news. I had a chesnut horse, the grandson of Childers, who won four plates, and ten by-matches; and a bay filly, who carried off the five years' old plate, and was expected to perform much greater exploits, when my groom broke her wind, because I happened to catch him selling oats for beer. This happiness was soon at an end; there was no pleasure when I lost, and, when I won, I could not much exalt myself by the virtues of my horse. I grew ashamed of the company of jockey-lords, and resolved to spend no more of my time in the stable.

It was now known that I had money, and would spend it, and I passed four months in the company of architects, whose whole business was to persuade me to build a house. I told them that I had more room than I wanted, but could not get rid of their importunities. A new plan was brought me every morning; till at last my constancy was overpowered, and I began to build. The happiness of building lasted but a little while, for though I love to spend, I hate to be cheated; and I soon found, that to build is to be robbed.

How I proceed in the pursuit of happiness, you shall hear when I find myself disposed to write.

I am, Sir, &c.

TIM. RANGER.

N°. 63. SATURDAY, JUNE 30, 1759.

THE natural progress of the works of men is from rudeness to convenience, from convenience to elegance, and from elegance to nicety.

The first labour is enforced by necessity. The savage finds himself incommoded by heat and cold, by rain and wind; he shelters himself in the hollow of a rock, and learns to dig a cave where there was none before. He finds the sun and the wind excluded by the thicket; and when the accidents of the chase, or the convenience of pasturage, leads him into more open places, he forms a thicket for himself, by planting stakes at proper distances, and laying branches from one to another.

The next gradation of skill and industry produces a house closed with doors, and divided by partitions; and apartments are multiplied and disposed according to the various degrees of power or invention; improvement succeeds improvement, as he that is freed from a greater evil grows impatient of a less, till ease in time is advanced to pleasure.

The mind, set free from the importunities of natural want, gains leisure to go in search of superfluous gratifications, and adds to the uses of habitation the delights of prospect. Then begins the reign of symmetry; orders of architecture are invented, and one part of the edifice is conformed to another, without any other reason, than that the eye may not be offended.

The passage is very short from elegance to luxury. Ionick and Corinthian columns are soon succeeded by gilt cornices, inlaid floors and petty ornaments, which show rather the wealth than the taste of the possessour.

Language proceeds, like every thing else, through improvement to degeneracy. The rovers who first took possession of a country, having not many ideas, and those not nicely modified or discriminated, were contented, if by general terms and abrupt sentences they could make their thoughts known to one another : as life begins to be more regulated, and property to become limited, disputes must be decided, and claims adjusted ; the differences of things are noted, and distinctness and propriety of expression become necessary. In time, happiness and plenty give rise to curiosity, and the sciences are cultivated for ease and pleasure ; to the arts, which are now to be taught, emulation soon adds the art of teaching ; and the studious and ambitious contend not only who shall think best, but who shall tell their thoughts in the most pleasing manner.

Then begin the arts of rhetorick and poetry, the regulation of figures, the selection of words, the modulation of periods, the graces of transition, the complication of clauses, and all the delicacies of style and subtilties of composition, useful while they advance perspicuity, and laudable while they increase pleasure, but easy to be refined by needless scrupulosity till they shall more embarrass the writer than assist the reader or delight him.

The first state is commonly antecedent to the practice of writing ; the ignorant essays of imperfect diction pass away with the savage generation that uttered them. No nation can trace their language beyond the second period, and even of that it does not often happen that many monuments remain.

The fate of the English tongue is like that of others. We know nothing of the scanty jargon of our barbarous ancestors ; but we have specimens of our language when it began to be adapted to civil and religious purposes, and find it such as might naturally be expected, artless and simple, unconnected and concise. The writers seem to have desired little more than to be understood, and, perhaps, seldom aspired to the praise of pleasing. Their verses were considered chiefly as memorial, and, therefore, did not differ from prose but by the measure or the rhyme.

In this state, varied a little according to the different purposes or abilities of writers, our language may be said to have continued to the time of Gower, whom Chaucer calls his master, and who, however obscured by his scholar's popularity, seems justly to claim the honour which has been hitherto denied him, of showing his countrymen that something more was to be desired, and that English verse might be exalted into poetry.

From the time of Gower and Chaucer, the English writers have studied elegance, and advanced their language, by successive improvements, to as much harmony as it can easily receive, and as much copiousness as human knowledge has hitherto required. These advances have not been made at all times with the same diligence or the same success. Negligence has suspended the course of improvement, or affectation turned it aside; time has elapsed with little change, or change has been made without amendment. But elegance has been long kept in view with attention as near to constancy as life permits, till every man now endeavours to excel others in accuracy, or outshine them in splendour of style, and the danger is, lest care should too soon pass to affectation.

TO THE IDLER.

SIR,

As nature has made every man desirous of happiness, I flatter myself, that you and your readers cannot but feel some curiosity to know the sequel of my story; for though, by trying the different schemes of pleasure, I have yet found nothing in which I could finally acquiesce; yet the narrative of my attempts will not be wholly without use, since we always approach nearer to truth as we detect more and more varieties of errour.

When I had sold my racers, and put the orders of architecture out of my head, my next resolution was to be a *fine gentleman.* I frequented the polite coffee-houses, grew acquainted with all the men of humour, and gained the right of bowing familiarly to half the nobility. In this new scene of life my great labour was to learn to laugh. I had been used to consider laughter as the effect of merriment; but I soon learned that it is one of the arts of adulation, and, from laughing only to show that I was pleased, I now began to laugh when I wished to please. This was at first very difficult. I sometimes heard the story with dull indifference, and, not exalting myself to merriment by due gradations, burst out suddenly into an awkward noise, which was not always favourably interpreted. Sometimes I was behind the rest of the company, and lost the grace of laughing by delay, and sometimes, when I began at the right time, was deficient in loudness or in length. But, by diligent imitation of the best models, I attained at last such flexibility of muscles, that I was always a welcome auditor of a story, and got.the reputation of a good-natured fellow.

This was something; but much more was to be done,

that I might be universally allowed to be a fine gentleman. I appeared at court on all publick days; betted at gaming-tables; and played at all the routs of eminence. I went every night to the opera, took a fiddler of disputed merit under my protection, became the head of a musical faction, and had sometimes concerts at my own house. I once thought to have attained the highest rank of elegance, by taking a foreign singer into keeping. But my favourite fiddler contrived to be arrested, on the night of a concert, for a finer suit of clothes than I had ever presumed to wear, and I lost all the fame of patronage by refusing to bail him.

My next ambition was to sit for my picture. I spent a whole winter in going from painter to painter, to bespeak a whole length of one, and a half length of another; I talked of nothing but attitudes, draperies and proper lights; took my friends to see the pictures after every sitting; heard every day of a wonderful performer in crayons and miniature, and sent my pictures to be copied; was told by the judges that they were not like, and was recommended to other artists. At length, being not able to please my friends, I grew less pleased myself, and at last resolved to think no more about it.

It was impossible to live in total idleness: and wandering about in search of something to do, I was invited to a weekly meeting of virtuosos, and felt myself instantaneously seized with an unextinguishable ardour for all natural curiosities. I ran from auction to auction, became a critick in shells and fossils, bought a *Hortus siccus* of inestimable value, and purchased a secret art of preserving insects, which made my collection the envy of the other philosophers. I found this pleasure mingled with much vexation. All the faults of my life were for nine months circulated through the town with the most active malignity, because I happened to catch a moth of peculiar variegation; and because I once out-bid all the lovers of shells, and carried-off a nautilus, it was hinted that the validity of my uncle's will ought to be disputed. I will not deny that

I was very proud both of the moth and of the shell, and gratified myself with the envy of my companions, perhaps, more than became a benevolent being.   But in time I grew weary of being hated for that which produced no advantage, gave my shells to children that wanted playthings, and suppressed the art of drying butterflies, because I would not tempt idleness and cruelty to kill them.

I now began to feel life tedious, and wished to store myself with friends, with whom I might grow old in the interchange of benevolence.   I had observed that popularity was most easily gained by an open table, and, therefore, hired a French cook, furnished my sideboard with great magnificence, filled my cellar with wines of pompous appellations, bought every thing that was dear before it was good, and invited all those who were most famous for judging of a dinner.   In three weeks my cook gave me warning, and, upon inquiry, told me that Lord Queasy, who dined with me the day before, had sent him an offer of double wages.   My pride prevailed ; I raised his wages, and invited his lordship to another feast.   I love plain meat, and was, therefore, soon weary of spreading a table of which I could not partake.   I found that my guests, when they went away, criticised their entertainment, and censured my profusion; my cook thought himself necessary, and took upon him the direction of the house ; and I could not rid myself of flatterers, or break from slavery, but by shutting up my house, and declaring my resolution to live in lodgings.

After all this, tell me, dear Idler, what I must do next ; I have health, I have money, and I hope that I have understanding ; yet, with all these, I have never been able to pass a single day which I did not wish at an end before sun-set.   Tell me, dear Idler, what I shall do.

I am
Your humble servant,
TIM. RANGER.

N°. 65. SATURDAY, JULY 14, 1759.

THE sequel of Clarendon's history, at last happily published, is an accession to English literature equally agreeable to the admirers of elegance and the lovers of truth; many doubtful facts may now be ascertained, and many questions, after long debate, may be determined by decisive authority. He that records transactions in which himself was engaged, has not only an opportunity of knowing innumerable particulars which escape spectators, but has his natural powers exalted by that ardour which always rises at the remembrance of our own importance, and by which every man is enabled to relate his own actions better than another's.

The difficulties through which this work has struggled into light, and the delays with which our hopes have been long mocked, naturally lead the mind to the consideration of the common fate of posthumous compositions.

He who sees himself surrounded by admirers, and whose vanity is hourly feasted with all the luxuries of studied praise, is easily persuaded that his influence will be extended beyond his life; that they who cringe in his presence will reverence his memory, and that those who are proud to be numbered among his friends, will endeavour to vindicate his choice by zeal for his reputation.

With hopes like these, to the executors of Swift was committed the history of the last years of queen Anne, and to those of Pope, the works which remained unprinted in his closet. The performances of Pope were burnt by those whom he had, perhaps, selected from all mankind as most likely to publish them; and the history had likewise perished, had not a straggling transcript fallen into busy hands.

The papers left in the closet of Pieresc supplied his heirs with a whole winter's fuel; and many of the labours of the learned Bishop Lloyd were consumed in the kitchen of his descendants.

Some works, in deed, have escaped total destruction, but yet have had reason to lament the fate of orphans exposed to the frauds of unfaithful guardians. How Hale would have borne the mutilations which his Pleas of the Crown have suffered from the editor, they who know his character will easily conceive[f].

The original copy of Burnet's history, though promised to some publick library[g], has been never given ; and who then can prove the fidelity of the publication, when the authenticity of Clarendon's history, though printed with the sanction of one of the first universities of the world, had not an unexpected manuscript been happily discovered, would, with the help of factious credulity, have been brought into question by the two lowest of all human beings, a scribbler for a party, and a commissioner of excise[h]?

Vanity is often no less mischievous than negligence or dishonesty. He that possesses a valuable manuscript, hopes to raise its esteem by concealment, and delights in the distinction which he imagines himself to obtain by keeping the key of a treasure which he neither uses nor imparts. From him it falls to some other owner, less vain but more negligent, who considers it as useless lumber, and rids himself of the encumbrance.

Yet there are some works which the authors must consign unpublished to posterity, however uncertain be the event, however hopeless be the trust. He that writes the history of his own times, if he adheres steadily to truth, will write that which his own times will not easily

---

[f] See Preface.

[g] It would be proper to reposite, in some public place, the manuscript of Clarendon, which has not escaped all suspicion of unfaithful publication. The manuscript of Clarendon is now in the Bodleian library at Oxford, and the editor of the present edition has it before him while writing this note. He may likewise add ,that a new and emended edition is now printing from the original MS. at the Clarendon press. December, 1824.

[h] See Preface.

Dr Johnson's hatred of the excise reminds us of John Wesley's wailing philippic against turnpike gates, which he denounced as the most cruel of impositions on the way-faring man.

endure. He must be content to reposite his book, till all private passions shall cease, and love and hatred give way to curiosity.

But many leave the labours of half their life to their executors and to chance, because they will not send them abroad unfinished, and are unable to finish them, having prescribed to themselves such a degree of exactness as human diligence can scarcely attain. " Lloyd", says Burnet, " did not lay out his learning with the same diligence as he laid it in." He was always hesitating and inquiring, raising objections and removing them, and waiting for clearer light and fuller discovery. Baker, after many years passed in biography, left his manuscripts to be buried in a library, because that was imperfect which could never be perfected.

Of these learned men, let those who aspire to the same praise imitate the diligence, and avoid the scrupulosity. Let it be always remembered that life is short, that knowledge is endless, and that many doubts deserve not to be cleared. Let those whom nature and study have qualified to teach mankind, tell us what they have learned while they are yet able to tell it, and trust their reputation only to themselves.

N°. 66.　SATURDAY, JULY 21, 1759.

No complaint is more frequently repeated among the learned, than that of the waste made by time among the labours of antiquity. Of those who once filled the civilized world with their renown, nothing is now left but their names, which are left only to raise desires that never can be satisfied, and sorrow which never can be comforted.

Had all the writings of the ancients been faithfully delivered down from age to age, had the Alexandrian library been spared, and the Palatine repositories remained unimpaired, how much might we have known of which we are now doomed to be ignorant! how many laborious inquiries, and dark conjectures; how many collations of broken hints and mutilated passages might have been spared! We should have known the successions of princes, the revolutions of empires, the actions of the great, and opinions of the wise, the laws and constitutions of every state, and the arts by which publick grandeur and happiness are acquired and preserved; we should have traced the progress of life, seen colonies from distant regions take possession of European deserts, and troops of savages settled into communities by the desire of keeping what they had acquired; we should have traced the gradations of civility, and travelled upward to the original of things by the light of history, till in remoter times it had glimmered in fable, and at last sunk into darkness.

If the works of imagination had been less diminished, it is likely that all future times might have been supplied with inexhaustible amusement by the fictions of antiquity. The tragedies of Sophocles and Euripides would all have shown the stronger passions in all their diversities; and the comedies of Menander would have furnished all the maxims of domestick life. Nothing would have been necessary to moral wisdom but to have studied these great masters, whose knowledge would have guided doubt, and whose authority would have silenced cavils.

Such are the thoughts that rise in every student, when his curiosity is eluded, and his searches are frustrated; yet it may, perhaps, be doubted, whether our complaints are not sometimes inconsiderate, and whether we do not imagine more evil than we feel. Of the ancients, enough remains to excite our emulation and direct our endeavours. Many of the works which time has left us, we know to have been those that were most esteemed, and which antiquity itself considered as models; so that, having the originals, we may without much regret lose the imitations. The obscurity which the want of contemporary writers often produces, only darkens single passages, and those commonly of slight importance. The general tendency of every piece may be known; and though that diligence deserves praise which leaves nothing unexamined, yet its miscarriages are not much to be lamented; for the most useful truths are always universal, and unconnected with accidents and customs.

Such is the general conspiracy of human nature against contemporary merit, that, if we had inherited from antiquity enough to afford employment for the laborious, and amusement for the idle, I know not what room would have been left for modern genius or modern industry; almost every subject would have been pre-occupied, and every style would have been fixed by a precedent from which few would have ventured to depart. Every writer would have had a rival, whose superiority was already acknowledged, and to whose fame his work would, even before it was seen, be marked out for a sacrifice.

We see how little the united experience of mankind hath been able to add to the heroick characters displayed by Homer, and how few incidents the fertile imagination of modern Italy has yet produced, which may not be found in the Iliad and Odyssey. It is likely, that if all the works of the Athenian philosophers had been extant, Malbranche and Locke would have been condemned to be silent readers of the ancient metaphysicians; and it is apparent, that, if the old writers had all remained, the Idler could not have written a disquisition on the loss[1].

[1] There was a weighty meaning in that fiction of the Stoics, of a grand periodic year, in which all events should be re-acted in the same mode and order as before. There is nothing new under the sun. Whatever is, or shall be, is only an imitation, or, at best, a re-production of something that has been. The moralist who speculates on the contingencies of human conduct can only divine the future from what has already been acted on the earth. The philosopher, leaning on principles which Science styles immutable, is confined within the narrow bounds of created matter. Why then should Reason make us undervalue that Revelation which carries us upwards to Creation's birth, and bears us downward to a period when time shall be no longer? ED.

N°. 67   SATURDAY, JULY 28, 1759.

TO THE IDLER.

SIR,

IN the observations which you have made on the various opinions and pursuits of mankind, you must often, in literary conversations, have met with men who consider dissipation as the great enemy of the intellect; and maintain, that, in proportion as the student keeps himself within the bounds of a settled plan, he will more certainly advance in science.

This opinion is, perhaps, generally true; yet, when we contemplate the inquisitive nature of the human mind, and its perpetual impatience of all restraint, it may be doubted whether the faculties may not be contracted by confining the attention; and whether it may not sometimes be proper to risk the certainty of little for the chance of much. Acquisitions of knowledge, like blazes of genius, are often fortuitous. Those who had proposed to themselves a methodical course of reading, light by accident on a new book, which seizes their thoughts and kindles their curiosity, and opens an unexpected prospect, to which the way which they had prescribed to themselves would never have conducted them.

To enforce and illustrate my meaning, I have sent you a journal of three days' employment, found among the papers of a late intimate acquaintance; who, as will plainly appear, was a man of vast designs, and of vast performances, though he sometimes designed one thing, and performed another. I allow that the Spectator's inimitable productions of this kind may well discourage all subsequent journalists; but, as the subject of this is different from that of any which the Spectator has given us, I leave it to you to publish or suppress it.

Mem. The following three days I purpose to give up to reading; and intend, after all the delays which have obtruded themselves upon me, to finish my Essay on the Extent of the Mental powers; to revise my Treatise on Logick; to begin the Epick which I have long projected; to proceed in my perusal of the Scriptures with Grotius's Comment; and at my leisure to regale myself with the works of classicks, ancient and modern, and to finish my Ode to Astronomy.

Monday.] Designed to rise at six, but, by my servant's laziness, my fire was not lighted before eight, when I dropped into a slumber that lasted till nine; at which time I arose, and, after breakfast, at ten, sat down to study, purposing to begin upon my Essay; but, finding occasion to consult a passage in Plato, was absorbed in the perusal of the Republick till twelve. I had neglected to forbid company, and now enters Tom Careless, who, after half an hour's chat, insisted upon my going with him to enjoy an absurd character, that he had appointed, by an advertisement, to meet him at a particular coffee-house. After we had for some time entertained ourselves with him, we sallied out, designing each to repair to his home; but, as it fell out, coming up in the street to a man whose steel by his side declared him a butcher, we overheard him opening an address to a genteelish sort of young lady, whom he walked with: " Miss, though your father is master of a coal-lighter, and you will be a great fortune, 'tis true; yet I wish I may be cut into quarters if it is not only love, and not lucre of gain, that is my motive for offering terms of marriage." As this lover proceeded in his speech, he misled us the length of three streets, in admiration at the unlimited power of the tender passion, that could soften even the heart of a butcher. We then adjourned to a tavern, and from thence to one of the publick gardens, where I was regaled with a most amusing variety of men possessing great talents, so discoloured by affectation, that they only made them eminently ridiculous; shallow things, who, by continual dissipation, had annihilated the few ideas nature had given them, and yet were celebrated for wonderful pretty gentlemen; young ladies extolled for their wit, because they were handsome; illiterate empty women as well as men, in high life, admired for their knowledge, from their being resolutely positive; and women of real understanding so far from pleasing the polite million, that they frightened them away, and were left solitary. When we quitted this entertaining scene, Tom pressed me, irresistibly, to sup with him. I reached home at twelve, and then reflected, that, though indeed I had, by remarking various characters, improved my insight into human nature, yet still I had neglected the studies proposed, and accordingly took up my Treatise on Logick, to give it the intended revisal, but found my spirits too much agitated, and could not forbear a few satirical lines, under the title of The Evening's Walk.

Tuesday.] At breakfast, seeing my Ode to Astronomy lying on my desk, I was struck with a train of ideas, that I thought might contribute to its improvement. I immediately rang my bell to forbid all visitants, when my servant opened the door, with, " Sir, Mr. Jeffery Gape." My cup dropped out of one hand, and my poem out of the other. I could scarcely ask him to sit; he told me he was going to walk, but, as there was a likelihood of rain, he would sit with me; he said, he intended at first to have called at Mr. Vacant's, but as he had not seen me a great while, he did not mind coming out of his way to wait on me; I made him a bow, but thanks for the favour stuck in my throat. I asked him if he had been to the coffee-house; he replied, Two hours.

Under the oppression of this dull interruption, I sat looking wishfully at the clock; for which, to increase my satisfaction, I had chosen the inscription, " Art is long, and life is short;" exchanging questions and answers at long intervals, and not without some hints that the weather-glass promised fair weather. At half an hour after three he told me he would trespass on me for a dinner, and desired me to send to his house for a bundle of papers, about inclosing a common upon his estate, which he would read to me in the evening. I declared myself busy, and Mr. Gape went away.

Having dined, to compose my chagrin I took up Virgil, and several other classicks, but could not calm my mind, or proceed in my scheme. At about five I laid my hand on a Bible that lay on my table, at first with coldness and insensibility; but was imperceptibly engaged in a close attention to its sublime morality, and felt my heart expanded by warm philanthropy, and exalted to dignity of sentiment. I then censured my too great solicitude, and my disgust conceived at my acquaintance, who had been so far from designing to offend, that he only meant to show kindness and respect. In this strain of mind I wrote An Essay on Benevolence, and An Elegy on Sublunary Disappointments. When I had finished these, at eleven, I supped, and recollected how little I had adhered to my plan, and almost questioned the possibility of pursuing any settled and uniform design; however, I was not so far persuaded of the truth of these suggestions, but that I resolved to try once more at my scheme. As I observed the moon shining through my window, from a calm and bright sky spangled with innumerable stars, I indulged a pleasing meditation on the splendid scene, and finished my Ode to Astronomy.

Wednesday.] Rose at seven, and employed three hours in perusal of the Scriptures with Grotius's Comment; and after breakfast fell into meditation concerning my projected Epick; and being in some doubt as to the particular lives of some heroes, whom I proposed to celebrate, I consulted Bayle and Moreri, and was engaged two hours in examining various lives and characters, but then resolved to go to my employment. When I was seated at my desk, and began to feel the glowing succession of poetical ideas, my servant brought me a letter from a lawyer, requiring my instant attendance at Gray's Inn for half an hour. I went full of vexation, and was involved in business till eight at night; and then, being too much fatigued to study, supped, and went to bed.

Here my friend's Journal concludes, which, perhaps, is pretty much a picture of the manner in which many prosecute their studies. I therefore resolved to send it you, imagining, that, if you think it worthy of appearing in your paper, some of your readers may receive entertainment by recognising a resemblance between my friend's conduct and their own. It must be left to the Idler accurately to ascertain the proper methods of advancing in literature; but this one position, deducible from what has been said above, may, I think, be reasonably asserted, that he who finds himself strongly attracted to any particular study, though it may happen to be out of his proposed scheme, if it is not trifling or vicious, had better continue his application to it, since it is likely that he will, with much more ease and expedition, attain that which a warm inclination stimulates him to pursue, than that at which a prescribed law compels him to toil[k].

I am, &c.

~~~~~~~~~~~~~~~~~~~~~

N°. 68. SATURDAY, AUGUST 4, 1759.

AMONG the studies which have exercised the ingenious and the learned for more than three centuries, none has been more diligently or more successfully cultivated than the art of translation; by which the impediments which bar the way to science are, in some measure, removed, and the multiplicity of languages become less incommodious.

Of every other kind of writing the ancients have left us models which all succeeding ages have laboured to imitate; but translation may justly be claimed by the moderns as their own. In the first ages of the world instruction was commonly oral, and learning traditional, and what was not written could not be translated. When alphabe-

---

[k] This paper, which is evidently throughout allusive to the Idler's own broken resolutions, was the composition of Bennet Langton, for whom Johnson cherished the fondest regard. In his admiration he ventured even to exclaim, " Sit anima mea cum Langtono." Boswell, iv.—ED.

tical writing made the conveyance of opinions and the transmission of events more easy and certain, literature did not flourish in more than one country at once, or distant nations had little commerce with each other; and those few whom curiosity sent abroad in quest of improvement, delivered their acquisitions in their own manner, desirous, perhaps, to be considered as the inventors of that which they had learned from others.

The Greeks for a time travelled into Egypt, but they translated no books from the Egyptian language; and when the Macedonians had overthrown the empire of Persia, the countries that became subject to Grecian dominion studied only the Grecian literature. The books of the conquered nations, if they had any among them, sunk into oblivion; Greece considered herself as the mistress, if not as the parent of arts, her language contained all that was supposed to be known, and, except the sacred writings of the Old Testament, I know not that the library of Alexandria adopted any thing from a foreign tongue.

The Romans confessed themselves the scholars of the Greeks, and do not appear to have expected, what has since happened, that the ignorance of succeeding ages would prefer them to their teachers. Every man, who in Rome aspired to the praise of literature, thought it necessary to learn Greek, and had no need of versions when they could study the originals. Translation, however, was not wholly neglected. Dramatick poems could be understood by the people in no language but their own, and the Romans were sometimes entertained with the tragedies of Euripides and the comedies of Menander. Other works were sometimes attempted; in an old scholiast there is mention of a Latin Iliad; and we have not wholly lost Tully's version of the poem of Aratus; but it does not appear that any man grew eminent by interpreting another, and perhaps it was more frequent to translate for exercise or amusement, than for fame.

The Arabs were the first nation who felt the ardour of translation: when they had subdued the eastern provinces of the Greek empire, they found their captives wiser than themselves, and made haste to relieve their wants by imparted knowledge. They discovered that many might grow wise by the labour of a few, and that improvements might be made with speed, when they had the knowledge of former ages in their own language. They, therefore, made haste to lay hold on medicine and philosophy, and turned their chief authors into Arabick[1]. Whether they attempted the poets is not known ; their literary zeal was vehement, but it was short, and probably expired before they had time to add the arts of elegance to those of necessity.

The study of ancient literature was interrupted in Europe by the irruption of the Northern nations, who subverted the Roman empire, and erected new kingdoms with new languages. It is not strange that such confusion should suspend literary attention ; those who lost, and those who gained dominion, had immediate difficulties to encounter, and immediate miseries to redress, and had little leisure, amidst the violence of war, the trepidation of flight, the distresses of forced migration, or the tumults of unsettled conquest, to inquire after speculative truth, to enjoy the amusement of imaginary adventures, to know the history of former ages, or study the events of any other lives. But no sooner had this chaos of dominion sunk into order, than learning began again to flourish in the calm of peace. When life and possessions were secure, convenience and enjoyment were soon sought, learning was found the highest gratification of the mind, and translation became one of the means by which it was imparted.

At last, by a concurrence of many causes, the European world was roused from its lethargy ; those arts which had been long obscurely studied in the gloom of monasteries became the general favourites of mankind ; every nation

---

[1] Some popular information on the interesting subject of Arabian Literature, is collected in the third part of Harris's Philological Inquiries. Mr. Hallam's History of the Middle Ages is a rich storehouse for these points.—Ed.

vied with its neighbour for the prize of learning; the epidemical emulation spread from south to north, and curiosity and translation found their way to Britain.

****

N°. 69. SATURDAY, AUGUST 11, 1759.

HE that reviews the progress of English literature, will find that translation was very early cultivated among us, but that some principles, either wholly erroneous or too far extended, hindered our success from being always equal to our diligence.

Chaucer, who is generally considered as the father of our poetry, has left a version of Boethius on the Comforts of Philosophy, the book which seems to have been the favourite of the middle ages, which had been translated into Saxon by King Alfred, and illustrated with a copious comment ascribed to Aquinas. It may be supposed that Chaucer would apply more than common attention to an author of so much celebrity, yet he has attempted nothing higher than a version strictly literal, and has degraded the poetical parts to prose, that the constraint of versification might not obstruct his zeal for fidelity.

Caxton taught us typography about the year 1474. The first book printed in English was a translation. Caxton was both the translator and printer of the Destruction of Troye; a book which, in that infancy of learning, was considered as the best account of the fabulous ages, and which, though now driven out of notice by authors of no greater use or value, still continued to be read in Caxton's English to the beginning of the present century.

Caxton proceeded as he began, and, except the poems of Gower and Chaucer, printed nothing but translations from the French, in which the original is so scrupulously followed, that they afford us little knowledge of our own language: though the words are English, the phrase is foreign.

As learning advanced, new works were adopted into
our language, but I think with little improvement of the
art of translation, though foreign nations and other languages offered us models of a better method; till in the
age of Elizabeth we began to find that greater liberty was
necessary to elegance, and that elegance was necessary to
general reception; some essays were then made upon the
Italian poets, which deserve the praise and gratitude of
posterity.

But the old practice was not suddenly forsaken : Hol-
land filled the nation with literal translation; and, what is
yet more strange, the same exactness was obstinately
practised in the versions of the poets.   This absurd labour
of construing into rhyme was countenanced by Jonson in
his version of Horace; and whether it be that more men
have learning than genius, or that the endeavours of that
time were more directed towards knowledge than delight,
the accuracy of Jonson found more imitators than the
elegance of Fairfax; and May, Sandys and Holiday, confined themselves to the toil of rendering line for line, not
indeed with equal felicity, for May and Sandys were
poets, and Holiday only a scholar and a critick.

Feltham appears to consider it as the established law
of poetical translation, that the lines should be neither
more nor fewer than those of the original; and so long had
this prejudice prevailed, that Denham praises Fanshaw's
version of Guarini as the example of a *new and noble
way*, as the first attempt to break the boundaries of custom, and assert the natural freedom of the Muse.

In the general emulation of wit and genius which the
festivity of the Restoration produced, the poets shook off
their constraint, and considered translation as no longer
confined to servile closeness.   But reformation is seldom
the work of pure virtue or unassisted reason.   Translation
was improved more by accident than conviction.   The
writers of the foregoing age had at least learning equal to
their genius; and, being often more able to explain the
sentiments or illustrate the allusions of the ancients, than

to exhibit their graces and transfuse their spirit, were, perhaps, willing sometimes to conceal their want of poetry by profusion of literature, and, therefore, translated literally, that their fidelity might shelter their insipidity or harshness. The wits of Charles's time had seldom more than slight and superficial views; and their care was to hide their want of learning behind the colours of a gay imagination; they, therefore, translated always with freedom, sometimes with licentiousness, and, perhaps, expected that their readers should accept sprightliness for knowledge, and consider ignorance and mistake as the impatience and negligence of a mind too rapid to stop at difficulties, and too elevated to descend to minuteness.

Thus was translation made more easy to the writer, and more delightful to the reader; and there is no wonder if ease and pleasure have found their advocates. The paraphrastick liberties have been almost universally admitted; and Sherbourn, whose learning was eminent, and who had no need of any excuse to pass slightly over obscurities, is the only writer who, in later times, has attempted to justify or revive the ancient severity.

There is undoubtedly a mean to be observed. Dryden saw very early that closeness best preserved an author's sense, and that freedom best exhibited his spirit; he, therefore, will deserve the highest praise, who can give a representation at once faithful and pleasing, who can convey the same thoughts with the same graces, and who, when he translates, changes nothing but the language[m].

***

N°. 70. SATURDAY, AUGUST 18, 1759.

FEW faults of style, whether real or imaginary, excite the malignity of a more numerous class of readers, than the use of hard words.

[m] Much research on this branch of literature is exhibited in Lord Woodhouselee's Principles of Translation.

If an author be supposed to involve his thoughts in voluntary obscurity, and to obstruct, by unnecessary difficulties, a mind eager in pursuit of truth; if he writes not to make others learned, but to boast the learning which he possesses himself, and wishes to be admired rather than understood, he counteracts the first end of writing, and justly suffers the utmost severity of censure, or the more afflictive severity of neglect.

But words are hard only to those who do not understand them; and the critick ought always to inquire, whether he is incommoded by the fault of the writer or by his own.

Every author does not write for every reader; many questions are such as the illiterate part of mankind can have neither interest nor pleasure in discussing, and which, therefore, it would be an useless endeavour to level with common minds, by tiresome circumlocutions or laborious explanations; and many subjects of general use may be treated in a different manner, as the book is intended for the learned or the ignorant. Diffusion and explication are necessary to the instruction of those who, being neither able nor accustomed to think for themselves, can learn only what is expressly taught; but they who can form parallels, discover consequences, and multiply conclusions, are best pleased with involution of argument and compression of thought; they desire only to receive the seeds of knowledge which they may branch out by their own power, to have the way to truth pointed out, which they can then follow without a guide.

The Guardian directs one of his pupils, " to think with the wise, but speak with the vulgar." This is a precept specious enough, but not always practicable. Difference of thoughts will produce difference of language. He that thinks with more extent than another will want words of larger meaning; he that thinks with more subtilty will seek for terms of more nice discrimination; and where is the wonder, since words are but the images of things, that he who never knew the original should not know the copies?

. Yet vanity inclines us to find faults any where rather than in ourselves. He that reads and grows no wiser, seldom suspects his own deficiency; but complains of hard words and obscure sentences, and asks why books are written which cannot be understood?

Among the hard words which are no longer to be used, it has been long the custom to number terms of art. " Every man," says Swift, " is more able to explain the subject of an art than its professors; a farmer will tell you, in two words, that he has broken his leg; but a surgeon, after a long discourse, shall leave you as ignorant as you were before." This could only have been said, by such an exact observer of life, in gratification of malignity, or in ostentation of acuteness. Every hour produces instances of the necessity of terms of art. Mankind could never conspire in uniform affectation; it is not but by necessity that every science and every trade has its peculiar language. They that content themselves with general ideas may rest in general terms; but those, whose studies or employments force them upon closer inspection, must have names for particular parts, and words by which they may express various modes of combination, such as none but themselves have occasion to consider.

Artists are indeed sometimes ready to suppose that none can be strangers to words to which themselves are familiar, talk to an incidental inquirer as they talk to one another, and make their knowledge ridiculous by injudicious obtrusion. An art cannot be taught but by its proper terms, but it is not always necessary to teach the art.

That the vulgar express their thoughts clearly, is far from true; and what perspicuity can be found among them proceeds not from the easiness of their language, but the shallowness of their thoughts. He that sees a building as a common spectator, contents himself with relating that it is great or little, mean or splendid, lofty or low; all these words are intelligible and common, but they convey no distinct or limited ideas; if he attempts, without the terms of architecture, to delineate the parts, or enumerate the ornaments, his narration at once becomes unintelligible. The terms, indeed, generally displease, because they are understood by few; but they are little understood, only because few that look upon an edifice examine its parts, or analyze its columns into their members.

The state of every other art is the same; as it is cursorily surveyed or accurately examined, different forms of expression become proper. In morality it is one thing to discuss the niceties of the casuist, and another to direct the practice of common life. In agriculture, he that instructs the farmer to plough and sow, may convey his notions without the words which he would find necessary in explaining to philosophers the process of vegetation; and if he, who has nothing to do but to be honest by the shortest way, will perplex his mind with subtile speculations; or if he, whose task is to reap and thrash, will not be contented without examining the evolution of the seed and circulation of the sap; the writers whom either shall consult are very little to be blamed, though it should sometimes happen that they are read in vain.

N°. 71. SATURDAY, AUGUST 25, 1759.

Celan le selve angui, leoni, ed orsi
Dentro il lor verde.   TASSO, L'AMINTA.

DICK SHIFTER was born in Cheapside, and, having passed reputably through all the classes of St. Paul's school, has been for some years a student in the Temple. He is of opinion, that intense application dulls the faculties, and thinks it necessary to temper the severity of the law by books that engage the mind, but do not fatigue it. He has, therefore, made a copious collection of plays, poems, and romances, to which he has recourse when he fancies himself tired with statutes and reports; and he seldom inquires very nicely whether he is weary or idle.

Dick has received from his favourite authors very strong

impressions of a country life ; and though his furthest excursions have been to Greenwich on one side, and Chelsea on the other, he has talked for several years, with great pomp of language and elevation of sentiments, about a state too high for contempt and too low for envy, about homely quiet and blameless simplicity, pastoral delights and rural innocence.

His friends, who had estates in the country, often invited him to pass the summer among them, but something or other had always hindered him ; and he considered, that to reside in the house of another man was to incur a kind of dependence inconsistent with that laxity of life which he had imaged as the chief good.

This summer he resolved to be happy, and procured a lodging to be taken for him at a solitary house, situated about thirty miles from London, on the banks of a small river, with corn-fields before it and a hill on each side covered with wood. He concealed the place of his retirement, that none might violate his obscurity, and promised himself many a happy day when he should hide himself among the trees, and contemplate the tumults and vexations of the town.

He stepped into the post-chaise with his heart beating and his eyes sparkling, was conveyed through many varieties of delightful prospects, saw hills and meadows, corn-fields and pasture, succeed each other, and for four hours charged none of his poets with fiction or exaggeration. He was now within six miles of happiness, when, having never felt so much agitation before, he began to wish his journey at an end, and the last hour was passed in changing his posture and quarrelling with his driver.

An hour may be tedious, but cannot be long. He at length alighted at his new dwelling, and was received as he expected ; he looked round upon the hills and rivulets, but his joints were stiff and his muscles sore, and his first request was to see his bed-chamber.

He rested well, and ascribed the soundness of his sleep to the stillness of the country. He expected from that time nothing but nights of quiet and days of rapture, and, as soon as he had risen, wrote an account of his new state to one of his friends in the Temple.

" Dear Frank,

" I never pitied thee before. I am now, as I could wish every man of wisdom and virtue to be, in the regions of calm content and placid meditation ; with all the beauties of nature soliciting my notice, and all the diversities of pleasure courting my acceptance ; the birds are chirping in the hedges, and the flowers blooming in the mead ; the breeze is whistling in the wood, and the sun dancing on the water. I can now say, with truth, that a man, capable of enjoying the purity of happiness, is never more busy than in his hours of leisure, nor ever less solitary than in a place of solitude.

I am, dear Frank, &c."

When he had sent away his letter, he walked into the wood, with some inconvenience, from the furze that pricked his legs, and the briars that scratched his face. He at last sat down under a tree, and heard with great delight a shower, by which he was not wet, rattling among the branches : This, said he, is the true image of obscurity ; we hear of troubles and commotions, but never feel them.

His amusement did not overpower the calls of nature, and he, therefore, went back to order his dinner. He knew that the country produces whatever is eaten or drunk, and, imagining that he was now at the source of luxury, re- solved to indulge himself with dainties which he supposed might be procured at a price next to nothing, if any price at all was expected ; and intended to amaze the rusticks with his generosity, by paying more than they would ask. Of twenty dishes which he named, he was amazed to find that scarcely one was to be had ; and heard, with astonish- ment and indignation, that all the fruits of the earth were sold at a higher price than in the streets of London.

His meal was short and sullen ; and he retired again to

his tree, to inquire how dearness could be consistent with abundance, or how fraud should be practised by simplicity. He was not satisfied with his own speculations, and, returning home early in the evening, went a while from window to window, and found that he wanted something to do.

He inquired for a newspaper, and was told that farmers never minded news, but that they could send for it from the alehouse. A messenger was despatched, who ran away at full speed, but loitered an hour behind the hedges, and at last coming back with his feet purposely bemired, instead of expressing the gratitude which Mr. Shifter expected for the bounty of a shilling, said, that the night was wet, and the way dirty, and he hoped that his worship would not think it much to give him half-a-crown.

Dick now went to bed with some abatement of his expectations; but sleep, I know not how, revives our hopes, and rekindles our desires. He rose early in the morning, surveyed the landscape, and was pleased. He walked out, and passed from field to field, without observing any beaten path, and wondered that he had not seen the shepherdesses dancing, nor heard the swains piping to their flocks.

At last he saw some reapers and harvest-women at dinner. Here, said he, are the true Arcadians; and advanced courteously towards them, as afraid of confusing them by the dignity of his presence. They acknowledged his superiority by no other token than that of asking him for something to drink. He imagined that he had now purchased the privilege of discourse, and began to descend to familiar questions, endeavouring to accommodate his discourse to the grossness of rustick understandings. The clowns soon found, that he did not know wheat from rye, and began to despise him; one of the boys, by pretending to show him a bird's nest, decoyed him into a ditch; and one of the wenches sold him a bargain.

This walk had given him no great pleasure; but he hoped to find other rusticks less coarse of manners, and less mischievous of disposition. Next morning he was accosted by an attorney, who told him that, unless he made farmer Dobson satisfaction for trampling his grass, he had orders to indict him. Shifter was offended, but not terrified; and, telling the attorney that he was himself a lawyer, talked so volubly of pettyfoggers and barrators, that he drove him away.

Finding his walks thus interrupted, he was inclined to ride, and, being pleased with the appearance of a horse that was grazing in a neighbouring meadow, inquired the owner, who warranted him sound, and would not sell him, but that he was too fine for a plain man. Dick paid down the price, and, riding out to enjoy the evening, fell with his new horse into a ditch; they got out with difficulty, and, as he was going to mount again, a countryman looked at the horse, and perceived him to be blind. Dick went to the seller, and demanded back his money; but was told, that a man who rented his ground must do the best for himself; that his landlord had his rent though the year was barren; and that, whether horses had eyes or no, he should sell them to the highest bidder.

Shifter now began to be tired with rustick simplicity, and on the fifth day took possession again of his chambers, and bade farewell to the regions of calm content and placid meditation.

N°. 72. SATURDAY, SEPTEMBER 1, 1759.

MEN complain of nothing more frequently than of deficient memory; and, indeed, every one finds that many of the ideas which he desired to retain have slipped irretrievably away; that the acquisitions of the mind are sometimes equally fugitive with the gifts of fortune; and that a short intermission of attention more certainly lessens knowledge than impairs an estate.

To assist this weakness of our nature, many methods have been proposed, all of which may be justly suspected of being ineffectual; for no art of memory, however its effects have been boasted or admired, has been ever adopted into general use, nor have those who possessed it appeared to excel others in readiness of recollection or multiplicity of attainments.

There is another art of which all have felt the want, though Themistocles only confessed it. We suffer equal pain from the pertinacious adhesion of unwelcome images, as from the evanescence of those which are pleasing and useful; and it may be doubted whether we should be more benefited by the art of memory or the art of forgetfulness.

Forgetfulness is necessary to remembrance. Ideas are retained by renovation of that impression which time is always wearing away, and which new images are striving to obliterate. If useless thoughts could be expelled from the mind, all the valuable parts of our knowledge would more frequently recur, and every recurrence would reinstate them in their former place.

It is impossible to consider, without some regret, how much might have been learned, or how much might have been invented, by a rational and vigorous application of time, uselessly or painfully passed in the revocation of events, which have left neither good nor evil behind them, in grief for misfortunes either repaired or irreparable, in resentment of injuries known only to ourselves, of which death has put the authors beyond our power.

Philosophy has accumulated precept upon precept, to warn us against the anticipation of future calamities. All useless misery is certainly folly, and he that feels evils before they come may be deservedly censured; yet surely to dread the future is more reasonable than to lament the past. The business of life is to go forwards: he who sees evil in prospect meets it in his way; but he who catches it by retrospection turns back to find it. That which is feared may sometimes be avoided, but that which is regretted to-day may be regretted again to-morrow.

Regret is indeed useful and virtuous, and not only allowable but necessary, when it tends to the amendment of life, or to admonition of errour which we may be again in danger of committing. But a very small part of the moments spent in meditation on the past, produce any reasonable caution or salutary sorrow. Most of the mortifications that we have suffered, arose from the concurrence of local and temporary circumstances, which can never meet again; and most of our disappointments have succeeded those expectations, which life allows not to be formed a second time.

It would add much to human happiness, if an art could be taught of forgetting all of which the remembrance is at once useless and afflictive; if that pain which never can end in pleasure could be driven totally away, that the mind might perform its functions without incumbrance, and the past might no longer encroach upon the present.

Little can be done well to which the whole mind is not applied; the business of every day calls for the day to which it is assigned; and he will have no leisure to regret yesterday's vexations who resolves not to have a new subject of regret to-morrow.

But to forget or to remember at pleasure, are equally beyond the power of man. Yet as memory may be assisted by method, and the decays of knowledge repaired by stated times of recollection, so the power of forgetting is capable of improvement. Reason will, by a resolute contest, prevail over imagination, and the power may be obtained of transferring the attention as judgment shall direct.

The incursions of troublesome thoughts are often violent and importunate; and it is not easy to a mind accustomed to their inroads to expel them immediately by putting better images into motion; but this enemy of quiet is above all others weakened by every defeat; the reflection which has been once overpowered and ejected, seldom returns with any formidable vehemence.

Employment is the great instrument of intellectual dominion. The mind cannot retire from its enemy into total vacancy, or turn aside from one object but by passing to another. ' The gloomy and the resentful are always found among those who have nothing to do, or who do nothing. We must be busy about good or evil, and he to whom the present offers nothing will often be looking backward on the past.

Nº. 73. SATURDAY, SEPTEMBER 8, 1759.

THAT every man would be rich if a wish could obtain riches, is a position which I believe few will contest, at least in a nation like ours, in which commerce has kindled an universal emulation of wealth, and in which money receives all the honours which are the proper right of knowledge and of virtue.

Yet, though we are all labouring for gold as for the chief good, and, by the natural effort of unwearied diligence, have found many expeditious methods of obtaining it, we have not been able to improve the art of using it, or to make it produce more happiness than it afforded in former times, when every declaimer expatiated on its mischiefs, and every philosopher taught his followers to despise it.

Many of the dangers imputed of old to exorbitant wealth, are now at an end. The rich are neither waylaid by robbers, nor watched by informers; there is nothing to be dreaded from proscriptions, or seizures. The necessity of concealing treasure has long ceased; no man now needs counterfeit mediocrity, and condemn his plate and jewels to caverns and darkness, or feast his mind with the consciousness of clouded splendour, of finery which is useless till it is shown, and which he dares not show.

In our time, the poor are strongly tempted to assume the appearance of wealth, but the wealthy very rarely desire to be thought poor; for we are all at full liberty to display riches by every mode of ostentation. We fill our houses with useless ornaments, only to show that we can

buy them ; we cover our coaches with gold, and employ
artists in the discovery of new fashions of expense ; and
yet it cannot be found that riches produce happiness.

Of riches, as of every thing else, the hope is more than
the enjoyment : while we consider them as the means to
be used, at some future time, for the attainment of felicity, we press on our pursuit ardently and vigorously,
and that ardour secures us from weariness of ourselves ;
but no sooner do we sit down to enjoy our acquisitions,
than we find them insufficient to fill up the vacuities of
life.

One cause which is not always observed of the insufficiency of riches is, that they very seldom make their
owner rich. To be rich, is to have more than is desired,
and more than is wanted, to have something which may
be spent without reluctance, and scattered without care,
with which the sudden demands of desire may be gratified,
the casual freaks of fancy indulged, or the unexpected
opportunities of benevolence improved.

Avarice is always poor, but poor by her own fault.
There is another poverty to which the rich are exposed
with less guilt by the officiousness of others. Every man,
eminent for exuberance of fortune, is surrounded from
morning to evening, and from evening to midnight, by
flatterers, whose art of adulation consists in exciting artificial wants, and in forming new schemes of profusion.

Tom Tranquil, when he came to age, found himself in
possession of a fortune, of which the twentieth part might
perhaps have made him rich. His temper is easy, and his
affections soft ; he receives every man with kindness, and
hears him with credulity. His friends took care to settle
him by giving him a wife, whom, having no particular inclination, he rather accepted than chose, because he was
told that she was proper for him.

He was now to live with dignity proportionate to his
fortune. What his fortune requires or admits Tom does
not know, for he has little skill in computation, and none
of his friends think it their interest to improve it. If he

was suffered to live by his own choice, he would leave every thing as he finds it, and pass through the world distinguished only by inoffensive gentleness. But the ministers of luxury have marked him out as one at whose expense they may exercise their arts. A companion, who had just learned the names of the Italian masters, runs from sale to sale, and buys pictures, for which Mr. Tranquil pays, without inquiring where they shall be hung. Another fills his garden with statues, which Tranquil wishes away, but dares not remove. One of his friends is learning architecture by building him a house, which he passed by, and inquired to whom it belonged; another has been for three years digging canals and raising mounts, cutting trees down in one place, and planting them in another, on which Tranquil looks with a serene indifference, without asking what will be the cost. Another projector tells him that a waterwork, like that of Versailles, will complete the beauties of his seat, and lays his draughts before him: Tranquil turns his eyes upon them, and the artist begins his explanations; Tranquil raises no objections, but orders him to begin the work, that he may escape from talk which he does not understand.

Thus a thousand hands are busy at his expense, without adding to his pleasures. He pays and receives visits, and has loitered in publick or in solitude, talking in summer of the town, and in winter of the country, without knowing that his fortune is impaired, till his steward told him this morning, that he could pay the workmen no longer but by mortgaging a manor.

No. 74. SATURDAY, SEPTEMBER 15, 1759.

In the mythological pedigree of learning, memory is made the mother of the muses, by which the masters of ancient wisdom, perhaps, meant to show the necessity of storing the mind copiously with true notions, before the imagina-

tion should be suffered to form fictions or collect embellishments ; for the works of an ignorant poet can afford
nothing higher than pleasing sound, and fiction is of no
other use than to display the treasures of memory.

The necessity of memory to the acquisition of knowledge is inevitably felt and universally allowed, so that
scarcely any other of the mental faculties are commonly
considered as necessary to a student : he that admires the
proficiency of another, always attributes it to the happiness of his memory ; and he that laments his own defects,
concludes with a wish that his memory was better.

It is evident, that when the power of retention is weak,
all the attempts at eminence of knowledge must be vain ;
and as few are willing to be doomed to perpetual ignorance, I may, perhaps, afford consolation to some that have
fallen too easily into despondence, by observing that such
weakness is, in my opinion, very rare, and that few have
reason to complain of nature as unkindly sparing of the
gifts of memory.

In the common business of life, we find the memory of
one like that of another, and honestly impute omissions not
to involuntary forgetfulness, but culpable inattention ; but
in literary inquiries, failure is imputed rather to want of
memory than of diligence.

We consider ourselves as defective in memory, either
because we remember less than we desire, or less than we
suppose others to remember.

Memory is like all other human powers, with which no
man can be satisfied who measures them by what he can
conceive, or by what he can desire. He whose mind is
most capacious, finds it much too narrow for his wishes ; he
that remembers most, remembers little compared with
what he forgets. He, therefore, that, after the perusal of a
book, finds few ideas remaining in his mind, is not to consider the disappointment as peculiar to himself, or to resign
all hopes of improvement, because he does not retain what
even the author has, perhaps, forgotten.

He who compares his memory with that of others, is

often too hasty to lament the inequality. Nature has sometimes, indeed, afforded examples of enormous, wonderful and gigantick memory. Scaliger reports of himself, that, in his youth, he could repeat above a hundred verses, having once read them; and Barthius declares, that he wrote his comment upon Claudian without consulting the text. But not to have such degrees of memory is no more to be lamented, than not to have the strength of Hercules, or the swiftness of Achilles. He that, in the distribution of good, has an equal share with common men, may justly be contented. Where there is no striking disparity, it is difficult to know of two which remembers most, and still more difficult to discover which reads with greater attention, which has renewed the first impression by more frequent repetitions, or by what accidental combination of ideas either mind might have united any particular narrative or argument to its former stock.

But memory, however impartially distributed, so often deceives our trust, that almost every man attempts, by some artifice or other, to secure its fidelity.

It is the practice of many readers to note, in the margin of their books, the most important passages, the strongest arguments, or the brightest sentiments. Thus they load their minds with superfluous attention, repress the vehemence of curiosity by useless deliberation, and by frequent interruption break the current of narration or the chain of reason, and at last close the volume, and forget the passages and marks together.

Others I have found unalterably persuaded, that nothing is certainly remembered but what is transcribed; and they have, therefore, passed weeks and months in transferring large quotations to a commonplace-book. Yet, why any part of a book, which can be consulted at pleasure, should be copied, I was never able to discover. The hand has no closer correspondence with the memory than the eye. The act of writing itself distracts the thoughts, and what is read twice is commonly better remembered than what is transcribed. This method, therefore, consumes time without assisting memory.

The true art of memory is the art of attention. No man will read with much advantage, who is not able, at pleasure, to evacuate his mind, or who brings not to his author an intellect defecated and pure, neither turbid with care, nor agitated by pleasure. If the repositories of thought are already full, what can they receive? If the mind is employed on the past or future, the book will be held before the eyes in vain. What is read with delight is commonly retained, because pleasure always secures attention; but the books which are consulted by occasional necessity, and perused with impatience, seldom leave any traces on the mind.

N°. 75. SATURDAY, SEPTEMBER 22, 1759.

IN the time when Bassora was considered as the school of Asia, and flourished by the reputation of its professors and the confluence of its students, among the pupils that listened round the chair of Albumazar was Gelaleddin, a native of Tauris, in Persia, a young man amiable in his manners and beautiful in his form, of boundless curiosity, incessant diligence, and irresistible genius, of quick apprehension and tenacious memory, accurate without narrowness, and eager for novelty without inconstancy.

No sooner did Gelaleddin appear at Bassora, than his virtues and abilities raised him to distinction. He passed from class to class rather admired than envied by those whom the rapidity of his progress left behind ; he was consulted by his fellow-students as an oraculous guide, and admitted as a competent auditor to the conferences of the sages.

After a few years, having passed through all the exercises of probation, Gelaleddin was invited to a professor's seat, and entreated to increase the splendour of Bassora. Gelaleddin affected to deliberate on the proposal, with which, before he considered it, he resolved to comply ; and next morning retired to a garden planted for the recreation of the students, and, entering a solitary walk, began to meditate upon his future life.

" If I am thus eminent," said he, " in the regions of literature, I shall be yet more conspicuous in any other place; if I should now devote myself to study and retirement, I must pass my life in silence, unacquainted with the delights of wealth, the influence of power, the pomp of greatness, and the charms of elegance, with all that man envies and desires, with all that keeps the world in motion, by the hope of gaining or the fear of losing it. I will, therefore, depart to Tauris, where the Persian monarch resides in all the splendour of absolute dominion: my reputation will fly before me, my arrival will be congratulated by my kinsmen and my friends; I shall see the eyes of those who predict my greatness sparkling with exultation, and the faces of those that once despised me clouded with envy, or counterfeiting kindness by artificial smiles. I will show my wisdom by my discourse, and my moderation by my silence; I will instruct the modest with easy gentleness, and repress the ostentatious by seasonable superciliousness. My apartments will be crowded by the inquisitive and the vain, by those that honour and those that rival me; my name will soon reach the court; I shall stand before the throne of the emperour: the judges of the law will confess my wisdom, and the nobles will contend to heap gifts upon me. If I shall find that my merit, like that of others, excites malignity, or feel myself tottering on the seat of elevation, I may at last retire to academical obscurity, and become, in my lowest state, a professor of Bassora."

Having thus settled his determination, he declared to his friends his design of visiting Tauris, and saw with more pleasure than he ventured to express, the regret with which he was dismissed. He could not bear to delay the honours to.which he was destined, and, therefore, hastened away, and in a short time entered the capital of Persia. He was immediately immersed in the crowd, and passed unobserved to his father's house. He entered, and was received, though not unkindly, yet without any excess of fondness or exclamations of rapture. His father had, in his absence, suffered many losses, and Gelaleddin was considered as an additional burden to a falling family.

When he recovered from his surprise, he began to display his acquisitions, and practised all the arts of narration and disquisition: but the poor have no leisure to be pleased with eloquence; they heard his arguments without reflection, and his pleasantries without a smile. He then applied himself singly to his brothers and sisters, but found them all chained down by invariable attention to their own fortunes, and insensible of any other excellence than that which could bring some remedy for indigence.

It was now known in the neighbourhood that Gelaleddin was returned, and he sat for some days in expectation that the learned would visit him for consultation, or the great for entertainment. But who will be pleased or instructed in the mansions of poverty? He then frequented places of publick resort, and endeavoured to attract notice by the copiousness of his talk. The sprightly were silenced, and went away to censure, in some other place, his arrogance and his pedantry; and the dull listened quietly for a while, and then wondered why any man should take pains to obtain so much knowledge which would never do him good.

He next solicited the visiers for employment, not doubting but his service would be eagerly accepted. He was told by one that there was no vacancy in his office; by another, that his merit was above any patronage but that of the emperour; by a third, that he would not forget him; and by the chief visier, that he did not think literature of any great use in publick business. He was sometimes admitted to their tables, where he exerted his wit and diffused his knowledge; but he observed, that where, by endeavour or accident, he had remarkably excelled, he was seldom invited a second time.

He now returned to Bassora, wearied and disgusted, but confident of resuming his former rank, and revelling again in satiety of praise. But he who had been neglected at Tauris, was not much regarded at Bassora; he was considered as a fugitive, who returned only because he could live in no other place; his companions found that they had formerly overrated his abilities, and he lived long without notice or esteem.

N°. 76. SATURDAY, SEPTEMBER 29, 1759.

TO THE IDLER.

SIR,

I WAS much pleased with your ridicule of those shallow criticks, whose judgment, though often right as far as it goes, yet reaches only to inferior beauties, and who, unable to comprehend the whole, judge only by parts, and from thence determine the merit of extensive works. But there is another kind of critick still worse, who judges by narrow rules, and those too often false, and which, though they should be true, and founded on nature, will lead him but a very little way toward the just estimation of the sublime beauties in works of genius; for whatever part of an art can be executed or criticised by rules, that part is no longer the work of genius, which implies excellence out of the reach of rules. For my own part, I profess myself an Idler, and love to give my judgment, such as it is, from my immediate perceptions, without much fatigue of thinking; and I am of opinion that, if a man has not those perceptions right, it will be vain for him to endeavour to supply their place by rules, which may enable him to talk more learnedly, but not to distinguish more acutely. Another reason which has lessened my affection for the study of criticism is, that cri-

ticks, so far as I have observed, debar themselves from
receiving any pleasure from the polite arts, at the same
time, that they profess to love and admire them: for these
rules, being always uppermost, give them such a propensity
to criticise, that, instead of giving up the reins of their imagination into their author's hands, their frigid minds are
employed in examining whether the performance be according to the rules of art.

To those who are resolved to be criticks in spite of nature, and, at the same time, have no great disposition to
much reading and study, I would recommend to them to
assume the character of connoisseur, which may be purchased at a much cheaper rate than that of a critick in
poetry. The remembrance of a few names of painters,
with their general characters, with a few rules of the academy, which they may pick up among the painters, will go
a great way towards making a very notable connoisseur.

With a gentleman of this cast, I visited last week the
Cartoons at Hampton-court; he was just returned from
Italy, a connoisseur of course, and of course his mouth
full of nothing but the grace of Raffaelle, the purity of
Domenichino, the learning of Poussin, the air of Guido,
the greatness of taste of the Carraccis, and the sublimity
and grand contorno of Michael Angelo; with all the rest
of the cant of criticism, which he emitted with that volu-
bility which generally those orators have who annex no
ideas to their words.

As we were passing through the rooms, in our way to
the gallery, I made him observe a whole length of Charles
the First by Vandyke, as a perfect representation of the
character as well as the figure of the man. He agreed it
was very fine, but it wanted spirit and contrast, and had
not the flowing line, without which a figure could not possibly be graceful. When we entered the gallery, I thought
I could perceive him recollecting his rules by which he
was to criticise Raffaelle. I shall pass over his observation of the boats being too little, and other criti-
cisms of that kind, till we arrive at St. Paul preaching.

" This," says he, " is esteemed the most excellent of all the cartoons; what nobleness, what dignity, there is in that figure of St. Paul! and yet what an addition to that nobleness could Raffaelle have given, had the art of contrast been known in his time! but, above all, the flowing l ɪ e which constitutes grace and beauty! You would not have then seen an upright figure standing equally on both legs, and both hands stretched forward in the same direction, and his drapery, to all appearance, without the least art of disposition." The following picture is the Charge to Peter. " Here," says he, " are twelve upright figures; what a pity it is that Raffaelle was not acquainted with the pyramidal principle! He would then have contrived the figures in the middle to have been on higher ground, or the figures at the extremities stooping or lying, which would not only have formed the group into the shape of a pyramid, but likewise contrasted the standing figures. Indeed," added he, " I have often lamented that so great a genius as Raffaelle had not lived in this enlightened age, since the art has been reduced to principles, and had had his education in one of the modern academies; what glorious works might we have then expected from his divine pencil!"

I shall trouble you no longer with my friend's observations, which, I suppose, you are now able to continue by yourself. It is curious to observe, that, at the same time that great admiration is pretended for a name of fixed reputation, objections are raised against those very qualities by which that great name was acquired.

Those criticks are continually lamenting that Raffaelle had not the colouring and harmony of Rubens, or the light and shadow of Rembrant, without considering how much the gay harmony of the former, and affectation of the latter, would take from the dignity of Raffaelle; and yet Rubens had great harmony, and Rembrant understood light and shadow: but what may be an excellence in a lower class of painting, becomes a blemish in a higher; as the quick, sprightly turn, which is the life and beauty of epigrammatick compositions, would but ill suit with the majesty of heroick poetry.

To conclude; I would not be thought to infer, from any thing that has been said, that rules are absolutely unnecessary; but to censure scrupulosity, a servile attention to minute exactness, which is sometimes inconsistent with higher excellency, and is lost in the blaze of expanded genius.

I do not know whether you will think painting a general subject. By inserting this letter, perhaps, you will incur the censure a man would deserve, whose business being to entertain a whole room, should turn his back to the company, and talk to a particular person [n].

I am, Sir, &c.

N°. 77. SATURDAY, OCTOBER 6, 1759.

EASY poetry is universally admired; but I know not whether any rule has yet been fixed, by which it may be decided when poetry can be properly called easy. Horace has told us, that it is such as " every reader hopes to equal, but after long labour finds unattainable." This is a very loose description, in which only the effect is noted; the qualities which produce this effect remain to be investigated.

Easy poetry is that in which natural thoughts are expressed without violence to the language. The discriminating character of ease consists principally in the diction; for all true poetry requires that the sentiments be natural. Language suffers violence by harsh or by daring figures, by transposition, by unusual acceptations of words, and by any licence, which would be avoided by a writer of prose. Where any artifice appears in the construction of the verse, that verse is no longer easy. Any epithet which can be

[n] By Sir Joshua Reynolds.

ejected without diminution of the sense, any curious itera-
tion of the same word, and all unusual, though not ungram-
matical structure of speech, destroy the grace of easy
poetry.

The first lines of Pope's Iliad afford examples of many
licences which an easy writer must decline :

> Achilles' *wrath*, to Greece the *direful spring*
> Of woes unnumber'd, *heav'nly* Goddess sing ;
> The wrath which *hurl'd* to Pluto's *gloomy reign*
> The souls of *mighty* chiefs untimely slain.

In the first couplet the language is distorted by inver-
sions, clogged with superfluities, and clouded by a harsh
metaphor ; and in the second there are two words used in
an uncommon sense, and two epithets inserted only to
lengthen the line ; all these practices may in a long work
easily be pardoned, but they always produce some degree
of obscurity and ruggedness.

Easy poetry has been so long excluded by ambition of
ornament, and luxuriance of imagery, that its nature seems
now to be forgotten. Affectation, however opposite to
ease, is sometimes mistaken for it ; and those who aspire
to gentle elegance, collect female phrases and fashionable
barbarisms, and imagine that style to be easy which custom
has made familiar. Such was the idea of the poet who
wrote the following verses to a *countess cutting paper :*

> Pallas grew *vap'rish once and odd,*
>> She would not *do the least right thing*
> Either for Goddess or for God,
>> Nor work, nor play, nor paint, nor sing.

> Jove frown'd, and " Use (he cried) those eyes
>> So skilful, and those hands so taper ;
> Do something exquisite and wise"—
>> She bow'd, obey'd him, and cut paper.

> This vexing him who gave her birth,
>> Thought by all Heaven a *burning shame,*
> *What does she next,* but bids on earth
>> Her Burlington do just the same ?

Pallas, you give yourself *strange airs ;*
    But sure you'll find it hard to spoil
The sense and taste of one that bears
    The name of Savile and of Boyle.

Alas ! one bad example shown,
    How quickly all the sex pursue !
See, madam ! see the arts o'erthrown
    Between John Overton and *you.*

It is the prerogative of easy poetry to be understood as long as the language lasts ; but modes of speech, which owe their prevalence only to modish folly, or to the eminence of those that use them, die away with their inventors, and their meaning, in a few years, is no longer known.

Easy poetry is commonly sought in petty compositions upon minute subjects ; but ease, though it excludes pomp, will admit greatness. Many lines in Cato's soliloquy are at once easy and sublime :

    'Tis the Divinity that stirs within us ;
    'Tis Heaven itself that points out an hereafter,
    And intimates eternity to man.
    ———— If there's a Power above us,
    And that there is all Nature cries aloud
    Through all her works, he must delight in virtue,
    And that which he delights in must be happy.

Nor is ease more contrary to wit than to sublimity ; the celebrated stanza of Cowley, on a lady elaborately dressed, loses nothing of its freedom by the spirit of the sentiment:

    Th' adorning thee with so much art
      Is but a barb'rous skill ;
    'Tis like the pois'ning of a dart,
      Too apt before to kill.

Cowley seems to have possessed the power of writing easily beyond any other of our poets ; yet his pursuit of remote thought led him often into harshness of expression.

Waller often attempted, but seldom attained it; for he is too frequently driven into transpositions. The poets, from the time of Dryden, have gradually advanced in embellishment, and consequently departed from simplicity and ease.

To require from any author many pieces of easy poetry, would be indeed to oppress him with too hard a task. It is less difficult to write a volume of lines swelled with epithets, brightened by figures, and stiffened by transpositions, than to produce a few couplets graced only by naked elegance and simple purity, which require so much care and skill, that I doubt whether any of our authors have yet been able, for twenty lines together, nicely to observe the true definition of easy poetry.

N°. 78. SATURDAY, OCTOBER 13, 1759.

I HAVE passed the summer in one of those places to which a mineral spring gives the idle and luxurious an annual reason for resorting, whenever they fancy themselves offended by the heat of London. What is the true motive of this periodical assembly, I have never yet been able to discover. The greater part of the visitants neither feel diseases nor fear them. What pleasure can be expected more than the variety of the journey, I know not, for the numbers are too great for privacy, and too small for diversion. As each is known to be a spy upon the rest, they all live in continual restraint; and having but a narrow range for censure, they gratify its cravings by preying on one another.

But every condition has some advantages. In this confinement, a smaller circle affords opportunities for more exact observation. The glass that magnifies its object contracts the sight to a point; and the mind must be fixed upon a single character to remark its minute peculiarities. The quality or habit which passes unobserved in the tumult of successive multitudes, becomes conspicuous when it is offered to the notice day after day; and, perhaps, I have, without any distinct notice, seen thousands like my late companions; for when the scene can be varied at pleasure, a slight disgust turns us aside before a deep impression can be made upon the mind.

There was a select set, supposed to be distinguished by superiority of intellects, who always passed the evening together. To be admitted to their conversation was the highest honour of the place; many youths aspired to distinction, by pretending to occasional invitations; and the ladies were often wishing to be men, that they might partake the pleasures of learned society.

I know not whether by merit or destiny, I was, soon after my arrival, admitted to this envied party, which I frequented till I had learned the art by which each endeavoured to support his character.

Tom Steady was a vehement assertor of uncontroverted truth; and by keeping himself out of the reach of contradiction had acquired all the confidence which the consciousness of irresistible abilities could have given. I was once mentioning a man of eminence, and, after having recounted his virtues, endeavoured to represent him fully, by mentioning his faults. "Sir," said Mr. Steady, "that he has faults I can easily believe, for who is without them? No man, Sir, is now alive, among the innumerable multitudes that swarm upon the earth, however wise, or however good, who has not, in some degree, his failings and his faults. If there be any man faultless, bring him forth into publick view, show him openly, and let him be known; but I will venture to affirm, and, till the contrary be plainly shown, shall always maintain, that no such man is to be found. Tell not me, Sir, of impeccability and perfection; such talk is for those that are strangers in the world: I have seen several nations, and conversed with all ranks of people; I have known the great and the mean, the learned and the ignorant, the old and the young, the clerical and the lay; but I have never found a man without a fault; and I suppose shall die in the opinion, that to be human is to be frail." .

To all this nothing could be opposed. I listened with a hanging head; Mr. Steady looked round on the hearers with triumph, and saw every eye congratulating his victory; he departed, and spent the next morning in following those who retired from the company, and telling them, with injunctions of secrecy, how poor Spritely began to take liberties with men wiser than himself; but that he suppressed him by a decisive argument, which put him totally to silence.

Dick Snug is a man of sly remark and pithy sententiousness: he never immerges himself in the stream of conversation, but lies to catch his companions in the eddy: he is often very successful in breaking narratives and confounding eloquence. A gentleman, giving the history of one of his acquaintance, made mention of a lady that had many lovers: " Then," said Dick, " she was either handsome or rich." This observation being well received, Dick watched the progress of the tale; and, hearing of a man lost in a shipwreck, remarked, that " no man was ever drowned upon dry land."

Will Startle is a man of exquisite sensibility, whose delicacy of frame and quickness of discernment subject him to impressions from the slightest causes; and who, therefore, passes his life between rapture and horrour, in quiverings of delight, or convulsions of disgust. His emotions are too violent for many words; his thoughts are always discovered by exclamations. *Vile, odious, horrid, detestable,* and *sweet, charming, delightful, astonishing,* compose almost his whole vocabulary, which he utters with various contortions and gesticulations, not easily related or described.

Jack Solid is a man of much reading, who utters nothing but quotations; but having been, I suppose, too confident of his memory, he has for some time neglected his books, and his stock grows every day more scanty.

Mr. Solid has found an opportunity every night to repeat, from Hudibras,

> Doubtless the pleasure is as great
> Of being cheated, as to cheat;

and from Waller,

> Poets lose half the praise they would have got,
> Were it but known what they discreetly blot.

Dick Misty is a man of deep research, and forcible penetration. Others are content with superficial appearances; but Dick holds, that there is no effect without a cause, and values himself upon his power of explaining the difficult and displaying the abstruse. Upon a dispute among us, which of two young strangers was more beautiful, " You," says Mr. Misty, turning to me, " like Amaranthia better than Chloris. I do not wonder at the preference, for the cause is evident : there is in man a perception of harmony, and a sensibility of perfection, which touches the finer fibres of the mental texture ; and before reason can descend from her throne, to pass her sentence upon the things compared, drives us towards the object proportioned to our faculties, by an impulse gentle, yet irresistible ; for the harmonick system of the Universe, and the reciprocal magnetism of similar natures, are always operating towards conformity and union; nor can the powers of the soul cease from agitation, till they find something on which they can repose." To this nothing was opposed ; and Amaranthia was acknowledged to excel Chloris.

Of the rest you may expect an account from,

Sir, yours,

ROBIN SPRITELY.

SIR,

YOUR acceptance of a former letter on painting gives me encouragement to offer a few more sketches on the same subject.

Amongst the painters, and the writers on painting, there is one maxim universally admitted and continually inculcated. *Imitate nature* is the invariable rule; but I know none who have explained in what manner this rule is to be understood; the consequence of which is, that every one takes it in the most obvious sense, that objects are represented naturally when they have such relief that they seem real. It may appear strange, perhaps, to hear this sense of the rule disputed; but it must be considered, that, if the excellency of a painter consisted only in this kind of imitation, painting must lose its rank, and be no longer considered as a liberal art, and sister to poetry, this imitation being merely mechanical, in which the slowest intellect is always sure to succeed best: for the painter of genius cannot stoop to drudgery, in which the understanding has no part; and what pretence has the art to claim kindred with poetry, but by its powers over the imagination? To this power the painter of genius directs his aim; in this sense he studies nature, and often arrives at his end, even by being unnatural in the confined sense of the word.

The grand style of painting requires this minute attention to be carefully avoided, and must be kept as separate from it as the style of poetry from that of history. Poetical ornaments destroy that air of truth and plainness which ought to characterize history; but the very being of poetry consists in departing from this plain narration, and adopting every ornament that will warm the imagination. To desire to see the excellencies of each style united, to mingle the Dutch with the Italian school, is to join contrarieties which cannot subsist together, and which destroy the efficacy of each other. The Italian attends only to the invariable, the great and general ideas which are fixed and inherent in universal nature; the Dutch, on the contrary, to literal truth and a minute exactness in the detail, as I may say, of nature modified by accident. The attention to these petty peculiarities is the very cause of this naturalness so much admired in the Dutch pictures, which, if we suppose it to be a beauty, is certainly of a lower order, which ought to give place to a beauty of a superior kind, since one cannot be obtained but by departing from the other.

If my opinion was asked concerning the works of Michael Angelo, whether they would receive any advantage from possessing this mechanical merit, I should not scruple to say, they would not only receive no advantage, but would lose, in a great measure, the effect which they now have on every mind susceptible of great and noble ideas. His works may be said to be all genius and soul; and why should they be loaded with heavy matter, which can only counteract his purpose by retarding the progress of the imagination?

If this opinion should be thought one of the wild extravagancies of enthusiasm, I shall only say, that those who censure it are not conversant in the works of the great masters. It is very difficult to determine the exact degree of enthusiasm that the arts of painting and poetry may admit. There may, perhaps, be too great an indulgence, as well as too great a restraint of imagination ; and if the one produces incoherent monsters, the other produces what is full as bad, lifeless insipidity. An intimate knowledge of the passions, and good sense, but not common sense, must at last determine its limits. It has been thought, and I believe with reason, that Michael Angelo sometimes trangressed those limits ; and I think I have seen figures of him of which it was very difficult to determine whether they were in the highest degree sublime or extremely ridiculous. Such faults may be said to be the ebullitions of genius; but at least he had this merit, that he never was insipid, and whatever passion his works may excite, they will always escape contempt.

What I have had under consideration is the sublimest style, particularly that of Michael Angelo, the Homer of painting. Other kinds may admit of this naturalness, which of the lowest kind is the chief merit; but in paint-ing, as in poetry, the highest style has the least of common nature.

One may very safely recommend a little more enthu-siasm to the modern painters; too much is certainly not the vice of the present age. The Italians seem to have been continually declining, in this respect, from the time of Michael Angelo to that of Carlo Maratti, and from thence to the very bathos of insipidity to which they are now sunk; so that there is no need of remarking, that, where I mentioned the Italian painters in opposition to the Dutch, I mean not the moderns, but the heads of the old Roman and Bolognian schools; nor did I mean to include in my idea of an Italian painter, the Venetian school, which may be said to be the Dutch part of the Italian genius. I have only to add a word of advice to the painters, that, however excellent they may be in painting naturally, they would not flatter themselves very much upon it, and to the con-noisseurs, that when they see a cat or fiddle painted so finely, that, as the phrase is, " it looks as if you could take it up," they would not for that reason immediately compare the painter to Raffaelle and Michael Angelo.º

N°. 80.   SATURDAY, OCTOBER 27, 1759.

THAT every day has its pains and sorrows is universally experienced, and almost universally confessed; but let us not attend only to mournful truths; if we look impartially about us, we shall find that every day has likewise its pleasures and its joys.

* By Sir Joshua Reynolds.

The time is now come when the town is again beginning
to be full, and the rusticated beauty sees an end of her
banishment. Those whom the tyranny of fashion had condemned to pass the summer among shades and brooks, are
now preparing to return to plays, balls and assemblies,
with health restored by retirement, and spirits kindled by
expectation.

Many a mind, which has languished some months without emotion or desire, now feels a sudden renovation of its
faculties. It was long ago observed by Pythagoras, that
ability and necessity dwell near each other. She that
wandered in the garden without sense of its fragrance, and
lay day after day stretched upon a couch behind a green
curtain, unwilling to wake, and unable to sleep, now summons her thoughts to consider which of her last year's
clothes shall be seen again, and to anticipate the raptures
of a new suit; the day and the night are now filled with
occupation; the laces, which were too fine to be worn
among rusticks, are taken from the boxes and reviewed;
and the eye is no sooner closed after its labours, than whole
shops of silk busy the fancy.

But happiness is nothing, if it is not known, and very
little, if it is not envied. Before the day of departure a
week is always appropriated to the payment and reception
of ceremonial visits, at which nothing can be mentioned
but the delights of London. The lady who is hastening to
the scene of action flutters her wings, displays her prospects of felicity, tells how she grudges every moment of
delay, and, in the presence of those whom she knows condemned to stay at home, is sure to wonder by what arts
life can be made supportable through a winter in the
country, and to tell how often, amidst the ecstasies of an
opera, she shall pity those friends whom she has left behind. Her hope of giving pain is seldom disappointed;
the affected indifference of one, the faint congratulations
of another, the wishes of some openly confessed, and the
silent dejection of the rest, all exalt her opinion of her own
superiority.

But, however we may labour for our own deception, truth, though unwelcome, will sometimes intrude upon the mind. They who have already enjoyed the crowds and noise of the great city, know that their desire to return is little more than the restlessness of a vacant mind, that they are not so much led by hope as driven by disgust, and wish rather to leave the country than to see the town. There is commonly in every coach a passenger enwrapped in silent expectation, whose joy is more sincere, and whose hopes are more exalted. The virgin whom the last summer released from her governess, and who is now going between her mother and her aunt to try the fortune of her wit and beauty, suspects no fallacy in the gay representation. She believes herself passing into another world, and images London as an elysian region, where every hour has its proper pleasure, where nothing is seen but the blaze of wealth, and nothing heard but merriment and flattery; where the morning always rises on a show, and the evening closes on a ball; where the eyes are used only to sparkle, and the feet only to dance.

Her aunt and her mother amuse themselves on the road, with telling her of dangers to be dreaded, and cautions to be observed. She hears them as they heard their predecessors, with incredulity or contempt. She sees that they have ventured and escaped; and one of the pleasures which she promises herself is to detect their falsehoods, and be freed from their admonitions.

We are inclined to believe those whom we do not know, because they have never deceived us. The fair adventurer may, perhaps, listen to the Idler, whom she cannot suspect of rivalry or malice; yet he scarcely expects to be credited when he tells her, that her expectations will likewise end in disappointment.

The uniform necessities of human nature produce, in a great measure, uniformity of life, and for part of the day make one place like another; to dress and to undress, to eat and to sleep, are the same in London as in the country. The supernumerary hours have, indeed, a great variety both of pleasure and of pain. The stranger, gazed on by multitudes at her first appearance in the Park, is, perhaps, on the highest summit of female happiness; but how great is the anguish when the novelty of another face draws her worshippers away! The heart may leap for a time under a fine gown; but the sight of a gown yet finer puts an end to rapture. In the first row at an opera, two hours may be happily passed in listening to the musick on the stage, and watching the glances of the company; but how will the night end in despondency when she, that imagined herself the sovereign of the place, sees lords contending to lead Iris to her chair! There is little pleasure in conversation, to her whose wit is regarded but in the second place; and who can dance with ease or spirit that sees Amaryllis led out before her? She that fancied nothing but a succession of pleasures, will find herself engaged without design in numberless competitions, and mortified, without provocation, with numberless afflictions.

But I do not mean to extinguish that ardour which I wish to moderate, or to discourage those whom I am endeavouring to restrain. To know the world is necessary, since we were born for the help of one another; and to know it early is convenient, if it be only that we may learn early to despise it. She that brings to London a mind well prepared for improvement, though she misses her hope of uninterrupted happiness, will gain in return an opportunity of adding knowledge to vivacity, and enlarging innocence to virtue.

N°. 81. SATURDAY, NOVEMBER 3, 1759.

As the English army was passing towards Quebec along a soft savanna between a mountain and a lake, one of the petty chiefs of the inland regions stood upon a rock surrounded by his clan, and from behind the shelter of the bushes contemplated the art and regularity of European war. It was evening, the tents were pitched: he observed the security with which the troops rested in the night, and the order with which the march was renewed in the morning. He continued to pursue them with his eye till they could be seen no longer, and then stood for some time silent and pensive.

Then turning to his followers, " My children," said he, " I have often heard from men hoary with long life, that there was a time when our ancestors were absolute lords of the woods, the meadows and the lakes, wherever the eye can reach or the foot can pass. They fished and hunted, feasted and danced, and when they were weary lay down under the first thicket, without danger and without fear. They changed their habitations, as the seasons required, convenience prompted, or curiosity allured them; and sometimes gathered the fruits of the mountain, and sometimes sported in canoes along the coast.

" Many years and ages are supposed to have been thus passed in plenty and security; when, at last, a new race of men entered our country from the great ocean. They inclosed themselves in habitations of stone, which our ancestors could neither enter by violence, nor destroy by fire. They issued from those fastnesses, sometimes covered, like the armadillo, with shells, from which the lance rebounded on the striker, and sometimes carried by mighty beasts which had never been seen in our vales or forests, of such strength and swiftness, that flight and opposition were vain alike. Those invaders ranged over the continent slaughtering, in their rage, those that resisted, and those that submitted, in their mirth. Of those that remained, some were buried in caverns, and condemned to dig metals for their masters; some were employed in tilling the ground, of which foreign tyrants devour the produce; and, when the sword and the mines have destroyed the natives, they supply their place by human beings of another colour, brought from some distant country to perish here under toil and torture.

" Some there are who boast their humanity, and content themselves to seize our chases and fisheries, who drive us from every tract of ground where fertility and pleasantness invite them to settle, and make no war upon us except when we intrude upon our own lands.

" Others pretend to have purchased a right of residence and tyranny; but surely the insolence of such bargains is more offensive than the avowed and open dominion of force. What reward can induce the possessour of a country to admit a stranger more powerful than himself? Fraud or terrour must operate in such contracts; either they promised protection which they never have afforded, or instruction which they never imparted. We hoped to be secured by their favour from some other evil, or to learn the arts of Europe, by which we might be able to secure ourselves. Their power they never have exerted in our defence, and their arts they have studiously concealed from us. Their treaties are only to deceive, and their traffick only to defraud us. They have a written law among them, of which they boast, as derived from Him who made the earth and sea, and by which they profess to believe that man will be made happy when life shall forsake him. Why is not this law communicated to us? It is concealed because it is violated. For how can they preach it to an Indian nation, when I am told that one of its first precepts forbids them to do to others what they would not that others should do to them?

" But the time, perhaps, is now approaching, when the pride of usurpation shall be crushed, and the cruelties of invasion shall be revenged. The sons of rapacity have now drawn their swords upon each other, and referred their claims to the decision of war; let us look unconcerned upon the slaughter, and remember that the death of every European delivers the country from a tyrant and a robber; for what is the claim of either nation, but the claim of the vulture to the leveret, of the tiger to the fawn? Let them then continue to dispute their title to regions which they cannot people, to purchase by danger and blood the empty dignity of dominion over mountains which they will never climb, and rivers which they will never pass. Let us endeavour, in the mean time, to learn their discipline, and to forge their weapons; and, when they shall be weakened with mutual slaughter, let us rush down upon them, force their remains to take shelter in their ships, and reign once more in our native country P."

* * *

Nº. 82. SATURDAY, NOVEMBER 10, 1759.

TO THE IDLER.

SIR,

DISCOURSING in my last letter on the different practice of the Italian and Dutch painters, I observed, that " the Italian painter attends only to the invariable, the great and general ideas which are fixed and inherent in universal nature."

I was led into the subject of this letter by endeavouring to fix the original cause of this conduct of the Italian masters. If it can be proved that by this choice they selected the most beautiful part of the creation, it will show how much their principles are founded on reason, and, at the same time, discover the origin of our ideas of beauty.

I suppose it will be easily granted, that no man can

---

p " How far the seizing on countries already peopled, and driving out or massacring the innocent and defenceless natives, merely because they differed from their invaders in language, in religion, in customs, in government or in colour; how far such a conduct was consonant to nature, to reason or to Christianity, deserved well to be considered by those who have rendered their names immortal by thus civilizing mankind." Blackstone, Com. ii. 7.

I love the University of Salamanca, said Johnson, with warm emotion, for when the Spaniards were in doubt as to the lawfulness of their conquering America, the University of Salamanca gave it as their opinion, that it was not lawful. Boswell, i. 434.

The untaught eloquence of Indian feeling is well preserved in the language of Gertrude of Wyoming.

judge whether any animal be beautiful in its kind, or deformed, who has seen only one of that species: this is as conclusive in regard to the human figure; so that if a man, born blind, was to recover his sight, and the most beautiful woman was brought before him, he could not determine whether she was handsome or not; nor, if the most beautiful and most deformed were produced, could he any better determine to which he should give the preference, having seen only those two. To distinguish beauty, then, implies the having seen many individuals of that species. If it is asked, how is more skill acquired by the observation of greater numbers? I answer that, in consequence of having seen many, the power is acquired, even without seeking after it, of distinguishing between accidental blemishes and excrescences which are continually varying the surface of Nature's works, and the invariable general form which Nature most frequently produces, and always seems to intend in her productions.

Thus, amongst the blades of grass or leaves of the same tree, though no two can be found exactly alike, yet the general form is invariable: a naturalist, before he chose one as a sample, would examine many, since, if he took the first that occurred, it might have, by accident or otherwise, such a form as that it would scarcely be known to belong to that species; he selects, as the painter does, the most beautiful, that is, the most general form of nature.

Every species of the animal, as well as the vegetable creation, may be said to have a fixed or determinate form towards which nature is continually inclining, like various lines terminating in the centre; or it may be compared to pendulums vibrating in different directions over one central point; and as they all cross the centre, though only one passes through any other point, so it will be found that perfect beauty is oftener produced by nature than deformity; I do not mean than deformity in general, but than any one kind of deformity. To instance in a particular part of a feature: the line that forms the ridge of the nose is beautiful when it is straight; this then is the central form, which is oftener found than either concave, convex or any other irregular form that shall be proposed. As we are then more accustomed to beauty than deformity, we may conclude that to be the reason why we approve and admire it, as we approve and admire customs and fashions of dress for no other reason than that we are used to them; so that, though habit and custom cannot be said to be the cause of beauty, it is certainly the cause of our liking it; and I have no doubt but that, if we were more used to deformity than beauty, deformity would then lose the idea now annexed to it, and take that of beauty; as, if the whole world should agree that *yes* and *no* should change their meanings, *yes* would then deny, and *no* would affirm.

Whoever undertakes to proceed further in this argument, and endeavours to fix a general criterion of beauty respecting different species, or to show why one species is more beautiful than another, it will be required from him first to prove that one species is really more beautiful than another. That we prefer one to the other, and with very good reason, will be readily granted; but it does not follow from thence that we think it a more beautiful form; for we have no criterion of form by which to determine our judgment. He who says a swan is more beautiful than a dove, means little more than that he has more pleasure in seeing a swan than a dove, either from the stateliness of its motions, or its being a more rare bird; and he who gives the preference to the dove, does it from some association of ideas of innocence that he always annexes to the dove; but, if he pretends to defend the preference he gives to one or the other by endeavouring to prove that this more beautiful form proceeds from a particular gradation of magnitude, undulation of a curve, or direction of a line, or whatever other conceit of his imagination he shall fix on as a criterion of form, he will be continually contradicting himself, and find at last, that the great Mother of Nature will not be subjected to such narrow rules. Among the various reasons why we prefer one part of her works to another, the most general, I believe, is habit and custom; custom makes, in a certain sense, white black, and black white; it is custom alone determines our preference of the colour of the Europeans to the Æthiopians; and they, for the same reason, prefer their own colour to ours. I suppose nobody will doubt, if one of their painters were to paint the goddess of beauty, but that he would represent her black, with thick lips, flat nose, and woolly hair; and, it seems to me, he would act véry unnaturally if he did not; for by what criterion will any one dispute the propriety of his idea? We, indeed, say, that the form and colour of the European is preferable to that of the Æthiopian; but I know of no reason we have for it, but that we are more accustomed to it. It is absurd to say, that beauty is possessed of attractive powers, which irresistibly seize the corresponding mind with love and admiration, since that argument is equally conclusive in favour of the white and the black philosopher.

The black and white nations must, in respect of beauty, be considered as of different kinds, at least a different species of the same kind; from one of which to the other, as I observed, no inference can be drawn.

Novelty is said to be one of the causes of beauty: that novelty is a very sufficient reason why we should admire, is not denied; but, because it is uncommon, is it, therefore, beautiful? The beauty that is produced by colour, as when we prefer one bird to another, though of the same form, on account of its colour, has nothing to do with this argument, which reaches only to form. I have here considered the word *beauty* as being properly applied to form alone. There is a necessity of fixing this confined sense; for there can be no argument, if the sense of the word is extended to every thing that is approved. A rose may as well be said to be beautiful, because it has a fine smell, as a bird because of its colour. When we apply the word *beauty* we do not mean always by it a more beautiful form, but something valuable on account of its rarity, usefulness, colour, or any other property. A horse is said to be a beautiful animal; but, had a horse as few good qualities as'

a tortoise, I do not imagine that he would be then esteemed beautiful.

A fitness to the end proposed, is said to be another cause
of beauty ; but supposing we were proper judges of what
form is the most proper in an animal to constitute strength
or swiftness, we always determine concerning its beauty,
before we exert our understanding to judge of its fitness.

From what has been said, it may be inferred, that the
works of nature, if we compare one species with another,
are all equally beautiful ; and that preference is given
from custom, or some association of ideas : and that, in
creatures of the same species, beauty is the medium or
centre of all various forms.

To conclude, then, by way of corollary : If it has been
proved, that the painter, by attending to the invariable and
general ideas of nature, produces beauty, he must, by re-
garding minute particularities and accidental discriminations, deviate from the universal rule, and pollute his can-
vass with deformity[q].

* * *

N°. 83.   SATURDAY, NOVEMBER 17, 1759.

TO THE IDLER.

SIR,

    I SUPPOSE you have forgotten that many weeks
ago I promised to send you an account of my companions
at the Wells. You would not deny me a place among the
most faithful votaries of idleness, if you knew how often I
have recollected my engagement, and contented myself to
delay the performance for some reason which I durst not
examine because I knew it to be false ; how often I have
sat down to write, and rejoiced at interruption ; and how
often I have praised the dignity of resolution, determined
at night to write in the morning, and deferred it in the
morning to the quiet hours of night.

            q By Sir Joshua Reynolds.

I have at last begun what I have long wished at an end, and find it more easy than I expected to continue my narration.

Our assembly could boast no such constellation of intellects as Clarendon's band of associates. We had among us no Selden, Falkland or Waller; but we had men not less important in their own eyes, though less distinguished by the publick; and many a time have we lamented the partiality of mankind, and agreed that men of the deepest inquiry sometimes let their discoveries die away in silence, that the most comprehensive observers have seldom opportunities of imparting their remarks, and that modest merit passes in the crowd unknown and unheeded.

One of the greatest men of the society was Sim Scruple, who lives in a continual equipoise of doubt, and is a constant enemy to confidence and dogmatism. Sim's favourite topick of conversation is the narrowness of the human mind, the fallaciousness of our senses, the prevalence of early prejudice, and the uncertainty of appearances. Sim has many doubts about the nature of death, and is sometimes inclined to believe that sensation may survive motion, and that a dead man may feel though he cannot stir. He has sometimes hinted that man might, perhaps, have been naturally a quadruped; and thinks it would be very proper, that at the Foundling Hospital some children should be inclosed in an apartment in which the nurses should be obliged to walk half upon four and half upon two legs, that the younglings, being bred without the prejudice of example, might have no other guide than nature, and might at last come forth into the world as genius should direct, erect or prone, on two legs or on four.

The next, in dignity of mien and fluency of talk, was Dick Wormwood, whose sole delight is to find every thing wrong. Dick never enters a room but he shows that the door and the chimney are ill-placed. He never walks into the fields but he finds ground ploughed which is fitter for pasture. He is always an enemy to the present fashion.

.He holds that all the beauty and virtue of women will soon be destroyed by the use of tea [r]. He triumphs when he talks on the present system of education, and tells us, with great vehemence, that we are learning words when we should learn things. He is of opinion that we suck in errours at the nurse's breast, and thinks it extremely ridiculous that children should be taught to use the right hand rather than the left.

Bob Sturdy considers it as a point of honour to say again what he has once said, and wonders how any man, that has been known to alter his opinion, can look his neighbours in the face. Bob is the most formidable disputant of the whole company; for, without troubling himself to search for reasons, he tires his antagonist with repeated affirmations. When Bob has been attacked for an hour with all the powers of eloquence and reason, and his position appears to all but himself utterly untenable, he always closes the debate with his first declaration, introduced by a stout preface of contemptuous civility. "All this is very judicious; you may talk, Sir, as you please; but I will still say what I said at first." Bob deals much in universals, which he has now obliged us to let pass without exceptions. He lives on an annuity, and holds that *there are as many thieves as traders*; he is of loyalty unshaken, and always maintains, that *he who sees a Jacobite sees a rascal.*

Phil Gentle is an enemy to the rudeness of contradiction and the turbulence of debate. Phil has no notions of his own, and, therefore, willingly catches from the last speaker such as he shall drop. This flexibility of ignorance is easily accommodated to any tenet; his only difficulty is, when the disputants grow zealous, how to be of two contrary opinions at once. If no appeal is made to his judgment, he has the art of distributing his attention and his smiles in such a manner, that each thinks him of

---

[r] Dr. Johnson was, as he has humorously described himself, " a hardened and shameless tea-drinker." See his amusing Review of a Journal of Eight Days' Journey and his Reply to a paper in the Gazetteer, May 26, 1757.

his own party; but if he is obliged to speak, he then observes that the question is difficult; that he never received so much pleasure from a debate before; that neither of the controvertists could have found his match in any other company; that Mr. Wormwood's assertion is very well supported, and yet there is great force in what Mr. Scruple advanced against it. By this indefinite declaration both are commonly satisfied; for he that has prevailed is in good humour; and he that has felt his own weakness is very glad to have escaped so well.

I am, Sir, yours, &c.

ROBIN SPRITELY.

N°. 84. SATURDAY, NOVEMBER 24, 1759.

BIOGRAPHY is, of the various kinds of narrative writing, that which is most eagerly read, and most easily applied to the purposes of life.

In romances, when the wide field of possibility lies open to invention, the incidents may easily be made more numerous, the vicissitudes more sudden, and the events more wonderful; but from the time of life when fancy begins to be overruled by reason and corrected by experience, the most artful tale raises little curiosity when it is known to be false*; though it may, perhaps, be sometimes read as a model of a neat or elegant style, not for the sake of knowing what it contains, but how it is written; or those that

---

* It is somewhere recorded of a retired citizen, that he was in the habit of again and again perusing the incomparable story of Robinson Crusoe without a suspicion of its authenticity. At length a friend assured him of its being a work of fiction. What you say, replied the old man mournfully, may be true; but your information has taken away the only comfort of my age.

——— Pol, me occidistis, amici,
Non servastis, ait; cui sic extorta voluptas,
Et demtus per vim mentis gratissimus error.   Hor. Lib. ii. Ep. ii. 138.

are weary of themselves, may have recourse to it as a pleasing dream, of which, when they awake, they voluntarily dismiss the images from their minds.

The examples and events of history press, indeed, upon the mind with the weight of truth; but when they are reposited in the memory, they are oftener employed for show than use, and rather diversify conversation than regulate life. Few are engaged in such scenes as give them opportunities of growing wiser by the downfal of statesmen or the defeat of generals. The stratagems of war, and the intrigues of courts, are read by far the greater part of mankind with the same indifference as the adventures of fabled heroes, or the revolutions of a fairy region. Between falsehood and useless truth there is little difference. As gold which he cannot spend will make no man rich, so knowledge which he cannot apply will make no man wise.

The mischievous consequences of vice and folly, of irregular desires and predominant passions, are best discovered by those relations which are levelled with the general surface of life, which tell not how any man became great, but how he was made happy; not how he lost the favour of his prince, but how he became discontented with himself.

Those relations are, therefore, commonly of most value in which the writer tells his own story. He that recounts the life of another, commonly dwells most upon conspicuous events, lessens the familiarity of his tale to increase its dignity, shows his favourite at a distance, decorated and magnified like the ancient actors in their tragick dress, and endeavours to hide the man that he may produce a hero.

But if it be true, which was said by a French prince, "that no man was a hero to the servants of his chamber," it is equally true, that every man is yet less a hero to himself. He that is most elevated above the crowd by the importance of his employments, or the reputation of his genius, feels himself affected by fame or business but as they influence his domestick life. The high and low, as they have the same faculties and the same senses, have no less similitude in their pains and pleasures. The sensations are the same in all, though produced by very different occasions. The prince feels the same pain when an invader seizes a province, as the farmer when a thief drives away his cow. Men thus equal in themselves will appear equal in honest and impartial biography; and those whom fortune or nature places at the greatest distance may afford instruction to each other.

The writer of his own life has, at least, the first qualification of an historian, the knowledge of the truth; and though it may be plausibly objected that his temptations to disguise it are equal to his opportunities of knowing it, yet I cannot but think that impartiality may be expected with equal confidence from him that relates the passages of his own life, as from him that delivers the transactions of another.

Certainty of knowledge not only excludes mistake, but fortifies veracity. What we collect by conjecture, and by conjecture only, can one man judge of another's motives or sentiments, is easily modified by fancy or by desire; as objects imperfectly discerned take forms from the hope or fear of the beholder. But that which is fully known cannot be falsified but with reluctance of understanding, and alarm of conscience: of understanding, the lover of truth; of conscience, the sentinel of virtue.

He that writes the life of another is either his friend or his enemy, and wishes either to exalt his praise or aggravate his infamy: many temptations to falsehood will occur in the disguise of passions, too specious to fear much resistance. Love of virtue will animate panegyrick, and hatred of wickedness imbitter censure. The zeal of gratitude, the ardour of patriotism, fondness for an opinion, or fidelity to a party, may easily overpower the vigilance of a mind habitually well disposed, and prevail over unassisted and unfriended veracity.

But he that speaks of himself has no motive to falsehood or partiality except self-love, by which all have so often been betrayed, that all are on the watch against its artifices. He that writes an apology for a single action, to confute an accusation, to recommend himself to favour, is, indeed, always to be suspected of favouring his own cause; but he that sits down calmly and voluntarily to review his life for the admonition of posterity, or to amuse himself, and leaves this account unpublished, may be commonly presumed to tell truth, since falsehood cannot appease his own mind, and fame will not be heard beneath the tomb.

N°. 85. SATURDAY, DECEMBER 1, 1759.

ONE of the peculiarities which distinguish the present age is the multiplication of books. Every day brings new advertisements of literary undertakings, and we are flattered with repeated promises of growing wise on easier terms than our progenitors.

How much either happiness or knowledge is advanced by this multitude of authors, it is not very easy to decide.

He that teaches us any thing which we knew not before, is undoubtedly to be reverenced as a master.

He that conveys knowledge by more pleasing ways, may very properly be loved as a benefactor; and he that supplies life with innocent amusement, will be certainly caressed as a pleasing companion.

But few of those who fill the world with books have any pretensions to the hope either of pleasing or instructing. They have often no other task than to lay two books before them, out of which they compile a third, without any new materials of their own, and with very little application of judgment to those which former authors have supplied.

That all compilations are useless, I do not assert. Particles of science are often very widely scattered. Writers of extensive comprehension have incidental remarks upon topicks very remote from the principal subject, which are often more valuable than formal treatises, and which yet are not known because they are not promised in the title. He that collects those under proper heads is very laudably employed, for, though he exerts no great abilities in the work, he facilitates the progress of others, and by making that easy of attainment which is already written, may give some mind, more vigorous or more adventurous than his own, leisure for new thoughts and original designs.

But the collections poured lately from the press have been seldom made at any great expense of time or inquiry, and, therefore, only serve to distract choice without supplying any real want.

It is observed that " a corrupt society has many laws;" I know not whether it is not equally true, that " an ignorant age has many books." When the treasures of ancient knowledge lie unexamined, and original authors are neglected and forgotten, compilers and plagiaries are encouraged, who give us again what we had before, and grow great by setting before us what our own sloth had hidden from our view.

Yet are not even these writers to be indiscriminately censured and rejected. Truth like beauty varies its fashions, and is best recommended by different dresses to different minds ; and he that recalls the attention of mankind to any part of learning which time has left behind it, may be truly said to advance the literature of his own age. As the manners of nations vary, new topicks of persuasion become necessary, and new combinations of imagery are produced; and he that can accommodate himself to the reigning taste, may always have readers who, perhaps, would not have looked upon better performances.

To exact of every man who writes, that he should say something new, would be to reduce authors to a small number ; to oblige the most fertile genius to say only what is new would be to contract his volumes to a few pages. Yet, surely, there ought to be some bounds to repetition ; libraries ought no more to be heaped for ever with the same thoughts differently expressed, than with the same books differently decorated.

The good or evil which these secondary writers produce is seldom of any long duration, As they owe their existence to change of fashion, they commonly disappear when a new fashion becomes prevalent. The authors that in any nation last from age to age are very few, because there are very few that have any other claim to notice than that they catch hold on present curiosity, and gratify some accidental desire, or produce some temporary conveniency.

But however the writers of the day may despair of future fame, they ought at least to forbear any present mischief. Though they cannot arrive at eminent heights of excellence, they might keep themselves harmless. They might take care to inform themselves before they attempt to inform others, and exert the little influence which they have for honest purposes.

But such is the present state of our literature, that the ancient sage, who thought *a great book a great evil*, would now think the multitude of books a multitude of evils. He would consider a bulky writer who engrossed a year, and a swarm of pamphleteers who stole each an hour, as equal wasters of human life, and would make no other difference between them, than between a beast of prey and a flight of locusts.

Nº. 86. SATURDAY, DECEMBER 8, 1759.

TO THE IDLER.

SIR,

    I AM a young lady newly married to a young gentleman. Our fortune is large, our minds are vacant, our dispositions gay, our acquaintances numerous, and our relations splendid. We considered that marriage, like life, has its youth; that the first year is the year of gaiety and revel, and resolved to see the shows and feel the joys of London, before the increase of our family should confine us to domestick cares and domestick pleasures.

Little time was spent in preparation; the coach was harnessed, and a few days brought us to London, and we alighted at a lodging provided for us by Miss Biddy Trifle, a maiden niece of my husband's father, where we found apartments on a second floor, which my cousin told us would serve us till we could please ourselves with a more commodious and elegant habitation, and which she had taken at a very high price, because it was not worth the while to make a hard bargain for so short a time.

Here I intended to lie concealed till my new clothes were made, and my new lodging hired; but Miss Trifle had so industriously given notice of our arrival to all her acquaintance, that I had the mortification next day of seeing the door thronged with painted coaches and chairs with coronets, and was obliged to receive all my husband's relations on a second floor.

Inconveniencies are often balanced by some advantage: the elevation of my apartments furnished a subject for conversation, which, without some such help, we should have been in danger of wanting. Lady Stately told us how many years had passed since she climbed so many steps. Miss Airy ran to the window, and thought it charming to see the walkers so little in the street; and Miss Gentle went to try the same experiment, and screamed to find herself so far above the-ground.

They all knew that we intended to remove, and, therefore, all gave me advice about a proper choice. One street was recommended for the purity of its air, another for its freedom from noise, another for its nearness to the Park, another because there was but a step from it to all places of diversion, and another because its inhabitants enjoyed at once the town and country.

I had civility enough to hear every recommendation with a look of curiosity, while it was made, and of acquiescence, when it was concluded, but in my heart felt no other desire than to be free from the disgrace of a second floor, and cared little where I should fix, if the apartments were spacious and splendid.

Next day a chariot was hired, and Miss Trifle was despatched to find a lodging. She returned in the afternoon, with an account of a charming place, to which my husband went in the morning to make the contract. Being young and unexperienced, he took with him his friend Ned Quick, a gentleman of great skill in rooms and furniture, who sees, at a single glance, whatever there is to be commended or censured. Mr. Quick, at the first view of the house, declared that it could not be inhabited, for the sun in the afternoon shone with full glare on the windows of the dining-room.

Miss Trifle went out again, and soon discovered another lodging, which Mr. Quick went to survey, and found, that, whenever the wind should blow from the east, all the smoke of the city would be driven upon it.

A magnificent set of rooms was then found in one of the streets near Westminster-Bridge, which Miss Trifle preferred to any which she had yet seen; but Mr. Quick, having mused upon it for a time, concluded that it would be too much exposed in the morning to the fogs that rise from the river.

Thus Mr. Quick proceeded to give us every day new testimonies of his taste and circumspection; sometimes the street was too narrow for a double range of coaches; sometimes it was an obscure place, not inhabited by persons of quality. Some places were dirty, and some crowded; in some houses the furniture was ill-suited, and in others the stairs were too narrow. He had such fertility of objections that Miss Trifle was at last tired, and desisted from all attempts for our accommodation.

In the mean time I have still continued to see my company on a second floor, and am asked twenty times a day when I am to leave those odious lodgings, in which I live tumultuously without pleasure, and expensively without honour. My husband thinks so highly of Mr. Quick, that he cannot be persuaded to remove without his approbation; and Mr. Quick thinks his reputation raised by the multiplication of difficulties.

In this distress to whom can I have recourse? I find my temper vitiated by daily disappointment, by the sight of pleasures which I cannot partake, and the possession of riches which I cannot enjoy. Dear Mr. Idler, inform my husband that he is trifling away, in superfluous vexation, the few months which custom has appropriated to delight; that matrimonial quarrels are not easily reconciled between those that have no children; that wherever we settle he must always find some inconvenience; but nothing is so much to be avoided as a perpetual state of inquiry and suspense.

I am, Sir,
Your humble servant,
PEGGY HEARTLESS.

N°. 87. SATURDAY, DECEMBER 15, 1759.

OF what we know not, we can only judge by what we know. Every novelty appears more wonderful as it is more remote from any thing with which experience or testimony has hitherto acquainted us; and, if it passes further beyond the notions that we have been accustomed to form, it becomes at last incredible.

We seldom consider that human knowledge is very narrow, that national manners are formed by chance, that uncommon conjunctures of causes produce rare effects, or that what is impossible at one time or place may yet happen in another. It is always easier to deny than to inquire. To refuse credit confers for a moment an appearance of superiority, which every little mind is tempted to assume when it may be gained so cheaply as by withdrawing attention from evidence, and declining the fatigue of comparing probabilities. The most pertinacious and vehement demonstrator may be wearied in time by continual negation; and incredulity, which an old poet, in his address to Raleigh, calls *the wit of fools*, obtunds the argument which it cannot answer, as woolsacks deaden arrows though they cannot repel them.

Many relations of travellers have been slighted as fabulous, till more frequent voyages have confirmed their veracity; and it may reasonably be imagined, that many ancient historians are unjustly suspected of falsehood, because our own times afford nothing that resembles what they tell[t].

Had only the writers of antiquity informed us, that there was once a nation in which the wife lay down upon the burning pile only to mix her ashes with those of her husband, we should have thought it a tale to be told with that of Endymion's commerce with the moon. Had only a single traveller related, that many nations of the earth were black, we should have thought the accounts of the Negroes and of the Phœnix equally credible. But of black men the numbers are too great who are now repining under English cruelty; and the custom of voluntary cremation is not yet lost among the ladies of India.

Few narratives will either to men or women appear more incredible than the histories of the Amazons; of female nations of whose constitution it was the essential and fundamental law to exclude men from all participation, either of publick affairs or domestick business; where female armies marched under female captains, female farmers gathered the harvest, female partners danced together, and female wits diverted one another.

Yet several ages of antiquity have transmitted accounts of the Amazons of Caucasus; and of the Amazons of America, who have given their name to the greatest river in the world, Condamine lately found such memorials, as can be expected among erratick and unlettered nations, where events are recorded only by tradition, and new

---

[t] *Le vrai n'est pas toujours le vraisemblable.* The researches of Gibbon, Rennel and Mitford, the travels of Bruce and Belzoni have fully proved the truth of this maxim in the case of Herodotus.

swarms, settling in the country from time to time, confuse and efface all traces of former times.

To die with husbands, or to live without them, are the two extremes which the prudence and moderation of European ladies have, in all ages, equally declined; they have never been allured to death by the kindness or civility of the politest nations, nor has the roughness and brutality of more savage countries ever provoked them to doom their male associates to irrevocable banishment. The Bohemian matrons are said to have made one short struggle for superiority; but, instead of banishing the men, they contented themselves with condemning them to servile offices; and their constitution, thus left imperfect, was quickly overthrown.

There is, I think, no class of English women from whom we are in any danger of Amazonian usurpation. The old maids seem nearest to independence, and most likely to be animated by revenge against masculine authority; they often speak of men with acrimonious vehemence, but it is seldom found that they have any settled hatred against them, and it is yet more rarely observed that they have any kindness for each other. They will not easily combine in any plot; and if they should ever agree to retire and fortify themselves in castles or in mountains, the sentinel will betray the passes in spite, and the garrison will capitulate upon easy terms, if the besiegers have handsome swordknots, and are well supplied with fringe and lace.

The gamesters, if they were united, would make a formidable body; and, since they consider men only as beings that are to lose their money, they might live together without any wish for the officiousness of gallantry or the delights of diversified conversation. But as nothing would hold them together but the hope of plundering one another, their government would fail from the defect of its principles; the men would need only to neglect them, and they would perish in a few weeks by a civil war.

I do not mean to censure the ladies of England as de-

fective in knowledge or in spirit, when I suppose them
unlikely to revive the military honours of their sex. The
character of the ancient Amazons was rather terrible than
lovely; the hand could not be very delicate that was only
employed in drawing the bow and brandishing the battle-
axe; their power was maintained by cruelty, their courage was deformed by ferocity, and their example only
shows that men and women live best together.

* * * * *

N°. 88. SATURDAY, DECEMBER 22, 1759.

* *Hodie quid egisti?*

WHEN the philosophers of the last age were first congre-
gated into the Royal Society, great expectations were
raised of the sudden progress of useful arts; the time was
supposed to be near, when engines should turn by a perpetual motion, and health be secured by the universal medicine; when learning should be facilitated by a real character, and commerce extended by ships which could reach
their ports in defiance of the tempest.

But improvement is naturally slow. The society met
and parted without any visible diminution of the miseries
of life. The gout and stone were still painful, the ground
that was not ploughed brought no harvest, and neither
oranges nor grapes would grow upon the hawthorn. At
last, those who were disappointed began to be angry; those
likewise who hated innovation were glad to gain an opportunity of ridiculing men who had depreciated, perhaps with
too much arrogance, the knowledge of antiquity. And it
appears, from some of their earliest apologies, that the
philosophers felt with great sensibility the unwelcome importunities of those who were daily asking, "What have
ye done?"

The truth is, that little had been done compared with
what fame had been suffered to promise; and the question

could only be answered by general apologies and by new hopes, which, when they were frustrated, gave a new occasion to the same vexatious inquiry.

This fatal question has disturbed the quiet of many other minds. He that in the latter part of his life too strictly inquires what he has done, can very seldom receive from his own heart such an account as will give him satisfaction.

We do not indeed so often disappoint others as ourselves. We not only think more highly than others of our own abilities, but allow ourselves to form hopes which we never communicate, and please our thoughts with employments which none ever will allot us, and with elevations to which we are never expected to rise; and when our days and years have passed away in common business or common amusements, and we find at last that we have suffered our purposes to sleep till the time of action is past, we are reproached only by our own reflections; neither our friends nor our enemies wonder that we live and die like the rest of mankind; that we live without notice, and die without memorial; they know not what task we had proposed, and, therefore, cannot discern whether it is finished.

He that compares what he has done with what he has left undone, will feel the effect which must always follow the comparison of imagination with reality; he will look with contempt on his own unimportance, and wonder to what purpose he came into the world; he will repine that he shall leave behind him no evidence of his having been, that he has added nothing to the system of life, but has glided from youth to age among the crowd, without any effort for distinction.

Man is seldom willing to let fall the opinion of his own dignity, or to believe that he does little only because every individual is a very little being. He is better content to want diligence than power, and sooner confesses the depravity of his will than the imbecility of his nature.

From this mistaken notion of human greatness it proceeds, that many who pretend to have made great advances in wisdom so loudly declare that they despise themselves. If I had ever found any of the self-contemners much irritated or pained by the consciousness of their meanness, I should have given them consolation by observing, that a little more than nothing is as much as can be expected from a being, who, with respect to the multitudes about him, is himself little more than nothing. Every man is obliged by the Supreme Master of the universe to improve all the opportunities of good which are afforded him, and to keep in continual activity such abilities as are bestowed upon him. But he has no reason to repine, though his abilities are small and his opportunities few. He that has improved the virtue, or advanced the happiness of one fellow-creature, he that has ascertained a single moral proposition, or added one useful experiment to natural knowledge, may be contented with his own performance, and, with respect to mortals like himself, may demand, like Augustus, to be dismissed at his departure with applause.

N°. 89. SATURDAY, DECEMBER 29, 1759.

'Ανέχου καὶ ἀπέχου.   Epict.

How evil came into the world; for what reason it is that life is overspread with such boundless varieties of misery; why the only thinking being of this globe is doomed to think merely to be wretched, and to pass his time from youth to age in fearing or in suffering calamities, is a question which philosophers have long asked, and which philosophy could never answer.

Religion informs us that misery and sin were produced together. The depravation of human will was followed by a disorder of the harmony of nature; and by that providence which often places antidotes in the neighbourhood of poisons, vice was checked by misery, lest it should swell to universal and unlimited dominion.

A state of innocence and happiness is so remote from all that we have ever seen, that though we can easily conceive it possible, and may, therefore, hope to attain it, yet our speculations upon it must be general and confused. We can discover that where there is universal innocence, there will probably be universal happiness; for, why should afflictions be permitted to infest beings who are not in danger of corruption from blessings, and where there is no use of terrour nor cause of punishment? But in a world like ours, where our senses assault us, and our hearts betray us, we should pass on from crime to crime, heedless and remorseless, if misery did not stand in our way, and our own pains admonish us of our folly.

Almost all the moral good, which is left among us, is the apparent effect of physical evil.

Goodness is divided by divines into soberness, righteousness and godliness. Let it be examined how each of these duties would be practised, if there were no physical evil to enforce it.

Sobriety, or temperance, is nothing but the forbearance of pleasure; and if pleasure was not followed by pain, who would forbear it? We see every hour those in whom the desire of present indulgence overpowers all sense of past and all foresight of future misery. In a remission of the gout, the drunkard returns to his wine, and the glutton to his feast; and if neither disease nor poverty were felt or dreaded, every one would sink down in idle sensuality, without any care of others, or of himself. To eat and drink, and lie down to sleep, would be the whole business of mankind.

Righteousness, or the system of social duty, may be subdivided into justice and charity. Of justice one of the Heathen sages has shown, with great acuteness, that it was impressed upon mankind only by the inconveniencies which injustice had produced. " In the first ages," says he, " men acted without any rule but the impulse of desire; they practised injustice upon others, and suffered it from others in their turn; but in time it was discovered, that the pain of suffering wrong was greater than the pleasure of doing it; and mankind, by a general compact, submitted

to the restraint of laws, and resigned the pleasure to es_
cape the pain."

Of charity it is superfluous to observe, that it could have
no place if there were no want; for 'of a virtue which
could not be practised, the omission could not be culpable. Evil is not only the occasional, but the efficient cause
of charity; we are incited to the relief of misery by the
consciousness that we have the same nature with the sufferer, that we are in danger of the same distresses, and
may sometimes implore the same assistance.

Godliness, or piety, is elevation of the mind towards
the Supreme Being, and extension of the thoughts to another life. The other life is future, and the Supreme
Being is invisible. None would have recourse to an invisible power, but that all other subjects have eluded their
hopes. None would fix their attention upon the future,
but that they are discontented with the present. If the
senses were feasted with perpetual pleasure, they would
always keep the mind in subjection. Reason has no authority over us, but by its power to warn us against evil.

In childhood, while our minds are yet unoccupied, religion is impressed upon them, and the first years of almost
all who have been well educated are passed in a regular
discharge of the duties of piety. But as we advance forward into the crowds of life, innumerable delights solicit
our inclinations, and innumerable cares distract our attention; the time of youth is passed in noisy frolicks; manhood is led on from hope to hope, and from project to
project; the dissoluteness of pleasure, the inebriation of
success, the ardour of expectation, and the vehemence of
competition, chain down the mind alike to the present
scene, nor is it remembered how soon this mist of trifles
must be scattered, and the bubbles that float upon the
rivulet of life be lost for ever in the gulph of eternity. To
this consideration scarcely any man is awakened but by
some pressing and resistless evil. The death of those from
whom he derived his pleasures, or to whom he destined
his possessions, some disease which shows him the vanity

of all external acquisitions, or the gloom of age, which intercepts his prospects of long enjoyment, forces him to fix his hopes upon another state; and when he has contended with the tempests of life till his strength fails him, he flies at last to the shelter of religion.

That misery does not make all virtuous, experience too certainly informs us; but it is no less certain that of what virtue there is, misery produces far the greater part. Physical evil may be, therefore, endured with patience, since it is the cause of moral good; and patience itself is one virtue by which we are prepared for that state in which evil shall be no more [u].

***

N°. 90. SATURDAY, JANUARY 5, 1760.

IT is a complaint which has been made from time to time, and which seems to have lately become more frequent, that English oratory, however forcible in argument, or elegant in expression, is deficient and inefficacious, because our speakers want the grace and energy of action.

Among the numerous projectors who are desirous to refine our manners, and improve our faculties, some are willing to supply the deficiency of our speakers [x]. We have had more than one exhortation to study the neglected art of moving the passions, and have been encouraged to believe that our tongues, however feeble in themselves, may, by the help of our hands and legs, obtain an uncontroulable dominion over the most stubborn audience, animate the insensible, engage the careless, force tears from the obdurate, and money from the avaricious.

---

[u] For a fuller exposition of Johnson's sentiments on this dark and deep subject, see his Review of Soame Jenyns' Nature and Origin of Evil.

[x] Johnson might here be glancing at the oratorical lectures of the modern *Rhetor* Sheridan, whose plans he delighted incessantly to ridicule. See Boswell. Many acute remarks occur in Hume's Essay on Eloquence.

If by sleight of hand, or nimbleness of foot, all these wonders can be performed, he that shall neglect to attain the free use of his limbs may be justly censured as criminally lazy. But I am afraid that no specimen of such effects will easily be shown. If I could once find a speaker in 'Change-Alley raising the price of stocks by the power of persuasive gestures, I should very zealously recommend the study of his art; but having never seen any action by which language was much assisted, I have been hitherto inclined to doubt whether my countrymen are not blamed too hastily for their calm and motionless utterance.

Foreigners of many nations accompany their speech with action; but why should their example have more influence upon us than ours upon them? Customs are not to be changed but for better. Let those who desire to reform us show the benefits of the change proposed. When the Frenchman waves his hands and writhes his body in recounting the revolutions of a game at cards, or the Neapolitan, who tells the hour of the day, shows upon his fingers the number which he mentions; I do not perceive that their manual exercise is of much use, or that they leave any image more deeply impressed by their bustle and vehemence of communication.

Upon the English stage there is no want of action; but the difficulty of making it at once various and proper, and its perpetual tendency to become ridiculous, notwithstanding all the advantages which art and show, and custom and prejudice can give it, may prove how little it can be admitted into any other place, where it can have no recommendation but from truth and nature.

The use of English oratory is only at the bar, in the parliament, and in the church. Neither the judges of our laws nor the representatives of our people would be much affected by laboured gesticulation, or believe any man the more because he rolled his eyes, or puffed his cheeks, or spread abroad his arms, or stamped the ground, or thumped his breast, or turned his eyes sometimes to the ceiling and sometimes to the floor.   Upon men intent only upon truth, the arm of an orator has little power ; a credible testimony, or a cogent argument will overcome all the art of modulation, and all the violence of contortion.

It is well known that, in the city which may be called the parent of oratory, all the arts of mechanical persuasion were banished from the court of supreme judicature. The judges of the Areopagus considered action and vociferation as a foolish appeal to the external senses, and unworthy to be practised before those who had no desire of idle amusement, and whose only pleasure was to discover right.

Whether action may not be yet of use in churches, where the preacher addresses a mingled audience, may deserve inquiry.   It is certain that the senses are more powerful as the reason is weaker ; and that he whose ears convey little to his mind, may sometimes listen with his eyes till truth may gradually take possession of his heart. If there be any use of gesticulation, it must be applied to the ignorant and rude, who will be more affected by vehemence than delighted by propriety.   In the pulpit little action can be proper, for action can illustrate nothing but that to which it may be referred by nature or by custom. He that imitates by his hand a motion which he describes, explains it by natural similitude ; he that lays his hand on his breast, when he expresses pity, enforces his words by a customary allusion.   But theology has few topicks to which action can be appropriated ; that action which is vague and indeterminate will at last settle into habit, and habitual peculiarities are quickly ridiculous.

It is, perhaps, the character of the English to despise trifles ; and that art may surely be accounted a trifle which is at once useless and ostentatious, which can seldom be practised with propriety, and which, as the mind is more cultivated, is less powerful.   Yet as all innocent means are to be used for the propagation of truth, I would not deter those who are employed in preaching to common

congregations from any practice which they may find persuasive : for, compared with the conversion of sinners,
propriety and elegance are less than nothing.

* * * * * * * * * *

N°. 91. SATURDAY, JANUARY 12, 1760.

IT is common to overlook what is near, by keeping the
eye fixed upon something remote.   In the same manner
present opportunities are neglected, and attainable good is
slighted, by minds busied in extensive ranges, and intent
upon future advantages.   Life, however short, is made
still shorter by waste of time, and its progress towards
happiness, though naturally slow, is yet retarded by unnecessary labour.

   The difficulty of obtaining knowledge is universally confessed.   To fix deeply in the mind the principles of science,
to settle their limitations, and deduce the long succession
of their consequences ; to comprehend the whole compass
of complicated systems, with all the arguments, objections
and solutions, and to reposite in the intellectual treasury
the numberless facts, experiments, apophthegms and positions, which must stand single in the memory, and of
which none has any perceptible connexion with the rest,
is a task which, though undertaken with ardour and pursued with diligence, must at last be left unfinished by the
frailty of our nature.

   To make the way to learning either less short or less
smooth, is certainly absurd ; yet this is the apparent effect
of the prejudice which seems to prevail among us in favour of foreign authors, and of the contempt of our native
literature, which this excursive curiosity must necessarily
produce.   Every man is more speedily instructed by his
own language, than by any other ; before we search the
rest of the world for teachers, let us try whether we may
not spare our trouble by finding them at home.

   The riches of the English language are much greater

than they are commonly supposed. Many useful and valuable books lie buried in shops and libraries, unknown
and unexamined, unless some lucky compiler opens them
by chance, and finds an easy spoil of wit and learning. I
am far from intending to insinuate, that other languages
are not necessary to him who aspires to eminence, and
whose whole life is devoted to study; but to him who
reads only for amusement, or whose purpose is not to deck
himself with the honours of literature, but to be qualified
for domestick usefulness, and sit down content with subordinate reputation, we have authors sufficient to fill up
all the vacancies of his time, and gratify most of his wishes
for information.

Of our poets I need say little, because they are, perhaps,
the only authors to whom their country has done justice.
We consider the whole succession from Spenser to Pope
as superior to any names which the continent can boast;
and, therefore, the poets of other nations, however familiarly they may be sometimes mentioned, are very little read,
except by those who design to borrow their beauties.

There is, I think, not one of the liberal arts which may
not be competently learned in the English language. He
that searches after mathematical knowledge may busy himself among his own countrymen, and will find one or other
able to instruct him in every part of those abstruse sciences. He that is delighted with experiments, and wishes
to know the nature of bodies from certain and visible effects, is happily placed where the mechanical philosophy
was first established by a publick institution, and from
which it was spread to all other countries.

The more airy and elegant studies of philology and criticism have little need of any foreign help. Though our
language, not being very analogical, gives few opportunities for grammatical researches, yet we have not wanted
authors who have considered the principles of speech; and
with critical writings we abound sufficiently to enable pedantry to impose rules which can seldom be observed, and
vanity to talk of books which are seldom read.

But our own language has, from the Reformation to the present time, been chiefly dignified and adorned by the works of our divines, who, considered as commentators, controvertists, or preachers, have undoubtedly left all other nations far behind them. No vulgar language can boast such treasures of theological knowledge, or such multitudes of authors at once learned, elegant and pious. Other countries and other communions have authors, perhaps, equal in abilities and diligence to ours; but if we unite number with excellence, there is certainly no nation which must not allow us to be superior. Of morality little is necessary to be said, because it is comprehended in practical divinity, and is, perhaps, better taught in English sermons than in any other books, ancient and modern. Nor shall I dwell on our excellence in metaphysical speculations, because he that reads the works of our divines will easily discover how far human subtilty has been able to penetrate.

Political knowledge is forced upon us by the form of our constitution; and all the mysteries of government are discovered in the attack or defence of every minister. The original law of society, the rights of subjects and the prerogatives of kings, have been considered with the utmost nicety, sometimes profoundly investigated, and sometimes familiarly explained.

Thus copiously instructive is the English language; and thus needless is all recourse to foreign writers. Let us not, therefore, make our neighbours proud by soliciting help which we do not want, nor discourage our own industry by difficulties which we need not suffer.

N°. 92.   SATURDAY, JANUARY 19, 1760.

WHATEVER is useful or honourable will be desired by many who never can obtain it; and that which cannot be obtained when it is desired, artifice or folly will be diligent to counterfeit. Those to whom fortune has denied gold and diamonds decorate themselves with stones and metals, which have something of the show, but little of the value; and every moral excellence or intellectual faculty has some vice or folly which imitates its appearance.

Every man wishes to be wise, and they who cannot be wise are almost always cunning. The less is the real discernment of those whom business or conversation brings together, the more illusions are practised; nor is caution ever so necessary as with associates or opponents of feeble minds.

Cunning differs from wisdom as twilight from open day. He that walks in the sunshine goes boldly forward by the nearest way; he sees that where the path is straight and even, he may proceed in security, and where it is rough and crooked he easily complies with the turns, and avoids the obstructions. But the traveller in the dusk fears more as he sees less; he knows there may be danger, and, therefore, suspects that he is never safe, tries every step before he fixes his foot, and shrinks at every noise lest violence should approach him. Wisdom comprehends at once the end and the means, estimates easiness or difficulty, and is cautious or confident in due proportion. Cunning discovers little at a time, and has no other means of certainty than multiplication of stratagems and superfluity of suspicion. The man of cunning always considers that he can never be too safe, and, therefore, always keeps himself enveloped in a mist, impenetrable, as he hopes, to the eye of rivalry or curiosity.

Upon this principle, Tom Double has formed a habit of eluding the most harmless question. What he has no inclination to answer, he pretends sometimes not to hear, and endeavours to divert the inquirer's attention by some other subject; but if he be pressed hard by repeated interrogation, he always evades a direct reply. Ask him whom he likes best on the stage; he is ready to tell that there are several excellent performers. Inquire when he was last at the coffee-house; he replies, that the weather has been bad lately. Desire him to tell the age of any of his acquaintance; he immediately mentions another who is older or younger.

Will Puzzle values himself upon a long reach. He fore-sees every thing before it will happen, though he never relates his prognostications till the event is past. Nothing has come to pass for these twenty years of which Mr. Puzzle had not given broad hints, and told at least that it was not proper to tell. Of those predictions, which every conclusion will equally verify, he always claims the credit, and wonders that his friends did not understand them. He supposes very truly that much may be known which he knows not, and, therefore, pretends to know much of which he and all mankind are equally ignorant. I desired his opinion yesterday of the German war, and was told, that if the Prussians were well supported, something great may be expected; but that they have very powerful enemies to encounter; that the Austrian general has long experience, and the Russians are hardy and resolute; but that no human power is invincible. I then drew the con-versation to our own affairs, and invited him to balance the probabilities of war and peace. He told me that war requires courage, and negociation judgment, and that the time will come when it will be seen, whether our skill in treaty is equal to our bravery in battle. To this general prattle he will appeal hereafter, and will demand to have his foresight applauded, whoever shall at last be conquered or victorious.

With Ned Smuggle all is a secret. He believes himself watched by observation and malignity on every side, and rejoices in the dexterity by which he has escaped snares that never were laid. Ned holds that a man is never de-ceived if he never trusts, and, therefore, will not tell the name of his tailor or his hatter. He rides out every morning for the air, and pleases himself with thinking that nobody knows where he has been. When he dines with a friend, he never goes to his house the nearest way, but walks up a by-street to perplex the scent. When he has a coach called, he never tells him at the door the true place to which he is going, but stops him in the way that he may give him directions where nobody can hear him.   The price of what he buys or sells is always concealed. He often takes lodgings in the country by a wrong name, and thinks that the world is wondering where he can be hid.   All these transactions he registers in a book, which, he says, will some time or other amaze posterity.

It is remarked by Bacon, that many men try to procure reputation only by objections, of which, if they are once admitted, the nullity never appears, because the design is laid aside.   " This false feint of wisdom," says he, " is the ruin of business."   The whole power of cunning is privative ; to say nothing, and to do nothing, is the utmost of its reach.   Yet men thus narrow by nature, and mean by art, are sometimes able to rise by the miscarriages of bravery and the openness of integrity ; and by watching failures and snatching opportunities, obtain advantages which belong properly to higher characters.

N°. 93. SATURDAY, JANUARY 26, 1760.

SAM SOFTLY was bred a sugar-baker; but succeeding to a considerable estate on the death of his elder brother, he retired early from business, married a fortune, and settled in a country-house near Kentish-town.   Sam, who formerly was a sportsman, and in his apprenticeship used to frequent Barnet races, keeps a high chaise, with a brace of seasoned geldings.   During the summer months, the principal passion and employment of Sam's life is to visit, in this vehicle, the most eminent seats of the nobility and gentry in different parts of the kingdom, with his wife and some select friends.   By these periodical excursions Sam gratifies many important purposes.   He assists the several pregnancies of his wife ; he shows his chaise to the best advantage ; he indulges his insatiable curiosity for finery, which, since he has turned gentleman, has grown upon him to an extraordinary degree; he discovers taste and spirit, and, what is above all, he finds frequent opportunities of displaying to the party, at every house he sees, his knowledge of family connexion. At first, Sam was contented with driving a friend between London and his villa. Here he prided himself in pointing out the boxes of the citizens on each side of the road, with an accurate detail of their respective failures or successes in trade; and harangued on the several equipages that were accidentally passing. Here, too, the seats, interspersed on the surrounding hills, afforded ample matter for Sam's curious discoveries. For one, he told his companion, a rich Jew had offered money; and that a retired widow was courted at another, by an eminent dry-salter. At the same time he discussed the utility, and enumerated the expenses, of the Islington turnpike. But Sam's ambition is at present raised to nobler undertakings.

When the happy hour of the annual expedition arrives, the seat of the chaise is furnished with Ogilvy's Book of Roads, and a choice quantity of cold tongues. The most alarming disaster which can happen to our hero, who thinks he *throws a whip* admirably well, is to be overtaken in a road which affords no *quarter* for wheels. Indeed, few men possess more skill or discernment for concerting and conducting a *party of pleasure*. When a seat is to be surveyed, he has a peculiar talent in selecting some shady bench in the park, where the company may most commodiously refresh themselves with cold tongue, chicken and French rolls; and is very sagacious in discovering what cool temple in the garden will be best adapted for drinking tea, brought for this purpose, in the afternoon, and from which the chaise may be resumed with the greatest convenience. In viewing the house itself, he is principally attracted by the chairs and beds, concerning the cost of which his minute inquiries generally gain the clearest information. An agate table easily diverts his eyes from the most capital strokes of Rubens,

and a Turkey carpet has more charms than a Titian.
Sam, however, dwells with some attention on the family
portraits, particularly the most modern ones ; and as this
is a topick on which the housekeeper usually harangues in
a more copious manner, he takes this opportunity of improving his knowledge of intermarriages. Yet, notwithstanding this appearance of satisfaction, Sam has some
objection to all he sees. One house has too much gilding ;
at another, the chimney-pieces are all monuments ; at a
third, he conjectures that the beautiful canal must certainly
be dried up in a hot summer. He despises the statues at
Wilton, because he thinks he can see much better carving
in Westminster Abbey. But there is one general objection which he is sure to make at almost every house, particularly at those which are most distinguished. He allows
that all the apartments are extremely fine, but adds, with
a sneer, that they are too fine to be inhabited.

Misapplied genius most commonly proves ridiculous.
Had Sam, as Nature intended, contentedly continued in
the calmer and less conspicuous pursuits of sugar-baking,
he might have been a respectable and useful character.
At present he dissipates his life in a specious idleness,
which neither improves himself nor his friends. Those
talents, which might have benefited society, he exposes
to contempt by false pretensions. He affects pleasures
which he cannot enjoy, and is acquainted only with those
subjects on which he has no right to talk, and which it is
no merit to understand [y].

[y] This humorous paper was written by Mr. Thomas Warton, who is said
to have sketched from a character in real life, distantly related to himself.—
Drake's Essays, Vol. II.

N°. 94. SATURDAY, FEBRUARY 2, 1760.

It is common to find young men ardent and diligent in the pursuit of knowledge; but the progress of life very often produces laxity and indifference; and not only those who are at liberty to choose their business and amusements, but those likewise whose professions engage them in literary inquiries, pass the latter part of their time without improvement, and spend the day rather in any other entertainment than that which they might find among their books.

This abatement of the vigour of curiosity is sometimes imputed to the insufficiency of learning. Men are supposed to remit their labours, because they find their labours to have been vain; and to search no longer after truth and wisdom, because they at last despair of finding them.

But this reason is, for the most part, very falsely assigned. Of learning, as of virtue, it may be affirmed, that it is at once honoured and neglected. Whoever forsakes it will for ever look after it with longing, lament the loss which he does not endeavour to repair, and desire the good which he wants resolution to seize and keep. The Idler never applauds his own idleness, nor does any man repent of the diligence of his youth.

So many hindrances may obstruct the acquisition of knowledge, that there is little reason for wondering that it is in a few hands. To the greater part of mankind the duties of life are inconsistent with much study; and the hours which they would spend upon letters must be stolen from their occupations and their families. Many suffer themselves to be lured by more sprightly and luxurious pleasures from the shades of contemplation, where they find seldom more than a calm delight, such as, though greater than all others, its certainty and its duration being reckoned with its power of gratification, is yet easily quit-

ted for some extemporary joy, which the present moment
offers, and another, perhaps, will put out of reach.

It is the great excellence of learning, that it borrows
very little from time or place; it is not confined to season
or to climate, to cities or to the country, but may be cultivated and enjoyed where no other pleasure can be obtained. But this quality, which constitutes much of its
value, is one occasion of neglect; what may be done at all
times with equal propriety, is deferred from day to day,
till the mind is gradually reconciled to the omission, and
the attention is turned to other objects. Thus habitual
idleness gains too much power to be conquered, and the
soul shrinks from the idea of intellectual labour and intenseness of meditation.

That those who profess to advance learning sometimes
obstruct it, cannot be denied; the continual multiplication
of books not only distracts choice, but disappoints inquiry.
To him that has moderately stored his mind with images,
few writers afford any novelty; or what little they have to
add to the common stock of learning, is so buried in the
mass of general notions, that, like silver mingled with the
ore of lead, it is too little to pay for the labour of separation; and he that has often been deceived by the promise
of a title, at last grows weary of examining, and is tempted
to consider all as equally fallacious.

There are indeed some repetitions always lawful, because they never deceive. He that writes the history of
past times, undertakes only to decorate known facts by
new beauties of method or of style, or at most to illustrate
them by his own reflections. The author of a system,
whether moral or physical, is obliged to nothing beyond
care of selection and regularity of disposition. But there
are others who claim the name of authors merely to disgrace it, and fill the world with volumes only to bury letters in their own rubbish. The traveller, who tells, in a
pompous folio, that he saw the Pantheon at Rome, and
the Medicean Venus at Florence; the natural historian,

who, describing the productions of a narrow island, recounts all that it has in common with every other part of the world; the collector of antiquities, that accounts every thing a curiosity which the ruins of Herculaneum happen to emit, though an instrument already shown in a thousand repositories, or a cup common to the ancients, the moderns and all mankind; may be justly censured as the persecutors of students, and the thieves of that time which never can be restored.

N°. 95. SATURDAY, FEBRUARY 9, 1760.

TO THE IDLER.

MR. IDLER,

IT is, I think, universally agreed, that seldom any good is gotten by complaint; yet we find that few forbear to complain, but those who are afraid of being reproached as the authors of their own miseries. I hope, therefore, for the common permission to lay my case before you and your readers, by which I shall disburden my heart, though I cannot hope to receive either assistance or consolation.

I am a trader, and owe my fortune to frugality and industry. I began with little; but by the easy and obvious method of spending less than I gain, I have every year added something to my stock, and expect to have a seat in the common-council at the next election.

My wife, who was as prudent as myself, died six years ago, and left me one son and one daughter, for whose sake I resolved never to marry again, and rejected the overtures of Mrs. Squeeze, the broker's widow, who had ten thousand pounds at her own disposal.

I bred my son at a school near Islington; and when he had learned arithmetick, and wrote a good hand, I took him into the shop, designing, in about ten years, to retire to Stratford or Hackney, and leave him established in the business.

For four years he was diligent and sedate, entered the shop before it was opened, and when it was shut, always examined the pins of the window. In any intermission of business it was his constant practice to peruse the leger. I had always great hopes of him, when I observed how sorrowfully he would shake his head over a bad debt, and how eagerly he would listen to me when I told him that he might at one time or other become an alderman.

We lived together with mutual confidence, till, unluckily, a visit was paid him by two of his school-fellows, who were placed, I suppose, in the army, because they were fit for nothing better: they came glittering in their military dress, accosted their old acquaintance, and invited him to a tavern, where, as I have been since informed, they ridiculed the meanness of commerce, and wondered how a youth of spirit could spend the prime of life behind a counter.

. I did not suspect any mischief. I knew my son was never without money in his pocket, and was better able to pay his reckoning than his companions; and expected to see him return triumphing in his own advantages, and congratulating himself that he was not one of those who expose their heads to a musket bullet for three shillings a day.

He returned sullen and thoughtful; I supposed him sorry for the hard fortune of his friends; and tried to comfort him, by saying that the war would soon be at an end, and that, if they had any honest occupation, half-pay would be a pretty help. He looked at me with indignation; and snatching up his candle, told me, as he went up stairs, that *he hoped to see a battle yet.*

Why he should hope to see a battle, I could not conceive, but let him go quietly to sleep away his folly. Next day he made two mistakes in the first bill, disobliged a customer by surly answers, and dated all his entries in the journal in a wrong month. At night he met his military companions again, came home late, and quarrelled with the maid.

From this fatal interview he has gradually lost all his laudable passions and desires. He soon grew useless in the shop, where, indeed, I did not willingly trust him any longer; for he often mistook the price of goods to his own loss, and once gave a promissory note instead of a receipt.

I did not know to what degree he was corrupted, till an honest tailor gave me notice that he had bespoke a laced suit, which was to be left for him at a house kept by the sister of one of my journeymen. I went to this clandestine lodging, and found, to my amazement, all the ornaments of a fine gentleman, which I know not whether he has taken upon credit, or purchased with money subducted from the shop.

This detection has made him desperate. He now openly declares his resolution to be a gentleman; says that his soul is too great for a counting-house; ridicules the conversation of city taverns; talks of new plays, and boxes and ladies; gives duchesses for his toasts; carries silver, for readiness, in his waistcoat-pocket; and comes home at night in a chair, with such thunders at the door, as have more than once brought the watchmen from their stands.

Little expenses will not hurt us; and I could forgive a few juvenile frolicks, if he would be careful of the main; but his favourite topick is contempt of money, which, he says, is of no use but to be spent. Riches, without honour, he holds empty things; and once told me to my face, that wealthy plodders were only purveyors to men of spirit.

He is always impatient in the company of his old friends, and seldom speaks till he is warmed with wine; he then entertains us with accounts that we do not desire to hear, of intrigues among lords and ladies, and quarrels between officers of the guards; shows a miniature on his snuff-box, and wonders that any man can look upon the new dancer without rapture.

All this is very provoking; and yet all this might be borne, if the boy could support his pretensions. But, whatever he may think, he is yet far from the accomplishments which he has endeavoured to purchase at so dear a

rate. I have watched him in publick places. He sneaks
in like a man that knows he is where he should not be; he
is proud to catch the slightest salutation, and often claims
it when it is not intended. Other men receive dignity
from dress, but my booby looks always more meanly for
his finery. Dear Mr. Idler, tell him what must at last become of a fop, whom pride will not suffer to be a trader,
and whom long habits in a shop forbid to be a gentleman.

I am, Sir, &c.

TIM WAINSCOT.

N°. 96. SATURDAY, FEBRUARY 16, 1760.

> * *Qui se volet esse potentem,*
> *Animos domet ille feroces:*
> *Nec victa libidine colla*
> *Fœdis submittat habenis.*   BOETHIUS.

HACHO, a king of Lapland, was in his youth the most renowned of the Northern warriors. His martial achievements remain engraved on a pillar of flint in the rocks of
Hanga, and are to this day solemnly carolled to the harp
by the Laplanders, at the fires with which they celebrate
their nightly festivities. Such was his intrepid spirit, that
he ventured to pass the lake Vether to the isle of Wi-
zards, where he descended alone into the dreary vault in
which a magician had been kept bound for six ages, and
read the Gothick characters inscribed on his brazen mace.
His eye was so piercing, that, as ancient chronicles report,
he could blunt the weapons of his enemies only by looking
at them. At twelve years of age he carried an iron vessel
of a prodigious weight, for the length of five furlongs, in
the presence of all the chiefs of his father's castle.

Nor was he less celebrated for his prudence and wisdom. Two of his proverbs are yet remembered and repeated among Laplanders. To express the vigilance of
the Supreme Being, he was wont to say, " Odin's belt is

always buckled." To show that the most prosperous condition of life is often hazardous, his lesson was, " When you slide on the smoothest ice, beware of pits beneath." He consoled his countrymen, when they were once preparing to leave the frozen deserts of Lapland, and resolved to seek some warmer climate, by telling them, that the eastern nations, notwithstanding their boasted fertility, passed every night amidst the horrours of anxious apprehension, and were inexpressibly affrighted, and almost stunned, every morning, with the noise of the sun while he was rising.

His temperance and severity of manners were his chief praise. In his early years he never tasted wine; nor would he drink out of a painted cup. He constantly slept in his armour, with his spear in his hand; nor would he use a battle-ax whose handle was inlaid with brass. He did not, however, persevere in this contempt of luxury; nor did he close his days with honour.

One evening, after hunting the gulos or wild-dog, being bewildered in a solitary forest, and having passed the fatigues of the day without any interval of refreshment, he discovered a large store of honey in the hollow of a pine. This was a dainty which he had never tasted before; and being at once faint and hungry, he fed greedily upon it. From this unusual and delicious repast he received so much satisfaction, that, at his return home, he commanded honey to be served up at his table every day. His palate, by degrees, became refined and vitiated; he began to lose his native relish for simple fare, and contracted a habit of indulging himself in delicacies; he ordered the delightful gardens of his castle to be thrown open, in which the most luscious fruits had been suffered to ripen and decay, unobserved and untouched, for many revolving autumns, and gratified his appetite with luxurious desserts. At length he found it expedient to introduce wine, as an agreeable improvement, or a necessary ingredient, to his new way of living; and having once tasted it, he was tempted, by little and little, to give a loose to the excesses of intoxication. His general simplicity of life was changed; he perfumed his apartments by burning the wood of the most aromatick fir, and commanded his helmet to be ornamented with beautiful rows of the teeth of the raindeer. Indolence and effeminacy stole upon him by pleasing and imperceptible gradations, relaxed the sinews of his resolution, and extinguished his thirst of military glory.

While Hacho was thus immersed in pleasure and in repose, it was reported to him, one morning, that the preceding night a disastrous omen had been discovered, and that bats and hideous birds had drunk up the oil which nourished the perpetual lamp in the temple of Odin. About the same time, a messenger arrived to tell him, that the king of Norway had invaded his kingdom with a formidable army. Hacho, terrified as he was with the omen of the night, and enervated with indulgence, roused himself from his voluptuous lethargy, and, recollecting some faint and few sparks of veteran valour, marched forward to meet him. Both armies joined battle in the forest where Hacho had been lost after hunting; and it so happened, that the king of Norway challenged him to single combat, near the place where he had tasted the honey. The Lapland chief, languid and long disused to arms, was soon overpowered; he fell to the ground; and before his insulting adversary struck his head from his body, uttered this exclamation, which the Laplanders still use as an early lesson to their children: " The vitious man should date his destruction from the first temptation. How justly do I fall a sacrifice to sloth and luxury, in the place where I first yielded to those allurements which seduced me to deviate from temperance and innocence! The honey which I tasted in this forest, and not the hand of the king of Norway, conquers Hacho[a]."

---

[a] By Mr. Thomas Warton.

N°. 97. SATURDAY, FEBRUARY 23, 1760.

IT may, I think, be justly observed, that few books disappoint their readers more than the narrations of travellers.
One part of mankind is naturally curious to learn the sentiments, manners, and condition of the rest; and every
mind that has leisure or power to extend its views, must
be desirous of knowing in what proportion Providence has
distributed the blessings of nature, or the advantages of
art, among the several nations of the earth.

This general desire easily procures readers to every
book from which it can expect gratification. The adventurer upon unknown coasts, and the describer of distant
regions, is always welcomed as a man who has laboured for
the pleasure of others, and who is able to enlarge our
knowledge and rectify our opinions; but when the volume
is opened, nothing is found but such general accounts as
leave no distinct idea behind them, or such minute enu-
merations as few can read with either profit or delight.

Every writer of travels should consider, that, like all
other authors, he undertakes either to instruct or please,
or to mingle pleasure with instruction. He that instructs
must offer to the mind something to be imitated, or something to be avoided; he that pleases must offer new images
to his reader, and enable him to form a tacit comparison of
his own state with that of others.

The greater part of travellers tell nothing, because their
method of travelling supplies them with nothing to be told.
He that enters a town at night, and surveys it in the
morning, and then hastens away to another place, and
guesses at the manners of the inhabitants by the entertainment which his inn afforded him, may please himself
for a time with a hasty change of scenes, and a confused
remembrance of palaces and churches; he may gratify his
eye with a variety of landscapes, and regale his palate
with a succession of vintages; but let him be contented to
please himself without endeavouring to disturb others.

Why should he record excursions by which nothing could be learned, or wish to make a show of knowledge, which, without some power of intuition unknown to other mortals, he never could attain?

Of those who crowd the world with their itineraries, some have no other purpose than to describe the face of the country; those who sit idle at home, and are curious to know what is done or suffered in distant countries, may be informed by one of these wanderers, that on a certain day he set out early with the caravan, and in the first hour's march saw, towards the south, a hill covered with trees, then passed over a stream, which ran northward with a swift course, but which is probably dry in the summer months; that an hour after he saw something to the right which looked at a distance like a castle with towers, but which he discovered afterwards to be a craggy rock; that he then entered a valley, in which he saw several trees tall and flourishing, watered by a rivulet not marked in the maps, of which he was not able to learn the name; that the road afterward grew stony, and the country uneven, where he observed among the hills many hollows worn by torrents, and was told that the road was passable only part of the year; that going on they found the remains of a building, once, perhaps, a fortress to secure the pass, or to restrain the robbers, of which the present inhabitants can give no other account than that it is haunted by fairies; that they went to dine at the foot of a rock, and travelled the rest of the day along the banks of a river, from which the road turned aside towards evening, and brought them within sight of a village, which was once a considerable town, but which afforded them neither good victuals nor commodious lodging.

Thus he conducts his reader through wet and dry, over rough and smooth, without incidents, without reflection; and, if he obtains his company for another day, will dismiss him again at night, equally fatigued with a like succession of rocks and streams, mountains and ruins.

This is the common style of those sons of enterprise,

who visit savage countries, and range through solitude and desolation; who pass a desert, and tell that it is sandy; who cross a valley, and find that it is green. There are others of more delicate sensibility, that visit only the realms of elegance and softness; that wander through Italian palaces, and amuse the gentle reader with catalogues of pictures; that hear masses in magnificent churches, and recount the number of the pillars or variegations of the pavement. And there are yet others, who, in disdain of trifles, copy inscriptions elegant and rude, ancient and modern; and transcribe into their book the walls of every edifice, sacred or civil. He that reads these books must consider his labour as its own reward; for he will find nothing on which attention can fix, or which memory can retain.

He that would travel for the entertainment of others, should remember that the great object of remark is human life. Every nation has something peculiar in its manufactures, its works of genius, its medicines, its agriculture, its customs and its policy. He only is a useful traveller, who brings home something by which his country may be benefited; who procures some supply of want, or some mitigation of evil, which may enable his readers to compare their condition with that of others, to improve it whenever it is worse, and whenever it is better to enjoy it.

N°. 98. SATURDAY, MARCH 1, 1760.

TO THE IDLER.

SIR,

I AM the daughter of a gentleman, who during his lifetime enjoyed a small income which arose from a pension from the court, by which he was enabled to live in a genteel and comfortable manner.

By the situation of life in which he was placed, he was frequently introduced into the company of those of much greater fortunes than his own, among whom he was always received with complaisance, and treated with civility.

At six years of age I was sent to a boarding-school in the country, at which I continued till my father's death. This melancholy event happened at a time when I was by no means of sufficient age to manage for myself, while the passions of youth continued unsubdued, and before experience could guide my sentiments or my actions.

I was then taken from school by an uncle, to the care of whom my father had committed me on his dying-bed. With him I lived several years; and, as he was unmarried, the management of his family was committed to me. In this character I always endeavoured to acquit myself, if not with applause, at least without censure.

At the age of twenty-one, a young gentleman of some fortune paid his addresses to me, and offered me terms of marriage. This proposal I should readily have accepted, because from vicinity of residence, and from many opportunities of observing his behaviour, I had, in some sort, contracted an affection for him. My uncle, for what reason I do not know, refused his consent to this alliance, though it would have been complied with by the father of the young gentleman; and, as the future condition of my life was wholly dependant on him, I was not willing to disoblige him, and, therefore, though unwillingly, declined the offer.

My uncle, who possessed a plentiful fortune, frequently hinted to me in conversation, that at his death I should be provided for in such a manner that I should be able to make my future life comfortable and happy. As this promise was often repeated, I was the less anxious about any provision for myself. In a short time my uncle was taken ill, and though all possible means were made use of for his recovery, in a few days he died.

The sorrow arising from the loss of a relation, by whom I had been always treated with the greatest kindness, however grievous, was not the worst of my misfortunes. As he enjoyed an almost uninterrupted state of health, he was the less mindful of his dissolution, and died intestate ; by which means his whole fortune devolved to a nearer relation, the heir at law.

Thus excluded from all hopes of living in the manner with which I have so long flattered myself, I am doubtful what method I shall take to procure a decent maintenance. I have been educated in a manner that has set me above a state of servitude, and my situation renders me unfit for the company of those with whom I have hitherto conversed. But, though disappointed in my expectations, I do not despair. I will hope that assistance may still be obtained for innocent distress, and that friendship, though rare, is yet not impossible to be found.

I am, Sir,
Your humble servant,
SOPHIA HEEDFUL*.

N°. 99. SATURDAY, MARCH 8, 1760.

As Ortogrul of Basra was one day wandering along the streets of Bagdat, musing on the varieties of merchandise which the shops offered to his view, and observing the different occupations which busied the multitudes on every side, he was awakened from the tranquillity of meditation by a crowd that obstructed his passage. He raised his eyes, and saw the chief visier, who, having returned from the divan, was entering his palace.

Ortogrul mingled with the attendants, and being supposed to have some petition for the visier, was permitted to enter. He surveyed the spaciousness of the apartments, admired the walls hung with golden tapestry, and the floors covered with silken carpets, and despised the simple neatness of his own little habitation.

Surely, said he to himself, this palace is the seat of hap-

---

* By an unknown correspondent.

piness, where pleasure succeeds to pleasure, and discontent and sorrow can have no admission. Whatever Nature has provided for the delight of sense, is here spread forth to be enjoyed. What can mortals hope or imagine, which the master of this palace has not obtained? The dishes of luxury cover his table, the voice of harmony lulls him in his bowers; he breathes the fragrance of the groves of Java, and sleeps upon the down of the cygnets of Ganges. He speaks, and his mandate is obeyed; he wishes, and his wish is gratified; all whom he sees obey him, and all whom he hears flatter him. How different, Ortogrul, is thy condition, who art doomed to the perpetual torments of unsatisfied desire, and who hast no amusement in thy power that can withhold thee from thy own reflections! They tell thee that thou art wise; but what does wisdom avail with poverty? None will flatter the poor, and the wise have very little power of flattering themselves. That man is surely the most wretched of the sons of wretchedness, who lives with his own faults and follies always before him, and who has none to reconcile him to himself by praise and veneration. I have long sought content, and have not found it; I will from this moment endeavour to be rich.

Full of this new resolution, he shut himself up in his chamber for six months, to deliberate how he should grow rich; he sometimes proposed to offer himself as a counsellor to one of the kings of India, and sometimes resolved to dig for diamonds in the mines of Golconda. One day, after some hours passed in violent fluctuation of opinion, sleep insensibly seized him in his chair; he dreamed that he was ranging a desert country in search of some one that might teach him to grow rich; and as he stood on the top of a hill shaded with cypress, in doubt whither to direct his steps, his father appeared on a sudden standing before him. Ortogrul, said the old man, I know thy perplexity; listen to thy father; turn thine eye on the opposite mountain. Ortogrul looked, and saw a torrent tumbling down the rocks, roaring with the noise of thunder, and scattering its foam on the impending woods. Now, said his father, behold the valley that lies between the hills. Ortogrul looked, and espied a little well, out of which issued a small rivulet. Tell me now, said his father, dost thou wish for sudden affluence, that may pour upon thee like the mountain torrent, or for a slow and gradual increase, resembling the rill gliding from the well? Let me be quickly rich, said Ortogrul; let the golden stream be quick and violent. Look round thee, said his father, once again. Ortogrul looked, and perceived the channel of the torrent dry and dusty; but following the rivulet from the well, he traced it to a wide lake, which the supply, slow and constant, kept always full. He waked, and determined to grow rich by silent profit and persevering industry.

Having sold his patrimony, he engaged in merchandise, and in twenty years purchased lands; on which he raised a house, equal in sumptuousness to that of the visier, to which he invited all the ministers of pleasure, expecting to enjoy all the felicity which he had imagined riches able to afford. Leisure soon made him weary of himself, and he longed to be persuaded that he was great and happy. He was courteous and liberal; he gave all that approached him hopes of pleasing him, and all who should please him hopes of being rewarded. Every art of praise was tried, and every source of adulatory fiction was exhausted. Ortogrul heard his flatterers without delight, because he found himself unable to believe them. His own heart told him its frailties, his own understanding reproached him with his faults. How long, said he, with a deep sigh, have I been labouring in vain to amass wealth which at last is useless! Let no man hereafter wish to be rich, who is already too wise to be flattered.

N°. 100. SATURDAY, MARCH 15, 1760.

TO THE IDLER.

SIR,

THE uncertainty and defects of language have produced very frequent complaints among the learned; yet there still remain many words among us undefined, which are very necessary to be rightly understood, and which produce very mischievous mistakes when they are erroneously interpreted.

I lived in a state of celibacy beyond the usual time. In the hurry first of pleasure, and afterwards of business, I felt no want of a domestick companion; but becoming weary of labour, I soon grew more weary of idleness, and thought it reasonable to follow the custom of life, and to seek some solace of my cares in female tenderness, and some amusement of my leisure in female cheerfulness.

The choice which has been long delayed is commonly made at last with great caution. My resolution was, to keep my passions neutral, and to marry only in compliance with my reason. I drew upon a page of my pocket-book a scheme of all female virtues and vices, with the vices which border upon every virtue, and the virtues which are allied to every vice. I considered that wit was sarcastick, and magnanimity imperious; that avarice was economical, and ignorance obsequious; and having estimated the good and evil of every quality, employed my own diligence, and that of my friends, to find the lady in whom nature and reason had reached that happy mediocrity which is equally remote from exuberance and deficience.

Every woman had her admirers and her censurers; and the expectations which one raised were by another quickly depressed; yet there was one in whose favour almost all suffrages concurred. Miss Gentle was universally allowed to be a good sort of woman. Her fortune was not large, but so prudently managed, that she wore finer clothes, and saw more company, than many who were known to be twice as rich. Miss Gentle's visits were every where welcome ; and whatever family she favoured with her company, she always left behind her such a degree of kindness as recommended her to others. Every day extended her acquaintance ; and all who knew her declared, that they never met with a better sort of woman.

To Miss Gentle I made my addresses, and was received with great equality of temper. She did not in the days of courtship assume the privilege of imposing rigorous commands, or resenting slight offences. If I forgot any of her injunctions, I was gently reminded ; if I missed the minute of appointment, I was easily forgiven. I foresaw nothing in marriage but a halcyon calm, and longed for the happiness which was to be found in the inseparable society of a good sort of woman.

The jointure was soon settled by the intervention of friends, and the day came in which Miss Gentle was made mine for ever. The first month was passed easily enough in receiving and repaying the civilities of our friends. The bride practised with great exactness all the niceties of ceremony, and distributed her notice in the most punctilious proportions to the friends who surrounded us with their happy auguries.

But the time soon came when we were left to ourselves, and were to receive our pleasures from each other ; and I then began to perceive that I was not formed to be much delighted by a good sort of woman. Her great principle is, that the orders of a family must not be broken. Every hour of the day has its employment inviolably appropriated ; nor will any importunity persuade her to walk in the garden at the time which she has devoted to her needlework, or to sit up stairs in that part of the forenoon which she has accustomed herself to spend in the back parlour. She allows herself to sit half an hour after breakfast, and an hour after dinner ; while I am talking or reading to her, she keeps her eye upon her watch, and when the minute of departure comes, will leave an argument unfinished, or the intrigue of a play unravelled. She once called me to supper when I was watching an eclipse, and summoned me at another time to bed when I was going to give directions at a fire.

Her conversation is so habitually cautious, that she never talks to me but in general terms, as to one whom it is dangerous to trust. For discriminations of character she has no names: all whom she mentions are honest men and agreeable women. She smiles not by sensation, but by practice. Her laughter is never excited but by a joke, and her notion of a joke is not very delicate. The repetition of a good joke does not weaken its effect; if she has laughed once, she will laugh again.

She is an enemy to nothing but ill-nature and pride; but she has frequent reason to lament that they are so frequent in the world. All who are not equally pleased with the good and the bad, with the elegant and gross, with the witty and the dull, all who distinguish excellence from defect, she considers as ill-natured; and she condemns as proud all who repress impertinence or quell presumption, or expect respect from any other eminence than that of fortune, to which she is always willing to pay homage.

There are none whom she openly hates, for if once she suffers, or believes herself to suffer, any contempt or insult, she never dismisses it from her mind, but takes all opportunities to tell how easily she can forgive. There are none whom she loves much better than others; for when any of her acquaintance decline in the opinion of the world, she always finds it inconvenient to visit them; her affection continues unaltered, but it is impossible to be intimate with the whole town.

She daily exercises her benevolence by pitying every misfortune that happens to every family within her circle of notice; she is in hourly terrours lest one should catch cold in the rain, and another be frighted by the high wind. Her charity she shows by lamenting that so many poor wretches should languish in the streets, and by wondering what the great can think on that they do so little good with such large estates.

Her house is elegant, and her table dainty, though she has little taste of elegance, and is wholly free from vicious luxury; but she comforts herself that nobody can say that her house is dirty, or that her dishes are not well drest.

This, Mr. Idler, I have found, by long experience, to be the character of a good sort of woman, which I have sent you for the information of those by whom a *good sort of woman* and a *good woman*, may happen to be used as equivalent terms, and who may suffer by the mistake, like

Your humble servant,

TIM WARNER.

Nº. 101.. SATURDAY, MARCH 22, 1760.

* Carpe hilaris : fuget heu! non revocanda dies.

OMAR, the son of Hussan, had passed seventy-five years in honour and prosperity. The favour of three successive califs had filled his house with gold and silver; and, whenever he appeared, the benedictions of the people proclaimed his passage.

Terrestrial happiness is of short continuance. The brightness of the flame is wasting its fuel; the fragrant flower is passing away in its own odours. The vigour of Omar began to fail, the curls of beauty fell from his head, strength departed from his hands, and agility from his feet. He gave back to the calif the keys of trust and the seals of secrecy; and sought no other pleasure for the remains of life than the converse of the wise, and the gratitude of the good.

The powers of his mind were yet unimpaired. His chamber was filled by visitants, eager to catch the dictates of experience, and officious to pay the tribute of admiration. Caled, the son of the viceroy of Egypt, entered every day early, and retired late. He was beautiful and eloquent; Omar admired his wit, and loved his docility. Tell me, said Caled, thou to whose voice nations have listened, and whose wisdom is known to the extremities of Asia, tell me how I may resemble Omar the prudent. The arts by which you have gained power and preserved it, are to you no longer necessary or useful; impart to me the secret of your conduct, and teach me the plan upon which your wisdom has built your fortune.

Young man, said Omar, it is of little use to form plans of life. When I took my first survey of the world, in my twentieth year, having considered the various conditions of mankind, in the hour of solitude I said thus to myself, leaning against a cedar which spread its branches over my head: Seventy years are allowed to man; I have yet fifty remaining: ten years I will allot to the attainment of knowledge, and ten I will pass in foreign countries; I shall be learned, and, therefore, shall be honoured; every city will shout at my arrival, and every student will solicit my friendship. Twenty years thus passed will store my mind with images, which I shall be busy through the rest of my life in combining and comparing. I shall revel in inexhaustible accumulations of intellectual riches; I shall find new pleasures for every moment, and shall never more be weary of myself. I will, however, not deviate too far from the beaten track of life, but will try what can be found in female delicacy. I will marry a wife beautiful as the Houries, and wise as Zobeide; with her I will live twenty years within the suburbs of Bagdat, in every pleasure that wealth can purchase and fancy can invent. I will then retire to a rural dwelling, pass my last days in obscurity and contemplation, and lie silently down on the bed of death. Through my life it shall be my settled resolution, that I will never depend upon the smile of princes; that I will never stand exposed to the artifices of courts; I will never pant for publick honours, nor disturb my quiet with affairs of state. Such was my scheme of life, which I impressed indelibly upon my memory.

The first part of my ensuing time was to be spent in search of knowledge; and I know not how I was diverted from my design. I had no visible impediments without, nor any ungovernable passions within. I regarded knowledge as the highest honour and the most engaging pleasure; yet day stole upon day, and month glided after month, till I found that seven years of the first ten had vanished, and left nothing behind them. I now postponed my purpose of travelling; for why should I go abroad while so much remained to be learned at home? I immured myself for four years, and studied the laws of the empire. The fame of my skill reached the judges; I was found able to speak upon doubtful questions, and was commanded to stand at the footstool of the calif. I was heard with attention, I was consulted with confidence, and the love of praise fastened on my heart.

I still wished to see distant countries, listened with rapture to the relations of travellers, and resolved some time to ask my dismission, that I might feast my soul with novelty; but my presence was always necessary, and the stream of business hurried me along. Sometimes I was afraid lest I should be charged with ingratitude; but I still proposed to travel, and, therefore, would not confine myself by marriage.

In my fiftieth year I began to suspect that the time of travelling was past, and thought it best to lay hold on the felicity yet in my power, and indulge myself in domestick pleasures. But at fifty no man easily finds a woman beautiful as the Houries, and wise as Zobeide. I inquired and rejected, consulted and deliberated, till the sixty-second year made me ashamed of gazing upon girls. I had now nothing left but retirement, and for retirement I never found a time, till disease forced me from publick employment.

Such was my scheme, and such has been its consequence. With an insatiable thirst for knowledge, I trifled away the years of improvement; with a restless desire of seeing different countries, I have always resided in the same city; with the highest expectation of connubial felicity, I have lived unmarried; and with unalterable resolutions of contemplative retirement, I am going to die within the walls of Bagdat.

N°. 102. SATURDAY, MARCH 29, 1760.

IT very seldom happens to man that his business is his pleasure. What is done from necessity is so often to be done when against the present inclination, and so often fills the mind with anxiety, that an habitual dislike steals upon us, and we shrink involuntarily from the remembrance of our task. This is the reason why almost every one wishes to quit his employment; he does not like another state, but is disgusted with his own.

From this unwillingness to perform more than is required of that which is commonly performed with reluctance, it proceeds that few authors· write their own lives. Statesmen, courtiers, ladies, generals and seamen have given to the world their own stories, and the events with which their different stations have made them acquainted. They retired to the closet as to a place of quiet and amusement, and pleased themselves with writing, because they could lay down the pen whenever they were weary. But the author, however conspicuous, or however important, either in the publick eye or in his own, leaves his life to be related by his successors, for he cannot gratify his vanity but by sacrificing his ease.

It is commonly supposed that the uniformity of a studious life affords no matter for a narration: but the truth is, that of the most studious life a great part passes without study. An author partakes of the common condition of humanity; he is born and married like another man; he has hopes and fears, expectations and disappointments, griefs and joys, and friends and enemies, like a courtier or a statesman; nor can I conceive why his affairs should not excite curiosity as much as the whisper of a drawing-room or the factions of a camp.

Nothing detains the reader's attention more powerfully than deep involutions of distress, or sudden vicissitudes of fortune; and these might be abundantly afforded by memoirs of the sons of literature. They are entangled by contracts which they know not how to fulfil, and obliged to write on subjects which they do not understand. Every publication is a new period of time, from which some increase or declension of fame is to be reckoned. The gradations of a hero's life are from battle to battle, and of an author's from book to book.

Success and miscarriage have the same effects in all conditions. The prosperous are feared, hated and flattered; and the unfortunate avoided, pitied and despised. No sooner is a book published than the writer may judge of the opinion of the world. If his acquaintance press round him in publick places, or salute him from the other side of the street; if invitations to dinner come thick upon him, and those with whom he dines keep him to supper; if the ladies turn to him when his coat is plain, and the footmen serve him with attention and alacrity; he may be sure that his work has been praised by some leader of literary fashions.

Of declining reputation the symptoms are not less easily observed. If the author enters a coffee-house, he has a box to himself; if he calls at a bookseller's, the boy turns his back; and, what is the most fatal of all prognosticks,. authors will visit him in a morning, and talk to him hour after hour of the malevolence of criticks, the neglect of merit, the bad taste of the age and the candour of posterity.

All this, modified and varied by accident and custom, would form very amusing scenes of biography, and might recreate many a mind which is very little delighted with conspiracies or battles, intrigues of a court, or debates of a parliament; to this might be added all the changes of the countenance of a patron, traced from the first glow which flattery raises in his cheek, through ardour of fondness, vehemence of promise, magnificence of praise, excuse of delay, and lamentation of inability, to the last chill look of final dismission, when the one grows weary of soliciting, and the other of hearing solicitation.

Thus copious are the materials which have been hitherto suffered to lie neglected, while the repositories of every family that has produced a soldier or a minister are ransacked, and libraries are crowded with useless folios of state-papers which will never be read, and which contribute nothing to valuable knowledge.

I hope the learned will be taught to know their own strength and their value, and, instead of devoting their lives to the honour of those who seldom thank them for their labours, resolve at last to do justice to themselves.

Nº. 103. SATURDAY, APRIL 5, 1760.

Respicere ad longæ jussit spatia ultima vitæ.   Juv. Sat. x. 275.

MUCH of the pain and pleasure of mankind arises from the conjectures which every one makes of the thoughts of others ; we all enjoy praise which we do not hear, and resent contempt which we do not see. The Idler may, therefore, be forgiven, if he suffers his imagination to represent to him what his readers will say or think when they are informed that they have now his last paper in their hands.

Value is more frequently raised by scarcity than by use. That which lay neglected when it was common, rises in estimation as its quantity becomes less. We seldom learn the true want of what we have till it is discovered that we can have no more.

This essay will, perhaps, be read with care even by those who have not yet attended to any other ; and he that finds this late attention recompensed, will not forbear to wish that he had bestowed it sooner.

Though the Idler and his readers have contracted no close friendship, they are, perhaps, both unwilling to part. There are few things not purely evil, of which we can say, without some emotion of uneasiness, *this is the last.* Those who never could agree together, shed tears when mutual discontent has determined them to final separation; of a place which has been frequently visited, though without pleasure, the last look is taken with heaviness of heart; and the Idler, with all his chilness of tranquillity, is not wholly unaffected by the thought that his last essay is now before him.

The secret horrour of the last is inseparable from a thinking being, whose life is limited, and to whom death is dreadful. We always make a secret comparison between a part and the whole; the termination of any period of life reminds us that life itself has likewise its termination; when we have done any thing for the last time, we involuntarily reflect that a part of the days allotted us is past, and that as more is past there is less remaining.

It is very happily and kindly provided, that in every life there are certain pauses and interruptions, which force consideration upon the careless, and seriousness upon the light; points of time where one course of action ends, and another begins; and by vicissitudes of fortune or alteration of employment, by change of place or loss of friendship, we are forced to say of something, *this is the last.*

An even and unvaried tenour of life always hides from our apprehension the approach of its end. Succession is not perceived but by variation; he that lives to-day as he lived yesterday, and expects that, as the present day is, such will be the morrow, easily conceives time as running in a circle and returning to itself. The uncertainty of our duration is impressed commonly by dissimilitude of condition; it is only by finding life changeable that we are reminded of its shortness.

This conviction, however forcible at every new impression, is every moment fading from the mind; and partly by the inevitable incursion of new images, and partly by voluntary exclusion of unwelcome thoughts, we are again exposed to the universal fallacy; and we must do another thing for the last time, before we consider that the time is nigh when we shall do no more.

As the last Idler is published in that solemn week which the Christian world has always set apart for the examination of the conscience, the review of life, the extinction of earthly desires, and the renovation of holy purposes; I hope that my readers are already disposed to view every incident with seriousness, and improve it by meditation; and that, when they see this series of trifles brought to a conclusion, they will consider that, by outliving the Idler, they have passed weeks, months and years, which are now no longer in their power; that an end must in time be put to every thing great as to every thing little; that to life must come its last hour, and to this system of being its last day, the hour at which probation ceases, and repentance will be vain; the day in which every work of the hand, and imagination of the heart shall be brought to judgment, and an everlasting futurity shall be determined by the past [b].

THE IDLER. N°. 22 [c].

MANY naturalists are of opinion, that the animals which we commonly consider as mute, have the power of imparting their thoughts to one another. That they can express general sensations is very certain; every being that can utter sounds, has a different voice for pleasure and for pain. The hound informs his fellows when he scents his game; the hen calls her chickens to their food by her cluck, and drives them from danger by her scream.

Birds have the greatest variety of notes; they have, indeed, a variety, which seems almost sufficient to make a speech adequate to the purposes of a life which is regulated by instinct, and can admit little change or improvement. To the cries of birds, curiosity or superstition has been always attentive; many have studied the language of the feathered tribes, and some have boasted that they understood it.

[b] This most solemn and impressive paper may be profitably compared with the introduction of Bishop Heber's first Bampton-Lecture.

[c] This was the original N°. 22, but on the republication of the work in volumes, Dr. Johnson substituted what now stands under that head.

The most skilful or most confident interpreters of the
sylvan dialogues have been commonly found among the
philosophers of the east, in a country where the calmness
of the air, and the mildness of the seasons, allow the student to pass a great part of the year in groves and bowers.
But what may be done in one place by peculiar opportunities, may be performed in another by peculiar diligence.
A shepherd of Bohemia has, by long abode in the forests,
enabled himself to understand the voice of birds; at least
he relates with great confidence a story, of which the credibility is left to be considered by the learned.

" As I was sitting" said he, " within a hollow rock, and
watching my sheep that fed in the valley, I heard two vultures interchangeably crying on the summit of the cliff.
Both voices were earnest and deliberate. My curiosity
prevailed over my care of the flock; I climbed slowly and
silently from crag to crag, concealed among the shrubs, till
I found a cavity where I might sit and listen without suffering or giving disturbance."

" I soon perceived, that my labour would be well repaid;
for an old vulture was sitting on a naked prominence, with
her young about her, whom she was instructing in the
arts of a vulture's life, and preparing, by the last lecture,
for their final dismission to the mountains and the skies."

"My children," said the old vulture, " you will the less
want my instructions, because you have had my practice
before your eyes; you have seen me snatch from the farm
the household fowl; you have seen me seize the leveret in
the bush, and the kid in the pasture; you know how to fix
your talons, and how to balance your flight when you are
laden with your prey. But you remember the taste of
more delicious food; I have often regaled you with the
flesh of man." "Tell us," said the young vultures, "where
man may be found, and how he may be known; his flesh is
surely the natural food of a vulture. Why have you never
brought a man in your talons to the nest?" " He is too
bulky," said the mother; " when we find a man, we can
only tear away his flesh, and leave his bones upon the

ground." " Since man is so big," said the young ones,
" how do you kill him? You are afraid of the wolf and of
the bear, by what power are vultures superior to man? is
man more defenceless than a sheep?" " We have not the
strength of man," returned the mother, " and I am sometimes in doubt whether we have the subtilty; and the vultures would seldom feast upon his flesh, had not nature, that
devoted him to our uses, infused into him a strange ferocity, which I have never observed in any other being that
feeds upon the earth. Two herds of men will often meet
and shake the earth with noise, and fill the air with fire.
When you hear noise and see fire, with flashes along the
ground, hasten to the place with your swiftest wing, for
men are surely destroying one another; you will then find
the ground smoking with blood, and covered with car-
casses, of which many are dismembered and mangled for
the convenience of the vulture." " But when men have
killed their prey," said the pupil, "why do they not eat it?
When the wolf has killed a sheep, he suffers not the vulture to touch it till he has satisfied himself. Is not man
another kind of wolf?" " Man," said the mother, " is the
only beast who kills that which he does not devour, and
this quality makes him so much a benefactor to our species." " If men kill our prey and lay it in our way," said
the young one, " what need shall we have of labouring for
ourselves?" " Because man will, sometimes," replied the
mother, " remain for a long time quiet in his den. The
old vultures will tell you when you are to watch his motions. When you see men in great numbers moving close
together, like a flock of storks, you may conclude that they
are hunting, and that you will soon revel in human blood."
" But still," said the young one, " I would gladly know the
reason of this mutual slaughter. I could never kill what
I could not eat." " My child," said the mother, " this is
a question which I cannot answer, though I am reckoned
the most subtle bird of the mountain. When I was young,
I used frequently to visit the aerie of an old vulture, who
dwelt upon the Carpathian rocks; he had made many ob-

servations; he knew the places that afforded prey round his habitation, as far in every direction as the strongest wing can fly between the rising and setting of the summer sun; he had fed year after year on the entrails of men. His opinion was, that men had only the appearance of animal life, being really vegetables with a power of motion; and that as the boughs of an oak are dashed together by the storm, that swine may fatten upon the fallen acorns, so men are by some unaccountable power driven one against another, till they lose their motion, that vultures may be fed. Others think they have observed something of contrivance and policy among these mischievous beings; and those that hover more closely round them, pretend, that there is, in every herd, one that gives directions to the rest, and seems to be more eminently delighted with a wide carnage. What it is that entitles him to such pre-eminence we know not; he is seldom the biggest or the swiftest, but he shows by his eagerness and diligence that he is, more than any of the others, a friend to the vultures."

END OF VOL. IV.

TALBOYS AND WHEELER.

Lightning Source UK Ltd.
Milton Keynes UK
UKHW010631171218
334136UK00011B/539/P